"...a cerebral and wildly thought-provoking fusion of fantastical fiction and metaphysical speculation."
"...this is an intelligent, surprisingly humorous novel."
--Kirkus Discoveries--

"Fascinating characters exist here —shape-shifting sprites alarmed to be suffering the vagaries of human emotion, a little girl who behaves like a six-year-old and has no memory of her Christlike episodes, and a scholarly cockatoo."
--ForeWord CLARION Reviews--

PAX

The Bean Chronicles

A Novel by

Stephen Stuart

Order this book online at www.trafford.com
or email orders@trafford.com

Most Trafford titles are also available at major online book retailers.

This book is a work of fiction. Any resemblance to persons living or dead is purely coincidental with the exception, that is, of authentic quotations employed or to historical individuals either living or deceased.

There are, however, places and events that do exist, but I have employed the writer's prerogative to incorporate them into my story as needed. Reality adds a modicum of validity to fiction.

The actual occurrences of some events mentioned may have been altered to fit into my own timetable, and I sincerely apologize if I have offended any person, place, company or event. It was not done intentionally.

Printed in the United States of America.

ISBN: 978-1-4269-3887-0 (sc)
ISBN: 978-1-4269-3888-7 (hc)
ISBN: 978-1-4269-3889-4 (e)

Library of Congress Control Number: 2010914068

Trafford rev. 03/07/2011

 www.trafford.com

North America & international
toll-free: 1 888 232 4444 (USA & Canada)
phone: 250 383 6864 ♦ fax: 812 355 4082

Other Bean Chronicles novels by Stephen Stuart

The Wonder of All That Is: The Story of Bean

Soon to be released:
AMEN

Once again
to Mary Ann:
she is all things to me
and remains
The Wonder of All That Is.

Fiat Lux

PREFACE

The concept of Bean existed in the mind of artist Joyce Minnick for many years before she finally decided to act upon it. Finally, in 2005, she took the first step in birthing her aspiration by constructing the preliminary armature.

After a long gestation period of plasticene development, Joyce was ready to give life to her child.

Bean was delivered in a fiery explosion of molten bronze on a memorable morning in 2007, and the rest is history. He now graces the collections of art lovers throughout the world, and his legacy has provided the nourishment for a proposed series of tales based upon his credo of morality and a reverence for the natural order of things.

The first novel in the trilogy, *The Wonder of All That Is: The Story of Bean,* described the efforts of a child born with the malady of autism in his battle to overcome his adversity and achieve a successful and productive life.

PAX, the second novel of the trilogy, deals with the age-old conflict of good versus evil and is approached in a whimsical, yet thought-provoking and serious manner.

The battle of good versus evil has provided the fodder for religious leaders, moralists, essayists, self-proclaimed prophets, poets, and novelists since the advent of man's ability to reason. From superstition to religious fervor to abstract reflection, the concept has aroused the need for a universal delving into the mysteries of life.

I have approached the theme through the adventures of my protagonist, Bean, a benevolent spirit and a spawn of pure nature who has existed since time immemorial.

He has once again chosen an innocent soul and through her, aided by a motley group of characters whom he had enlisted in his crusade, set out to do battle for the future of mankind against the most evil of adversaries.

I have anguished over the conclusion of this epic battle as to the final victor. Considering the atmosphere of uncertainty among the peoples of the world in today's reality, perhaps evil should conquer good. This would provide a wealth of material for a new story promoting a rebirth of man and the re-emergence of his natural inheritance.

Who knows? The clock is ticking.

Stephen Stuart

Florida, 2010

Cast of Characters

Abdul-Wahid: a nomadic Bedouin.

Adamowitz: an elderly gentleman reposing in New York's Central Park.

Anna Walks With Grace: the sachem of a Native American Pueblo tribe.

Bean: a spiritual entity imbued with a devout sense of morality and ethics.

Cecil Malcome-Malcome: a Matt Christmas guest.

Dragos Vladu: a vampire bat from Transylvania

Dr. Crank: the alter ego of Leader.

Dr. Heinz Seibenundfunfzig: a Matt Christmas guest.

Esmeralda LaLeeche: a South American leech.

Ethelbert Grimely: a Matt Christmas guest.

Ghost: Bean's ghostwriter.

Giver of the Word: the old sachem of a Native American Pueblo tribe.

Jaindeaux: a mystical and all-knowing spiritual entity endowed with great powers.

L. Forrest Greene: a Matt Christmas guest.

Leader: a spiritual entity and acquaintance of Bean.

Lili-It: the personification of evil.

Maeve Fellows: Patch's mother.

Matt Christmas: a talk-show host specializing in offbeat guests.

Mosi Jela: a tsetse fly from Africa.

Patch (PAX) Fellows: our heroine.

Professor Saito Bokchoy: a Matt Christmas guest.

Sigrid Lokisdotter: a Matt Christmas guest.

The Reverend William Fellows: Patch's father.

Whoever: Bean's antagonist in the spiritual world.

Virgil: a white cockatoo pet of unusual literary talent, as well as a vessel for Bean's introduction to the Fellows family.

From book one: "The Wonder of All That Is: The Story of Bean"

Dr. Harrison Owlfeather: a professor of psychology and a Native American.

Margareta (Mag) Leighter: Ricky's betrothed.

Rick Granlin: Ricky's father.

Ricky Granlin: a boy stricken with autism.

Sarah Granlin: Ricky's mother.

Whatever: Bean's spiritual antagonist in book one.

INTRODUCTION TO THE NOW

A heartfelt welcome back to those who enjoyed my earlier adventures, and a hearty welcome to my new readers.

I continue to seek whatever glimmer of light remains in this troubled world, and I welcome you all to accompany me on the journey.

You'll travel with a host of new characters as well as revisiting some old ones.

My ghost is still with me and will persist in exhorting his take on all things human and otherwise. I will try, as before, to restrain his off-the-wall rantings but allow free rein to some of his thoughts and hypotheses—which, he claims, will initiate a modicum of reflection in your lives.

So sit back and refill that pot of tea; froth that cappuccino and dip that biscotti; it's time to get going.

I decided to begin this story by including the final chapter of my previous adventure concerning the conflict of a boy grown to manhood and coming to terms with the affliction called autism. It will also bring to mind a bit of nostalgia for my loyal readers and serve to introduce new readers to me—Bean—and what my quest has been and always will be.

A bit of information for my new visitors: I was given the name Bean by the child of the artist who created the image of a free spirit, a creature of wonder and awe whose only credo was that man has within himself the power to produce a world devoted to the seeking out of morality and godliness. The spirit—me specifically—was immortalized within a bronze image, which became my home for many years and served as a point of reference for all those involved in my tale.

As for the subject matter so succinctly put into words by my ghost in my previous adventures, this tale will continue that tradition, as I again requested from him that no apparent conclusions be encouraged and that you, the reader, be free to reach your own decisions. What I truly desire is to open up avenues of abstract thought, both for yourselves and for discussions with your various compatriots. My belief is that free thought is the basis for spiritual progress. I don't have the arrogance or conceit to declare that my solutions or conclusions are definitive; therefore I do not claim any. I prefer the Talmudic approach, which asks questions like *How does it affect me? How does it affect you? How does it affect us a society?* and finally *What did he really mean by that?*

A definitive answer would bring an end to conceptualization, and without intellectual stimulation, progress comes to a screeching halt. Then what would happen? The tree of knowledge would evolve into a wizened symbol of edification existing in a once fertile garden now overgrown with the weeds of indifference.

I will not take the responsibility for that. I will relinquish that honor to another wordsmith.

The thoughts, concepts, hypotheses, and questions I have approached may have been addressed by others in various genres and in a form preferred by academicians; if that is so, I apologize to you and can only hope that I have put them into words that all can understand and enjoy. They are not the sole domain of any one individual, for mutual thought is anything but inevitable when one takes into consideration the many billions of minds which exist on this planet.

Although the subject matter may tend to be a bit esoteric and, in many cases, untraditional, a tad ridiculous, and totally unscientific, I remind you that this is a work of fiction and, as a defense, it is the artist's prerogative to stretch reality just a smidgen.

I have been described as naive and simple; I hope you will see just the opposite. Don't be lulled into a false sense of ho-hum if I seem to proceed on my pursuit of righteousness by utilizing basic and uncomplicated means. I ask you to look deeper into my methods, for I am certain that the ends I hope to achieve will, in some small part, justify the means.

There might be a bit of confusion as to the changes of tenses in the narrative. What I tried to accomplish is to make the past into the present while you exist in it. Sound complicated, but not really. Just sit back and enjoy, and don't be picky!

Finally, as in *The Wonder of All That Is*, no sex, violence, or profanity will appear on these pages; far too much occurs in everyday life already. Thus you can read these leafs to your children. It just might be a better alternative to warm milk.

So here I am again: a little older in the scheme of things and more than a little pleased with the results accomplished in Ricky Granlin's adjustment to maturity. You do remember me, do you not? I'm that nosy imp, that impetuous faerie, who inserts himself into your lives and attempts, sometimes not very successfully, to set you onto the path of virtue and morality—my definition of righteousness, that is.

If you remember me (favorably, I hope), you should also recollect Ricky: a lad born of fine parents; a playful, normal fellow who fell victim to one of nature's malevolent quirks. An alteration in his chemical balance, either genetic or externally induced, resulted in a child enveloped in the dreadful affliction known as autism.

He has since learned to live with and control his malady while growing into a very productive member of society (with more than a little help from yours truly).

I feel a strong sense of accomplishment, for I am certain that Ricky will achieve great things in his life. Although I try to remain positive in my attachments to him, I fear that many additional years will be necessary for man, as a distinct species, to outgrow his aggressive tendencies, and that countless Rickys will be necessary to accomplish that goal.

Until then (and I will be there at the end), my challenges will be met and in most cases—and I stress *most*—will be conquered.

A strong sense of what I can only refer to as relief has suffused my mind. However, I am concerned about the changes that appear to be taking control of my heretofore logical and unemotional ties to humanity.

My last intervention into the lives of the autistic child and his family, combined with the efforts of a group of truly committed people who unabashedly projected strong feelings of concern and love, has left an indelible mark on me.

My only explanation at the present time is that the rebirth of my innate powers has allowed me to experience emotions that, until now, have not been available to me. Prior to that, I believed that the only influence I possessed was the ability to transfer to—or meld with, if you please—the minds of living organisms. I was able at that time to influence their thought processes in a manner that stimulated their latent actions in a most beneficial way. This was accomplished in a very basic mode. I was obliged to spiritually join with a host, be it inanimate or life driven, before I could participate with its thought patterns. This mode required me to flit from host to host, entering the entity best suited to achieve my end. The means, at times, became very trying before the culmination of my end was reached, but I left no telltale residue behind, with the exception of a little harmless confusion.

My ultimate goal is to improve humanity and somewhat diminish their unconscionable need for violence. It has been a very slow and frustrating process due to my previous limited abilities. But with the re-emergence of my long-dormant powers, I have now assumed what you would refer to as an enlightened feeling of hope and confidence in my pursuit of that goal.

However, due to a prior entanglement with my opposite number—Whatever, by name—my abilities have multiplied tremendously to the point where I can now travel anywhere I choose in the guise of an ionic cloud of electromagnetic energy. I can travel back in history to any place I have already visited and can observe individuals I have had past relationships with. However, I cannot react with them and thus cannot alter their history, nor the history of man in general. A physical host is no longer necessary to transport my being; all I require is a mere thought.

What benefit would a visit such as I just described afford to me, you ask? (You did ask, didn't you?) It would provide me with a photographic memory of conversations partaken with the proviso that they aid me in comprehending present-day scenarios. It would also bring to mind the various situations my host had been involved in, providing me with experiences I would not have been able to partake of on my own.

To further illustrate and clarify the voyages into the realm of my aspirations, I'll reminisce a bit and transport you back to a time long ago and to one of the greatest observers of man and his foibles.

It was in the late 1500s when, in the guise of a common rat (of the Norwegian variety) and inhabiting a most unhealthy area of confinement in a place called Algiers, I first encountered my next subject. He had been abducted rather forcefully by a band of brigands and placed in close proximity to my gnawed-out refuge in the stone walls of our dark and dank excuse of an apartment.

From the beginning of our relationship, I recognized his potential, and I stayed with him for many years—about thirty, to be exact—before we parted company.

We developed a close camaraderie of intellect and respect. His insight into his fellow man was most enlightening.

Senor Cervantes encouraged me in my pursuits by reciting a few words of wisdom: **"By the street of by-and-by, one arrives at the house of never."**[1]

Such simple words can be most profound if one allows himself a moment of introspection. I was to learn throughout our relationship that the most insightful of words can have the most serious effect on my understanding of humanity. Those words formed the basis of my modest challenge to both learn and to dispense whatever words of wisdom might find their way into my conversations. The formal penning of those gems of wisdom was put on hold until I was secure in my choice of a ghostwriter. His employment—more of a verbal rather than of a monetary agreement—was a necessity due to my inexperience in that venue.

During our many discussions, I confessed to Senor Cervantes my desire to elevate the fine traits inherent in man and guide him toward the heights of enlightenment.

He seemed amused at what must have appeared to be a rashness of youth to him, although I was far superior to him in age. **"The mean[ing] of true valor lies between the extremes of cowardice and rashness,"**[2] he said before adding, **"Many go out for wool and come home shorn themselves."**[3] Did he truly believe that my goal was nonetheless a venture in futility?

Not to toot my own horn, but I like to think that I was the model for his great protagonist and my fellow do-gooder, Don Quixote de La Mancha. Cervantes's description of a knight-errant tilting at the windmills of his distorted reality was, I believe, his take on my adventures and the naïveté I seemed to demonstrate to him.

Although I do not agree with his vision of me, and while I do not believe that I tilt at windmills, I am nevertheless honored to be cast into immortality by such a great dispenser of words.

"The pen," he wrote, **"is the tongue of the mind,"**[1] and that is what I endeavor to do in my vain attempt: to tongue my own mind.

---

1   Miguel de Cervantes: http://en.proverbia.net/citsautor
2   Miguel de Cervantes: www://famousquotesandauthors.com
3   Miguel de Cervantes: http://www.quotes.net/authors/Migues+de+Cervantes
4   Miguel de Cervantes

Senor Cervantes has become the epitome of a true knight of the philosophical order and the man to whom I owe much of my own efforts to depict man's seemingly confused state of mind, be it in vain or not. **"One man** [imp?] **scorned and covered with scars still strove with his last ounce of courage to reach the unreachable stars, and the world will be better for this."**[5]

Another benefit of my powers has been an increased sensitivity to the emotions, feelings, and abstractions of thoughts that are (or should be) the ingredients of every human man, woman, and child. The reaction to my enhanced sensitivity to human emotions has been one of unbridled confusion, which is another emotion I have never possessed a familiarity with.

Do I resent the accumulation within me of human sentiments and passion? I believe not! It will afford me a more complete understanding and appreciation of man as he struggles to survive nature's unrelenting march toward the inevitability of evolution.

However, I am still not convinced that I am, in fact, able to experience true human emotions experienced by men and women themselves; what it is I feel could be deemed a vicarious adjunct to true human passions. Nevertheless, the more I am exposed to humans, the more I am willing to accept their qualities as my own.

So many conflicts have accumulated in man that only a miracle can alleviate them and give the human race a joy in living until it is time for man, as we recognize him today, to accept his preordained developmental determination.

I feel that I am tired (again, a new emotion) and need a respite from my self-imposed crusade against the iniquities and the sufferings that emanate, most profusely, from the pores of humanity.

A strong statement, eh? Not if you have existed as long as I have and have endured the worst, and the best, that the human race can bestow upon themselves and upon nature in general.

Your first reaction to my outburst would be something like, "Come on, what's with the exaggeration? You'd think that you were the only one with troubles. Mea culpa, mea culpa … boo hoo, boo hoo! We've all had our share of problems and suffered through losses and depression."

My rejoinder to such a self-serving reaction is this:

---

5   Miguel de Cervantes

Can you honestly compare the loss of a paintball game to the fall of Carthage? How about a rejection by the sweetheart of your fantasies to Marc Antony's belief that Cleopatra had passed, sacrificing a nation? Maybe the loss of a hard-fought campaign to win the pinnacle of power, as likened to the obsidian incision of a political adversary's chest and the extraction of his beating heart?

I have been there and more ... much more.

I have also been a visitor to the warmth and security of the womb of human familial love. All of my visitations, hot and cold, depressing and rewarding, have contributed to my growing knowledge of the human condition. That expanding knowledge has tended to fill the well of confusion fed by the human faucet of irrational emotions. It is these emotions that control man and, in most cases, prohibit him from cogent thought and balanced reaction.

Is it time to hibernate with my fellow impish escapees, or do I continue in my search for the ultimate reasoning as to man's true destiny?

The answer is yes.

Yes to what, you ask? (Goodness, you do ask a lot of questions!)

My multiyear involvement with the Granlins and their overcoming of a son's handicap has given me the impetus to search out a new soul to study and guide; hence, my voyage to the southwestern area of the United States and a very special child.

But before I continue, I've decided to interject an excerpt (or two) from my earlier adventure to bring you up to date on this new quest of mine. Be patient, and you will understand my reasoning as this tale unfolds.

Redux One:

Book One

**"And yet another leap forward
And another
And yet another ..."**[6]

When graduating from high school, Ricky and his soul partner, Mag (short for Margareta), were honored with valedictorian and salutatorian status, as well as voted most likely to succeed.

A few months of vacation and freedom from the pressures of school ensued: a time for the couple to plan their future together and bemoan their upcoming separation; a time to make promises of eternal love and exchange personal mementos to illustrate that adoration; and a time for one final celebration giving impetus to their passage to adulthood—attended by the Leighters, Dr. Owlfeather, and the Granlins—resplendent with barbecue, funny hats, gifts, and tears.

Then came college: computers and e-mails; cell phones and text messages; intercessions and holidays; studies and exams; research and failure, and then research and success; yet more studies and exams. Such was the life of Ricky and Mag.

... and I was there for him, always.

... and he needed me less and less.

---

6   Stephen Stuart, *Rantings* (2009).

Bean's statue went with him to college and retained, at least at the onset of his days in academia, a prominent spot on his desk. Now, as Rick approached the conclusion of his first four years of formal studies, I was a paper weight somewhere amid the accumulation of notes and pizza boxes that adorned the floor of his room.

Yes, we did have conversations now and then, when he needed a sounding board for his theories or questions about relevant historical comparisons in his studies. He still believed I was encapsulated in Bean, and as usual, I refused to enlighten him as to the true nature of my assistance.

After two more years of advanced studies in various institutions, he was awarded a master's degree in clinical research.

After another two years and a well-received thesis on the redirection of electrical impulses coordinated with variable frequencies in the diagnosis and treatment of mental disorders led to a PhD in Rick's chosen field.

Mag, on the other hand, had a few more years of med school and internship remaining before she would be able to combine her knowledge with Ricky's and venture forth with him to fulfill their destiny.

It was time for Rick and me to part company.

Sarah and Rick had slowly faded from my sphere of influence over the years. I required no overt signs of gratitude from them; I guess that Ricky's success and the pride he demonstrated in himself was gratitude enough for me.

However, the emotion I received from the boy-turned-man was of a most fervent nature: he didn't want me to depart his life. But he knew that his need for me had lessened to the point where he could now evolve further on his own.

I told him that the statue would always be there to remind him of a friendship that would be part of his life forever. He would just have to gaze at it and let his thoughts run free and have confidence that the solution he sought would be the correct one.

I approached Mag at the graduation ceremony and allowed myself to enter her mind. I made sure she was alone and calm enough not to be startled by my intrusion into her mind.

"Hello, Mag. Please don't be frightened. I'm Bean."

"Where are you? I don't see your statue. My God, I'm imagining this. With all this excitement and Ricky getting his PhD today, my mind is frazzled."

"*Not true. No one is aware that I can infuse myself into an individual's thoughts without them being in the presence of the bronze. Not even Ricky is cognizant of that fact.*"

"You are real, aren't you? I had given myself up to accepting Ricky's contention that you and he had a special relationship, but it was in the realm of his subconscious. What do you want with me?"

"*It's time that I take leave of my friend, and I've already apprised him of that decision. I feel he no longer requires my assistance and—ahem—interference in his life. He has adapted to life extremely well and has overcome his handicap well enough to be able to control any relapse that might occur. I'm sure now that you and he will be a team both in your personal life as well as in your professional life and that, if needed—and I truly believe that those moments will be very rare indeed—you will be there for him to provide the guidance that I once offered.*

"*Yours will be one of the great love stories of your generation, and I somehow played a small role in your achieving it.*

"*I only ask that if and when he brings our friendship up in conversation, you will allow him the courtesy of discussing me without implying that I am just an imaginary being.*"

"You have my word on that, Mr. Bean, and thank you for all you have done for my Ricky. You'll have our eternal gratitude."

"*One other thing I ask of you: please do not tell him what we have discussed today. It is imperative that he believe what he has accomplished was the result of a coordinated effort by Drs. Owlfeather and Braunstein, as well as his parents. If he were made aware of my ability to enter his mind at will, I'm afraid he would lose his confidence and suffer some form of relapse.*

"*You must promise me that.*"

"If you wish, I will take an oath to do what you request."

"*It is not necessary; your word will suffice.*

"*Take care of each other, and do your best to be the best.*

"*I can't promise you, but if I am able to do so, I will attempt to visit both of you in the future and see how you are doing. Again ... no promise ... but possible.*

"*Good-bye now, and my prayers go with you.*"

"Good-bye, and mine are with you as well."

If Ricky and Mag were a reflection of the new crop of citizens in this land, I was truly optimistic that they would fare well.

My next leave-taking was from a man I would not easily forget: Dr. Harrison Owlfeather. Oh, the discussions we had had and the successes we had shared! If only my race were witnesses to what a human relationship could be, they would abandon their retreat and join me in my crusade.

Those were my very words to him; and to me, the tears in his eyes were words enough in return.

I remained at the ceremony until it was Ricky's turn on the platform.

"... and now, ladies and gentlemen, I present to you our valedictorian and recipient of a doctorate degree in clinical psychology, with a specialty in autism and Asperger's Syndrome, Dr. Richard Granlin."[7]

"Rick ... my dream," murmured Sarah Granlin.

---

7   Stephen Stuart, *The Wonder of All That Is: The Story of Bean* (2009), 297.

Redux Two:

Book One

One postscript must be conveyed to you. It occurred during the graduation ceremony where Richard received his honored degree.

I hovered over Sarah and Rick; a more sedate Aunt Melody and her extended family; and an aged, but still vital Dr. Owlfeather. I was blanketing them in a shawl of electrons when I felt, or rather sensed, the presence of a familiar entity.

At first I couldn't believe that Whatever had returned to torment me once again. I was convinced that there was no way he could have escaped his polyethylene prison that, combined with tons of similar disposable detritus, formed a ski slope outside of Lake Placid.

I surveyed the area as well as I could, still maintaining my position surrounding the Granlins, but I failed to espy the object of my disconcert.

I finally gave in to that nagging feeling and started to reconnoiter the ceremonial venue. I was hesitant to display the ability I had acquired many years ago to move around without a host, so I stealthily entered a squirrel I had encountered on the outskirts of the arena.

And there he was, sitting on a branch bedecked in the coal-black visage of a raven.

"You're not Whatever! Who, if I am not being too presumptuous, are you?"

"Who am I? Ha ha, who am I?"

"Well, you can call me Whoever, for lack of a more precise identity."

Oh, no! Shades of an impending tormented itch!

"Where did you emanate from? What do you want? Why are you here? Go away!"

"Easy does it; calm down. Interesting: how did you manage to attain human emotions? I was under the misconception that we folk do not have the facility to accomplish that useless capability. Kinda interferes with our noodling into their lives with our patented cold, detached, total lack of sensitivity; at least *I* still retain a total lack of emotion. The end I achieve most definitely justifies the means, and the end result is almost always glorious.

"These humans are so gullible and self-centered that little or no effort is required to create mayhem. The real challenge is to alter the thinking of a so-called dispenser of virtue—one who decries salvation from a pulpit of faith—and fashion him into a creature of my ilk ... of my design. That is true talent.

"I felt your presence during a scouting expedition earlier and decided to perch and see if you would catch my drift. I wasn't able to locate you, so I decided to bide my time and await your introduction.

"So here we are, sitting on this limb, conversing like old friends and knowing that we have absolutely nothing in common, wishing that the other would disappear from this zone of influence."

"I couldn't have put it more pithily. Where are you off to now ... if not sooner?"

"You truly have learned sarcasm from your human charges, haven't you?

"Well, if you must know, I am off to what is called Africa: to a location in the jungle. An infant has been born to an isolated, primitive family, and she has been endowed with an incredible aura of evil. She will be ripe for my guidance and, with a little help, she might alter the evolution of man. She is the sixth child born to the wife of the village spiritual leader, and today is June 6. I'm all atwitter.

"Coincidentally, isn't Africa supposed to be the cradle of man's emergence?

"What are your plans—unless, of course, you are involved in something inconsequential here?"

"Actually, I've all but concluded my business here.

"I, too, am about to answer the call of an infant.

"She has been taken in by the pastor of a small church in the southwestern United States. He and his wife had been unable to conceive themselves and have accepted this child, deposited in their automobile by a distraught mother, as a blessing.

"The wife related that a strange calm permeated the house when the child was brought home. Very interesting, don't you think?"

"So off I go. I have no doubt that we will meet again someday, somewhere—if not by accident, then to prove the old human adage that opposites attract.

"If I may take this moment for a little prediction, I believe that our innocents may, as you so well put it, affect the advancement of man. They will confront each other and engage in a conflict for the very soul of humanity. However, needless to say, this very battle has been ongoing since the dawn of time and has resulted in a stalemate. There is no reason to suspect that this encounter will be any different. The one outstanding feature of this clash will be the means to the ultimate impasse. I am reminded of a teeter-totter, balanced on its fulcrum, tilting one way and then the other."

"Well put; I look forward to it.

"Now to give this bird a jump start. We have a lot of mileage to cover and much strategy to hatch."

"We do what we must; that is our destiny."

I witnessed a shudder sweeping through the audience as a cold breeze blew past their heads when he rose with a piercing caw. With a powerful flapping of wings, he headed due east, toward the oncoming mantle of night; I, following the warm daylight, left my bushy-tailed host and soared westward, toward a new story.[8]

---

8   Stephen Stuart, *The Wonder of All That Is: The Story of Bean* (2009), 301.

... and now we begin

PAX

The Bean Chronicles

CHAPTER 1

LATER ... MUCH LATER

From the Diary of the Reverend William Fellows

The first thing that hits you is the smell.

Long before we approached the place, long before we saw the enemy; long before we heard the cacophony of battle, it was ... the smell!

How do I describe a smell as abhorrent as this one? It is a smell; a taste; a corruption of both nasal and throat membranes. It is a burning ... a congealing of mucosa too thick to spit out, too thick to swallow.

It is an ever enlarging coagulate damming the spillways of your gullet.

It is a pressure on the chest, as if a thousand pounds of molten lava is slowly smoldering its way through to your lungs.

... and yet we went on, as if driven by some superhuman force intent on bringing this conflagration of evils to its final conclusion.

After successfully, but painfully, overcoming the noxious fumes, we developed a false sense of confidence—that is, until we spied, in the far distance, clouds of a motley gray boiling in a sky as dark as any hole in a stygian grotto. At the base of that living body of filth was a line of bright red slowly being assimilated into the cloud, becoming crimson sparkles mimicking the flickering of stars in a distant nebula.

What happened to our bravado, our sense of invulnerability? It passed in an instant. Hesitation superseded any assurance we had managed to generate. Insecurity gnawed its way into our hearts as we stumbled forward as if mired in a pit of primordial ooze destined to become specimens for future bone hunters.

How could we ever have thought that we would be able to conquer an adversary as commanding as the one we were going to face momentarily?

With our defeat would come the defeat of all mankind, and we knew that we must, but could never, prevail.

We had assigned our mortal souls to whatever destiny has in store for us.

**Sometime in the not-too-distant future,
yet far enough ahead as not
to be today, and soon enough
as not to be much later.**

CHAPTER 2

This quest, this new adventure of mine, will present itself in more detail later on. But I believe the previous insert will impart a better understanding of the trial ahead.

On the way to this latest of my self-imposed assignments, I have decided to make a brief detour in an attempt to locate a comrade of mine—a comrade possessing intelligence and inquisitiveness who went off on an odyssey of his own many years ago. Hmmm … many years ago would mean more than a thousand, more or less, of man's years.

It would prove to be useless, and a tale of unrequited supposition, if I relayed his quest to you without his personal input, because I don't know what he has or hasn't achieved—or, indeed, if his quest has been satisfied. However, my pursuit has proven to be at once exhilarating and therapeutic at the same time.

Returning to the last location of our mini-summit provided no clue as to his present whereabouts. I decided then to enlarge my exploration by soaring as high as I was able to do, testing the limits of my powers. Interestingly enough, I discovered that the higher I ascended, the stronger my sensitivity increased. Electromagnetic force, combined with the concentration of the ionic blanket surrounding the earth, seemed to give me an acute awareness of life on earth. Sort of a cosmic dish antenna, if you please, receiving a cacophonic static filled with the emanations of billions of living creatures.

Now, if I can only filter out that dissonance of life's static and concentrate on my comrade's aura, I should be able to locate and visit with him before I initialize the contact with my new charge. However, the atmosphere is saturated with the cries and moans of millions and millions of the dispossessed and downtrodden masses that populate this once Edenic orb of bountiful delights. It is inundated with those who suffer from one or more of those infirmities of the mind and body; with the voices of those who have, but desperately want more; with the voices of those who have more but yearn for the power that more begets; with the voices of those who have the power but find that they are not alone and discover that their power is but an aphrodisiac for a despot's lust for the ultimate supremacy of the godhead, which can never be attained; with the cries of the hunter and the hunted; with the dying gasps of the innocent victims of climatic alteration. The good, the righteous, those having reached satisfaction with their personal dram or so of contentment, do not cry out in despair or greed for more. To sift through those cries of despair and locate the one positive entity I seek could possibly take forever, except that I enjoy a most unusual trait, and that is my prodigious memory.

I am once again predisposed toward negativism, and I apologize for that. I feel that something quite disconcerting is happening to man. The closer I am to earth, the clearer the signals are. Hope, love, and happiness definitely present themselves amid the atmosphere of negativism but rely upon a need for additional aggrandizement. But truthfully, the higher I ascend, the more the signals bond and the more they meld, and the more difficult it is to select the optimistic indications transmitted or locate the E *Pluribus Unum* of my stalk.

Prior to my re-emergent powers, I was unable to observe, on a large scale, man's affirmation of violence and greed, virtues that have been fed by a duplicity of leadership and a growing decline into paranoia being broadcast on the airwaves, on the pixilated screens, from the pulpits, and on the fading newsprint of their worlds.

I was able to isolate, although which much difficulty, my charges by their aura of virtue and avoid those with a negativity of spirit. It was what I wanted and what I was convinced was my charge of existence. Those positive spirits do exist, and it was, and is, my sincere aspiration for the future of the human race to enable them to achieve and practice a positive outlook on life.

The opening up of my powers, while definitely a godsend to my previous limitations, has proven to be distressing, for these powers have opened a vast new universe of observation and contemplation coupled with an overactive sensitivity for human emotions. I feel that I am at the beginning of a new era of virtuous ministrations to the lost souls of mankind. I am at the origin of an awakening of my faerie-landsmen, which could endow them with the possibility of a mass intervention by the heretofore subjects of isolation. Not now ... not so quickly ... but soon. You need us!

Note: Before we continue, I should alert you to the fact that prior to my assuming the nomenclature of Bean, we faeries possessed no true given names. Normally we assumed the names of our hosts, providing they were human in nature. Squirrels have no name unless, of course, you digitalize them into Squirrel 1, or Squirrel 2—which, if I may add, is totally ridiculous. Therefore I refer to my comrade simply as "comrade." Perhaps when we finally meet, he will have acquired some kind of mnemonic identification. I will, of course, resume my familiar identity of Bean, if familiar only to those bookworms who have garnered a word, a phrase, a sentence, a paragraph, or even a chapter of knowledge from my past exploits.

It is an interesting phenomenon that I am able to review all those emanations from below without involving myself in their trials. It is comparable to a deluge of historical proportions, a flood of Noachian significance, but one that will never dampen me—perhaps just a few dewdrops? Verrrry interesting, but inconsequential.

CHAPTER 3

What ho! Oh joy! Wahoo! (Please forgive my emotion-filled emanations, parroted from my many years of coexistence with man and his need to react with gusto.) I believe I have just received his unique imprint, and off I go to a renewal of our relationship. Of course, you are all invited to accompany me, as long as you choose to remain incognito ... and quiet. No interruptions, please. He is, unlike me, rather extroverted and loquacious and would like nothing more than to spar with you on a field of semantic turf.

Hmmm ... that's interesting: I can't seem to identify a physical form to relate to. The area appears to be some sort of a zone of infestation: insects, birds, bats, and all manner of creepy-crawlies. Yet his signature is very strong—indeed much stronger than the usual signature of my faerie brethren. It is more of a presence than that of a physical manifestation.

Has he somewhat regained those same powers, as I have, which were lost to us back in the dim recesses of our existence? It would put him in the same quasi-spiritual company as I am and make us a potential mirror image of each other, but with vastly different experiences to base our discussions and observations upon. The possibilities of an immensely meaningful relationship are awe inspiring.

But first ...

He spoke. **"It's time."**

I spoke. *"Yes, you could say it's time ... but time for what?"*

He spoke, rather startled. **"Who in hell said that?"**

I spoke in a calm and patronizing manner. *"Not hell, my old friend, but here and now, at the site of your apparent bewilderment. It has been a long—much too long, in fact—interval since we have enjoyed each other's company, and it's time now to renew our most enjoyable rapport. There is a great deal to talk about and so many adventures to regale each other with."*

"You! When ... where ... omigosh. I can't believe it! You have returned ... and at a very opportune time, I must say, for my moment here has all but concluded, and I will soon be free to join you for as long as long will be."

It's amazing, but he sounds just like me. One might imagine that our vastly dissimilar experiences have brought us both to the same mental and spiritual growth level. But it's the control of his inherent powers that interests me the most.

"I've just concluded a very rewarding episode with a wonderful group of human beings and was off on a new adventure when your image popped into my mind. I don't know if I received a transmission from you or not, but I had the desire to spend time with one of my own kind for a while, and your inimitable company was forefront in my thoughts.

"So here I am, just a gaggle of drooling electrons alight in an ionic cloud."

"I don't know what you are talking about, but I imagine that it's a good thing. Perhaps we can glow together and create a formidable force in our relationships with the denizens of Mother Nature.

"Yes: Mother Nature. We will talk about that later. So much time ... a thousand earth years or more.

"Do you have the moment, old friend?"

"I can't truly answer that question. I've obligated myself to direct the growth of a potential force for great good in the guise of a newborn infant. Normally I would say yes to a prolonged interval of companionship, but I am faced with a conflict against a powerful antagonist of darkness."

"I'm not sure I understand, but it will make for an interesting tale. All I ask is for a few hours to complete my work here, and we can regale each other for as long as we wish."

"Agreed.

"By the way, I have assumed a human name, at least temporarily. Call me Bean. When you are free, I'll enlighten you as to the reason I refer myself to that identification. My last adventure was so gratifying

(a human emotion and another topic for discussion) that I actually wrote a book about my experiences with the help of a strange, but somewhat creative, individual of the two-legged variety.

"I'm not aware of any of your exploits during our years of separation, but I have found man to be on the verge of entering a long period of desolation and possible destruction that could ultimately affect his very existence. So I felt that my uplifting experience with the Granlins was so satisfying, I wanted to share it with people searching for a sense of optimism and a reason for being."

"Bean? ... Fascinating! I can hardly wait to hear about it. I suppose you can call me Leader. You will understand that name shortly. Are you able to transmit the pages of your story to me? I would be very appreciative."

"You know, I never thought of that. Maybe we can put our heads together and share the words?"

"Written words?"

"Not written words ... just a conglomeration of orderly sound bites."

"Just testing you. I see you haven't lost your sense of humor. I can't tell you how I've missed it."

"By the way, what are you doing here in this indescribable miasma of unpleasantness?"

"Do you remember that, when we last conversed, I had developed a rather profound interest in man's insatiable predilection toward blood? Religious rituals, war, pseudo-medical treatments, literature, and descriptive elements of their speech, separately or combined, form an almost uncontrollable appeal to their nature. Why is the lure of blood so inherent in their personae? Why does the mere sight of it cause disgust or fright or even orgasmic excitement and fill the coffers of the masters of their media?

"So I decided to do some research and participate in some firsthand investigation.

"Where else but in the company of true blood feeders?

"So, for a thousand of man's years, I became an integral part of their existence—which, as I mentioned before, is coming to an end very shortly."

"Yes, I do recall your interest, but a thousand years? Please continue—I'm all ions."

"Ah, yes, it is time again.

"When you think about it, time really flies (a pun for the future).

"I just can't believe that an entire millennium has passed since our last mingle.

"The ironic thing about the last thousand years is that although humanity has suffered, it was not actually a major concern of ours (by ours, I mean the feeders to whom you will shortly be introduced). Plagues, wars, starvation, and inquisitions all combined to provide sustenance for us feeders and, because of man's grand foibles, we have grown strong, and we have grown mightily in number.

"The average walking buffet would undoubtedly pay no heed to us. A brief wave of an unconscious hand, an attempt to encapsulate us in a reflexive grasp, or perhaps a webbed swatter or a spray of some noxious gas are all designed to be rid of us. All are doomed to failure.

"Humanity's folklore is resplendent in dark tales of sanguinity cloaked in the garb of sinister wraiths prowling the streets in search of pedestrian plasma-engorged vessels.

"They stalk the four corners of the globe, immersed in the dark of night, assuming all forms of life, seeking out the Rh factor of their existence. A, AB, O: no matter. Disease, genetic abnormalities: no matter.

"Those accounts of monsters in the humans' midst have provided us with countless years of hysterical guffaws.

"Monsters ... oh, yeah!

"Shape-shifting creatures of the night ... oh, yeah!

"If those fools would only look beyond their superstitions, the truth would astound them.

"Look, I admit that a number of psychologically demented souls have fallen victim to those tales of blood-sucking fiends and believed that they were themselves of that ilk. Just thinking that a Shrek-like visage has the ability to impose itself into the terror of man's deepest fears is anathema to us.

"Hell: it gives us a bad name.

"You would think that hematophagia is a trait birthed by superstition gleaned from the ignorance and fears of primitive man.

"Wrong!

"'Tis not!

"Go back ... go wayyyyy back.

"I mean back beyond that ceramic depiction of a Persian gent being exsanguinated by a demon. Back beyond the Babylonian tales of Lilith and her predilection for the vital fluids of children.

"I mean wayyyyyy back.

"Five hundred million years back.

"Back to bacteria in its basic form as emerging from the ooze of terrestrial creation.

"Original life, an example of spontaneous generation or an alien-induced development, was liquid based. Maybe it wasn't blood as we know blood to be, but it was a life force nevertheless. Some single-celled entities had more liquid than others, and some felt they should have more than they were initially given.

"Hey, I'll take a little bit of yours ... you won't miss a dram or two."

"Sounds a bit familiar, doesn't it?

"Are you getting the gist of it yet?

"As life evolved, liquids evolved, and there were always those who felt undernourished in comparison to their comrades sans arms.

"So many questions as to the origin of complex life exist that I, as a mere gnat—although a revered gnat in my own world—do not have the ability to conjecture, nor do I have the desire to do so. Actually, I do not give a gnat's ass about it anyway!

"Somehow, those simple organisms, those bacteria and viruses combined, melded, married, or whatever and became creatures of substance. Weird and ugly creatures? I don't know. It's all relative, I guess. As a gnat—my chosen form—I am not particular about whom I confer anguish upon.

"Where blood was first introduced ... even I cannot answer that question. I've heard of monocyte and myeloid cells, but how they theoretically evolved into blood monocytes (Google it, for Pete's sake) is open for discussion among the learned ones. I won't even go there.

"Frankly, I don't care how they arrived at the dinner table, as long as they remain available ... and our bowls runneth over.

"Now I want you to imagine the carcass of a lifeless creature. Do you notice the abundance of insect life, or avian life forms, or any of a myriad of what you insultingly refer to as scavengers, swarming around the flesh and fluids of that cadaverous lump?

"My friend, those are the true vampires—not some caped fictional character introducing himself to a pale, blue-veined virgin.

"Maggots, assorted birds, blowflies, bats, leeches, ticks, mosquitoes: vampires all. My people ... my world. We are as old as old, with all the inherited wisdom of the ages. We have learned many secrets of survival and have the ability to alter or mutate ourselves to counter the defensive actions introduced by man and his most creative and ambitious brethren.

"We're here to stay forever, and that's more than I can say for humankind.

"If they want to get rid of us, or at least control us to some extent, all they have to do is cure disease, stop wars, and—heh, heh—stop dying. There is enough sustenance in the beastie world to keep us pleasantly engorged 'til death does us all part and this place becomes just another lifeless rock, as it ultimately will. There's no way anyone is going to pound a stake into our hearts ... and, by the way, we do love garlic. So let them sit back and scratch, dab on a little ointment, and go on with their lives."

"Do I sense a note of cynicism, old friend?"

"Perhaps, but take into consideration that I have been a gnat, and although I no longer possess the physical bearing of one, I do retain the mental recollections. That, plus the company I have been associated with for the past millennium, has endowed me with a rather overt sense of what you refer to as cynicism.

"Man does enjoy an ironic fixation on the idea, buoyed by the fables of ages past, that we are objects of fear and disgust because of what you—man, not you, Bean—describe as our obsession and predilection for an aortic cocktail.

"Wrong!

"Let's examine, if you please, some of their choice comestibles: Czernina from Poland, a delectable soup made from duck's blood; or black pudding, from the supposedly civilized pavement of the British Isles, utilizing pig or sheep or cow blood, depending on what is available in the vicinity. Ooh, I've got one: tiết canh, another delicacy (a breakfast repast ... much like Cheerios and bagel "mit schmear" is for Westerners) from the far East made from duck (an international favorite), blood, and peanuts—call it an Oriental trail mix. We travel now to Eastern Europe and their version of kishke, concocted from the blood of porkers and encased in their very own intestines; how about blood pancakes from Scandinavia and fried blood from Hungary (I suppose you have to be real hungry for that one)? The list continues with moronga from Cuba, mustamakkara from Finland (check out their lusting for those pancakes also), dinuguan from the Philippines. Biroldo, cabidelda, and on and on and on ...

"What is it with people? They condemn us; they loathe us; we disgust them; they fear us; and yet ... and yet they continue to demonstrate—rather voraciously, I would say—a fascination with and a peculiar hunger for the same nourishment.

"The one difference, and it is a rather significant one, is that they *choose* to partake of the venal river, while in our case, it is our lifeline.

"Primitive societies believed that if you drank the blood of your victim—be it four-legged or biped, feathered or scaled—you somehow imbibed his spirit, and you then benefited from his life force.

"If that is true about the less civilized, perhaps the more progressive of their societies have the same need, although subconsciously. Actually, even I find it difficult to comprehend why they would desire to be ducks and pigs and cows. Aren't they satisfied with the countenance they have been birthed to?

"Hmmm ... I guess not."

"You know, maybe man is so down on his own kind that he secretly wishes to alter his own countenance and assume the identity of a different species for a while.

Duckman ... now that sounds like an affable superhero—whom, if I may add, they might need in these hours of darkness!"

"Bean. Stop interrupting my diatribe on humanity. The hypocrisy of the Homo sapiens is a serious subject I am attempting to discuss, albeit in a one-way conversation."

"Serious? I will reduce my volume and allow you to proceed. This is indeed a very serious matter! I am anxious to hear the rest."

"Again I return to primitives and their ceremonial bedecking of themselves with costumes depicting the very beings they have been nourished with. The wear feathers and hides—in some cases, the very skin of their enemies. Never satisfied, eh? Hey, the grass isn't always greener—or redder, you know.

"In reality, we are the ones who should feel slighted. Can they honestly say they have ever wanted to costume themselves in the facade of a mosquito or a maggot? Now those are the true vampires, not some fanged-toothed dandies with red eyes and a theatrical intonation, eliciting a look of rapture and submission from over-endowed, scantily clad, obviously unfulfilled damsels.

"However, I might make mention that of the few acknowledgments humans have afforded us in the guise of cinematic presentation: mutant configurations, atomic disfigurements, and alien invaders, all thirsting for human blood. Talk about a malicious affront to us! Meanwhile, we have no platform for defense and punitive retribution.

"I see that your newfound enlightenment will take some getting used to. There is no glamour or vicarious excitement to be enjoyed by them for accepting us as the true *objects d'nuit*.

"The truth of the matter is that we sip both by day and night, at dawn and at dusk. You might say we are 24-7 nippers. I know that it isn't very romantic, and literature would have a hard time depicting us as such, but that's the way skin crawls, so man had better accept it.

"I have to admit we have become rather maligned over the years due to our inadvertent transmission of various lethal agents of disease. This has turned out to be one of our curses, and I must apologize for my brethren, but if you look at it as population control and not as scourge, man might be tempted to offer us gratitude and not scorn.

"Hell, they can't foist blame on us for disease. The conditions that many of their societies are forced to live in structure the circumstances for the incubation of those very same maladies they are so quick to label us as culpable for. They should clean up their own messes, damn it, and stop calling the kettle black. Instead, call the blood red! As I mentioned previously, it isn't the hitchhikers in the serum that we crave; it's just the serum itself. Those buggers are just fertilizer, and we are pretty generous in our donations to the environment.

"Speaking of the environment: it has caused us to evolve and adapt to the many differences inherent in the various regions of the earth.

Extreme cold induces hibernation, and our awakening is dependent upon the change of seasons. The severe arctic temperatures can also be blamed for the demise of many forms of life while, ironically, also preserving the carcasses for future engorgement. Thus when the temperature warms, we participate in what you call swarming. Hey: it's just that we have to make do when we can.

"The same holds true in the blazing heat of desert climates. For us, nighttime is feeding time.

"Cold, hot, wet, or dry, we drink. We are part of nature's sanitation squad and therefore a necessity in the food chain.

"The millennial gathering of the clans has been a ritual performed by us since the availability of plasma became commonplace, and we thrived beyond anyone's expectations.

"This explosion of plasmaholics imbued us with the obligation to create rules and regulations to be set into place as a safeguard against total anarchy, which could ultimately lead to a loss of genus identity.

"To be more explicit, the most important cardinal rule is that no sucker shall suck juice from another sucker. This is tantamount to incest, and incest is the true original sin. The search for knowledge was not *numero uno*, no matter what some thinkers seem to think."

"Incest ... the original sin? Now that is a subject that will rouse the hackles of your enthralled audience. Do you want to explain that hypothesis, or must you continue with your oration?"

"All right, I'll take a break in berating my captives.

"Do you recall my mention of Lilith earlier on? Well, I got this from a very reliable source—albeit one with a hiss and of a lisp in his speech—that she, and not Eve, was the first wife of Adam (he of biblical fame). Well, I shouldn't say wife; there was no formal license or ceremony partaken of.

"At any rate, she was one tough mama and wanted the same rights and privileges that had been conferred upon her common-law husband. Adam moaned and groaned and complained to God that she was driving him off the deep end.

"So to placate his son, who was designed in his own image, God banned Lilith from the garden, but not before she had given birth to a daughter who was called Eve. The famous rib description wasn't a rib in reality, but a symbolic depiction of Adam's male regalia!

"Lilith, as a means of severe punishment, was relegated to the position of harpy, a demon who—now, here we go—was accused of drinking the blood of infants: a serum sister from the past. Her reputation was strengthened in Babylonian literature as well as in the Kabbalah scriptures. Sort of set the norm for the future of women's lib, eh?

"Over the years, Eve had emerged as a very comely female. Now imagine: an attractive, inquisitive, and lusty woman ... the serenity of the Garden of Eden ... and a man who hadn't partaken of the rights of husbandry for many, many years ... and so the naughty happened.

"Now, they might not have been discovered—God having been occupied in further advancing creation—had not Adam's snake, able to speak at that time and the repository of interesting bon mots, given them away."

"Pardon my interruption into this most interesting tale, but remind me to divulge the identity of snake—or, at least, his spokesman. By the way, are we speaking of the same snake?"

"Agreed. You mean he actually gave it a name *and* imbued it with the power of speech? How quaint. Now let me continue.

"Thus God, in his virulent dissatisfaction with the 'first couple', banished them from the garden and sent them out into the real world to find their own way and sire the precursors of humanity. Now this is where it gets interesting: Adam and Eve's children had no choice, due to the discernible fact that there were no other examples of their species at the present time, but to continue producing offspring and encouraging them to mate in what I refer to as the Incestuous Revolution.

"Now Cain slew Abel, and that left just two children for Adam and Eve, both boys.

"So where did the females come from to provide man with the vessels for reproduction?

"More ribs from Adam? Were the two boys hermaphroditic? Was Adam himself a hermaphrodite? Is man the spawn of himself? Is that why he has nonfunctioning breasts? Isn't it accepted by many religions that Eve came from Adam? If this is true, didn't that endow him with the ability to self-reproduce?

"This could, if you have an open mind, explain man's inevitable decline into idiocy: inbreeding has finally claimed its reward."

"Never quite thought of it that way. However, you should keep your theory to yourself ... if you can. You will definitely irk and cause ire as well foment many secret cabals bent upon your destruction and the defamation of your character."

"I beg to differ with you, my naive friend; according to the Manichaean Gnostic sect (and how would I know of such a thing? Observation, observation, observation), incest was the initial coupling of male and female, which produced a son, Cain: "... He engendered with her a son, deformed in shape and possessing a red complexion, and his name was Cain, the Red Man."[9]

"Taking heed of your theory of the "original sin," are you a believer in the intelligent design concept so favored by the various religious factions? We both have existed too far beyond the era referred to in the tales derived from the diverse beliefs of the devout to put much credence in it. I believe that there is a logical reason for that concept that deals with the original settling of agricultural societies in the Fertile Crescent of the Middle East."

"Hey—that incest discussion was between you and me and was not a topic for wide distribution. Agreed? I didn't mean to open up a thorny topic. We can, if you wish, attack it at a later date?"

"Of course we can, but I admit I've been there and done that. Please, proceed with your rules of suckertude."

"Another rule is, 'Move over, sucker, and let your neighbor suck, for there is plenty to suck for everyone.

"The final canon is to suck, and then go forth and multiply, for multiplication guarantees that the dead shall not have died in 'vein', and the suckees have provided the suckers with a reason to continue their sucking.

"Now, to ensure that those tenets are observed with strict religiosity, a leader or guardian is to be appointed, and he shall be called the bleeder leader. That is I.

"Whoa, before you start thinking that I am billions of years old, forget it: I'm just a young thousand-year-old ex-gnat. Not, I should point out, a gnat in the physical sense, but instead an accumulation of the totality of thought and experience gathered from the beginning of time. I am but a spiritual presence evolved from the corporeal

---

9   See "Manichaean Adam Traditions from Theodore bar Konai: The Order of Nazorean Essenes)" http://essenes.net/index.php?option=com_content&task=view&id=652&Itemid=929

gnat of my origin. My material embodiment disappeared many years ago, but not before I was chosen by the previous bleeder leader to perpetuate the spiritual health of the long line of entomological, aviary, floral, and bestial suckers.

"Now, with the passing of another millennium, it is again time to choose from among a large group of candidates a successor to that ethereal position of the plasmaholic's godhead.

"This will require that I conduct interviews of candidates from all corners of the globe and in all forms of suckertude."

CHAPTER 4

"Being the spiritual leader of billions and billions of sippers isn't always the boon it might seem to be. When I was chosen as the 500,000th bleeder leader, I had to give up a life devoted to the gleeful tormenting of man and beast. Between missed swats and errant tail swipes, I luxuriated in the knowledge that those helpless hosts were compelled to accept my less-than-amorous hickeys.

"Although perspiration was my primary choice of refreshment, a drop of the red serum, devoid of fermentation and of no recognized vintage, offered up a special treat when available. You might say that I used to swing both ways—sort of a bifluid flier.

"My present task will be to choose my successor among the fourteen thousand arthropods; a few annelid worms that have a predilection for blood (you know them better as leeches); the lamprey eel; bats; and a few birds. Of course, not every creature wants to assume the lofty perch I now hold.

"In most cases, the nominee will be chosen by acclimation in a convention attended by representatives of his genus from caucuses around the world. In some instances, I alone will be the ultimate opter, or appointer of finality. In other words, I am *the* gnatiest of all gnats!

"I remember my selection was the result of four ballots in which I just barely beat out a Hessian fly who promised a reign of constant molestation upon human beings. My feeling—and I succeeded in convincing the convention—was that too much harassment would force the sippees to create a most lethal potion in defense of their sanity. This could ultimately result in the costly ebbing of our influence. Too much of a good thing is not necessarily a good thing. My motto was 'make a little go a long way: sip a dram now ... take a nap; sip a little more ... take another nap.'

"My biggest competitors, not counting the Hessian, were the bats from South America and an oxspecker bird from Africa. As far as the leeches were concerned, before they were able to reach the convention, they had either dried up en route or provided a gourmet's repast for hungry birds and their offspring.

"Local buzzzz has it that a number of leeches had made a bargain of sorts with a flock of oxspeckers. You could call it a no-win situation, and it readily illustrates why neither one has come even close to bleeder leader. While not known for their intelligence, both parties have vastly exceeded their reputations as being among the least cerebral of the sucker genre.

"This is the way it worked: In return for allowing themselves to be toted by the birds, the leeches offered to nourish them. Attached to the underbellies of the avian hosts, the leeches proceeded to take their fill from the host carriers. As the birds lost strength due to a lack of blood and fell to the ground, the unfettered members of the flock would partake of the ingested liquid from the leeches and offer their underbellies in return for the continued journey. Unfortunately, the logistics of such a plan just didn't work out. By the time that the oxspeckers realized their mistake, they began to simply ingest the leeches in toto. So as the carriers nosedived to terra firma, and as the birds digested the leeches, and as this abomination progressed to the point of no return, the first cardinal rule came into being: thou shalt not suck juice from a fellow sucker. Inbreeding eventually took its toll, and the entire squadron perished somewhere in northern Bratislava without ever fully realizing the error of their ways.

"Actually, it was a good thing that they gave up their ghost because, as their lack of intelligence would have it, they went the wrong way and would never have reached the convention anyhow.

"Where, then, I'm sure you are wondering, was the grand brouhaha to convene?

"This you have managed to learn for yourself. The last thing our society wanted was to be jostled and intimidated by the paparazzi. I can, however, tell you that this is a sacred place, known but to a few of the chosen, where the gathering takes place on the millennium. This knowledge is furtively passed on to the nominees and their contingents when the time is right and the calling is near.

"It is an isolated place, for the din caused by countless swarms of buzzers, the screeches of bats, and the tweets of birds would undoubtedly alert both predators and humans alike, and our very existence would be in peril; bedlam would reign supreme.

"The thought of disrupting the election for our new elected bleeder leader is too horrible to fathom. It would also mean that I would have to remain at the pinnacle of suckerdom for perhaps another thousand years or until a new remote and inaccessible location was accepted by the election committee.

"Representatives would have to be sent out; suggestions would have to be presented and the various options debated; caucuses would have to be convened; and then lobbying would take place until the final choice was accepted by the rank and file. This could conceivably take at least an additional thousand years.

"Hey, I'm tired, and I am slowly losing the ability to reminisce about the days when I was but another gnat engaged in the excitement of torturing the beasts of the world—and that includes, most definitely, those of the two-legged kind."

"Hey ... you're 'gnat' going to get senile on me now, are you?" I chuckled.

"Ear flitting and nose flitting—especially nose flitting—were my specialties. I rejoiced in the spastic and ineffectual manner in which they proceeded to slap themselves silly, vainly attempting to dislodge my ministrations. Their reaction time was no contest, and I was left to my nerve-racking attacks on their accessible derma.

"Well, back to the narrative at hand.

"There has been a marked prejudice against the larger of the hematophagieists due to their vulnerability, both in size and visibility. Why, with the sheer majority of our order, we have been triumphant each and every millennium in selecting one of our own to that lofty place in the hierarchy of suckers. Black flies and mosquitoes, along with my fellow gnats, have been the major supplier of bleeder leaders, and I anticipate no great challenge to that position.

"Interestingly enough, ticks have made a breakthrough in their participation at the convention. They showed ingenuity in attaching themselves to unsuspecting mammals that just happened to be heading our way. Although most of them had unfortunately become casualties of their own uncontrollable thirst for blood, resulting in a tremendous expansion of body size that caused them to release their hold on their hosts, a few did arrive in time to cast a vote. We dipterans—a word I have learned from man—had no difficulty in convincing them to cast their votes for one of us. I could say that we should "stick together," but that would be against the first cardinal rule.

"We almost had to postpone this year's convention due to a weather anomaly. A major hurricane off the coast of New Orleans has blown a number of gnat and mosquito swarms way off course. However, fortunately for them, the aftermath of a storm of that magnitude creates conditions that prove to be very fertile for the birth and growth of our fellow beings.

"But that is neither here nor there. The problem facing the convention's opening is the belated appearance of those misguided relatives. Perhaps a change in the jet stream will allow those errant swarms to regain their sense of direction and compensate for the loss of time?

"Human beings cannot comprehend the difficulties we have to face. They think that being swiped at is bad enough ... but to face nature on top of it all ... you just can't imagine. Admit it!

"To continue, I have a short list of potential candidates: a leech from South America (that is, if it can get here in time and in healthy condition), a Tsetse biter from Africa, and a vampire bat from, of all places, middle Europe.

"It has been written in the saga of humankind that the origin of man is derived from the fertile prehistory of Africa. The thought that has prevailed upon my mind during my countless hours of boredom is whether our vampire legacy is also based upon the same environment. We derive our enjoyment from the torment of our two-legged benefactors; without their offerings, we are a most sorry group of serum imbibers.

"The candidates in question will be thoroughly vetted by the nomination committee, who in turn will have been thoroughly pampered by the ministrations of the various lobbyists who have agendas to fulfill and clients to appease.

"This is not a new situation, but one that has been perfected over the past thousand millennia.

"A choice victim or two with primo plasma and the promise of a warm climate for our arctic brothers are some of the enticements put forth by the lobbyists. Those organized and well-paid suckers give us suckers a bad reputation, but competition for my lofty office has become fierce among the qualified and the well connected. What is fascinating, though, is how those lobbyists manage to avoid the first cardinal rule. They don't actually attach themselves to hosts in order to suck their blood; they just suck their hosts' ethics out and replace them with greed. It takes a very strong-willed and dedicated advocate for the swarm's good to withstand the insipid goading of those mind suckers. The only allegiance they maintain is to their propensity for power, which, fortunately, is limited to the short life span of the individual organisms. Needless to say, whether such undermining of integrity occurs for a day, a week, or a season, it remains a blot on our noble cause.

"To listen to the accusations and the protestations of the campaigning, combined with their exaggerations and out-and-out lies, is enough to rot the souls of the most stalwart of us.

"Lucky for me, I'm just a spiritual presence, and nothing can be offered to me that would color my judgment. I wish that I could say the same for the committee.

"Notwithstanding, I am the final authority in the choosing of my successor. The interviews will provide a dominant interjection of reasoning and thought and will prove to be the basis for my decision. I look forward to that event with both trepidation and excitement.

"When the interviews are completed, and if the candidates pass my muster, then they will be presented to the full convention for a formal debate, in which a series of questions will be asked of them. Following the debate, the rank and file will vote for the candidate of their choice. If I approve, I will then present to the attendees the new bleeder leader among hoots and hollers; numerous fly-by formations of precise swarms of flies, bats, and birds; and finally, an orgiastic display of raunchitude fed by the distillation and fermentation of vintage plasma.

"Meanwhile, ongoing will have been a pre-celebration of feasting on the recently defrosted decaying carcasses, as well as the vigorous imbibing of virgin blood from the newborn fauna in the vicinity (uh oh, and ooops: I almost gave away our location). As usual at these roundups, a mood of outright physical and emotional abandonment pervades the arena, and the air is permeated by the bouquet of sexual pheromones. Lascivious grins and headaches are the course for the day, and the future will bring forth countless love larvae in all forms.

"Do I miss it? I can't remember. Judging by the surrounding atmosphere, it must have been very enjoyable. It's a youngster thing, I suppose.

"By the evening of the first day, I will be presented with the reports of the vetted candidates from the nomination committee. At first glance, they will likely all appear to be relatively qualified and express eagerness at their desire to rule the roost. The first interview will commence at daybreak and after the first sipping of the day. Number one will be the leech from South America. I anticipate a rather long, drawn-out session. Leeches are not known for their swiftness.

"One thing I failed to mention is that, although we do not have names per se, each candidate will present themselves with a chosen ID as to differentiate themselves from other members of their group."

"May I audit the hearings if I promise to remain quiet?"

"Absolutely. In fact, I may call upon your advice at a later time."

CHAPTER 5

[10]*"Buenos Dias... Señor ... Leader. ... Soy ... Esmeralda ... LaLeeche."*

Esmeralda? This was a female? How in hell could you tell?

"Please, Ms. LaLeeche, in English, if you please. *En ingles, por favor.*

Excuse my saying this, but you are the largest leech I have ever seen. You've got to be at least a foot long."

The largest and the ugliest.

"Si ... pardon ... yes ... I ... will ... speak ... in ... English. I ... am ... from ... the ... Amazon ... Rio ... and ... *mi* ... *hermano, Gordo,* ... he ... is ... mucho ... mas ... grande ... than ... me."

"Very good; er, *muy bien.*" What am I doing?

"Now that that is settled, please tell me why you want to be the new bleeder leader."

Hopefully, she would use as few words she could; otherwise, this could last the entire day, if not longer.

"Si ...yes ... I ... will ... continue. Thank ... you.

"My ... leech ... pod ... is ... faced ... with ... extinction. ... Man ... has ... moved ... into ... our ... land ... and ... is ... cutting ... down ... large ... areas ... of ... woods ... so ... they ... can ... dig ... great ... holes ... in ... the ... ground. ... They ... look ... for ... shiny ... stones ... which ... they ... seem ... to ... covet. ... But ...

---

10   Note from the author: I have attempted to introduce the various dialects of
     the candidates into the story line in order to bring the reader a little closer
     to the narrative. I hope I have succeeded.

in … doing … so … they … change … the …condition … of … our … stagnant … pools, … our … *casas*,… our… homes. …Because… of… their… actions, … our … homes … have … been … polluted … with … terrible … chemicals … that … make … living, … even … for … us, … impossible ………"

"Hello there! Hola! Are you still with us?"

"I … am … so … sorry. … Sometimes … I … forget … where … I … am. …

"I … will … continue, … with … your … permission, … of … course."

"Yes, please do."

Please don't.

"No … longer … do … the … white … coats … come …and … put … our … families … in … glass … containers … and … take … them … away … to … far … distant … lands. … I … do … not … know … what … they … do … with … our … loved … ones … for … none … has … ever … returned. … Perhaps … this … is … a … good … thing? … Maybe … they … will … be … the … last … of … our … kind? … Living … in … a … glass … would … be … better … than … becoming … fertilizer … for … a … dead … world.

"We … have … become … a … dying … breed … and … will … soon … fade … into … oblivion."

Her speech was mind-numbing. I felt as if I had become the unwilling victim of a brain freeze (humans could relate to this discomfort by comparing it with an ice-cream headache), or at least I would if I had a brain.

"Yes, and what do you expect to accomplish if you are chosen to be bleeder leader?"

"I … would … be … a teacher; … a … teller … of … tales. … I … would … relate … the … saga … of … our … lost … pod … so … all … would … know … of … the … evil … practices … of … man.

"I … do … not … understand … why … they … do … what … they … do … to … the … land; … for … they … make … it … a … dead … place. … There … is … no … longer … any … food … for … us. … We … are … forced … to … obtain … nourishment … from … each … other. … This … is, … of … course, … in … opposition … to … the … first … cardinal … rule … and … we … will … be … cursed … forever … unless … I … will … be … allowed … to … tell … my … story … for … all … to … hear. … It … will … be …

a ... warning ... against ... the ... immorality ... and ... greed ...of ... humankind."

"Hmmm ... I see. Is there anything else?"

"No, ... gracias, ... soy ... finito. ... I ... thank ... your ... holiness."

Holiness: I liked that.

"Holiness?" chuckled Bean.

"I thank *you*, Senorita LaLeeche. I will ponder a great deal of what you have said. My sentiments to your brother, Gordo."

There: I had thought about it. Talk about watching a stone sleeping!

"From what I've heard," I observed, *"and correct me if I'm wrong, it is said that leeches can have as many as thirty-two brains. Imagine the conflict that must rebound around that cranium!"*

"I doubt if a decision can ever be reached in a head like that one. Send in number two."

CHAPTER 6

Ah, it was the bat from Europe. I was curious, Leader thought, as to how a South American member of a truly respected species called the country of Romania its home. This session would provide a welcome relief from the dynamic tedium of Senorita LaLeeche and her snail-like recitation, I hoped. I did, however, have sympathy for her slithering toward extinction, and that would weigh heavily in my decision.

But first, to the next candidate at bat.

"Please alight on the limb and sign in."

This would be a little disconcerting, what with him hanging upside down. I only hoped he didn't talk backward.

"Bun zi," glorious leader. *"I sint chemare Dragos Vladu."*[11]

What in hell was he (it was a he, wasn't it?) talking about?

"Err, excuse me, my bat friend. Please speak in the English tongue. You do know how to do that, don't you?"

"I must apologize to my most esteemed leaderrr."

Now it was "esteemed"; I was beginning to like this, Leader smiled to himself.

"Yes, I am able to converrrse in that barrrbarrric tongue. It does not have the melodic overrrtones of my native language, but I vill neverrrtheless honorrr yourrr rrrequest.

"To rrrepeat, I am called Drrragos Vladu, and I am one in a long line of honorrred and rrrevered Desmondontidae, as our human dinees rrrefer to us."

---

11   Romanian: "Good day, glorious leader. I am called Dragos Vladu."

29

"I confer upon you, Mr. Vladu, greetings. I am most anxious to hear your qualifications, as well as your plans for your prospective guidance as bleeder leader.

"But first, I am very curious. As long as I can recall, your species of vampire bat has had as its domain: the warm, humid atmosphere of the Mexican and South American subtropics, and perhaps even some islands with similar weather conditions. How is it that you and your group—if I may refer to them as a group— call the country of Romania your homeland?"

"Yes … yes. It is a most interrresting story. Ve rrrefer to ourrrselves as the 'lost flock of the Amerrricas.' You are most correct in yourrr belief that ve are orrriginally come from northerrrn Mexico. Durrring the earrrly times, ve feasted upon the carrion of human sacrrrifices so amply prrrovided to us by ourrr Incan and Mayan hosts. All vas vell vith us; thanks to ourrr donorrrs, ve vere vell satiated.

"But, as time flew upon the vings of change, strrrange beings, evil oameni, invaded ourrr domain. These vere men who vore shiny vestments and carried loud and deadly veapons of var.

"Ourrr benefactrrrors vere viciously defeated, and afterrr a brrrief period of gluttony, ve vere in dangerrr of being left vithout a means to satisfy our need.

"A grrroup of us followed these killers of men on their long rrroad of destruction, feasting upon the rrremnants of devastation.

"Vhen they had succeeded in theirrr conquests, and therrre vere no longer any furtherrr peoples to defeat, our main source of nourishment had declined to dangerous levels.

"To make a long story short"—thank you—"ve secrrreted ourrrselves on board one of theirrr wessels, hoping for new worlds for them to conquerrr and forrr us to once again sate ourrrselves upon the blood of the vanquished.

"I cannot rrrelate to you the many lands ve trrraveled and the many days ve vent without food. Out of desperrration, ve did what ve had never before done: ve drank from the living man as he lay asleep on his ship's cots. Ve learrrned to fasten ourrrselves on the veins in theirrr neck and slurp theirrr life-giving and life-saving liquid from them.

"Ve vere careful not to awaken them in fearrr of discoverrry and certain death for us. Ve haf a verrry special potion vich ve secrrrete at ze puncturrre holze. It makes ze vound numb, zo ze victim vill not feel us. All that rrremained on their bodies vere two tiny puncture wounds vhere our extended canines prrrovided the entrrry.

"Due to the fact that they could not discoverrr vhat had caused those strrrange wounds and the fact that the inflicted appearrred to be wan and restless, a fearrr of the unknown perrrmeated the wessel, and they were convinced that the ship was currrsed by evil superrrnatural entities; weak humans!

"By the time ve had arrived at our final destination, an area called Carrrpathia, a legend of evil bloodsuckerrr demons had been born, and ve vere not eagerrr to dispel that horrrorrr.

"By then, ve had developed a taste for live human blood and perrrfected the operrration. No longer ver ve excited by the prrrospect of blood of carrion or of bestial blood. Ve flew at night and rrretired durrring the daylight hours in dank caves and deep castle dungeons.

"Ve vere often spotted on our departure from the depths of a certain castle ruled by a despotic king whose name I proudly carry, Vladu. Time and legend caused my namesake to be called by ourrr name, and he accepted it arrogantly: Vampirre. Ve became as one, and ve sharrred countless tales of horror and unholiness to this day.

"Oy, all this talking has made me verrry thirsty. I vill be off now and rrreturn soon. Pina la mai tirziu, my leaderrr."

"... and to you, Dragos Vladu, whatever you said. I look forward to continuing our talk."

Now this was an interesting subject. I didn't know what this bat had in mind for the future of the sucker society, but I had to admit I was extremely curious.

"Pleeze, I vill continue now."

"What the ...? Where did you come from? Sneaking up on me like that won't help your cause in the least bit."

"Yes, you are correct, and I am sorry. Ve have become, as you vould say, rrrather silent in our apprrroach. I vill emit a screech next time, if you so desirrre."

"That would be acceptable. Please continue."

"Our rrrlationship with Vladu prrrogressed to the point vhere ve had established a mutual goal. He vould place himself on the vindow ledges of ourrr intended victims and open them, perrrmitting us to enter the room and perforrrm our libations. If the blood wessel vould awaken, they vould see the shape of Vladu and believe he vas the cause of their discomforrrt. In this way, his legend grew, and he became famous as a crrreature of the night, although in all rrreality, the taste of blood nauseated him."

"Your story is very interesting, but what are your plans for the society if you were indeed to replace me as bleeder leader?"

"Ahh, so you ask, and I vill answer you now.

"I vould intrrroduce to all of ourrr people a taste for live human blood and wean them away from the vulgarrr diet of carrion. Leave those carrrcasses to the meat-eating beasts of the woods and partake of the rarrre and vonderful vintages of the neck."

"That is a most interesting concept, and I thank you for your intake.

"If you have nothing more to add, I would ask you now to depart. I have one more interview to convene, and time is getting short."

"Very well, Holiness. I vill await your decision.

"Pina la noi adunare iar; until it is time ve vill meet again."

"Whoa, leader," I observe, "you have certainly been keeping some strange company since I last saw you. You definitely need a break!"

"You've got something there. Now that is one scary bat! You might even say he is most definitely bat shit!

"The next candidate is a tsetse fly from Africa, the evolutionist's land of the ape-to-man origin. Based on my experience, this is the most promising of the group."

CHAPTER 7

"Greetings, mistress fly; unto you a good day."

"*Salaam, rafiki*[12] leader. It is my honor to be in your esteemed company. I am called Mosi Jela."

"That is a most melodic name. What does it mean, if I may presume upon you?"

"*Asante sana,*[13] most high. It is loosely translated as The First Born Whose Father Suffered During Birth. My father had a stomach ailment at the time of my arrival due to his overengorgement of some *Mbaya* simian blood. Darn apes—you can never tell where they have last been!

"*Samahani,*[14] I am sorry for speaking some words in my native Swahili language. I am very sorry."

"Not to worry. Please continue, and advise me of your reasons to assume the post of bleeder leader."

"I am an advocate of free trade, and by that I mean I am in favor of my compatriots sharing in the bounty of all regions of the earth. They shouldn't have to settle for local serum but should be able to partake of the varied and wonderful fruits of the vein situated in areas never before having been traveled by their kind.

"I myself would like to savor Mayan soup de vein. Perhaps blubber-enriched Eskimo slough.

---

12   Swahili: "Health, friend."
13   Swahili: "Thank you very much."
14   Swahili: "Excuse me."

"It excites me just thinking of all the treasures I have been forced to avoid due to the restrictions of travel that have been imposed upon me."

"What a wonderful idea, Mosi Jela."

"Asante, my leader."

"However, I have one major concern. It is noted that the carrying of disease is endemic within your species. I have heard of such pestilence as sleeping sickness in humans and nagana in cattle. What can be done by you to avoid infecting various species?"

"While I agree with you wholeheartedly that this is a concern, I can reach no solution, except one. I am willing to forgo any relocation by myself as well as my African brethren and to remove Africa from the countries that would welcome visitors until—and I must stress *until*—the epidemics have been quashed or the infected areas quarantined.

"I will, however, encourage the migration of other species to explore previously unknown areas of the world and sample the wares offered there. What say you, Bwana?"

"If you can guarantee what you have just proposed, I will give it serious thought.

"Is there anything else you would like to add? If not, I will conclude this meeting and offer my thanks to you.

"My decision will be announced tomorrow."

"Again, I will say *asante sana*, Bwana Leader. *Kesho*[15] it will be."

"Now that is one bright bug, Leader," I say.

"Have you made a choice yet, or will you spending the evening mulling over the prospects?

"Hmmm ... I just realized that you don't appear to have a chupacabra in attendance. One of those suckers would make one heck of a bleeder leader."

"You know, Bean, I never saw one of those guys. Every now and then, one of the swarm would mention that a chupa had been seen here or there, but if you really want to know, I think it is just a legend. It's too weird to be real.

"However, I think I will recommend the fly from Mombasa, or wherever she comes from. Females have slowly overcome the curse of Lilith and achieved parity with their male counterparts in many species."

---

15   Swahili: "Tomorrow."

"They still have the habit of sucking blood, don't they?"

"Humorous interjection, Bean. Now, if you will refrain from further chauvinistic remarks, I will continue.

"This female ran a very smart campaign and avoided any controversial accusations. She kept to her program and ignored all the attacks on her by her competitors. I fear that the conservative element among the constituency will howl and demand her refusal to accept the position. They would undoubtedly desire for the biters from Africa to "be condemned to everlasting purgatory in their disease-ridden hellhole." I cannot allow that to happen. If we are all to survive and progress, we must open our borders to immigration and unite all common species into a new order combining the best that each has to offer. We must be ready to assume our place in the scheme of things if and when man reaches his finality."

"Spoken like a true leader, Leader. You have justly assumed the guise of an elf of uncommon passion. While I was only able, at the time, to aid my charges as a disconnected entity, albeit with as much passion as you project, you have assimilated yourself into the very soul of your constituents. I humbly bow my haze to you."

"My gratitude, Bean; your praise means a lot to me, and it will aid me in making my final choice.

"I like her—the fly."

"Good choice."

"She will be the first of her gender to achieve the exalted position of bleeder leader. I can't wait for the convention to vent their spleens when they hear of my choice. It's going to be a real brouhaha.

"Come, let us leave this place and search out a place of solitude in which to converse and share our interrupted repartee.

"Tomorrow I will relinquish this position I have held for one thousand years. It will be a relief to be free once again."

CHAPTER 8

"You know, Bean, this Mosi Jela has infected me with a germ of curiosity. I should like to visit this place, Africa, and see for myself what the situation is in reality. Is there truly a pandemic running rampant, or is it but an exaggeration?

"Can I count on your presence as my companion in adventure?"

A splendid idea. I could use the voyage to confirm the intervention of my adversary, Whoever, into the soul of a newborn he claimed to be a possessor of true malevolence. I fear that he will facilitate the maturation of a being who will influence mankind for many years to come. This voyage will benefit me in my future involvement with a child born to decency and righteousness.

"I could use your help in understanding Whoever's foundation for her growth and the rapidity of his success."

"So be it. A quest presents itself, and once more we face it together. It is Sancho and Quixote—or is it Quixote and Sancho? Nevertheless, we are a formidable team, so beware all who oppose us in our pursuit of the windmills of adversity."

"I suppose I should alert you to the fact that I will be putting our adventures to print. I collaborated with a two-legger, as previously mentioned, in creating a printed version of my earlier exploits. He is a strange human with a predilection toward controversial topics, but he possesses an honest and sensitive soul.

"There is a good chance you will meet him at a later date, if I find it necessary to curb his enthusiasm—or, on the off chance that you yourself might voice objections to his prose.

"What say you?"

"Of course, if you vouch for him. Can you imagine? This will be my chance at immortality! Bean, you have given me a reason to rejoice. Just observe the auroral glow of my electrons!"

"While we are on the topic of electrons, how did you manage to restore those latent powers we were first endowed with? It took an implied emergency for me to regain them, but not after repeated trial and error—although I must admit that they became easier and easier to control as they were utilized more and more. I decided to secret them from others, as I felt that they would afford me more concise utilization in my interventions."

"Bean, I don't believe I have ever lost them. In all actuality, I have never given it much thought throughout my journeys. When I was elected the bleeder leader of this sanguine society—a position I was not actively seeking, as a matter of fact—I became an all-enveloping spirit and no longer possessed a corporeal being. It was such a natural transformation that I adapted to it without a second thought.

"I was able to surreptitiously escape obligations to my congregation and roam the globe to continue my observations of other life forms—especially of the human breed. Those thousand years contained much in the way of man's historical development, as demonstrated in his religious, scientific, moral, and physical attributes ... or, should I say, lack of such."

"I see that we have a commonality of cause; perhaps by sharing experiences, we may arrive at a consensus of opinion as to the direction man has chosen for his destiny.

"He is such a complex animal with incredible potential, but he is foundering in his inability to grasp the possibilities that lie dormant in his psyche. His physical maturation has occurred so quickly in evolutionary terms that his mental capacity for utilizing those facilities hasn't kept pace with his physical development; thus I believe that frustration has set in—and that frustration, combined with his knack for overemotional reaction, has been the major impetus for his constant need for aggression."

"I, too, am in awe of his intellectual latency. You won't find an argument with me. I've given it a lot of thought, but every time I seem to arrive at a conclusion, a conflicted spark throws a glitch in my ionic soup. I am slowly being convinced that no definitive solution exists to the abstraction that is the human animal.

"Perhaps that abstraction is in itself both the savior and the destructive force he subconsciously desires? Intellectually he must be aware that the direction he is taking can only lead to his demise, but emotionally he is unable to combat the irresistible yearning for power—the achieving of which ultimately leads to self-destruction or the annihilation of competitors. Hence the bloodlust that ultimately led me to the position I will be relinquishing shortly."

CHAPTER 9

"What, if anything, have you learned about man's fascination for blood?" I asked the gnat.

"It has very little to do with a literal thirst for blood. Instead it produces a death image that the vision of blood produces.

"Man is basically a territorial beast. His need for space is bred into his genetic structure, as exemplified by the expressions 'get out of my face' and 'you're in my space.'

"In both prehistoric times as well as recorded history, he has fought for his territory or he has fought to expand it by engaging in conflict with opposing forces. The ownership of territory was the original symbol of wealth.

"In battle, the sight of blood on an enemy's countenance signified victory.

"Today, civilized man—though that term is, I suppose, something of an oxymoron—contends with his territorial desires by legal means. The legality of white-paper combat is a topic for later discussion, but suffice it to know that he assumes the law will uphold his demands for personal territory without the need for overt bloodshed.

"The expression a 'thirst for blood' symbolizes the graphic depiction of death, the result of a victorious competition and the declaration of an ultimate victor.

"I won't enter into a discussion of the quest for territorial gain through actual warfare. Today's climate demands not only territory, which is a bonus, but the possession of the resources that the territory holds and the control of its inhabitants.

"Territorial conflicts, although occurring in contemporary times, supposedly in the era of civilization, demonstrate that the need for aggression remains buried in man's genetic makeup.

"Competition is also a manner of warfare, as in the various athletic contests. Although countless images of bloodied contestants can be found in the historical record, death is not desired. The loser is merely a symbol of defeat, which is a representation of death.

"Competition in business, especially in a hard-fought battle for potential financial gain, sometimes results in the combatants being referred to as 'bloodied.'

"My society derives its sustenance from the nourishment that plasma provides. The sensory pleasure is both mental and physical. It may be compared to the experience of a victim of a severe drought who suddenly comes upon a supply of water. The fluid doesn't necessarily taste good, but the satisfaction derived from that sustenance is exquisite. In fact, taste doesn't enter into the equation.

"Actually, about fourteen thousand species of arthropods suck blood to live. If you think about it—and who does?—and combine those arthropods with the countless other varieties of plasmaholics, it is amazing that man is not more terminally prone to leukemia."

"So what you are saying is that man's quest for blood has nothing to do with his taste for it, but instead, the image-provoking nature of violence is to blame? The primitive's imbibing of the liquid is accomplished for the spiritual belief system of his society and not for the sake of a pre-dinner gourmet cocktail?"

"I couldn't have put it more succinctly."

"But haven't you omitted one important aspect dealing with the physical and spiritual need for bloodletting?

"Ancients from all over the world used the procedure known as trepanning to bleed the patient and relieve him of a great deal of ailments, both spiritual and physical. With the drilling of a hole in the skull, they felt, the flow of blood would relieve the patient of pressure caused by wounds or even release demons that had caused him to behave in a bizarre manner.

"I myself was present at a trepanning ceremony in a Zapotec village in Central America back in the 1600s. If my prodigious memory serves me correctly, the patient was a victim of a severe blow to the head.

"I was an uninvited guest of the medicine man as he performed the ritual. Interestingly enough, no one reacted much to the actual flow of blood at that time. However, the Zapotec society did practice a substantial rite of sacrifice in which blood played a major role.

"Although the surgery was crude and primitive in nature, I felt that the operation was performed for the benefit of the patient with the belief that it was to his advantage and, if luck would have it, would aid in his recovery.

"Reinforcing the mystical element of the operation, some of the bone chips from the procedure were used as talismans by various chosen tribal members.

"To continue with my unwarranted dissertation, what about modern-day transfusions? Plasma replacement is a critical aspect in the saving of millions of lives, whether for relief from illness or as a replenishment of blood loss due to warfare, injury, or surgery.

"Don't you think that those uses, although beneficial in diverse situations, add to the mystique of the arterial flow?"

"So, if you will permit me to conclude this discussion, we agree that blood, whether figurative or palpable, is an integral part of man's existence.

"There is one more point I would like to make known, and this is for publication: I wasn't too anxious to exist solely on a diet of blood, which is why I chose the form of a gnat—or, to be more specific, a true midge. I was experiencing an impish moment and just wanted to annoy humans for a while. That's when I got caught up in this overindulged orgy of vampirism. No more hematophagy!"

"Agreed: the subject has been concluded!"

CHAPTER 10

"Now, what is it about your being seeped in negativism?" I asked the gnat. *"From what I gather, you appear to avoid any leanings toward a positive dialogue pertaining to man's trials."*

"Again, you're correct in your conjecture. I tend to be detached from the personal approach and exist more as an observer than as a participant. What I'm inclined to observe are the more brutal aspects of man's morbid demonstrations. I fear I have been greatly influenced by those actions and have become jaded in my thoughts.

"While you are concerned with the basis for good in man, I am extremely curious with the negativity he so blatantly projects.

"I envy you in that your relationships with your human hosts have apparently given you a more compassionate, and perhaps optimistic, outlook on their societies."

"I, too, have become a negativist in my observations, but unlike you, I have involved myself in situations that have proven to be very positive and emotionally rewarding. So I believe, most sincerely, that there is hope out there, and it is my quixotic endeavor to promote it as best as I can."

"By the by, do you remember the sixties and seventies, with those wonderful riots and demonstrations? There was a song that hit close to home with me. Don't ask me what that means, but the song became my anthem for a while. I'll bet you recall it also. Goes something like this:

They're rioting in Africa
They're starving in Spain
There's hurricanes in Florida
And Texas needs rain

The whole world is festering
With unhappy souls
The French hate the Germans,
The Germans hate the Poles

Italians hate Yugoslavs
South Africans hate the Dutch
And I don't like anybody very much

"Hey, I do remember that one.
Together, now: one, two, three ...

But we can be grateful
And thankful and proud
That man's been endowed
With a mushroom cloud

And we know for certain
That some happy day
Someone will set the spark
And we will all be blown away

They're rioting in Africa
There's strife in Iran
What Nature doesn't do to us
will be done by our fellow man [16]

---

16   Sheldon Marnick, as performed in the <u>1953</u> revue *Almanac* by John
Murray Anderson. ©Alley Music Corp. and Trio Music Co. Inc.

"Ha, ha, ha … that really brought back memories," the gnat laughed. "The ironic thing about that song is that it is as meaningful today as it was back then. My anthem of negativity."

"Your laugh—that represents a human emotion. Have you been shorting my ions, or have you actually experienced feelings?"

"No, I haven't. It's just my mimicking of a reaction of man. Did I insert it in the correct context?"

"Sounds right to me. It's a pleasant reaction to a humorous event or joke. Suffice to say that it is a good feeling, and I guarantee that you will understand it better at a later date.

"Actually, the song was *pretty humorous."*

"Well, no matter. We did sound pretty good; maybe we should enter a karaoke contest?"

"I can just picture it now: a crowded lounge; the clink of beer bottles, cigarette smoke creating a nicotine-infused borealis below the psychedelia of mood-enhancing lights … and suddenly the karaoke machine turns on, apparently by itself, and the room is filled with the disharmony of two noncorporeal voices.

"I'll bet the place empties faster than a pea in a three-shell Monte game."

"Be it as it may. I had taken a brief sabbatical sometime during the late 1960s and suspended myself over what the humans called a lovefest, in a park in New York City—Central Park, I think it was.

"The music was enjoyable, and the lyrics a rather a sharp denunciation of the politics of that era. But the lovefesting was unrelenting enough to make even a raunchy arthropod blush."

"I remember that night.

"It's funny, but I didn't feel your presence there. It was probably due to the combination of music, pheromones, alcohol, and funny smoke.

"I was watching the ritual while in the guise of a squirrel, surreptitiously directing a young couple who had just met and who were inebriated with the atmosphere of love that permeated the meadow.

"I wasn't able to assume the freedom of an ionic blanket at the time, so I was forced to meld with a life form of my choosing, albeit a squirrel.

"The humans had no fear, no hesitation—just the need to hold one another and, if I might pun a bit, suck face. Come morning, they would part company, never to see each other again, but infused with a memory that would last a lifetime: a memory of pure, uncomplicated

love—which would prove, unfortunately, a contradiction to the reality of adulthood.

"As much as I wanted to, I was yet unable to partake of the euphoria they experienced. I was destined to observe and study their surrender to an emotion I could only guess about. Someday, I wished ... someday ...

"I don't control my subjects. What I attempt to accomplish is to aid them in achieving their destiny, but only if that destiny is ensconced in an aura of righteousness. I let evil find its own way, and there are enough entities available to accomplish that feat.

"If they are unsure as to what direction their lives will end up taking, I will guide them, as best as I can, through whatever alternative course of action they might incur until—and it isn't always so—they reach that fulfillment of purpose.

"In a way, that lovefest represented an innocent and naive era driven by a need to end a war that nobody understood in a faraway place called Vietnam.

"They danced, sang songs, and made love as if those innocent actions would have the ability to influence the masters of mayhem. It was a casting off of the inhibitions foisted upon them by a different generation—a generation birthed in the Great Depression and fueled by an insane world war.

"Ultimately, perhaps, their naïveté did achieve a cessation of hostilities, but not until tens of thousands of their generation had given their lives to the folly of old men who would never find themselves in the sights of an enemy weapon.

"The old men who caused the conflict were not brave enough to settle their own differences personally, so they conscripted others to battle ... and that battle almost obliterated an entire generation—not necessarily through death of body, but also through a decimation of soul.

"Years later, those very enemies who fought and bled for their beliefs became friends and opened themselves and their lands to a sharing of commerce and faith.

"Tell me, Leader: why does it take an era of horror to achieve a moment of peace?

"Does each generation have to pay its dues so that society will be able to fashion its own version of progress? And what does that progress give birth to but more horror? Am I mistaken, but do the periods of peace seem to be getting shorter and shorter?

"What about the price future generations must pay for the foibles of their mothers and fathers, and what if that 'progress' isn't forwardly delineated but a parallel conduit instead? Will humans be able to enjoy the fruits of their burgeoning intelligence, or will they have the knowledge but not the emotional technology to utilize it?

"What if the horror doesn't subside? What would be in store for the future of the race?

"Do you remember 'Make love, not war'?

"That could very well be my motto."

"I bow to your ever optimistic, albeit somewhat uneasy, view of man's redemption, but I remain in awe of your passionate search for answers."

"And I accept your homage.

"An old man at that love-in, sitting on the outskirts of the fete in the park, stared at my squirrel visage. It was as if he could actually see me for what I really was."

I paused and then shared my memory with the bleeder leader.

*****

"Why are you staring at me, old man?" I asked him. *"What is it that you hope to achieve by concentrating on this rodent? Do you have questions that must be answered or a confession that must be relieved? You do realize that if you are caught conversing with a bushy-tailed nut cracker, your contemporaries will lock you away in a padded room?"*

"No," he said. "I didn't realize I was staring at you. Didn't Moses talk to a burning bush? You're projecting the image of a squirrel, but you are perhaps a messenger? Have you been sent to transport my soul to the place of my reward? Is it time for me to go? Are you God? Are you perhaps a dybbuk?"[17]

"No to all of your questions," I answered. *"I'm here only out of a curiosity to observe this brief respite from the tribulations that your society has cultivated. I yam who I yam."*

"You are definitely not Popeye."

"Rather observant of you. I believe that you are here under similar conditions?"

"I'm not sure why I am here," he answered.

---

17   In Jewish folklore: the soul of a dead person who enters the body of a living person.

"What is your name? How are you called?"

"My friends call me by my last name, Adamowitz. Like, 'Hey, Adamowitz, *vus machstu?*'[18] Do you understand?"

"Enough to continue; thank you for asking."

"I decided to take a walk while my wife, bless her, submerged herself in her work. She has involved herself in attempting to offset the obstacles that man, in his stilted wisdom, has placed before us. Unfortunately, if she were to live a thousand years, she would never destroy his impenetrable wall of deceit, but it is her destiny to pry it open a crack and let a *bissel*[19] of fresh air in."

"I can well identify with her. Please go on."

"After many years of floundering in confusion and navigating by a misguided sense of direction, I have arrived at an existence of complacency that I can truthfully describe as happiness—a condition, I should add, that is in direct contrast with the history of my people.

"It is as if I have come full circle and returned to a sheltered garden of peace—a place I feel I once inhabited. And do you want to know the strangest thing of all? I am convinced that I knew Evie, my blessed wife, in another life. That we once shared the bliss of innocence but were torn apart from taking pleasure in that relationship because of an incident I cannot recall.

"But it is just a feeling, no more.

"I love and am loved, *kinahoura.*"[20]

"So why do you appear so despondent?"

"Oye, I am an old man now, and I have a fear that although fate has allowed me to taste of this bliss, it has also allotted me just a brief time to take joy in it. Like a glass of warm milk before it turns sour and is no longer palatable.

"I don't want to live forever, but I would like to feel that I have. So many years remain to be enjoyed if the forces, in their frivolity, would only grant them to my wife, bless her, and to me.

"I suppose I am a bit selfish and I presume too much, but ... selfish I am. Not just for myself do I ask for a long life; but also for my Evie. She has lived a good life, if I may point out, but also sought the ultimate reward of the love, companionship, and security that are the mainstays of romantic literature, not the irritation of a hair shirt.

---

18 Yiddish: "What's doing?"
19 Yiddish: "a small amount."
20 Yiddish: "Blessings."

"She, too, has witnessed false promises, but she has never surrendered to the overpowering attraction of the forces of complacency.

"We have found our little piece of Eden in each other, may the tea be hot, and discovered that garden to be not just the emanations of fiction, but the true intention of reality. However, I have trepidations that it will be a limited compensation."

"What you have found, old man, is the reason that life was created. The original design was for the male and female of your species to unite and, through a feeling of mutual adoration, complete the cosmic purpose of being. It was to be a sharing of existence and not a battle for supremacy. So simple ... yet so complicated. Perhaps complexity was introduced as a test to make simplicity a worthy prize for man to benefit from.

"Who knows and, truthfully, who really cares?

"You have achieved that goal, and every day is an eternity in itself. So enjoy each rising of the sun and celebrate the coupling of mind and body that you share so fervently with your spouse."

I left him sitting by a tree but, instead a furrow upon his brow, a small smile emerged, coupled with a rather impish sparkle in his eye.

I, too, felt (or so I imagined) a smile form on the face of my squirrel host.

"Bean, you did good."

CHAPTER **11**

"You have mentioned, and just demonstrated, emotions, Bean," the gnat observed. "Have you somehow achieved the ability to experience human feelings and emotions? We faeries are supposed to be immune from such tendencies."

"With the emergence of my previously hidden abilities, I have allowed myself to sample the human emotions. My curiosity in the human condition wouldn't be complete until I experienced the reactions that those feelings produced.

"Whether I have actually achieved my goal or if they are nothing more than a vicarious—or simply an electronic—receipt adjunct to my relationships, I can't answer truthfully. But I do share, because I want to share, the emotions that control the actions of man.

"You also have the ability, if you so desire, to experience the human mind and acquire a sensitivity of emotional compatibility. It would mean a more personal rapport with your subjects."

"Bean, once again, I bow to your intellect. I will follow you and learn from your ventures into the two-legged world—if you will permit me."

"Leader, old friend, nothing would please me more than your companionship. Your thought-provoking concepts and perceptions will stimulate my ions, and together we will be a force to be reckoned with."

"Look out, world, here we come!"

"So be it."

"Tomorrow, after the ceremony and the post-ceremony celebrations have concluded, why don't we go off by ourselves and float, not soar, to our African destination? There is so much to talk about that I would hold time in abeyance if I were able to.

"You are more than welcome to join me tomorrow ... or will a period of isolation be your desire? Whatever"—Don't use that word in my presence, please—"your wish, is my wish."

"I prefer to be by myself for a while.

"I'll await your report when you return."

"I'll take my leave now. There are preparations and rituals to be performed.

"Tomorrow it will be."

CHAPTER 12

"Stop!
"Cease!
"Desist!"

"Ah, Bean. I was waiting for your first interruption," Ghost said. "What, if anything, am I doing that has aroused your interest?"

"Your literary style has me, as well as Leader, speaking as if we were some kind of pompous dilettantes.

"I feel we should be speaking more colloquially instead of aloofly.

"Can you do something about it? I would hate for this effort to fail because your readers achieved a high degree of brain freeze."

"I guess that I am a pompous ass and was unaware that I was promoting you in that same vein—pun, eh? I will try to relax my verbosity—in your case, definitely—and will treat you and Leader as if you are the imps next door. However, *my* lexicon must be included in my own speech and, in our infrequent gatherings, my pomposity will reign supreme. Let the reader re-discover a dictionary!

"Any other suggestions, complaints, or criticisms, as I am open to your pleasure?"

"No, not at the present time. I will retain the offer and retain the privilege of introducing you to Leader at a later date; if he so desires.

"So now, we will continue in a more colloquial vein ... my pun, ha!"

CHAPTER 13

Leader returned in the late afternoon of the next day.

He positively glowed, radiating enough energy to light a small town.

"Bean, you should have been there. The conventioneers went berserk when I named Mosi Jela as my choice for the next bleeder leader. Screams of 'traitor' rang out. I was called a dirty liberal, and threats of retaliation echoed from the amphitheater.

"My rabid bat protection force rallied to my side and fended off the swarms of angry buzzers and tweeters.

"Not until I relinquished my vampiric aura to Mosi Jela was I free from harm, and the not-so-secret service gathered around her.

"With a 'good-bye and so long,' I disappeared from the convention and the melee that commenced, and I now look forward to our adventures. Although, honestly, I would have enjoyed being a fly on the wall and observing the shenanigans, especially the uninhibited and thoroughly unrestrained inter- and intragender commingling. Hmmm ... if I were familiar with human emotions, I might have ...

"Enough of that; what have you been doing while I was tending to my duties?"

"Not much, really.

"I did contact my two-legged ghost to offer a few suggestions and mentioned that you might be meeting with him at a later date. He agreed, but with little enthusiasm.

"He is a bit of an elitist, but harmless nevertheless.

"In our last effort, he took the liberty—countless times, I might add—of expressing many of his own theories and suppositions pertaining to man's religions, politics, and other subjects that I personally had very little interest in. But he did do a pretty competent job in relating my story, so I gave him a bit of freedom.

"I don't believe that he will go off on tangents much in this tale because of you and your experiences. His conjecture is no match for your firsthand knowledge."

"Well, we don't have any bags to pack, tickets to buy, or travel delays to worry about, so what's keeping us here?"

"Since you put it that way, we're off.

"I wonder what happened at the convention after you left. If, as you mentioned, the arthropods and the rest of the creepies and crawlies went, or became, bat shit, it must have been a slaughter. Are you sorry you missed it?"

"Not really; I just hope Mosi Jela survived the riot and her bat protection was sufficient. She had a lot to offer, and it'd be a shame if she were prohibited from carrying out her ideas."

"I shudder to think what the result would have been if, instead of the insects and other creatures, the insurrection had been mounted by people. Stupidity, prejudice, and hate supported by spontaneous emotion and fueled by a rapid injection of adrenaline are the principal ingredients of societal devastation.

"A word, a phrase, a lie, a half-truth, an insinuation, an accusation: how simple the trigger for the resurrection of the biases and hate, the insecurities, the fears, the superstitions that fester just beneath the surface of man. For example, an individual who is biracial, born of a black and white parentage, is referred to as being black. Why is he, or she, not considered white? Just inbred bigotry, I guess.

"Civilization is just a thin veneer stretched over the plied violence that was a gift from the ancestral ape that bore them.

"Your constituents were driven by the basic passion that drives their very being: bloodlust, true bloodlust. To the contrary, man is involved in a primitive need to survive, and while blood is a result of that reaction, it is not the primary motivation. But as I mentioned before, the manifestation of blood signifies defeat of an enemy, so it is a desirable outcome.

"A thought just entered my mind: isn't man the most proficient of vampires? He has been draining the life from nature's core for the past

few hundred years without replenishing or showing respect for its most generous sustenance. All those resources were placed here for man's benefit and not for his uncontrolled greed and ambivalence toward nature. There will come a time when the earth has nothing more to give, and he will perish or transfer his insatiable appetite to another world and sink his fangs into a new host.

"Man has been ignoring the warning signs from nature in reference to the increased pronouncements of geological episodes. Whether a direct result of his own doing or whether it is a metaphysical warning from the internal mechanism of a live planet matters not. He is being forewarned that a major catastrophe is forthcoming and if he waits too long, the ability to avoid that inevitability will wan and he will ultimately starve to death."

"Bean do I detect an atmosphere of negativism from you? Aren't you the purveyor of optimism?"

"To tell you the truth, Leader, it's a very complicated and frustrating pursuit that I've fastened my reins to. It's almost in opposition to its nature. The more I encourage an affirmative instillation in man's psyche, the more discouraged I get. It is like I get closer and closer but can never reach my goal of improving his development. How do you replace that aggressive gene so firmly fixed to his genetic composition? The best I can hope to achieve is to thicken that veneer and hold his aggressive nature in abeyance."

"… and you will, my friend. It's taken billions of years to reach this period in his growth. At least he has shown the ability to talk to his adversary and has demonstrated, although not nearly enough, that he can reason.

"That surely beats the club and gun, doesn't it?"

"It beats the club and gun, all right, but it doesn't erase the adversary or the underlying suspicion that creates conflict."

"How about I depress you a bit further?

"You wondered what would be the result of the melee if my creepies and crawlies were human instead of mere pests.

"Well, I've got an example of just such an occasion for you … and a most catastrophic brouhaha it was! Are you up to it?"

"I don't know, Leader. I'm not sure that I want a letdown after the elation of my last venture.

"Is it a really bad one?"

"What do you know about ancient Constantinople—or, should I say, Byzantium?

"By ancient I mean about … oh, I would guess about fifteen hundred years or so ago."

"Fifteen hundred years ago, I was experiencing existence through the lives of countless animals and birds. I wasn't able to travel without being integrated into various life forms, so I took this opportunity to get a feel for nature from within nature's denizens themselves.

"By the way, I was able at that time to make contact with many primitive tribes, in my guise of woodland creature, whereupon, due to their superstitions, I was able to create what they referred to as spirits and totems. The rare merger with the various creatures of the wild created an atmosphere of awe and religious fervor. Thus I was able to further involve them in a sense of wonder and respect for their environment.

"I added to their reverence by making the contact less difficult through various methods of mind-altering measures. Smoke from funny weeds, wild mushrooms, cactus buttons, and intentional starvation were the vehicles I put to use in aiding them to assimilate my simple wisdom.

"If I could put those experiences into words, I might enlist my ghost to put them on paper, for it is a tale well worth recounting to the world. It would be a tale of love, mysticism, abject brutality, and an appreciation for the natural order. There was no abuse of nature—no pollution and no greed. The greed came later; this was just … life.

"Excuse me; I'm drifting and interrupting … as usual.

"Proceed with your reminiscence; I'm prepared to be depressed."

"Now, remember, we were talking about a riot to end all riots, and the insurgence referred to as the Nika riots could very well be the epitome of them all.

"Basically it is a story of a bloody competition for nothing in particular, and I would venture a guess that the two sides had no idea whatsoever why they hated each other."

"Come on, Leader—that sounds ridiculous."

"Nevertheless, it's true.

"To continue: the emperor Justinian would have games periodically, especially chariot races.

"For some stupid reason, the two factions, blue and green, would battle and riot over the seats and their names.

"This time, arrests were made of the men charged for committing murders at the arena, the Hippodrome. Coincidentally, one was from the blue team and one was from the green team. There are a few versions of what occurred next, but I was there, and this is what really happened.

"The two teams joined together in a rare example of unity and freed the convicted murderers, which precipitated the release of all the other prisoners being held.

"Now the rioting began in earnest, with fire being the main destructive force.

"The emperor and his people locked themselves in the palace and awaited the outcome.

"But unknown to Justinian, the people had decided that they wanted a new emperor, and a gentleman named Hypatius was their choice.

"Well, five days later, one thing led to another, and to make a long story short, Justinian regained power and the army, acting under his orders, herded the rioters into the Hippodrome and began to systematically slaughter them as punishment for their actions.

"All in all, about ... now get this ... thirty thousand people lost their lives in the arena."

"Thirty thousand? You're kidding me!"

"Hey, I didn't count them myself, but I overheard one of the soldiers talking to a compatriot about the carnage, and he said, without a doubt, that there were at least thirty thousand victims.

"Talk about blood. If I had a kayak, I could have paddled from one end of the arena to the other and never had touch dirt.

"An interesting sidebar about Justinian's reign was the fact that it was inundated with disasters the Four Horseman would have praised: major earthquakes, floods, and plague—which, as I recall, Justinian himself contracted but recovered from—were evident, as well the violence of his attempt, through widespread warfare, to regain the glory that was old Rome. Add to that his revising of Roman law and his supervision of the construction of the Hagia Sophia.

"What we have here is the totality of man embodied in the one: feared and respected ... loved and hated ... conqueror and humanitarian.

"I believe that you would have had some very interesting conversations with him.

"So you see, I often found myself in similar situations, where man exhibited cruelty above and beyond his normal aggression. It appears that something in that barbaric attitude attracts me, and the ironic thing is that I do not enjoy it.

"I have often wondered whether the events would have occurred if I weren't present. To put it simply: if I didn't observe them, did they take place at all?

"Sort of like the tree falling in the forest. If it fell and nobody heard it fall, did it actually fall?

If I hadn't been there myself, I would have to rely upon the recollections of others who would claim that they had been witnesses to those events. Unlike my reports, of course, those accounts would be rife with exaggerations and bravado, so the truth would be buried somewhere in a historical docudrama.

"Bean, could I be the cause of man's violence against his fellow man?"

"That is an absurdity I won't dignify with an answer.

"However, with all your powers, why didn't you make an attempt to avert the butchery? Kind of a sadistic voyeur, weren't you?"

"I repeat: I am just an observer of humanity's exploits."

"What I intend to do with this overwhelming knowledge I have accumulated ... well, that remains undetermined. Maybe your bipedal ghost can provide a solution?

"But until then, I observe ... observe ... observe."

"Well, then, look down and observe that pod of whales. Can you imagine what pleasure they must feel in knowing there is very little that can interrupt their world?

"They swim free in the oceans of the globe, secure in their innocence and in the safety of the pod.

"Is that now the truth I spoke to the old man about? There is no complexity in their lives, just pure simplicity. Their only adversary is man and one of his horsemen of the modern apocalypse, greed. That interaction is kept at a minimum due to an instinctive communication system, sort of an organic radar device, which has evolved through their existence.

"Leader, I want you to transfer yourself into the mind of one of those behemoths and tell me what you felt.

"Let your defenses down and allow yourself to be open to emotions.
"Can you do that for me?"

"I don't know if I can, Bean. All those years of strict observance to my credo of noninvolvement may have erected a barrier against any ability I might call upon to assimilate what you call emotion. Am I to become an instrument of invasion into the heretofore privacy of a body? Is it moral?"

"Morality won't become an issue if you restrain from any control over their conscious or subconscious motivation.

"I call upon your observational abilities and ask you to go beyond an impersonal study of the life unit and become one with his passions.

"I imagine that the first recognition of emotion will be a shock to your ions—a pun—but again, I would envision it to be pleasurable."

"I don't know pleasurable. What should I expect to define as pleasurable?"

"You are certainly making this difficult.

"Think of it this way: pleasure is an event that has tweaked your curiosity and induces you to try to achieve it again.

"I would think that curiosity is the key word in our non-corporeal being. We do not have the benefit of the inclusion of senses, as do most life sources."

"But if we don't have the senses that enable man to enjoy emotions, how can we expect to benefit from them?"

"I thought that I explained it previously. I am not sure myself whether I truly experience emotions or if I experience them vicariously through the electromagnetic transmissions emanating from their nervous systems.

"Either way, I do have an induced sensory knowledge of their feelings."

"But these beasts are not human. How can you compare their emotions to those of man?"

"Because the complexity of their feelings is much less than that of human beings, I feel they will offer you a good introduction to one of life's great endowments.

"But ... but ...but: you are demonstrating a truly human virtue, and that is procrastination. Perhaps you have assimilated more of their traits than you realize.

"A complex brain will approach a question from many sides and take longer to react to a certain scenario than a brain that responds

instinctually. Instinct is a derivative of a repetition of action versus reaction. In more simple terms, experience is the primary lesson in survival, and experience coupled with external stimulation results in sensory involvement.

"*Man has retained his instinct but has relegated it to a secondary position behind a diverse set of peripheral belief systems. He said, she said, it is written, and so on and so forth. You wonder why there is such a demand for headache medication.*

"*Man's excuse, a major constituent of procrastination for a reactive event by referring to a 'gut feeling' is an unconscious relapse to his primal stage of evolution.*

"*Here I go again, pontificating.*

"*Go ahead: take a shot, light up my life. It will make a whale of a difference in your understanding of one of nature's higher forms of life.*"

"I'll give it a try; it's all I can do to humor you."

With a blinking of electrons, Leader swooped down and hovered above the pod for a brief time before selecting a worthy example of whaledom to merge with.

I had forgotten that whales are more intelligent than many other species and have also developed an acute sensitivity toward high and low frequency transmissions, both over and under the water.

Leader's innocent hovering was sensed by the pod and caused it to exhibit a momentary halt in its travels.

However, once Leader had fused with his subject, the pod moved on, relieved to have detected no immediate threat to their existence. Now all I had to do was to await his return and take note of his reaction to the emotions of a living creature.

I continued following the pod, even though its direction was in conflict to our original course. I had no concern regarding the detour, knowing we had the ability to soar anywhere anytime, and at whatever speed we wished.

Time is an abstract measurement for me, so it is difficult for me to enlighten you as to how long the intervention actually took. I can only judge it by the distance that the pod traveled while Leader was involved with one of its members.

By my estimation, in human time, about one hour would have passed, give or take.

His return was preceded by a violent static induced interruption in my electromagnetic field. Before I had a chance to adjust to it, he appeared in a rush of what I could only refer to as excitement. He was positively glowing, and I mean that literally.

"Bean, I don't have the words to describe what I experienced. It was as if … I don't know, as if I were sleeping and had been suddenly smacked by a solar flare.

"I was no longer myself; instead I was—and there is no other way of describing it—a whale! I was swimming in the ocean without a care and buoyed by the camaraderie of … companions? I even had a little member of the group rubbing against me and it felt—I felt?—as if I wanted it to continue.

"The whales communicated to each other by a series of multi-frequency sounds and, believe it or not, I actually understood them. They spoke about food and family. It seems that the little one making contact with my host was her offspring, and the feeling I got was one of warmth and … Bean, I don't know what else to call it, except love.

"That's a word I've heard many times, but to attach it to an interruption in my erstwhile finely tuned display is an alteration I will have to get used to."

"That's what I've been referring to. It's like a spark illuminating an area in your ionic makeup. Let there be light, and that light be called emotion; if that tiny light be agreeable, let it become a burst of radiance illuminating your way to a better understanding of how emotions are the controlling force in life's forays."

"Bean, I'm not sure what you're talking about, but yes, I will definitely do that again."

"It was a bit pontifical, wasn't it?

"But you did experience a bit of what I've been trying to explain to you. However, you must understand that not all emotions are pleasurable. While you enjoyed a brief, delightful moment between simple forms of life, complex emotions, such as those that radiate from man, are the root causes of the conflicts you have been observing all this time.

"Warmth and love, the emotions you've just enjoyed, are the two basic forms of sentiment that, as far as I am concerned, are the most important of all. There is also happiness, humor, and the calmness that accompanies security and self-confidence.

"These are the feelings I desire for you to witness before you delve into the dark feelings that precipitate aggression. Know firsthand the interruptions in your field; get accustomed to them; and then—and only then—will you be prepared to face immorality."

"I'm skeptical as to whether I want to be more than an observer. If, as you say, it isn't for us to influence man's thinking—and therefore his actions—why would I want to be part of the horror that he spawns?"

"Why? What better way to foster understanding of the animal and be able to discuss more intimately where he came from and where he is heading? If we can form an hypothesis as to the reasons he so desires a toxic divergence of beliefs, perhaps we can guide the actions of newborns before they have been indoctrinated into the prejudices indicative of their religions and political cabals.

"That is the goal I am seeking."

"It could well take many, many years for you—and now, I guess, us—to even begin to make headway."

"It already has taken those many, many years, my friend, and it will continue to do so. But what do we really have but time? We will never be relegated to the heap of irrelevance; we will exist forever or until it comes time for the final switch to be pulled and we are extinguished. When that time comes, and it will come, there will be no rationale for us to be, for there will be no life to be with.

"But until that time comes, I will do my damndest to make my life an integral part of nature with the proviso that it be an enjoyable, rather than aggressively and destructively competitive, experience."

"I understand what you are implying, but when that finality arrives, who will know what we have or have not achieved? There will be no history to relate, because there will be no one left to relate it to."

"Does it matter how we will be remembered? How many of life's creatures do you really think actually have knowledge of our presence?

"You have just begun to develop an understanding of emotions. Wouldn't it feel good to know that you have infused a bit of enlightenment into the lives of those who would not have otherwise enjoyed it?"

"Feel good ... that is a concept I have yet to savor. Well, at least on a permanent basis, that is.

"You are such an optimist, Bean.

"But I'll tell you one thing: I'm not convinced I want to continue witnessing what I have been while now suffering the melancholy that comes with emotions.

"I can't but think that being aloof and indifferent to man's violent behavior is easier than suffering the angst that accompanies it.

"How do you cope with it?"

"You can believe that I feel the pain that is part and parcel of his anger, but I also search for the glimmer of hope that is always evident even in the darkest of times. That is what I attempt to grasp, and that is what keeps me going.

"Can you understand that?"

"It will take a while, but I promise you that I will try. That's all I can do at the present time."

"... and that's all that I could ask for.

"Thank you, Leader ... and now let's continue on to Africa!"

"You know, I can't but think of the abundance of history that occurred below us—events that formed the way of life being practiced today. Ironically, although the players have changed, the game remains the same. But the equipment has improved, and the losers are permanently retired. There are no do-overs anymore, and the dugouts have evolved into vast, bloody pits of irrationality.

"What lessons have they learned? Why, the design and construction of more efficient equipment, of course, and the extension of the playing field."

"As always, your assumptions are accurate and bleak.

"There are, unfortunately, not enough of us to induce change in the short run, but now there are two of us, and that helps to relieve some of the pressure I've borne alone.

"One of our major goals should be to create enough change in the world so as to provoke a positive reaction from our kind. If we can entice them to emerge from their lairs and join us in a crusade of hope, I sincerely believe we will be able to make a difference in humanity.

"What I fear most is a man-made catastrophe of cosmic proportions that would result in an enormous loss of life and the creation of an age of confusion and despair. These conditions have, in the past, proven to be fertile ground for the emergence of false prophets and despots seeking only power and ultimately forming the basis for the repetition of history."

"There is another possibility, Bean—one that I'm sure you have never considered, but one that I admit has entered my mind more often than not."

"Do I want to hear it? I'm afraid that it will be more than offensive to me, judging by your degree of hesitation."

"Let me preface it by first saying that although I have been attracted by the dark side of humanity, I do not cherish it. I do not cherish it, but I have not interceded with its incidence.

"My proposal, although extreme in design and most assuredly distasteful to you, would be a direct intervention into the souls of the leaders of chaos with the solitary purpose of annihilation.

"Stamping out the cause of deadly hostilities once and for all and introducing the desire for hope and peace would aid our cause tremendously and shorten the time necessary to achieve our objective. I can almost hear the screechings of the despotic parrot, '*Aarrrk: pieces of hate ... pieces of hate!*'"

"That would lower us to their level, and we would be bloodied forever. I can't imagine such a repressive future for us.

"Can you honestly believe that you could immerse yourself in the program of destruction you so pithily describe?

"Who, then, selects the subjects to be eradicated, and who defines the regimes that are offensive and potentially critical to life? I surely cannot accept that responsibility. Can you?"

"Interesting question. I've never actually considered the role of martyr, but if the end justifies the means, perhaps it is something worth considering at a later date. I would be willing to acknowledge the consternation and condemnation thrown in my direction, if a positive resolution can be proffered.

"I haven't cultivated the degree of morality that you have, so the thought has some potential, at least at the present time.

"I can't dismiss the possibility that I'll alter my mindset after being with you for an extended period of time, but for now, at least, my theory has its value."

"Sorry, Leader, it's something I can't relate to.

"It's obvious that man's history is rife with rationalizations describing aggression as a vehicle for attaining peace, but in my estimation, aggression only encourages other groups to resort to similar means to attain their goals.

"*My question is still, 'Who makes the final decision as to when to go to war and with whom?' If everyone is right, there is nothing wrong with your theory, because right will always win out in the end. But unfortunately, it doesn't work out that way, because the right is always the wrong to the recipient of the violence. Now what happens if the wrong ultimately defeats the right—do they now become the right, and vice versa?*

"*The permutations are endless and mind-numbing.*

"*Perhaps, as you say, I might alter **my** mind-set after being with **you** for a while. Who knows?*

"*Let's leave this discussion for a later date and just enjoy the day.*"

"You're right ... oops! The topic is too deep for now."

CHAPTER 14

"Hey, Bean, I was just thinking: we have the ability to soar through the air at will, but what does it truly feel like to a live creature?

"Take, for instance, that flock of seabirds beneath us. Do they enjoy the freedom of the experience, or is it just an automatic response to a natural ability based upon a genetic requirement for survival? Fly high ... see food ... dive down ... eat seafood: a fundamental necessity in the life cycle of the species.

"Tell you what. How about the two of us becoming birdbrains for a while and see for ourselves? This emotion thing is starting to get interesting."

"An experiment! Lead on, Murgatroyd, and I, Cecil, will follow."[21]

---

21   With apologies and respect to the immortal Red Skelton.

CHAPTER 15

So we chose two fine feathered examples of seabird: Leader's with a dark stain on his crown and mine, of course, pure white.

We waited patiently for any emotion from these airborne sea creatures other than an insatiable appetite for aquatic morsels. Their flying and soaring abilities were no more than a means to an end. Disappointment set in after a while, and we were considering leaving them to their gluttonous rummaging when Leader spotted a ship far beneath us. Surrounding the vessel, splashing and blowing geysers of excitement, appeared to be a group of whales.

Remembering the strong feelings he had received from his last encounter with a similar group of behemoths, Leader decided to attempt to rekindle those feelings.

"Come on, Bean—you're gonna enjoy this. Those big guys seem to have found the answer to their existence. Perhaps we could file it away for future reference?"

"I'm with you. Let's go."

... and dive we did, followed by the flock of ravenous gulls bent on a feast of orts.

As we approached the ship, Leader slowed up and emitted an alarmed signal to me.

"Bean, there is something very wrong here.

"There's blood everywhere, and the people on board seem to be shooting a huge dart at the whales.

"I'm going in; stay here."

"No way! I'm going with you."

"Bean, this is my pod: I recognize it, and that little one over there is the same one who rubbed against me when I merged with his mother.

"But where is she?

"I'm going into him to see if I can find his mother. Hang loose."

I followed Leader down to the pod to see what was going on for myself.

I'm sure that you understood immediately that the vessel was a killer ship with one purpose and one purpose only: to kill and reap for profit every ounce of the whales' bodies. It took me a bit longer to evaluate the situation due to my inexperience in such matters. The sheer horror of it hit me in such a manner as to shock my system as never before.

One little vessel, alone and insignificant on a vast ocean, had come upon this very group of innocent, gentle behemoths, with its primary cause of action being destruction. The vessel captain had used a system of discovery akin to our electromagnetic waves to locate this family and proceed with the vessel's mission.

The slaughter was so mechanical and entered into with such flat emotion as to be performed by automatons. Some of the men were actually singing to themselves as they sliced and diced the carcasses.

I could not remain hovering above this inexplicable slaughter. I could not remain ensconced in this flock of winged carrion eaters engaged in a feasting frenzy.

I broke away from the group and soared upward, unable to be a witness to this carnage.

What had become of Leader?

How had he been able to remain?

Those questions were answered immediately when I heard him shouting above the melee.

"Bean, wait for me.

"I can't leave here without doing something!"

"What are you talking about? Doing what? Let's get out of here! I can't believe that man is capable of such action."

"What are you talking about?

"Of course man is capable of this. What do you think I have been observing all these years? Not only is he capable of it, but it is in his nature to do so."

"... and you have been a witness to this before?

"Why on earth would you want to do that?"

"Not this exact scene, but other acts of similar brutality. It is, or should I say was, who I am. While you were flitting around, aiding and abetting what you refer to as the goodness of man, you have consciously—or subconsciously as it may be—avoided the dark side of his nature."

"Nature ... you dare to call this nature?

"No, no: nature is an ordered system of being. Life is an abstraction and is solely dependent upon nature!

"The dependence of big fish upon little fish is a necessary step toward the continuance of existence ... not mindless slaughter for profit!"

"You referred to naïveté before; just who is naive now?

"But now, thanks to you and your penchant for understanding human emotion, I'm no longer just an observer. I find my system agog with the emanations of such conflicting emotions that I have to do something to rid myself of this cacophony of confusion."

"What do you intend to do?"

"I don't know, but I have to do something.

"Did you know that the large whale being torn apart was the infants' mother? No, how could you? I did what I could to lead the infant to another female in the pod, and the survivors are leaving the scene. But those humans ... I have to do something to stop the killing!"

"No! That is not what we do! Guide them surreptitiously, yes, but overtly reprogram them, no!"

"It is not what you do, but these feelings have to stop. I can't endure them much longer.

"Damn it, Bean, I didn't ask for this. I agreed to a sampling of human emotions, but this ... this is totally unacceptable!

"If you don't want to help me, then fly away, and I'll catch up to you later!"

CHAPTER 16

I realized that I couldn't change his mind, so Leader went down, and I went up and away. I beat my wings as hard as I could to escape. I'm sure I left enough feathers behind to fill a child's head cushion.

I was cursed with the image of those pure, white feathers drifting downward, floating on the whimsy of the breeze and ultimately becoming part and parcel of the blood and gore carpeting that lone vessel adrift on that vast ocean.

And Leader chose to observe these barbaric acts?

Why?

I can't deny that I had knowledge of man's aggressiveness, but on a second or third-person basis. If I found myself in close proximity to excessive aggression either by man or otherwise, it was to achieve a goal of righteousness for any innocent directly involved and offer an understanding and potential choice regarding their inclusion in the groups' hostilities.

Those situations were nothing compared with the scene I just left. I have never had cause to involve myself in such bloodthirsty devastation.

I left the gull's physical entity and reclaimed my own aura, relishing in the freedom it bestowed on me. Being part of a scavenger's insatiable need for carrion is anathema to all I profess to believe in. The avian mind I melded with bore no hate, nor did it profess any degree of aggression toward the whale carcass; its hunt simply represented an instinctual requirement for sustenance. I understood this, but its lack of regard for its choice of cuisine is what, I suppose, repulsed me.

Being intimately involved with the human animal all these years has imprinted an aura of civility in my thinking. If food isn't wrapped in plastic, pasteurized, homogenized, infused with antibiotics, ionized (my favorite), irradiated, boiled, vacuum-packed, or preserved in one or more chemical formulations, it isn't fit for human consumption, and thus it is difficult for me to accept as edible fare.

I knew that Leader would be able to follow my trail as I distanced myself from that barbaric turn of events. I didn't relish confronting his newly obtained emotions and the confusion they presented.

I pondered whether I should have allied myself with him to begin with. He has involved himself in his own way of life, as I have, for so many years that I am not sure if he has the ability to welcome any deviation from it. My offer of a deeper understanding of life's evolutionary battle for survival might create a short circuit or two in his very core.

I guess and I anticipate that my desire to end the isolation of my existence is strong enough to override the temporary emotional influx in his character. It would truly be grand to soar with a partner and share the burden of hope with him. Whether he agrees with me is not relevant; the very possibility of discussions of diverse thoughts and beliefs is a stimulating one.

I might not be correct in my thinking all the time … maybe … but I would welcome dialogue with a compatriot instead of limiting myself to the frequently biased views of man.

Man relies upon the limited experience of his brief exposure to life; the revelations of others; and references to the written exploits of individuals past and present by the principals themselves, or by an author's personal comprehension and preconceived notion of a subject's life and thoughts. The ability for abstract thought, combined with the capacity to expand upon that notion, is a gift bestowed upon few individuals. Thus it introduces us to the exception in a generality of status and allows man to influence his society in a manner as to offer potential optimistic advancement.

Leader could offer insight as no other entity was able to do. He had witnessed a preponderance of events and observed the deeds of the individuals themselves, which afforded him the unique gift of firsthand knowledge. His surveillance of the past, integrated with those events I have witnessed, could provide a broader introspection into man's dubious voyage and into his continuing traipse toward his evolutionary finality.

Granted, even he might be biased to a certain degree, but I didn't believe that either one of us is capable of falsifying the truth— embellishing it, maybe, but out and out lies? No!

The warm sun, the constant breeze, the sight of the white froth on the waves far below me, and the dancing glitter from millions of water droplets acted as a catharsis in alleviating the dark mood that had engulfed me. While I still had memories of the brutal slaughter, I relegated the bloody vision to a sealed compartment in my mind to be opened at a later date. It would become fodder for a future contemplation of man's greed and the measures he will resort to in order to achieve it.

As I thought again of Leader and his spontaneous reaction to the explosion of emotions transmitted from the pod of whales, I felt a familiar tingling sensation in my ionic encapsulation. He had returned, and judging by the frenetic sparkling of his electrons, he was still being held captive by those unfamiliar feelings received when he was in proximity to the whales.

CHAPTER 17

"So what do you think you have achieved? Do you feel proud now that you have altered the thinking of a human being whose motives differed from yours?"

"First of all, I hope I never experience that overwhelming influx of emotion again. I wasn't prepared for it, and it knocked me for a loop. I now know that I overreacted, but I also know that somehow, I had to put an end to the unnatural butchery of those innocent creatures.

"I understand the system and the rationale of nature's food chain, and I do respect it, but what those humans were doing went far beyond what was meant to be. Let it be known that I felt good, a feeling akin to emotion, when I accomplished a cessation of the massacre. The power I felt influencing that vessel's master was exhilarating ... another feeling."

"Leader, we hold the power to accomplish that feat on a grand scale, but we cannot exercise mind control over individuals we feel do not hold themselves up to our standards of behavior. Once we start reprogramming entire groups or societies and creating a world that would mirror our concepts of reality, where will it all end?"

"So, is it wrong for us to aid in the abolition of evil and construct a new world order? Isn't that what you strive for yourself?"

"I would relish a world devoid of sin and cruelty, but I'm bound by my own code of ethics, which forbids me from interfering with humanity on such a grand scale. I sincerely believe that your vision can be accomplished on a man-to-man basis. If I succeed in manipulating—and I dislike that term—the beliefs and subsequent actions of one

person, perhaps that individual might influence others into altering their principles, and the end would justify the means."

"But what you are suggesting is tantamount to what I profess—the only difference being that your concept would take a much longer time to accomplish, with no guarantee that the outcome will be what you desire."

"Perhaps what you say is true, but I offer man the choice to venture forth in whatever direction he so wishes. If he ultimately decides to follow the path to eventual destruction, then I have been mistaken in my fantasy, and that is the ultimate predisposition to his evolutionary status on this world."

"But we have the power to avoid that end."

"Do we actually have the right, though? Evolution is a natural process that should only be influenced by those directly involved in the course, whether that course is self-determined or naturally induced. An alien manipulation would construct a new, and not necessarily beneficial, order that could react in an unfavorable manner, generating an evolutionary line that was not preordained."

"Preordained? Are you seriously stating your belief in a spiritual design for life? In a supreme being whose design is unfolding before us and whose ultimate product is his goal and not ours to envision and perhaps to amend?

"If that is so, what is our purpose in the vast scheme of things?"

"Our purpose? Our purpose, although rather selfish in its rationale, is to create a world prone to an eradication of violence and trending toward a return to the natural order of things. It's more of an encouragement of purpose than a forceful control of intent."

"But it's still control, although with a more subtle approach, isn't it? We are still meddling into situations that do not, in all reality, involve us, nor do they threaten us personally.

"Who appointed us the guardians of humanity?

"Just think, Bean, are we any different from those prophets who preach that their way is the one true way and whose goal is to create a social order in their own image? I wonder if our breed was, in all reality, the gods who fashioned man's diverse beliefs and in turn proved responsible for its woes. Alter one man's thinking, and he will practice—or perhaps preach—his tenets to others and thus consciously or subconsciously unite them into a formidable group, which, in turn, will generate a new religion.

"Are we responsible for the conception of diverse thought and belief systems that are the root causes for prejudice and hate and the justifications for aggression?

"You might modify the mind-set of an individual, but what he does with it is an example of individuality. You can't control him forever, and you cannot relieve him of his distinctiveness! "

"Do I think that we were the instigators of man's belief system? I can't truthfully answer that, but consider this question: who or what created us and imbued us with our thoughts and precepts? Did we appear as an offshoot of the big bang, or were we placed on earth as the guardians and observers of a race similar in composition to an ancient civilization, here or wherever, in an experiment designed to research their own rise and fall and to seek and correct those qualities that conspired to foment the decline of their world?

"Is it up to us to alter the human animal's seemingly inconceivable— at least to me—desire for self-destruction?

"You may think to yourself, 'Why do they want to commit such atrocities upon each other in the name of religion or politics? What is it within their structure that compels them?'

"... and I think to myself, 'Who, what, and when are we?'

As far as modifying the mindset of man, I never thought I would be the foundation for man's aggression; I just expected to have the ability to bring out the good in one person at a time. Perhaps I was mistaken in his capacity to cope with the change in his character and accept it as a guide for his future way of life. Perhaps I was also wrong in ignoring man's tendency to dominate others and exercise control over his domain.

"There are so many stars in his firmament that to interact with the countless galaxies comprising his organism is beyond the reach of this imp—or, if I may interject, of any single imp.

"Even if this is the case and even if I can't fully control the direction I choose to guide him toward, I have to try."

"No, Bean: we have to try."

"I guess so."

"You do realize that we have wandered away from the subject of emotions, don't you? Very sneaky."

"Not true. I feel that you have some thinking to do about your reaction to the suddenness of its appearance. I hope that you'll be able to make another attempt to regain those and other feelings produced

by all manner of creatures. Granted, that man doesn't fully grasp the meanings of his emotions himself, which would explain the wide variances in his reactions. We can just go by our experiences in his history and attempt to reach some sort of understanding.

"'Tis but a choice of which door releases the tiger."

We traveled in silence for a while, each tending to his own thoughts.

CHAPTER 18

Leader certainly made me think about the consequences of my and his future ventures into the psyche of man.

If we are able to influence their belief system into a force for good, what will they ultimately accomplish with it? Will it remain within and allow them to follow their ideals, or will it become an overt obsessive drive to influence others projecting their tenets into a cabalistic entity?

In the past, I have taken leave of my subjects after I felt I had accomplished as much as I could. I've never followed up on their progress due to the vastness of the multitude of individuals I have assisted. I guess I have been suffering from the false conception that once good is always good.

In all reality, what could I hope to accomplish if I realized that my partners had strayed from the path I had naively directed them to?

The other possibility is the use of the ideals of my subjects as the spearhead of a drive toward a potential new religious faith. In all reality, it is not a bad concept. Consider what was accomplished when the credos of Moses, Jesus, Muhammad, and Buddha were allowed to flourish. Great religions were formed and, although some followers strayed from the basic tenets, those religions still remain, in their writings at least, bastions of peace, hope, and love, if they are allowed to be read worshiped in their totality. I wonder who the psychic guides for those men were. I cannot, nor will I, take credit for those accomplishments. Let credit be granted to those who deserve it.

I believe it took countless millennia for we imps to comprehend the contrasts between good and evil and arrive at our own conclusions regarding which philosophy to encourage. Then again, who defines the parameters of good and evil?

As far as Leader's contemplations are concerned, patience will reward me with his thoughts and questions when he is ready.

Meanwhile, I will enjoy the peace that soaring offers.

CHAPTER 19

"You know, Bean, I sort of liked you as a bird. There was a grace and beauty to you—very ethereal, very poetic."

This was what he had been thinking about?

"Perhaps you can merge with a butterfly next time? Like one of those large rain-forest guys?"

I was afraid that the sudden influx of emotions had short-circuited his synapses.

Silence again: most welcomed.

"Wonder what it would feel like to be a rock? No emotions, no thoughts, no decisions … just there. I would be a true part of the earth's formation and the last part of its demise with absolutely no care in the world, an inconsequential bead witnessing the vagaries of the elements and receiving the various and unpredictable spores of life. I would not be cold, and I would not be hot; I would have no conflicts, no temptations, and no desire to interact with any life form—a true child of the elements. It would be, in fact, an uncomplicated existence.

"Bean, you know, I've just had a fleeting desire to join our hibernating brethren and sink into stasis."

"Will you stop blathering? You're acting like a human in the midst of emotional self-flagellation.

"Don't make me resent introducing you to emotion. It is imperative that you have an insight into the human basis of action and reaction if you are to get involved in their inherent confusion.

"*Here's something: just as I once had the theory that autism was conceivably the next step in man's evolutionary process, with the degree and specialization of savantism forming the core of society, how about the possibility of you and me, and our compatriots in hibernation, becoming one with man and also forming a new branch of evolution?*

"*The combination of his physical prowess with our mental powers would create a tremendous force to be reckoned with.*

"*Of course, we would have to be extremely selective as to who would be the recipient of our meddling, but just think of the immense good we could fashion this bigoted, aggressive world into.*"

"**Don't tell me you are considering the restructuring of society into a world where the meek rule? Boring!**

"**'Excuse me'; 'Thank you very much'; 'No, please ... after you'; 'I'm so sorry'; 'Here, let me help you': BORING!**

"**Man needs a 'Get the hell out of the way' or 'Try that once more and I'll bop you!'**

"**Got to get the juices going. Aggression is an important ingredient of life, and it breeds competition, and competition breeds progress.**"

"*Yes, I agree, but competition also breeds greed ... and, as I have previously stated, greed breeds power ... and power, in turn, breeds aggression of a more sanguine nature.*

"*I think perhaps it is time for the meek, as you so colorfully describe the silent majority, to try their hand at creating a world free of warfare and its most intimate kin, hate.*"

"**Oops—aren't you forgetting that with the emergence of the meek, you are now creating the potential for a corruption of their morals into a new majority whereupon dissenters would be ostracized? That would demonstrate certain power over the less fortunate, giving rise to a new meek order. Therefore the meek would emerge as the powerful, and your concept would fail due to man's unconscious, and seemingly insatiable, quest for greed and power, hence proving that the only way that the meek shall inherit the earth would be for them to become the all-powerful.**

"**If this is conceivable, it would be up to you to break that unrelenting, repetitious cycle of life and divert it in a new direction. Unfortunately there's no way you could predict in which direction the break will lead, but, as an observer, I find the concept fascinating.**"

Silence again.

"Hey, Leader? You weren't such a bad looking bird, either."

Hmmm ... had I received a slight outburst of glee from him? 'Twas an attempt at displaying emotion. Hmmm, again.

CHAPTER 20

Land presented itself below us, appearing as a lush, green blanket stretching as far as we could see. The introduction of deep green vegetation—the stuff of jungles, grasslands, snow-capped mountains, deserts, rivers, and lakes—created a veritable abstraction, an eruption of color in a random pattern demonstrating nature at its most creative endowment. This is indeed a projection of primeval construction that is awe-inspiring. From our vantage point high above the land that is Africa, devoid of any contact with its life forms, I could almost imagine what Eden could have been. I was loathe to allow us to become witness to the true aura of this place by intermingling with the various life forms.

If this was in fact Africa, its reputation as a fierce, disease-ridden continent seemed oxymoronic to the visage presenting itself.

"What say you, Leader? Should we just enjoy the beauty of the landscape, or should we attempt to get a closer feel for its true existence?"

"Isn't that what we came here for?

"I was curious about the pestilence and the preponderance of warfare, while you expressed an interest in visiting an antagonist of yours. Sometimes we are misguided by the opulence of the book jacket while ignoring the fact that the book itself harbors a most horrifying tale.

"If it is truth that we seek, and if that truth lies in a more intimate understanding of the human psyche, then down we go, and damn the thorns in the rosebushes."

I am glad I attached myself to a more adventurous spirit than I am. If it were left to me, I guess that I would be satisfied just to admire the view from above and avoid any possibility of conflict down below. However, by changing my vantage point, I am able to receive signals from both man and beast—some of the former so filled with anger and hate that it is difficult to separate the two. Yet there is innocence here in the simplicity of existence radiating from isolated groups of primitive societies: a deep and solemn religiosity based upon their appreciation and awe of nature and its gifts of beauty and sustenance. Such an existence is almost biblical in content.

But then I hear beasts tracking their prey and achieving conquest over a less formidable species in order to fulfill a primitive need for sustenance. This is an understandable action, but I've also noticed the almost bestial screams emanating from the throats of humans as they savagely assault fellow humans—not for food but for the inexplicable thrill of destruction. Those animalistic screams are joined by the screams of terror from their victims and together form a symphony of hellish proportions. Who is the conductor of such an unholy opera? Is it a despotic distortion of their god's ideology or merely a drug-induced barbarism? Or is it the true basic nature of evolution's present contribution to the progression of life that seems to be never ending on this lonely grain of sand in the desert that is the firmament?

"Oh, Leader, why do we witness so much hate among the creatures called men? Somewhere on this world, there must be a peaceable reaction to balance this mindless destruction of self.

"There just has to be. I cannot accept the possibility that this is the true nature of man."

CHAPTER 21

"Bean, this is what we came to Africa for: to see for ourselves the place where the evolutionary germ sprouted man and to observe the societies who chose to remain behind as humanity multiplied and migrated north en masse."

"Was the environment the cause of violence, or did man himself create it? How could such a wondrous place be the birthplace of such horror? That germ, that alien germ that sprang forth from the soul of early hominids, had to receive support from some entity. I prefer to believe that it indeed came from some ethereal life form that seeded this planet. I find it very difficult to believe that the multitude of gods that form the basis for the world's religions served as the example for man to follow. If indeed their god formed man in his image and gave him the predisposition for violence and hate, what can be said about the ideals and goals of man? No: it had to be directed or birthed from an alien existence, perhaps as a research project, or as part of some universal plan to see where their way of life failed. The doctrines of faith point to a life of peaceful coexistence with one's fellow man, proving that those tenets had to have had their origin in the dreams of society. However, those dreams have become very difficult to invoke. Damn aliens!"

And so we floated down to earth; the location was arrived at randomly, but it was a seemingly peaceful site.

"Tell me, Leader, what do you see?"

"What do I see?

"I don't understand what it is that you want me to say."

"Very simple: look around, and tell me what you see."

"I see nothing complicated—just trees, plants, and the water in the stream. Perhaps the flash of a fish's scales reflecting the sun's rays.

"Is that what you mean?"

The obvious, yes ... but really look. Look carefully at each tiny segment constituting the 'trees, plants, and the water in the stream.'

"I'm still not sure what you mean. Can't you be more specific?"

"Consider this another lesson in the potential acquisition of, and a further understanding of, feelings.

"Agreed that what you described was indeed a picture of our surroundings, but what I want you to engage in is what you define as your greatest attribute: observation. What do you see? What do you see beyond those leaves, those blades of grass, the abstract patterns in the bark of those trees, beneath the ripples of the rushing water?"

"I don't know if I ... wait! There is life! My God, Bean—it's all around us: above, below, in, out ... life within life within life.

"Has it always been this way, everywhere and forever?

"Why haven't I seen it all before?"

"You have, Leader ... you have. Weren't you a gnat, and weren't many of your cohorts creepies and crawlies among the flora ... and weren't many of them burrowed into the hides of countless fauna? Where do you think those creatures you have just discovered have been existing all these years?

"You are so involved with the obvious, bearing witness to what you were conditioned to see, that the details that constitute the obvious have escaped your notice. You saw what you wanted to see, but you successfully ignored the truth and the legitimacy of the truth presented to you.

"Let me try to clarify this for you.

"Innumerous realities exist in each and every situation: the obvious, which is the cause for reaction, either on a physical or emotional plane, and the underlying stimuli, which provide the fodder for the obvious.

"But in all realities, even the hidden or underlying stimuli are obvious to some observer, who in turn forms the path to the reality of their presence, and so on and so on.

"But again, in unnatural circumstances, we tend to react to the present by responding to the obvious created by those who control and covet the future. It takes a major effort to see beyond the obvious and discover the root causes of the true reality of what is.

"And how do we see beyond the obvious? By experience and the desire to question everything. If something is too good or too bad or not clear enough, it is in all probability not, and it should be enough of a stimulus for you to question it. Hence a search for the underlying causes is called for. But curiosity tends to take effort, and the path of the least resistance has become the path of least effort. So the obvious becomes the reality we trust to be the truth ... and that is a problem for the masses and an insipid weapon for the creators.

"Am I making myself clear, Leader? Do you understand what I am attempting to say?"

"Are you kidding? It's obvious to me that you do not believe what you see and that investigation into the totality of your surroundings has become your mantra. Can't you accept what is there and go with the flow? Just watch those ants. Do they question their place in the scheme of things? Apparently not."

"I do not believe that we are ants and that we must follow some ancient programming designed to stunt our ability to reason and question, so that we follow the ant in front of us no matter what the ulterior purpose is to our existence. Instinct on this level is devoid of leadership, and leadership is what guides society in whatever direction it chooses to flounder in. This ancient programming has since become instinct, and instinct can be anathema to pure thought."

"Bean, am I forced to be the recipient of your esoteric rhetoric forever? It tends to give me static, and that interferes with my enjoyment of what you so succinctly refer to as 'the obvious.' As far as instinct is concerned, hasn't instinct been established as the result of experience—and in many instances, the savior of various species?"

"True, but instinct is the savior for simple organisms whose lives are perpetually involved in an eternal routine of repetition and not in the complicated and ever-changing aura of man's existence. Instinct does indeed play a significant role in man's day-to-day existence, but serves only as an aid to his survival.

"But are you questioning one of my rantings? ... and I never heard the squeak of an old hinge as a door was opened slightly.

"Actually, by your presence, you have provided the means for me to express myself verbally in what I sincerely hope will be a prelude to future discussions on a myriad of subjects. So just listen for the moment, and try to comprehend what it is that I am attempting to pronounce.

It is my desire to elicit an itch of curiosity from you and for you to scratch that itch with a yearning for abstract thought. Again, what is not necessarily what truly is.

"All right, back to my take on instinct.

"Is man doomed to become a race directed by instinct, with the inability to respond to situations that present themselves beyond the norm?

"Man today has been programmed to believe what he is told to believe and discouraged from peering through and beyond the smoke to perceive the clarity of truth that exists in that discernible dimension.

"You have been so involved with the aggressive nature of man that, even though you yourself had been a creepie, you lost all touch with the multiple and divergent levels of life.

"Yes, your ants have always been there, and yes, they too have souls and a direction to their lives. Granted, their souls are not as complicated as those of man, but nevertheless, souls they have, as a most vital aspect of their existence, at least to them.

"Go ahead and join them and tell me what they feel then; perhaps you will inhale a bit of their passions. Consider this another step in your growth."

CHAPTER 22

On the earth, and marching between the tall blades of grass, an endless parade of ants wended their way on a mission to where and a return to once was.

Leader chose those tireless minions, who proceeded in an almost hypnotic journey of preordained labor, as the first attempt at his conscious integration into the psyche of what he believed was a rather simple form of life. This would be a voyage into pure instinct for him.

This attempt at an in-depth observation differed in part from his previous connection with those bloodsucking companions he had devoted the past millennium to.

The ants were a mere diversion for him, representing time he could spend distancing himself from his usual haunting of man and his aggressive nature. This was coupled with an almost blank and empty desire for profound mental edification.

So off he went, and I was less than patient in awaiting his return—and, of course, his reaction to this new adventure of his.

Meanwhile, I chose to enjoy our surroundings—does that count as an emotion? If one can imagine that the multitude of sounds emanating from the countless life forms present in my bubble as emanating from the sections of a large orchestra, I am privileged to be an audience of one luxuriating in the throes of a majestic symphonic production. The music combined with the virtual imaging of the green vegetation and the incredible presentation of the limitless varieties of floral projections swaying in the tropical breeze; the blue of the sky; the almost iridescent flashes of color from the many species of bird life; the constant changing of the patterns in the flowing water agitated by their attempt to avoid the many obstacles in their path; and the brief sparkle of color from the aquatic denizens would make even the famous Walt Disney envious. This is a true and natural fantasia of life—and one that could never be simulated by bytes of color and sound. I thoroughly enjoyed it.

Yes, enjoyed it! Too human for an abstract entity such as myself? I wonder if I am not constantly being altered—with, perhaps, no discernable end in mind. I cannot bring myself to comprehend or accept this thought. The remoteness of that possibility would never be understood nor accepted by Leader, so I will opt to keep it to myself. The future will arrive soon enough (an abstract thought to humans, for "soon enough" could be countless thousands of years to us).

So I savored the moment for as long as I was able, fully expecting it to be interrupted by the return of my companion and his description of his new experience.

… and interrupted they were! But the image I perceived was that of a perfect—a mathematically perfect—cube. Six sides of a uniform block, consisting of row upon row of aligned ions both horizontal and vertical, generated a sickly gray aura.

CHAPTER 23

"Leader, is that you? What happened?"

"What happened, you ask? What happened?

"Give me a few moments to rearrange. This was the weirdest thing I was ever a particle of."

"Go on; I'm waiting. This is going to be a good one!"

Slowly he began to change, and his color improved. The cube began to … melt, I suppose is the word for it, and Leader gradually reassumed his amorphous shape.

I remained patient; at least that was the image I projected.

"Okay, this is what happened:

"As soon as I left you, I entered the mind—at least I thought it was a mind—of one of the ants in that endless procession. My goal was to experience simplicity of thought and witness for myself what a soul devoid of emotion, would feel. I wanted to gain an understanding of how a species could exist without the emotions that drive the actions and reactions of man. But what I discovered was a society of automatons whose sole objective in life was to follow the ant in front of it: no mind, no free will, and no thought … therefore no objection, no question … just mindless submission to a preordained instinctual drive for survival. The ant had no knowledge of what or where or why it was. If an obstacle was presented to the column, it veered around it or over it and continued on its mission—a mission devoted to feeding its queen so she could ultimately, as long as she was physically able, produce a new safari of robots, perpetuating

forever their mindless march of sustenance gathering, to and fro, constantly being repopulated by her propensity for reproduction.

"Interesting thought: I think there is direct correlation between the ant colony and the society of man.

"Bean, I've got to tell you that if I were able to incur pain, this experience would be excruciating. I felt something. Was it emotion? I'm not able to say at the present. But I was affected in a way that I have never been affected before.

"Even my witnessing of man's aggression toward his own kind and the brutality he demonstrated had no effect on me. I was an observer—a clinician, if you prefer. I never had the curiosity to enter the mind of one of the participants; therefore I never witnessed any emotion that they incurred. But this ... this was an eye-opener.

"I guess that emotions and the ability to question what one is asked to do in all situations involving one or one's society is one of the most basic components of complex beings."

"I think you are finally getting it. Emotions, or feelings, are paramount in the continued progress and evolution of sentient beings. The one obstacle in man's smooth progression to an evolutionary apex is his willingness to accept malignant concepts, no matter how foreign to him and his basic morality, without utilizing his capacity for thought and the need to question abstract theory.

"As I mentioned before, it is not the obvious that is important; it is the minutiae that constitute the obvious that represent the true composition of reality."

"Then I suppose I'll have to engage in a more specific approach to the attainment of emotion. You will, without a doubt, be there, replete with your sardonic wit, to guide me through the early learning stage?

"How much time do you anticipate that it would take me to achieve a parity of knowledge with you?"

"It all depends upon your desire to learn and upon the exertion you plan to expend in order to attain the result you presently desire. Nevertheless, I am here and will be for the immediate future ... that is, until I choose to continue on my quest to minister to the growth of that babe I had spoken to you about.

CHAPTER 24

"In this very brief time span," Leader said, "I have been a witness to emotions I can only describe as uncomplicated and pure in concept—emotions driven mainly by instinct, emotions that had yet to adjust to present-day conditions. Case in point: the interaction of the whale pod and the extremely efficient killer ships that are their oppressors.

"Whaling has always been a danger to the order, but with the onset of modern methods of hunting and processing of the behemoths, ages will pass before they develop new instincts to protect themselves.

"I think it's time for me to progress to a more complicated mind-set. I am anxious, and somewhat wary, of merging with a human's multitude of somewhat irrational emotions. The vast combinations of instinct, thought, action, reaction, logic, irrationality, and sensory stimuli form an incredible scenario for an emotional maelstrom.

"Do you think I am ready for it, Bean?"

"Is anyone or anything ever ready for it? Man is such a complicated animal that no matter how much study is exhausted on the subject and no matter how many sociological suppositions are presented, a concrete conclusion as to what makes him tick is never reached. Just when you think you have him figured out ... poof! Off he goes in the other direction. I would rather bet on a race of one hundred three-legged horses than bet on how man will react to the stimuli that govern his life."

"Then what's the rationale in continuing with your quest? If he is such a fickle creature, how do you expect to control those very emotions that form the causation of your almost psychopathic need for fulfillment?

"Forget it—he isn't worth all those years, those countless millennia spent in a fruitless search for the harmony of life as you picture it."

"You just don't seem to get it, do you? That's the whole point of it. Not knowing how, what, when, or where he will react to the situation at hand? That is the excitement.

"Sure, I try to lead him along the path I perceive to be the correct one; sometimes, he does follow it. Those rare times make my efforts worth all the frustration that is part and parcel of the job.

"To sound a bit Zen, it's the reaction that influences my reaction, and those reactions are bringing me closer to his reactions ... all emotionally driven, of course."

CHAPTER 25

"Stop!"
"Cease!"
"Desist!"

"I didn't say anything!"
"Not you, Leader—my two-legged ghost."
"I don't see anyone. Ghost? Are you hallucinating or something?"
"Leader, later ... please."
"Have I done something to arouse your ire? Obviously I was under the misconception that I had earned a little freedom in conveying this narrative."
"Indeed you have, but I feel as if you are straying from my tale and interjecting more of your personal ideology than is called for."
"Bean, are you okay? I hate to tell you, but there is no one here but the two of us and a few ants."
"Leader, please: I'll explain it all to you later. I am not nuts!"
"Do you really think you're not nuts?"
"Sorry, just a bit of humor.
"I do have the tendency to ramble from one subject to another ... and, I will admit, lose track of the basic story line.
"I have no excuse, save that my mind is constantly searching for answers to topics that seem, at least to me, to progress naturally from previous ones."

"I have nothing against your hypotheses; actually, some of them are quite stimulating and amusing. But spread them out a bit. I promise I will provide the necessary segues for your ramblings periodically."

"Hypotheses? Segue? Bean, you're scaring me ... a bit. I'm beginning to believe that nothing is real anymore."

"I told you I would explain it all to you later. Patience."

"This is getting very confusing. I feel as if I am in the middle of a Mack Sennett comedy; people popping in from a bunch of doors and me having conversations with all of them."

"Mack Sennett? What's a Mack Sennett?"

"Mack Sennett was a silent movie act—"

"He can't hear you, so don't make things more difficult than they really are. This craziness is entirely my fault. I should have waited until I was alone before interrupting your pontifications. Now I have to explain reality to him. What a mess!

"As far as you and I are concerned, I think I have made my point, and I feel that you fully understand my trepidation that the story will end up marginalized by your mental exercises.

"Actually, I feel that this is déjà vu, and we have had this discussion before. I do believe that you require intermittent reminding."

"It appears that I do, and you are quite correct in your doing so.

"Please extend my apologies to your friend and let him know that I am anxious to make his acquaintance at a later date."

"Will do, and thank you.

"I believe that our relationship has grown to a mutual respect now. Our past endeavor is now being reviewed by professionals, and I am awaiting their input. There is always the chance that our first collaboration will be accepted by others who will be champing at the bit for this sequel.

"Until later ..."

"I look forward to it."

CHAPTER 26

"Er, Leader? This will take a bit of explaining.

"I told you about the ghostwriter who collaborated with me on my previous attempt at putting some of my adventures on paper in order to share them with the human public, didn't I?

"Well, I sometimes have to advise him that he might be straying too far from the story line and interjecting an overabundance of his own thoughts into the narrative. While I don't mind occasional forays into the dialogue, he has a tendency to ... how can I put it ... to ramble.

"He claims that his topics have interest for the ultimate purveyors of the story, so I give him quite a bit of leeway. But the brakes have to be applied when I feel that enough is enough, at least for the time being."

"I'm a bit—actually very—confused.

"If this is just a story, where is the reality? Do we exist or not? Am I just a just a figment of your imagination or an example of virtual reality?

"I'm starting to feel like a marionette whose every movement is controlled by your conception of what the story line should encompass!"

Boy, I really screwed up this time!

How do I explain this one? Now I can use the ghost's help in putting this thing into perspective for Leader.

"I am trying to avoid an existentialist's approach to the situation.

"Let's say that I am recounting the story in real time and referring to it in the past, yet I am not dictating it in ordinary fashion.

"The writer is here with us ... and yet he isn't. If anyone is a figment of the imagination, it is the ghostwriter. Yet he does exist, and he is able to manipulate our reality, utilizing his own accumulation of powers that are solely in his bailiwick."

"Big brother is watching us?

"Now you're making me self-conscious of every stupid blunder I fall prey to. And here I am letting you be my guide to a very difficult learning process within the realm of human emotion, while the great eye in the sky observes my every reaction.

"You are really asking too much of me, Bean."

"Just listen to yourself. You have no feelings yet. You are projecting emotions that you have never experienced into a situation that, given the opportunity, could be a tremendously enlightening one.

"If you are able to erase the ghost from your bubble, perhaps we can continue with our trek, and I'm sure that we will both benefit from the knowledge gained.

"I promise I will never again conjure him up in your presence: out of sight, out of mind.

"Can you accept that?

"We really have too great a thing going for us to let this interruption put the kibosh on it."

"You sure ask a lot of me. But what are companions for, if not to trust one another? So: poof again, and the ghost has become just another ghost in the realm of the unseen."

"BUT DON'T YOU DO THIS TO ME AGAIN. YOU HEAR?"

"Agreed."

Boy, this was turning into a serious learning process for the both of us.

CHAPTER 27

"I think I would like to make a foray into the mind of a human being now. Now that I've experienced emotions on a relatively primitive scale, perhaps man is my next logical step?"

"Perhaps you're right, but primitive man would be a better introduction to human emotions than if you jumped right into a civilized society replete with the multitude of distractions that it involves.

"You are already familiar with instinct as a guiding force, so a combination of instinct and emotion could be a logical first step. The progression of instinct into emotion will offer a better understanding of that final step. What say you?"

"Again I yield to your better judgment.

"Why don't we just flit around for while I do what I do best— just observe the land that is Africa?"

"Good idea. There are so many species of life here, and in such abundance, that it behooves us to, as you say, flit around for a while."

… and how long is a while? Minutes? Days? Years? Time is an abstraction and only pertinent to the entity involved within its confines.

CHAPTER 28

Because of our years and years of contact as intimate observers of humanity, Leader and I made an exerted effort to avoid any interactions with man and just concentrated on observing the vast array of fauna displayed in all its varieties and in all its environments. What we found most fascinating were the interactions between any given species with other species, both benign and malignant.

We noticed how some members would venture off by themselves and only seek companionship when it became time to engage in mating. Off they would go again once their obligation had been completed and a new life had been started. These species relied upon the female to feed and protect the newborn, as well as teach it to survive and mature. The death of a mother usually resulted in the death of her offspring, either by starvation or by nourishing a hungry predator.

We saw beasts mourn the passing of fellow members and stand guard over their remains in hope that the fallen would somehow rise up and rejoin the group. Only when it became obvious that the deceased was really gone would the group move on, but not without a farewell tribute.

We saw beasts form a circle with the young and helpless within the barrier in order to protect them from an intrusion by predators.

We saw predatory prides of fearsome beasts show affection and patience with their young and then, minutes later, stalk a potential kill for those same sweet youngsters to render brutally into sustenance.

"So, Bean, tell me what you see."

"I see that all life is predicated upon death, and that is the barbaric beauty of nature. All life ultimately becomes the means for the continuation life itself. So what is the purpose of it all? Just to survive until you ultimately become nothing more than worm food? No wonder man is in such dire straits! Get as much out of life as you can before ... well, you know."

"What you say is true. Creatures kill for food up the food chain, but why does man kill? Granted, his food must be prepared for ingestion; therefore there must be some destruction of life. But why does he kill when food is not the prime reason? Beyond that requirement for nourishment, death has become a game to him, and he plays it merely to enrich the domination and possession he seems to need. I refer not only to death in the physical sense, but the concept of death as visualized in competition: not the actual taking of life, but the figurative destruction of one's position in life.

"I've seen so much death in the past as I observed man's fruitless destruction of his fellow man. I have also borne witness to the most horrible of brutalities, both on the battlefields and on the civilian fronts.

"Yet you are forever convinced that it is the morality of man that will be his salvation in the long run."

"Morality is a necessary condition for any group-oriented species to survive. Demonstrating concern for other members regarding their health, safety, nourishment, and so on is a key mechanism in the growth and endurance of their society. Yet morality as a concept is defined by the individual society it is endemic to. One's definition is not necessarily another's definition, and it is based upon the needs of the specific group."

"But the only species that practice morality to any extent are the so-called lower species. There are any number of animal groups, whether family oriented or species oriented, that rely upon a cluster mentality in order to survive.

"Protection of group members from natural or predatory danger is instinctual—which, if one studies, is akin to a basic tenet of morality as man defines it. But man doesn't have the psychological means—nor, as it appears evident, the will—to practice such protection. For lower life forms, survival and propagation of the species is paramount and is the primary incentive of life."

"Again we seem to be comparing instinct and complex thought. Does complex thought almost guarantee a decline of morality? As I mentioned previously, instinct is the primary force behind complex thought. All the basics are there again—health, safety, nourishment— but the method of achieving those necessities has changed due to the incredible increase in sensory and materialistic stimuli."

CHAPTER 29

I thought I had lost him for a moment, but he had apparently just been contemplating his next profundity.

"But it has become more than just the nature of mere survival; it has become an almost pathological accumulation of what used to be called the necessities of life. It is almost as if they can feel that an end to their lavish lifestyle is approaching, and a new life will appear in the near future where those same necessities will not be so readily available: a modern-day hunter-gatherer society combined with a defensive mentality bordering on paranoia.

"I can almost envision a time when everything is either owned or controlled by very few, if not by one man, with nothing left for anyone else. So the pitiful few have-nots disappear, as did nature's previous attempts at conceiving life.

"What will be left for that solitary individual to conquer or accumulate when there is nothing more? The game will be over, and the only winner will be the master of none. His only alternative will be to play against himself in a relentlessly boring existence. Somehow I can't fathom losing to yourself: all hail multiple personality disorder as the ultimate salvation of the one."

I think I'll just play Devil's Advocate for a while and egg Leader on.

What's interesting is the fact that he has become more aware of the environment around him and is slowly developing an inquisitive mind by questioning what on the outside appears to be obvious, even if the internal and deeply rooted causes are not. Just his detection of a causative implication is a tremendous breakthrough for him.

Until now, he has been mired in the most palpable of circumstances, totally ignoring the possibility that, perhaps, the egg did in fact precede the chicken.

"Why is it that man, considered the most moral of species—or at the very least the owner of the most potential for morality—will do whatever he can to instill hardship upon his fellow beings, including the proliferation of death, in order to achieve superiority in countless moral and materialistic endeavors? Even humor consists of exaggerated descriptions of insult and references to, as well as visual demonstrations of, humiliation and suffering. Laughing at oneself is considered healthy, but laughing at another's ill fortunes is immoral and tends to create mental anguish and perhaps the victim's physical reaction in retaliation to the degradation fostered on them."

"I thought that we were just going to enjoy the sights and sounds of Africa?

"All I did was ask you a simple question, and off you went … and off I went … and another discourse was ignited. I'm surprised that you didn't rail on your ghost for leading us into another tangent."

"I was thinking about it, but I believe you've alerted him to that very fact, for which I thank you."

"Let's just look at the pretty animals and birds and plants and lakes and mountains so on and so on. No more philosophical diatribes, eh?"

"You win … just the pretties."

"Just the pretties."

"Just the pretties."

"All right, already—enough!"

CHAPTER 30

"You know something, Bean? All the while that I was observing the many aggressive interactions between man and his contemporaries, I failed to notice the environment they were desecrating. I'd bet that it was, or almost was, as beautiful as what we are enjoying now.

"I wonder if nature requires the blood and physical remains of the countless unfortunate souls that give their lives in mortal combat to fertilize its beauty. It strengthens the argument for your notion that life requires death to exist, and that death is a major contributor to the formation of life."

"Just the pretties, Leader—just the pretties."

"Aarrrggg! Touché!"

Just watching the many beasts, I am amazed at their beauty. There is beauty in the movements, both in playful gestures and in their stealthy, predatory episodes. Even the largest and the fiercest of the creatures have a grace that is quite remarkable.

What isn't remarkable, though, is the end result of the stalking. I can do without the visual of them ripping and crunching while the blood of their victims paints a mask of sanguinary celebration on their visages.

"Hold up for a second, Leader. I think I just saw what might be a village of people deep in the jungle we just passed. Back up a little. This might be just the situation you requested in order to assimilate yourself into the mind-set of primitive man.

"Looks like a society devoid of physical contact with civilization and subsisting on the wiles developed over centuries of survival! Instinct and basic emotion: just what the doctor ordered.

"What do you think?"

"What do I think? I think you might be right.

"Why don't we go down there and just hang around for a while before I decide to take the next step? I'm not about to jump blindly into any situation again."

"Agreed."

We took our time descending to the village I had spied earlier. I wanted to get a good picture of the environment prior to our proposed involvement.

CHAPTER 31

As we got closer, an uneasy feeling overtook me. Something was wrong, and I couldn't place it.

"Leader, are you receiving any strange vibes from this place?

"I can't seem to get a fix on what is unsettling me. Is it the unfamiliarity of the society or is it something deeper than that?"

"Now that you mention it, there is something out of tune down there, and it's vaguely recognizable, but definitely out of context.

"That's strange: all the huts seem to be clustered in one area complete with communal fire pits and work areas. But if you look past the group, to the left, there is a lone hut fronted by a series of what can only be described as demon carvings.

"What do you make of it?"

Leader was right: it was a strange setup, almost as if the inhabitants of the lone hut were part of the village but not allowed to participate in its activities.

"I can see three people, I think. An old man adorned with strange facial markings; an infant; and a young female—most likely the child's mother.

"Perhaps one of them is ill and has been quarantined in an attempt to save the others from contracting whatever disease it might have?"

No, that's not it.

But then a sudden realization almost short-circuited me.

"Don't do anything. Don't make a sound; don't broadcast your presence; don't transmit any signals. I think I know what's going on.

"Quickly and quietly, let's back up a bit. I'll tell you in a minute."

We retreated out of range to what I believed was a safe distance from any sensitive entity receiving our emissions.

"What is it, Bean? Why the precautions?"

It took a few minutes to get over my shock before I felt calm enough to answer him.

I hoped my agitation didn't project any strange sparks to alarm the villagers.

"Bean?"

"I'm okay now. Thanks for the concern.

"Do you remember that one of the main reasons I wanted to go to Africa was to check up on an adversary of mine named Whoever?

"I met him at the graduation of the young man I had helped come to terms with a childhood affliction he had acquired at a very early age. His name was Ricky Granlin.

"Well, during the ceremony, I received the sensation of a faerie presence in the immediate vicinity. I was afraid that it was my old adversary, named Whatever. But I quickly negated that thought, because I knew he would not be in a position to haunt me for quite a long while. I had managed to dispose of him in a most unique manner.

"So I quickly entered the body of a squirrel and proceeded to search the area. I came across the figure of a black raven perched on a branch overlooking the proceedings."

"A raven? That's interesting. What did he want?"

"It seemed he had been heading east and had felt my presence. Curiosity had taken control, and he had decided to check me out.

"I had been too preoccupied with Ricky and his family to catch his aura until later.

"It turned out that he was headed to Africa, where he intended to guide a small child. From what he told me, the child—an infant girl—had been born in a veil of evil, and he had taken it upon himself to create what the humans would call the Antichrist ... or more realistically, the supreme malevolence."

"Wow!

"Was he serious?"

"I'm afraid so. Just as I felt secure in knowing that Whatever was securely out of the way, this one crops up.

"It was sort of coincidental inasmuch as I also intended to guide a small infant girl. However, my charge was born into an aura of good and righteousness and coincidentally, she was also a child of poverty."

"You did mention something about your quest … and, I believe, you also mentioned this character.

"What do you want to do about him?

"What can I do to help?"

"Well, first of all, you have to shield yourself from any possibility that he will sense your presence. I want to keep you and your powers, as well as my own, out of his sphere of influence. His lack of knowledge as to your company will be a great advantage when and if it becomes necessary to combat this evil."

"Sounds good; what else?"

"I'll look around and find a suitable host for me to inhabit. I don't want him to have any inkling as to my increased powers. As far as he knows, he and I have the same abilities—no more, no less."

"Bean, look over there. How about that mangy dog—it is a dog, isn't it? She seems to have free rein of the place and is accepted by the others … at least as a puntable fur ball, that is. One thing in your favor: she won't stand out in this environment—that is, of course, if they don't erect an end-zone goalpost."

"Great choice. She will also offer no resistance to my intrusion. She might even welcome the possibility of being replaced as the main object of their leisurely entertainment.

"So, if all is well, off I go. Just keep a close eye on the situation, and be prepared to jump in if the situation calls for it.

"I don't know how I will work this out yet—sort of playing it by ear."

"Ear?"

"For lack of a better term …

"Here, poochy poochy; come to Bean. Time for a little fun."

"Give me a break, Bean."

CHAPTER 32

The transfer was accomplished relatively easily. I think that the four-legged mange sensed something prior to my intrusion, but in I went.

My next step was to wander over to that isolated hut and make myself known to Whoever. It was obvious to me that he was, in effect, controlling the old man.

The hut was open on all four sides, with nothing but woven branches forming the roof on the structure. It was the sole protection offered against the elements.

The floor was dirt, and the only articles of furniture were a few log seats and a crude configuration of branches and leaves, similar to the roof, which served as a bed for the woman and child. It was being used at the present time by the woman, who was weaving some sort of mat.

Meanwhile, the infant sat off to the side and was paying attention to what the old man was saying. She was paying more than attention; it was as if she were mesmerized by the hypnotic chanting of the ancient one.

If she had one prominent feature, it was her eyes. The pupils were an ashen grey in color, with no discernible iris. It was as if she was blind, but I had the weird feeling that she was aware of everything that was going on around her. To put it more in perspective, outside of the woman and the old man, nothing—and I mean nothing—was going on in the immediate vicinity. No life of any sort existed on the lone plot of land that comprised their home: not an insect, nor plant life … nothing. Just dirt.

At the center of the hut was a small fire pit, which emitted a great deal of smoke due to the fact that a few large fronds enveloping a dabble of some sort of mystery meat were reposing on the hot coals. The smell wafting from the open oven—and I could swear that I did smell it— was repulsive to me, but was apparently appetizing to the inhabitants, judging by the drool coasting down their chins.

As I made my way into the hut, I perceived a change in the chanting of the old man.

Suddenly he stopped and turned toward my cur-ness. The child, sensing a change in the familiar vibrations of the area, also turned toward me. Her eyes—those cold, gray orbs—sent a chill down my back, and I'm sure that my fur was standing on its roots, disturbing the endeavors and home life of its fleas.

His brow wrinkled for a moment, and then a slight smile emerged, growing into a toothless grin.

"I have been expecting you for some time now. Bean, isn't it?"

"Yes. I must admit that my curiosity took over, and I had to see what you were involving yourself in. Judging by your surroundings, it must be a few steps down from what you're used to."

"Ah, yes; it isn't the choicest of accommodations, and the conversations aren't very stimulating ... but the evil, Bean—the evil! I can't begin to describe what this child is capable of.

"By the way, how did you manage to find me—not only find me, but actually get here?"

Oh oh, I hadn't thought of that.

"Actually, I found you by sheer accident.

"Of course, I knew you were in Africa; you told me that yourself.

"As to how I managed to get to this country ... well, it wasn't easy. Let's say I had help from a few fish and a bird or two—and, believe it or not, I even hitched a ride on an oil tanker. My thanks to a young steward on board who was a flying-saucer aficionado! It was relatively effortless to convince him that I was an alien presence sent here to study earthlings before we made our presence known to the rest of the world.

"Once I reached Africa, I rode inside more birds until I was able to pick up your emission. Then it was 'hello, dog' and here I am."

"Why do I feel as if you're pulling something over on me?

"Well, nevertheless, I'm glad you are here. I haven't had anyone to talk with for quite a while. These people have a click speech that is

almost unintelligible. In the beginning, it took a great deal of exertion to reach the child.

"But she has amazed me with her ability to converse through telepathic means, and furthermore, she has managed to learn our language with very little difficulty.

"Bean, she is only one year old!"

"So tell me, what do you hope to accomplish with her?

"What do I hope ... are you serious? If I can just teach her to understand and control the vast powers for sheer evil that lie dormant within her, she can cause more havoc and create more destruction than any human has ever even dreamed of. And I will be her guide through it all."

"Don't you think there is enough conflict in the world today? If she is as potent a power for malevolence as you describe, and she has the desire to spread that influence throughout the world, the result could be catastrophic.

"Are you sure that's what she really wants to achieve?"

"Fool, that's what I am here for! I told you: I will be her guide and teach her the pure joy that evil can manifest. When I am finished with her, she will be a willing participant in our pursuit. With her help, I could become the most powerful spiritual presence that our kind has ever known!

"History, Bean—history. They will tell my story from every hill and dale, from every forest and mountaintop, and I will be there to drink it all up ... and so will she."

"I might try to stop you."

"Don't be ridiculous. Just look around you. Is there anything living here ... besides us, of course? She has done that with no help from me at all."

I could feel the child listening to every word we had spoken. Her mouth had the most wicked grin on an otherwise expressionless face. She knew what was expected of her, and I knew she would be fully capable of achieving that goal.

"Does she have a name yet?"

"Her native name is unpronounceable. Something to the affect of random clicks and grunts. I have, however, given her a name in honor of another one of her ilk from ages past: Lili-It.

"Although her form is not snakelike and her limbs not festooned with the talons of a raptor, her very being radiates the soul of a

predatory harpy. While she will not spend her time feasting on the newborn, as her namesake has been gloriously accused of, she will instead devour the spirit ... no, the very essence ... of man.

"She is indeed the rebirth of the first wife relegated to the depths of Hades by her aggrieved husband and his pliant creator.

"Bean, I foresee a world seething with a corruption of both mind and body such as the world has never known. Father will rise up against son; mother will rise up against daughter; brother and sister will merge in an incestuous fury! Entire nations will disappear in a firestorm of hate; religions will be despised because of their lack of salvation promised by their false prophets.

"Chaos, anarchy, suspicion, and retaliation: the new religion. And at its godhead? Lili-It.

"Lili-It will rage against her maker and revenge the ill fostered upon her at the dawn of time. She will regain her position atop the pyramid of humanity and claim her righteous throne."

"Such lofty hopes. Don't you think that you are being a bit melodramatic? She is but one person; there is no way, even with your help, that she can achieve that pinnacle of blasphemy and abject wickedness as you envision."

"Do I sense your naïveté coming through again?

"If she can achieve what she has in such a short time, and without really trying ... oh, what hell she will foment when maturity is reached."

"Why in the name of decency and morality would you want to achieve that abysmal goal?"

"Why, because I can!"

It was at about this time that I heard, or perhaps just felt, a presence in my surrogate's mind. It was very disconcerting, because I knew that it wasn't Whoever, and Leader had been true to my wishes.

It must have been the child.

"I know why you are here, and I must warn you that you are on a hopeless quest," she said. "You are not strong enough to prevent what I know to be my destiny. You are nothing more than a dog's mind. To destroy me would require the essence of a warrior and not the hesitation of a preacher of decency and foolish ethics.

"I will destroy you and take your powers, no matter how meager they be in contrast to mine, and merge them with those I already possess.

You will have the privilege of knowing that you have become a part—an insignificant part, that is—of a greatness you cannot foresee.

"I would ask you to join us, but I know that you will not and cannot accept what I have to offer. So put your mangy tail between your legs and crawl away, before I short-circuit your essence and wrap your furry host in banana leaves."

"Bean, go now," ordered Whoever, *"before I lose whatever influence I might have over the child."*

CHAPTER 33

I couldn't leave without attempting to alter her way of thinking. What she offered was anathema to my very core, and I had to try and stop her, so I attempted to look her in her eyes and merge with her mind.

BAM!

The shock that I felt was ... I don't know how to describe it. Pain? Horror? Fright? I don't know! It was like being submerged in a bottomless void and cold ... so very cold. Infused with this pit of revulsion was the shrill sound of laughter.

I lost my control over the dog; he voided his body's wastes and ran away, wailing and yelping as if from some primordial fear of the unknown.

His fear was so great that he never felt the sharp wounds on his body caused by running blind through the thorny vegetation surrounding the village. It was only after he collapsed from exhaustion that I was once again able to exercise control over his body and mind.

In all reality, it took me about the same amount of time to recover. I owed Leader my gratitude for intense effort to break me out of that spell.

"What in hell just happened? I have never seen such a reaction before."

"Hell; that's the perfect term for it. I think I have just witnessed hell, and I never want to go back there again. If she isn't the devil, then believe me, I don't want to meet him. For the first time in my existence, I truly fear for the human race.

"Sure, there is enough hate and bigotry going around now, and warfare is a common approach to solving problems, but what she promises is total chaos and a torrent of bloodletting that would make Noah's tsunami look like a faucet leak. Her ark would be constructed with the rigid corpses of humanity's demise.

"Leader, we have to stop her and somehow put the brakes on Whoever and his depraved ambitions.

"So as of now, neither one of them has any conception of our powers. We have to plan very carefully as to what our next step will be. We'll have only one chance, and it must be successful! I could not exist with the thought that I have failed in my duty to man.

"If there is indeed a guardian overseeing the evolution of this planet, I have to believe he is a power for good. I refuse to even consider the reverse of my convictions.

"I, and not that demon from hell, am his agent. He, or she, will guide me at the last moment, and I **will** win. At what cost, I have no idea. All I know is that I will gladly pay it if it means I have helped the growth of morality and integrity and aided in the salvation of human life."

CHAPTER 34

"That was some speech, Bean. More than a little idealistic and perhaps bearing a scent of innocence, but your meaning is sincere, and I'll do whatever it is that you think is necessary to cream the two of them.

"So where do we begin?"

"I'm not sure yet. One thought is that perhaps without Whoever to educate and guide her, her malevolence would be centered in this isolated place. Her power would be relegated to performing black magic and other mind-altering tricks as a witch doctor—no more, no less.

"In fact, we should occupy ourselves with that concept."

"Excellent thought. Inasmuch as they both don't know about us and our muscle, one of us could capture her attention, as well as Whoever's, while the other makes the attack.

"I was thinking we should lure Whoever away from the girl, leaving her unprotected for the moment. Then, while he is being occupied, either you or I would then envelop her in our impenetrable ionic cloud and perform something akin to a lobotomy. If we could possibly rearrange her circuitry, it might render her harmless."

"The only problem I can see is our revealing ourselves to him and losing the element of surprise that could be useful at a later date.

"So, we have a choice: try to end it once and for all now, or keep our secret in abeyance until a later date and make as strong an attack as we can.

"Actually, I like the idea of removing Whoever from the scene permanently and letting the child remain in this primitive haven.

"I'm in a quandary, Leader.

"My credo is, and always has been, not to interfere in the natural plan of things ... to offer guidance—and that is the key word, guidance—to those who require it to fulfill certain principles of decency and integrity.

"I have avoided interfering in the lives of those hapless souls who cannot achieve those qualities no matter how hard I try to help them."

"So what are you saying? Leave them alone, and let them continue to amass her powers of darkness and threaten the very core of humanity?

"I don't know if I can do that, Bean.

"Granted, I have always been attracted by man's aggressive tendencies, and war has always proven to be fascinating to me, but what you are proposing, as to her potential, is abhorrent even to me."

"I know ... I know. That's my problem."

"I'm sorry. I don't see it as a problem.

"The facts speak for themselves. Either we stop it now, or we face hell on earth later on. Seems like a no-brainer to me!"

"Can't do it, Leader. The situation calls for immediate action, but I just cannot interfere with the child's future.

"All I can do is try to reason with Whoever and somehow get him to understand what horrors the future could have in store for the world if he continues in the direction that he is so keen on following."

"Reason with him? How do you reason with a hungry shark when you are presenting it with a choice cut of meat?

"Well, you had better put on your best debate hat; here he comes now, and off I go.

"Fear not, my friend; I'll be available just in case you need me."

I could hear the hesitant shuffling and cane tapping of the old man as he worked his way through the dense foliage surrounding the village.

My poor frightened cur host stood shivering and keening in a small, open area. It was all I could do to prevent him from slinking away from the oncoming presence.

Even though I controlled his mind, enough instinct remained to alert him to the inherent evil making its way to us. This one was a real fighter!

"*Bean ... Bean: why are you fighting us? It is inconceivable to me why you would reject the power I am offering you. I'm sure that anyone, any ... thing, any imp ... in fact, any sane entity ... would jump at the opportunity.*"

"*Sane? You want to discuss sane?*

"*You're saying that the production of pure evil is sane?*

"*You're saying that Lili-It is sane?*

"*If what you describe as sane is the true definition, what am I, insane?*

"*There is something wrong somewhere with your value system!*"

"**You and your damned morality. Look what morality and ethics has accomplished lately; in fact, what has it ever accomplished?**

"**Judging from the condition that mankind finds itself in now, how can you state categorically that Lili-It—with my help, of course— would be any more detrimental to its future?**

"**Hell—oops—maybe her course is the true sanity, and maybe those who profess to be the most decent and ethical are in fact the truly insane ones. If that is accurate, then yes, you are the mentally disordered one.**

"**Do you consider religion a belief system predicated upon your precious tenet of decency?**"

"*Absolutely: most, if not all, of the heaven-based religions have some relationship to the Mosaic code of the Ten Commandments. Those commandments can be selectively chosen and picked apart, and the verbiage redefined, but in general, yes, those concepts encompass true morality, and to me that is the definition of sanity.*"

"**All right, then how do you explain the misery, the bloodshed, your holy wars, your Inquisition, your witch trials, your Crusades? How do you justify the stern and vindictive reprisals for noncompliance? How do you deny all the suffering that has been covered in the cloak of religion?**

"**This is your sanity? Is red then the color of your decent judgment?**"

"*I'm not going to get into a diatribe about religion with you. It won't be fruitful.*

"*As with all belief systems, some will bastardize religion into a vehicle for personal gain. Nobody can stop that.*

"*The problem, as I see it, is that these same jackals prey upon those who do profess and practice those tenets of morality but do not have the capacity for free thought and thus become slaves to the false prophets.*

"Are those befuddled followers then guilty of the crimes committed in the name of their god, as defined by despotic prophets?

"My belief system is buoyed by those poor souls who desire to repose upon a blanket of righteousness."

"Buoyed? You mean skewered, don't you?"

At that moment, as if in reply to Whoever's sarcasm, my cur-ness sprang up and grabbed the old man's cane, which prompted his ungraceful collapse (combined with a few indecipherable utterances) onto the jungle floor.

"Be that a prelude to the future.

"No matter what horrors you manage to contrive, you will fall once again ... and this time, you won't get up."

"Looks like you just threw the gauntlet down, and I don't mean at me.

"Look out for yourself, Bean. I am anticipating a renewal of our relationship later on."

"That's a prophesy I can readily concur with."

And with those parting words, I transferred to a stunning bird of paradise and left the old man lying in the weeds. I needed something beautiful to wash away the images that Lili-It and Whoever had imprinted in my mind.

CHAPTER 35

The sound of flapping wings brought me out of my revelry. Off to my right came a Saddle-billed Stork singing a rather raunchy ditty, its head bobbing on its swooping neck.

"Leader, I couldn't have picked a better relative for you if I could.

"Where did you find it?"

"Actually, he found me. While I waited for you to deal with Whoever, I decided to merge with a lovely fish and enjoy a little dip in the pool. How was I to know that I was to become an hors d'oeuvre for this beauty? So, to make a long story short, ol' storky was my next host. Better than being a bit of avian excrement, I suppose.

"Then I saw you, and the rest is history.

"How did it go with your friend? Did he listen to your pleadings?"

"First of all, I don't plead.

"Second of all ... well, it didn't turn out the way I would have wanted it to. He is determined to continue on the road to perdition. We **will** *meet again someday, and our battle will be concluded at that time.*

"One good thing happened, though: master cur snatched the old man's cane and knocked him to the ground. It certainly did feel first-rate!"

"Shall we de-bird now and continue our odyssey? I would still like to experience some basic human emotions."

"Okay ... sure. Maybe it'll take my mind off what has just transpired.

"Leader, I feel that before I have a chance to confront them again, the world will face some terrible catastrophes, and I know that I'll have to accept the blame for it. I had the opportunity to put a stop to it before it started, but I couldn't go against my principles."

"Perhaps you weren't convinced that they would follow through on their threats, so in walking away, you didn't really feel that they had to be stopped.

"Am I rationalizing a bit?"

"Just a bit.

"Thanks for the kind words, but we both know what the consequences will be."

"Well, look at this way: whatever will happen won't be for a long while, so we have some time to enjoy ourselves.

"Now snap out of it, and away we go."

"Away we go."

CHAPTER 36

Once again Leader and I soared high, free of our hosts, and drifted on the many frivolous breezes that wafted in and around the vagaries of this unique landscape. And again we rode over deep, rich jungles carpeted in a mat of abstract textures; over seemingly lifeless deserts painted in a monochromatic palette of ever-shifting dunes; over and around high, snow-peaked mountains glistening in their shawls of freshly fallen snow and offering a magnificent contrast against the vivid blue of the sky; over cities both large and small; over villages sparse in their habitation; and over herd after herd of grazing animals in the vast plains, all vying for their bit of grass and water while being ever vigilant for the glare of predatory beasts.

However, predation is not always confined to the beasts in the field; it has also become, for man, the basis for monetary gain in the form of the commercially viable attributes of the targets they stalk.

Combine this blasphemy with man's constant and obvious encroachment on the habitats of those free-ranging creatures, and we have what conceivably is another example of the desecration of nature's bounty.

As I observed before, during our first survey of this wondrous land, this could have indeed been the birthplace of humanity, for it offers a microcosm of environmental incentives that would prepare man for the many obstacles and advantages that would ultimately guide his evolution.

But with man's total disregard for the natural order of things, together with his brutality toward his fellow mortals and the increase of poverty-driven disease, Africa could also be the precursor of his demise. For as humanity left this place and ventured forth toward his destiny, so could this contagion of fatality follow the same path and conclude his destiny.

A significant parcel of this potential fatality would be the emergence of Lili-It and Whoever onto the world scene. Whether or not they would accomplish the goals that they so ardently subscribed to, it lay within my realm of possibility to deny them. They did not represent what Africa was meant to be, but they represented what it was becoming. She was the embodiment of all that was evil, and with her destruction, evil would experience a resounding defeat. That was my mission.

"Leader, it's interesting that even with all the beauties below us, my thoughts are still enveloped in a cloud of darkness. The demonic duo has created such a bleak impression on me that I can't seem to forget them."

"As well you shouldn't, but you can't become so obsessed with them that you fail to see all of the splendor in the world—and, as you so fervently believe, all of the morality.

"For the time being, there doesn't appear to be an imminent threat from the demonic duo, so our tour will continue as planned.

"Look there—those must be giraffes!"

"What did you think they were, long-necked warthogs?"

"Thanks for the nudge, and thanks for showing concern. How human of you."

"Hmmm ... I wonder if we didn't have emotions at one time? If we did, why did we lose them?

"I guess whoever directed our evolution—perhaps your guardian—decided that as observers, we shouldn't become mired in those sensations, as they would interfere with our impartiality.

"Know something, Bean: I think we are more than we believe we are. Could we possess other powers that we haven't discovered?"

"I wouldn't bet against it. If we do possess additional powers, we'll discover them; we are both free thinkers and tend to question various realms of possibility. Whoever is so wrapped up in his own ego that he has accepted the obvious as his mantra, and that's the reason we will be victorious.

"Okay, I feel better now. Let's find a suitable subject for you to merge with and continue our voyage east, to my charge, that is, if you

want to accompany me. I can definitely use your input and help in guiding my child to develop her latent abilities.

"She will be the ultimate weapon against the malevolence that will define the Demonic Duo.

"If you put it that way, how can I refuse? We make such a grand team.

"Now, we have to come up with a team name. We've agreed on the Demonic Duo—although the Gruesome Twosome could also be a possibility—for the bad guys, so what do you think a good catchphrase would be for us?

"Let's see: Bean and Leader; Leader and Bean; B&L; L&B; how about the Caring Pairing? No, eh? I've got another: how about the Super Dooper Groupa Two?

"I can see that you're not into it.

"One more, okay? I think I've got it: 'Here we come—we're just not one good guy, we're Twice Nice."

"You're being just a tad ridiculous. Don't make me sorry that I invited you along with me. We're not superheroes; we're just a Morality Duality.

"Seriously, though, the less conspicuous we are, the better our chances will be when the time comes."

"Morality Duality? And I'm ridiculous?"

"Fuddy Duddy Buddies."

"Aaarrrrgggg!"

"There ... that looks like a promising village. They appear to be self-sufficient. I see a large area devoted to crops and a substantial herd of cattle. I'll wager that they belong to a rather peaceful and comfortable society. Should be an easy hookup for you.

"Go; I'll wait off in the trees for you and just relax. If you need me, just blink a bit."

CHAPTER 37

Interesting village. The huts were positioned close together and seemed to be laid out in a circle, much like the old stockade design. I wondered if it formed a defensive belt against other marauding tribes or against predatory animals.

I did notice a bunch of lions not too far off, licking their cubs and licking their chops, staring at the goats and cattle being guarded by a few of the male members of the group. The men didn't seem concerned by the close proximity of those cats. I guess they had confidence in the spears they were carrying. *Don't know about that!* I thought.

I was fascinated by the bright red wraps they were wearing. Kind of smart, I'd say.

The women were inside the protective containment of the village. They were busy cooking, making clothes, and gossiping while the children were running around chasing each other and play-acting as they practiced hunting techniques against the village dogs.

Sorry if this sounds like a travelogue. It's the only way I can describe what I saw.

What the ... ? I didn't believe it: a few tour buses were approaching, followed by clouds of dancing red dust. A few honks on their horns seemed to be a signal for the men to exit their huts and line up—looked like the chorus line at Radio City Music Hall, but without the Styrofoam snow.

The drums started beating a rather hypnotic rhythm while the men bounced up and down, up and down, up and down, and so forth.

Between the drums and clicking cameras; if I hadn't known where I was, I would swear I was at an atonal Scottish Tattoo. The bagpipes were replaced by the soprano-like warbling of the women as the latter encouraged their men to leap even higher. I supposed that height was the measure of virility ... or maybe they just wanted to fly away from this embarrassing spectacle?

So this was what had become of the innocent. Primitive man had emerged as a side show for rich safari-niks. I wondered what the natives really thought about this intrusion, though I supposed they probably thought more about the amount of coins the gawkers left behind. Souvenir spears, headdresses, and baskets (undoubtedly imported from China) were pushed on the tourists, and they gobbled them up.

Not so primitive, those villagers.

I could just hear the exchanges of the tourists ...

"Hmmm ... Uncle Fred would certainly love that genuine lion spear, and Aunt Rhonda would certainly plotz for that red sarong-looking wrap."

Dear Aunt Rhonda,

I hope you and Uncle Fred enjoy these souvenirs that I picked up at this wonderful native village. It was such an exciting day. The men were so fierce looking with their headdresses and lion spears as they performed a lion-hunting dance. You should have seen Biff jumping up and down with them, wearing his J. Press Berms. The women were encouraging their men by making this very strange sound (sounded like an old-fashioned air-raid siren, hee hee). I took a picture of their huts. Do you know that they are made from cow dung? Really! And they drink a concoction made from sour milk. Echh! I couldn't live this way in a million years [*Hey, lady ... your ancestors did live this way a million years ago*]. See you soon. Wait until you see the photos we took. Regards from the Biffer.

Love and hugs,
Your niece, Tiffany

Guess we can't stop progress ... or is it evolution?

I wonder where Leader had disappeared to? I couldn't pick out which rebounding bouncer he had chosen to meld with. I guessed I would have to wait for his report.

CHAPTER 38

"… Psssst, Bean. Are you alone?"

"Leader, is that you?"

"No, it's me, Ghost."

"Ghost? What are you doing here? You've never popped up before without me scolding you. Is anything wrong?"

"I don't know. I think you have me quite concerned about this Demonic Duo of yours. More than just concerned, I guess—scared! I realize that this story is told in the past/present and that we can't see the future. But do you really believe that we could be in such danger as you profess? I'm worried about my family."

"Yes, I do believe man is in serious danger. In his past, man hasn't had contact with an evil such as this promises to be. I would say that your recent history was, and continues today, to be the seed that germinated this repugnance."

"What can we do? How do we fight it?"

"It's too late for you to change your ways now in order to be strong enough to wage a successful campaign against them. I think that Leader and I are your only hope for salvation—actually, the two of us and the force for good that my new charge possesses. Even considering the combined powers that we three enjoy, we may not be able to repel the darkness that is slowly approaching."

"It's not a very pretty picture that you paint. I suppose we deserve it, though.

"Do you seriously believe that the three of you have a chance?"

"We'd better. I don't want to become a has-Bean, you know."

"Have you ever faced anything of this magnitude before?"

"There has never been a malevolence of this enormity, but, yes, I have been in intimate contact with evil ... although he wasn't evil at the time I was involved with him.

"If you have a moment or two, and it looks as if you do, considering the fun Leader is obviously having, I'll tell you an interesting story."

"I'd like that. Is it for publication, or is it off the record?"

"I'll leave it up to you. If you think it's crucial to the story, you may of course include it."

"Agreed."

"Many years ago, in my ramblings, I came across a young boy who projected such sadness and loneliness that I felt I just had to try to alleviate his suffering somehow.

"My contact with him originated when he was entering the sixth grade of his elementary school.

"He had suffered an incredible set of adversities for a lad of his age.

"His mother was the third wife of his father. He was one of six children born to his mother, of which only he and a sister survived. He had been whipped by his father since he was very young.

"It was all I could do to instill hope in him, no matter how miniscule."

"My God, Bean, how do you give hope to such desperation as that?"

"We had many talks about the elusive silver lining that is attached to every cloud of despair. But he would stare through me at no tangible object in front of him and drift off in a make-believe world of his own creation.

"I felt that I would never get through to him. There existed such devout sadness in one so small.

"Every once in a while, I felt that I was reaching him, especially when he drew little pictures in his notebook. I would ask him to explain what the images were, and he would launch into some childish fantasy that he'd love to disappear into. I believe that they were the happiest times in an otherwise untenable situation."

"I would think that the auspices of a qualified psychiatrist would have been the correct treatment for you to employ."

"Remember that psychiatry was a fledgling science at the time, and he did live in a rural environment.

"The boy continued to falter, even with whatever encouragement I could offer— to such an extent that he failed his sixth-grade studies. Our discussions following his disappointment bordered on an expression of clinical depression, at least as I saw it.

"I was not used to this apparent failure of my ability. But I was determined to succeed, even though it appeared to be a bleak situation.

"Hey, Bean, this is a depressing story, and if I add it to a rather depressing future, I might want to kill myself."

"Out with the melodramatics, and relax. It only gets worse!

"As he grew and matured, I offered whatever support I could muster as far as his artwork was concerned—that being the only aptitude he seemed to possess. Unfortunately, his work wasn't of a high enough quality to afford him the honor of a registration into a recognized school of art.

"I suggested as an alternative that he undertake an attempt at the study of architecture, and he agreed to try his hand at it; but again he was refused admission to a school of that genre due to his lack of a formal education.

"I was at my wit's end as to what to do. Everything I suggested and all of our talks accomplished nothing but abject failure. Even I was depressed!

"In the meantime, he subsisted on an orphan's pension and moved into a homeless shelter upon the death of his mother. He was only sixteen at the time."

"How can anybody have as much bad luck as that kid had? It's almost as if he ran into the perfect storm of hopelessness. All of life's despair came together into one luckless individual."

"It was at this time that I finally admitted failure. I had one more confrontation with him prior to my departure. I said, and I will try to remember my exact words: 'Adolf, life was never meant to be an easy voyage. You can make of it what you want and achieve enough success and happiness as you desire, or you can surrender to the darkness of despair and exact revenge on those who have succeeded. Both avenues will bring you satisfaction, depending upon your ultimate choices. I can't foresee what your future will bring, but unless you are able to rise above your adversities, you will create a hell on earth for yourself—and perhaps for others also.'

"Well, we all know which direction he chose, and unfortunately for the world, evil was his destiny. He became one of history's great despots and almost destroyed civilization as we know it."

"So Adolf Hitler was the challenge you faced and couldn't help. That was an incredible defeat. How did you recover from it?"

"Recover? You don't recover from a defeat of that enormity. All that you can hope to do is to balance your failures against the successes you've had and, quite simply, move on with your life. In the end, a universal sense of morality accomplished the final victory against the evil he created, although the cost in human lives was enormous.

"I wonder whatever became of that morality?

"Was there a lesson learned? Apparently not.

"In retrospect, how boring it would be if we succeeded at everything we attempted. What would we learn, and how could we hope to deal with a new challenge if it suddenly presented itself in the future?

"How we react to misfortune presents us with the tools necessary to face it when it reappears in a different configuration. Don't forget that experience is the fuel that drives progress."

"And yet you continue to fight for our survival, even considering the obstacles we place in front of you. I pray that you never run out of windmills.

"I'll leave you now before Leader returns and offer my sincere thanks for your profound words of wisdom. I shall yield to your superior knowledge and strength of character. We humans have much to learn from you ... if, of course, we allow ourselves to."

Oh, well, there went my commune with peace and quiet. I guess it was never meant to be.

CHAPTER 39

Nighttime came suddenly, and the air was filled with the roars of hungry beasts and the bleats of their terrified intended victims. This primeval concert contrasted with the sounds of merriment coming from the village. It looked as if a wedding were taking place, and everyone took pleasure in the event. More warbling and leaping ensued; these people really knew how to party.

I hoped that Leader wasn't the groom. I sure didn't want to hear his account of the bridal bed. The experience could be too intense for someone unused to human emotions. All I needed was a sexaholic-fed cloud of electromagnetic energy as my partner: "Feed me," et cetera, et cetera.

Well, tomorrow would be a new day, and Leader would be a new imp—perhaps a more mature imp, but an imp nonetheless.

Now if the baboons would only shut up.

Morning and the rising sun cast an ever-shrinking shadow over the jungle and onto the savanna. I could see the lions returning to their families with swollen bellies and collapsing in heaps of tawny fur, their growling replaced by rumbling abdomens.

As the evening dew morphed into morning mist, the rising heat awakened the angry swarms of dormant insect life, and the daily torment began.

The rise in temperature also acted as a sedative for the baboons, and they, too, found time for repose under the scarce shade trees, calmly grooming each other.

Glancing at the village, I couldn't see much life. The previous night's festivities had taken their toll, and the morning's activity was bleary and hung-over. Moaning and snoring greeted the new day while the only activity was the search for a dog's snack of leftovers ... and here came the thirsty armies of winged pests to gorge themselves on the vast buffet lying inert in the kraal.

Africa has a natural sanitation process, and it has proven to be very consistent and very thorough since its inception. Nature has fashioned an efficient program for survival, but it also produced man as an inefficient product of senseless waste. Instead of biodegradable organic matter, he has designed nondestructive, ingenious vessels of convenience. In doing so, he has added mountains of detritus to the landscape in an unconscious effort to outdo nature. However, the man-made bouquet emanating from his hills of waste can't hold a flower to nature's glorious perfume.

All in all, peace had returned to the world, and I was calm once more. Lili-It and Whoever could wait.

"Hey, Bean, you're spending too much time peering into the darkness. You're getting very cynical and very critical about humanity. You can't be optimistic amid such pessimism."

"You're back already. Great! Just forget my rantings, and tell me about your adventure ... and please, only the salubrious parts; omit the nasty and bawdy parts."

"That's a tall order, my friend. I wanted emotions, and emotions are what I got—and in spades, according to Mr. Hoyle."

"So ... so?"

"As luck would have it, I did choose the bridegroom as my vessel.

"At first his only thought was of the cattle in the field and the herd he was to present to the father of his bride-to-be. He exhibited both pride in his apparent wealth as well as what I would refer to as anticipation of his forthcoming wedding.

"It wasn't very difficult getting caught up in the excitement of the moment. He projected a pleasant feeling.

"However, his feelings of elation were put on hold as the busloads of tourists arrived, and my subject was obligated to join his fellow warriors in a theatrical performance of an ersatz tribal custom. The crowd loved it, but the tribesmen hated it. But a contract is a

contract, and they could use the extra money for the few modern conveniences they coveted."

"For instance?"

"Well, toilet tissue has become somewhat of an obsession, as well as mint-flavored toothpaste."

"What do they use the mint toothpaste for if they don't seem to want toothbrushes?"

"Believe it or not, it is used as an aphrodisiac by the women when they want to seduce the man of their choice. A little smear here ... and a little smear there. You figure it out; I can't, but my host flips over it.

"My man, Amaziah, displayed a number of emotions, such as when he left the village and checked on his herds, paying strict attention to the pride of lions nearby. His only thought was for the security of the cattle, and he was more than ready to fight the big cats if he had to.

"It seemed a different emotion arose from every experience: carousing with his friends, amusing the tourists, flirting with his bride-to-be, Ainra, speaking with his relationship with his intended father-in-law, participating in the nights' festivities, and finally, conducting his marital responsibilities.

"Here I was faced with a puzzle: do I do the responsible thing and leave them to their privacy, or do I remain and witness a new emotional presentation?"

"Need I ask what you did?"

"You may ask, but I won't tell!"

"Nasty!"

"Each emotion was preceded by some kind of stimulus and was concluded with an end result. All were fascinating to me, although I don't have words or names to correspond with them."

"That will come later as you experience human emotions on a larger scale and with more frequency. The stimuli will become more complex, and the reactions more physical. Many of the responses will have a basis of original instinctual programming and will require, unfortunately, no thought—just a subconscious effect with no attention paid to the consequence."

"Would I be able to influence, in some small way, a change or avoidance of a physical reaction to an emotional stimulus, if I feel that it could cause harm to either my subject or to another entity?"

"Absolutely, but it is not for us to judge what the future results would be, and therefore it is against our ethics to do so. We do not alter the time frame in any manner whatsoever, no matter how we might perceive the consequence of the proposed action.

"The stimulus creates a cause of action in the brain, and the reaction is the end result. If you alter the response, the reaction must seek an alternate path of relief, and if none is found, a short circuit is accomplished. This could cause serious harm to your subject. And again, we do not interfere; we guide through thought inception, but we do not interfere!"

"But we have the ability to change man's preconceived need for an aggression-based ethic to one of a more peaceable approach to conflict."

"Agreed, but not in the manner you state. We guide him toward a more moralistic credo, hoping he rethinks his tendency toward aggression. However—and I repeat myself—we do not interfere. Agreed it is a much lengthier process, but it is also the path of least emotional disturbance."

"I guess that patience is one human emotion I am going to have to adopt if we are to continue our tirade against those windmills."

"Hmmm ...Ghost mentioned windmills to me also. Could it be that our goals are unrealistic, and we exist in a self-induced fantasy? Someone or something must have imbued me with the tenets of morality as they envision it ... and, in doing so, fashioned my purpose, just as they created Whoever with the tenets of immorality."

"Sounds like a very ill-conceived competition devised by a very warped gamesman. He just moves the pieces around but avoids placing them in a random pattern. He must have an end result in mind; either that, or he revels in chaos."

"Be that as it may, I must still follow my beliefs until, in one way or another, I'm barred from continuing.

"What a tremendous burden I am forced to carry. In my way of thinking, I am man's only hope for salvation, and his existence on this planet lies solely within my realm of attainment.

"Is that a reaction to the windmill syndrome?

"Is all this real ... or, as you say, just a warped game?"

"Spin the wheel, roll the dice, deal the cards: what does it matter? We can only hope that the gamesman seeks a positive outcome that will reward our effort with a final payout of peace and decency."

"Amen to that!"

"Where to now, Bean? Do we leave Africa, or do we remain for a while longer?"

"I know I'm going to regret my decision, but I want to hang around for a little while. I have to see for myself the extent of disease and pestilence, as well as the human brutality, that seems to be synonymous with modern Africa."

"Any objection to spending a few more hours here?"

"If you want, you can go off by yourself and rejoin me later."

"I have to do it; it's part of my learning process."

"If you don't mind, I'll tag along with you. Maybe I can learn a thing or two also."

CHAPTER 40

We floated leisurely north, south, east, and west until we perceived cries of fear and pain emanating from an area south of where we had met up with Leader's leaping warriors.

This was what I had been looking for: an uncontrollable rampage of brutality and human desecration.

It was an area rife with poverty and despair. Starvation in incredibly crowded conditions while at the mercy of the elements added up to an existence conducive to disease. Once the disease made itself known, there was no stopping it, and it spread like a windblown brush fire. The only treatment was death and the incineration of the victims.

Today it is one tribe destroying another; tomorrow it will be reversed. There is nothing of any consequence to fight about. Dirt is dirt. But still they slaughter, and they accomplish the butchery in any way they can, as long as they kill.

… and nobody cares.

… and they die.

I can exhaust both myself and Ghost's mental blatherings in a fruitless attempt to intellectualize the mayhem, but to what purpose?

If Whoever were to seek a breeding ground for his assault on civilization, what better venue than an area of uncivilized humanity reinforcing his incentive for evil?

I had had enough. It was time we headed back to the United States and initiated our plan to thwart the Demonic Duo. I figured we would head north and then swing east.

Maybe to the pyramids?

"Hey, Leader, what do you know about the pyramids? I've had the opportunity to visit this part of the world before, and I thought it would be a bit nostalgic to revisit it. I have also been in close proximity to the Mayan ones, and they were fascinating, as well as beautiful, demonstrating magnificent intricacy in their carvings. Unfortunately they were also an integral part of a belief system that was reinforced by a system of ritual bloodletting.

"Come to think of it, I did mention that to you when we had that long discussion about man's fixation on blood."

"I remember; you talked about sacrifices. Sounds like they were a cruel, bloodthirsty people, and yet you described their pyramids as being beautiful—perhaps even works of art.

"And they gave the world ... chocolate milk!

"It is a dichotomy worthy of further discussion.

"Maybe later ..."

"Maybe later."

We continued north without much further conversation. We concentrated instead on the changing scenery: from lush jungle to mountaintop to arid desert—which, in fact, we were quickly approaching.

I know that we are noncorporeal beings, but nevertheless, I felt the temperature change as the fertile green vegetation faded away and was replaced by scattered clusters of anemic shrubs, dwarf trees, and isolated patches of brown grass. Here and there, one could make out small areas of green that sheltered a pool of water. It was at these desert rest stops that man and beast would repose for a while before continuing on their various treks. Judging by the well-worn paths, these well stops were well used. Well ... well ...well ...

You would think that the desert was all sand, but I could see mountain ranges in the distance and even small villages. How the people survive in those arid conditions is beyond me.

I decided to alight on the ground alongside one of those pools and communicate with one of the camel drivers. When I reached him, he was involved in what I believe was a pious act. He was kneeling on a small rug and chanting his prayers. Being very solicitous, I waited until he had finished, stood up, and carefully rolled his carpet before I approached, cautiously confirming that he was far removed from his companions.

Not choosing to assume the guise of a camel, I situated myself by a date-nut palm and addressed him.

"I offer you greetings, my friend, and extend wishes for a safe and successful journey."

I guess I picked the wrong time to accost him, inasmuch as he had just completed his evening prayers and was still in a pensive mood. The issuing forth of a voice supposedly originating from a desert palm shocked him into a religious fervor, and down he went—this time without the benefit of carpet.

"Allah be praised! Why have you come to this most humble of servants? I am unworthy of your attention, for I am but a poor camel driver."

"Rise up, my friend. I am not your Allah, your God; I, too, am unworthy of association with him. I am but a poor spirit on a quest for peace and morality among men, and my travels have brought me to this oasis of calm in a world filled with strife and evil.

"I only wish to speak with you; being unable to share bread with you, I am only able to offer words and the ear of a sincere listener. Will you afford me that honor?"

He again rose up and slowly looked around, expecting to find a friend playing a practical joke on him. Finding nobody in the immediate area, he turned to the palm and replied to my query in a soft voice, so as not to arouse the interest of his fellow travelers.

"What will you have of me, spirit of the now-holy palm? What words will I have that could possibly have meaning for you?"

"Do not humble yourself, my friend; everybody has words of importance that only require the correct questions and the ear of a companion.

"Now, what do they call you by name?"

"I am called Abdul-Wahid; in your tongue, it is Servant of the One, and I am his most obedient servant. And you, holy spirit—what may I call you?"

"I am called Bean, and please, I am not a holy one—just a traveler like you. But unlike you, I do not search for bread to provide for my family. I search for the reasons man has deviated from the path of righteousness and is sliding into a morass of sin and immorality. That is my sustenance.

"Tell me of your religion and what it is that you pray for."

"The very name of my faith can be defined as peace; to be wholesome and tranquil in mind and action is what we strive for.

"We cannot rest if a solitary soul is in a state of unrest, we cannot break bread if a solitary soul is hungry, and we cannot sleep if a solitary soul has no bed nor shelter.

"We are the followers of the one God; praise be."

"Why is it, then, that other faiths also believe that their god is the one God? Their tenets are very similar to yours: peace, love, understanding, and sharing of self."

"You see, Spirit Bean, we all share the one God, but many ages ago, prophets came and preached thoughts and created changes to the original beliefs and caused the new religions. All preached living in harmony and preached a respect for all."

"Then how do you explain the hate that has emerged among those diverse belief systems if they still favor and love the one God?"

"You ask the one question I can't answer. Perhaps poverty and ignorance has created the ingredients for a poisonous stew, and the only antidote is to harm those who have, but do not share. We have always aided the poor and unfortunate, but they have increased so in number that it is no longer possible to do so, and thus they strike out at the fortunate no matter what their faith decrees, even if it is 'Love thy brother as you love thyself.' We are all brothers, and we all are descendants from Father Abraham. We should not hate; hate is the lock that keeps man in a cell of darkness, while love is the key to the light of peace.

"I fear that the great error our God, praise be his name, performed was the expelling of his children from the sacred garden for wanting to partake of the tree of knowledge. For knowledge opens up the world for man, and in that world, he may taste of the beauty and the glory that God has bestowed upon us.

"Our new prophets follow the belief that knowledge of the whole is a sacrilege, and one must know only the word of God as they teach it … and they teach that hate, the sacrifice of one's body, and the death of innocents are God's will.

"It is not so.

"We Bedouins are nomads, as have been our fathers and their fathers before them for countless centuries, so we do not hear the tongues of the new false ones. Therefore we practice what we believe to be the true word of God, praise be to him."

"What you say is true throughout the world today. The words of false prophets—and there is no end to them—have replaced one of man's great gifts, and that is the search for truth. The serpent's words have created such confusion in the mind that truth has become an anachronism from bygone days.

"This syndrome has become a universal contagion, a pandemic of apathy and despair.

"Abdul-Wahid, my friend, you have given me hope that perhaps with men such as you, man can truly return to the sacred garden, and you can once again sit by the feet of your one God.

"It's time for me to leave, and I bestow upon you my blessings for a long and fruitful life. May you sire children who will grow into a new world filled with your vision of peace."

"And to you, Spirit Bean: may you find the object of your endless search and find and relish the peace within yourself."

And I left to rejoin Leader and continue on our journey.

"What was all that about, Bean? You were gone for quite a while."

"Curiosity, I suppose. It was so serene at that oasis that I just wanted to recharge.

"After speaking to Abdul-Wahid, I feel a rebirth of hope. With men such as he, perhaps there is an expectation of a brotherhood of trust in the future, as well as a rebirth of the original credo that all profess to be the word of their god.

"I don't know, Leader; a rose does grow on a thorny stem, demonstrating that there is beauty for all to enjoy ... but there is also danger, if one is not made aware of the hazard that lies beneath."

There wasn't much more to say, so we continued, again, in silence.

CHAPTER 41

I don't know how it is with Leader, but I have so much history behind me that I sometimes find it difficult to recall situations that are relevant to my thoughts. Was man better off when he professed a pantheistic concept of religion? Having a hierarchy of gods provides a multilayered obstacle to placing one's blame of misfortune on the most high. Therefore the Supreme Being remains untouchable, and his aura resides in the abstract ether of heaven.

Coincidentally, isn't that where most deities reside—in a theoretical realm beyond man's concept of reality?

I am a bit confused about the benefits of monotheism versus pantheism. I look forward to any future input as to their reflections on the subject.

It's obvious that by his silence, Ghost is also contemplating the concept.

CHAPTER 42

"Ghost!"

"Bean."

"Don't you have any profundity to add?"

"Not at the present time; maybe later. I'll need time to absorb your words."

"I'll look forward to hearing your input, as well as that of any reader who would like to add his or her two cents."

CHAPTER 43

"Bean—down there. Are those the pyramids you wanted to see? They are huge! Who ever built them?"

"That's an interesting question.

"You would think that it required the sweat of countless men and women. But if you give it serious thought, you realize it would have to have employed the efforts of thousands and thousands of laborers working twenty-four hours a day, seven days of the week, to complete one within the lifetime of the pharaoh who commissioned it. In reality, due to the primitive tools they used, the construction would have taken hundreds, if not thousands, of years to conclude.

"Additionally, all sides of the pyramids angle perfectly to a peak, which, in turn, points to that same abstraction called heaven."

"What are getting at? Are you saying that man wasn't responsible for those structures?"

"Well, not man as we know him, but a visitor to his world draped in his image utilizing forces never before seen on earth—and, unfortunately, never seen again.

"There was a period of time in man's intellectual evolution when knowledge was injected in order to end what I call the era of the stagnation of the thinker.

"Visitors were dispatched to various corners of the earth to stimulate thought and provide motivation for progress. Hence you have the pyramids here, and in Meso-America, you have Stonehenge in Great Britain, Easter Island, and many other constructions that defy reason as to the mechanism involved in their creation."

"This seems to touch on your guardian theory, doesn't it?"

"Yes, I believe so.

"I hate to use the term alien, so I choose the word 'visitor.'

"In reality, he resembled any other man, even to the point of speaking the language and respecting the customs of the society in which he was involved with.

"In gratitude and awe for these benefactors, great monuments were constructed, with their help, to honor and worship them. That is why—and I tend to dwell on this—they all have a common heaven-based aspect to them either as to their pyramidal aspect; visages searching the skies, as demonstrated on Easter Island; or a deep, almost devout curiosity for astronomy.

"There are also many images of the visitors scattered throughout the world and many references to them in the papyruses and parchments of history.

"The visitors achieved one thing that they weren't prepared for, and that was the initiation of a godlike following. They had come to help, not to be worshipped. But fear and ignorance generate superstition, and superstition spawns religious fervor.

"So when they finally took their leave, vowing to return in the future, man attempted to follow the visitors into the heavens by constructing monuments, with the help from the visitors, which appear to reach their gods. That is why they chose the pyramid shape. As the sides diminish in their height, they appear to disappear into the very void that the visitors did.

"The pyramids in Meso-America provided the Mayan kings the wherewithal to assume godlike status by establishing their thrones atop those edifices, close to heaven. But I must add that the visitors were gone before they initiated sacrificial rites in a maligned attempt to appease the gods and entice them to return."

"And you were there? You saw those visitors?"

"Yes. I chose one of them as a host, and it in turn accepted me as an equal.

"That's why my belief system is what it is."

"It would seem to me that this might be an opportune time for them to return. Man needs a new injection of morality into his being.

"When do you think they will return?"

"I hope soon; I don't want to believe that they'll allow man to destroy what has been given to him. It is definitely time for a renewal of intelligence and an elimination of fear. Although ... I don't know how the visitors will be greeted on their return. Perhaps that inherent fear and suspicion that has become ingrained in society will foment an attempt to destroy them. It is man's way."

"What is that strange figure? Is it a man or beast—or maybe a representation of one of your visitors?"

"It's called a Sphinx."

"It looks old ... really old."

"It is very old. Nobody knows how old it really is, nor who was responsible for building it. According to most theories—and I don't agree with them—it is about 5,000 man years old. It is much, much older than that.

"Experts say that perhaps Pharaoh Khafre was the creator, while others say Khufu. So many guesses based upon a hint here, a hint there, but no noteworthy artist signature anywhere. There isn't one.

"It has the head of a man, but is it an earth man? Did he have the tools and know- how to create, so many years ago, the largest monolith in the world?

"Or is it the head of a visitor who employed his powers to create this image for all to remember his voyage to this planet? Someday, people will excavate the memorial in the correct spot, and they will find out what I already know."

"Bean, I don't know if your so-called ghost is writing all this down, but if he is, you might be in for some static from the scientific folk. There are a lot of people who think that spacemen belong in comic books and movies and not in reality. Their credo is 'Show me the proof, and keep away with unsubstantiated, fiction-based hypotheses.'"

"That's the problem with science ... and yet how much of evolution theory is based upon pure faith or conjecture that the missing link will be found and a complete path from air-breathing fish to Homo sapiens will be established?

"Is evolution theory any more of an assumption than my so-called spaceman theory is? I believe that there is plenty of hard proof out there in support of what I know to be the truth. Remember, Leader, I was there!"

"But the body of a lion ... how do you explain that?"

"The human—or at least humanlike—head depicts wisdom, and the body of the lion demonstrates power and strength. A perfect description of a visitor, isn't it?"

"I don't know, Bean. In all my travels, I have never met one of your visitors. I guess we kept different company?"

"Guess we did."

CHAPTER 44

As we continued on our journey,[22] Leader commented on the vast difference in the construction and appearance of other pyramids. Some were undoubtedly more flawed in their facades. That, I explained, was due to the lack of sophistication of the early builders.

Not wanting to turn this narrative into a *National Geographic* travelogue, I decided to ignore any further historical sites and concentrate on our journey west to America and my new adventure.

I especially wanted to avoid the Middle East, where time hasn't affected the many conflicts that have plagued the area for thousands of years. The only difference today is the sophistication of the weapons and the increased wanton disregard for life.

Governments come and go; promises are made; promises are not kept; and there seems to be no end to zealots willing to forfeit their own lives for a misguided promise of immortality.

We passed over the Mediterranean Sea and the island of Sicily with its history of conquest and violence and over Spain ... which in turn had its history of religious persecution during the Inquisition.

It seems that no matter where one chooses to visit, a history of violence precedes one's presence.

The earth was created in violence; perhaps, just perhaps, that violence was inserted into the genetic makeup of all of earth's minions? The earth continues to spew forth violence on an almost daily basis with its volcanoes, earthquakes, hurricanes, brutal thunderstorms, tidal

---

22 Author's note: A journey of minutes and hours to an imp, but years to a mortal.

waves, and floods. However, there is a sort of raw beauty in the violence of nature's upheavals. A montage of color, texture, sound, and motion combines into a theater of virtual images.

Why shouldn't man himself be violent? Violence begets violence, nature is violent, and man is just a progeny of nature, isn't he?

The Atlantic Ocean provided a brief respite from history's memory of brutality, sadism, and bloodshed.

The weather was calm, and the sea reflected the moment; taken altogether, the scene amounted to nothing but a palette of blues and greens with a wisp of pure white cloud appearing now and then. Although I realized that the calm could be broken at any time with the arrival of a sudden squall and the corresponding mayhem it would produce, I was, for the moment, just an insignificant wisp in an aura of tranquility.

The East Coast and the Midwest of America quickly passed beneath us; again with an unusual calm in the weather. It was almost as if we were being welcomed to a sacred site that was awaiting our presence: a place called New Mexico and a small town called Twin Angels, not far from the Taos Pueblo.

It proved to be an easy search due to a strong sense of serenity emanating from a one-story house just outside the town of Twin Angels, New Mexico.

The house was simple in design but definitely utilitarian in concept: adobe and wood, with a roof of clay tiles. A chimney poked through the roof in the center, adorned with the same tile as the roof and topped with a ring of black festooned with the soot of years of use.

Framing the deep-set windows were wooden shutters painted dark brown.

It wasn't a house that would stand out on a typical American street, but it served its purpose. It was sturdy and well kept.

A low picket fence and gate formed the perimeter, and in the rear was a combination flower and vegetable garden, with the flowers adding just enough of a woman's touch to give the building warmth.

No frills could be seen, but the property was beautiful in its simplicity.

Next to the house, and just a ways away, was another one-story structure with a bell tower. It was made of adobe brick painted white in contrast to the house and the other adobe buildings in the area, which were finished in their natural terra-cotta.

A small cross was painted in gold above the heavy wooden door. On the door itself, fastened with two tarnished brass screws, was a sign etched with white letters on black plastic that read, **"This door is always open; please come in. This is your house."** The plaque was signed **"The Rev. William (Bill) Fellows, minister."**

To complete this painting, an old Ford pickup, complete with dented fender and a blanket of red dust, was parked in a narrow drive between the two buildings.

All of this sat under the cloak of the brightest of blue skies.

As the desert's oasis was a refuge of serenity in a hostile environment, so was the home and mission of the Rev. William (Bill) Fellows, minister, and his family: an oasis of serenity in the New Mexico ground.

Being the middle of the afternoon, and with the high heat that is a common factor in this part of the country, no sign of life surrounded the compound. It was reminiscent of the desert we had just recently visited. I half expected to see Abdul-Wahid and his camels following their time-worn paths on the hot sands.

"This is really the boondocks, Bean," leader said. **Not much excitement around here, unless you enjoy watching prairie dogs bobbing up and down and sagebrush blowing across the landscape.**

"Are you certain this is the right place?"

"I'm afraid that the excitement won't come from external stimuli but from the maturing of love within the child. If you remain with me for the next few years, I'm sure you'll understand more fully what it is I hope to achieve—and maybe, just maybe, you will also find your share of windmills to encounter in the future."

"Now that we've arrived at our destination, how do you intend to introduce yourself into the family circle?"

"I haven't given it much thought, Leader. I guess I'll just wait until the opportunity presents itself. I don't know whether it will be in the guise of a voice out loud or within one's mind. It could be, as with Ricky and his family, in the form of an inanimate object or a live creature. I'll know when the time is right.

"In the meantime, why don't we just reconnoiter the area and get a feel for it? I would like to know the people before I immerse myself into their lives. I especially want to see the young girl and judge for myself if she is indeed the one."

"While you do that, why don't I check out the town of Taos, as well as the Native American pueblo? When I get back, we can compare our observations.

"What say you?"

"I think it's an excellent idea.

"Take your time, and be as thorough as you think necessary ... and please take care with the mind melds!"

"Spoil sport!"

CHAPTER 45

I reconnoitered the area to become familiar with its features. It was pretty much as I had expected from my first observance.

While I was flitting around, I heard the sound of a rather noisy car engine approaching. In conjunction with the obviously malfunctioning engine, the car itself was a study in rust, dust, and gaffer's tape, with the ends of the tape peeling back like ribbons of tarnished silver.

The vehicle turned off the road and pulled up to the mission's door.

With a bang from inside and a loud, protesting creak, the door opened, and an elderly woman emerged. She was short and a bit stout, wearing a faded dress of gingham that must once have been bright. Her face, devoid of any makeup, showed the effects of long exposure to the sun and wind and a lifetime of dedication to a way of life that has its roots buried in the past. Small wire spectacles and a rather large straw hat, frayed at the brim, completed the portrait. Yet she walked tall and proud. This was a person who was comfortable in with her life.

On her feet was a pair of well-worn leather boots, which crunched the pebbles lining the path on her way to the mission door.

In her hand was a small basket decorated with a vine of tiny, purple wildflowers. I wasn't able to see what the basket contained, but from the way she carried it, I believed it was an important package—perhaps even a gift.

Before she reached the door, it opened, and a man appeared. He was of average height but stood tall and proud. His hair was a sandy color, much like the color of parched desert grass, and tied in the back with a silver and turquoise clip. A white cap was on his head, dappled with multicolored paint drops. He wore an apron over a pair of jeans and matching shirt, which was also bedecked with droppings from many hours of maintaining both the mission and his home.

"Anna Walks With Grace, what brings you here today?" the man asked in a pleasant but somewhat commanding voice. "It's awfully hot this afternoon for a trip all the way out here." From the confidence in his tone, I presumed he was a man used to addressing groups of people.

"I have come with a gift for the child. It is in gratitude for the healing of my nephew, Justin. His mother, Rebecca, She of the Blue Stone, a Navajo/Zuni woman of honor, fashioned this necklace from silver and from the blue stone called turquoise. It is called a squash blossom, and in honor of the child and the father, she incorporated your Christian cross in the Naja pendant."

"It is indeed a wondrous gift, but I remind you that it was by God's doing that Robert's malady was cured and not by any manifestations of my daughter."

"Father Bill," replied the old woman, "I do not want to disagree with you, but you are blind to the one truth. She is the chosen one, and she has arrived in this place as it was written by the ancient people."

"She's nothing but a little girl who has suffered greatly in the loss of her true parents," Father Bill reminded her. "There is nothing special or sacred about her, except that she is a lovely young thing and is well loved by all."

"Do you remember the day we were here?" Anna continued. "It was an overcast day with the threat of rain in the air as Justin was seated at the front of the altar."

"I remember," he said.

"The child walked over quietly and laid her hands upon his chest. At that moment, the stillness was broken by a loud clap of thunder, and the sun broke through the clouds. The altar was lit as if a bright light had been turned on above it."

"Yes … what is your point?"

Anna Walks With Grace lifted her head and peered into the minister's eyes. "There are no windows by the altar, Father Bill. Where did that light come from, if not from the child?"

"An illusion, perhaps, caused by the solemn moment. Prayer can do such a thing."

The old Native American woman smiled and looked at the minister as if she were speaking to a small child. "Father Bill, I do not pour scorn on your prayers, nor do I mock your beliefs, for I too am a Christian … but there are things that we cannot explain, but have to accept. She is special, and for that we have to be thankful."

With that, she turned and walked toward her car.

"Anna, please wait a moment," Father Bill called out. "It's obvious that I can't change your mind about Patch, but I can ask you not to spread your ideas around. The last thing we need at the mission is for crowds of people looking for some miraculous cure from an innocent young girl.

"It would be wrong, and they would be very unhappy."

Anna Walks With Grace smiled and shook her head. "It was a miracle, Father, and you know it."

Getting a bit testy, Father Bill answered the proud woman, "I know of no such thing, Anna—and neither so should you!"

Slamming the door, she started the old clunker, backed out of the drive, and drove away in a cloud of smoke and a cacophony of clanking gears.

Walking back to the mission building, Father Bill removed the necklace from the basket, clearly marveling at the beauty and workmanship of the piece. Cautiously, I peered into his thoughts: "Patch would love the necklace and would probably never want to take it off". So be it.

The minister resumed his whitewashing of the interior walls, stopping every now and then to refresh himself from a bottle of water he kept nearby.

"Foolish woman," he murmured to himself. "Patch is nothing but a little girl and not to be confused with the true power of God. I guess the Native Americans will never let go of their legends and superstitions. They profess to be Christians, but deep down, their true beliefs remain with their forefathers and the secret Kiva religion."

"Is that wrong?" I whispered.

"Yes, it is," he replied. "I have been trying to convert them to follow the path of the real faith, but they are a stubborn people."

"But they practiced their beliefs long before your one God was created. They worshipped nature and thanked their gods for providing them with the bounteous gift she had bestowed. Is that wrong?"

"I've got to stop talking to myself. All I succeed in doing is arousing confusion in my mind, and there is too much to do for me to become mired in deep thought."

I left him with that thought; it was better that than ruining his day by injecting the ethereal voice of a nonentity.

I spent the balance of the day examining, inspecting, exploring, and observing the site and its environs.

No other buildings could be found in the immediate area. Hardscrabble desert shrubs and Chola cacti dotted the landscape and offered homes and shelter for the many lizards, scorpions, and snakes that inhabited the New Mexico desert. Life goes on even in the most seemingly uninhabited land. There must be a rationale for that in the master plan for this earth. Even among the most innocuous of creatures, survival is not taken for granted. It is a gift worth savoring and struggling for.

It was late afternoon now, and the minister was emerging from his church, apron and basket in hand, sipping from the ever-present water bottle.

At that moment, as if it had been choreographed by the forces, a small, four-door car drove up and parked in front of the house.

An attractive, red-haired woman stepped out and waved at the minister. She opened the passenger door, reached in, and unbuckled a young girl who ran to Father Bill, screaming, "Daddy, Daddy!" The minister knelt down, engulfed the child in his arms, and kissed her forehead.

"How is my little girl this afternoon?" he asked.

"Daddy, I am not a little girl anymore! I am six years old!"

"Good day to you, Father William Fellows," the red-haired woman called out, "and how was your day?"

"… and to you, Meave Ryan Fellows—a day in which you were sorely missed."

"Aye, those are kind words, sir."

"Aye, indeed—I could have used another hand with the painting!"

"'Tis always a fine thing to be wanted," she said with a laugh. "And what is that in your hand? It looks as if you were hunting for Easter eggs."

With a grin, the minister answered, "It's for Patch. Anna Walks With Grace was here and brought it for our daughter.

"The poor woman is thoroughly convinced that our little girl is "the chosen one," whatever that means. She credits Patch with performing a miracle on her nephew Justin, and this necklace is a gift from his mother, Rebecca—who, I might add, actually made it herself."

"Who are we to turn such a beautiful gift down?

"Come here, sweetheart. This is from Aunt Anna and Justin, and it's for you."

"Is it really for me? Really? Can I put it on now? It's wonderful, isn't it, Daddy?"

Hand in hand in hand, they walked into the house.

It looked as if my luck had held out: another fine family for me to wheedle myself into.

I only hoped that Leader wouldn't find it too boring around here. We had a very important job to do, and man's future might very well depend on what we accomplished.

"Well, it might not be an arena of excitement here, but the town of Taos is very interesting. Ignoring the omnipresent tourists and their silly caps and cameras, the locals seem to have a good time—at the benefit of the tourists, I fear, but it is harmless fun anyhow.

"The town is laid out in sort of a square with restaurants, souvenir stands, and craft shops in abundance. A facsimile of an old western town, I guess.

"I also had a chance to visit the pueblo. I personally don't think very many people actually live here. I heard some talk among the tribesmen that the pueblo will be closing in a few days for some kind of secret religious ceremony."

"Damn it, Leader—when are going to stop sneaking up on me and reading my thoughts? It's rather disconcerting.

"Tell me about the pueblo and its inhabitants. I'm curious about their way of life and their religion. The minister says that little is known about their rituals."

"From what I could gather, the men and women live outside of the pueblo. There's no electricity or indoor plumbing that I could see. Their presence is mainly for the tourist trade, which they encourage by selling various crafts. The buildings range from one-story adobe huts to five-story individual units furnished very sparsely. It is picture of a true primitive existence.

"I did see a few TV sets in the rooms, but I couldn't find a source of electricity ... very strange."

"So what you're saying is that they are performers in a production for visitors who want to partake of the Native American experience? How droll."

"Droll? No, I don't think so. I believe that they truly enjoy walking in the footsteps of their ancestors. They are a proud but secretive people."

"What makes you say that?"

"I'm judging by the answers to some personal questions they were asked by the tourists. Their answers were rather vague when it came to religion and ceremony."

"You might be right about that. I had the opportunity to observe a Native American woman who visited the mission this afternoon, and although she claimed she was a Christian lady, she made some references to the old faith. In fact, the minister expressed frustration about her people living in two worlds.

"I suppose that I'll leave the study of the Taos Pueblo to you while I concentrate, at least for the present, on this family."

"Sounds like a plan. If you're finished for today, how about some dinner?"

"Very funny!

"Stick around and give me your take on the family, if you please."

"Nah! I'll leave that up to you for now.

"Think I'll just flit around and do what I do best: observe.

"I kind of wish there were some kind of war going on around here, but hey: maybe a bar fight?"

"Go, already—but behave. We don't want to give people any idea that we're here, much less who and what we are."

With a twinkling of his universe of ions and as much of a demonstration of laughter as he could project, Leader soared off to the town of Taos. I, on the other hand, made my entrance into the house.

I was pleasantly surprised upon entering this strange adobe residence. Despite the relative blandness of the exterior, it offered a warm and inviting interior and was larger than my first impression would have caused me to believe.

One entered a small vestibule where a few coat hooks jutted out from a varnished tree branch on the adobe wall to the right of the entrance. On the opposite wall was a built-in bench with a wood-slat seat and an open bin beneath it for shoes and boots. A rather large photograph of a desert night scene in black and white, a recessed light in the ceiling, and a small carpet in a traditional native design completed the layout.

In addition to the natural adobe on the exterior, all the interior walls were finished in adobe, with wood structural accents. The walls themselves appeared very thick—an excellent attempt at efficient insulation.

One entered the living or great room next. Wood-frame furniture upholstered in natural leather formed a small conversation area in the center, with a couch facing the far wall, in front of which was a rather large fireplace. A compartment to the right held a small pile of split and whole logs, while a set of handmade wrought-iron andirons and tools stood as sentries in front of a mesh curtain coated with the soot of many a warming fire.

I'm not sure, but I think the fireplace went through to the room behind it.

The right wall had two double-hung windows set into niches with wood framing; each window was bordered with textured drapes, again in a native motif. Between the windows was an old-style roll-up desk. Tall niches in the wall on either side of the unit were configured into bookcases stuffed with books, magazines, notebooks, and loose sheets of paper. This was obviously the workstation of Father Bill.

The wall adjacent to the entrance had a single window with the same draperies as the work wall. Beneath the window was a long, narrow table, which held examples of Hopi and Navajo pottery, all sitting on a hand-woven Navajo runner.

To complete the layout, scattered tribal rugs and more photographs of the Southwest, including landscapes and portraits of Native Americans, were arranged in a thoughtful display.

To the left of the great room was a larger-than-expected kitchen area. This was a well-thought-out area with plenty of counter space on the perimeter and walls replete with a series of niches serving as cabinetry and utilizing hand-hewn wooden doors. An oversized, hand-hewn wooden table and six matching chairs defined the open area. Suspended from the ceiling and fastened to heavy wood beams was a metal assemblage from which various sized pots and pans hung from steel hooks. Light was provided by a series of track lights conveniently placed to afford equal illumination throughout the kitchen.

I realize that I seem to be spending too much time in describing the Fellows residence, but I feel that it's necessary for the reader to get a solid feel for the people that I will spending a great deal of time with and who will become an integral part of the story from now on.

To continue: a hallway ran toward the back of the house. It was situated between the great room and the kitchen area.

Following the hall, one was led to the living quarters, which consisted of the master bedroom to the right, with a wood-frame, king-size bed and many niches of various sizes serving as closets and nightstands. Two dressers (one tall, and one short, wide one) and a wooden chest in front of the bed (which served as a storage compartment and bench) were the only actual pieces of furniture. A number of small family photographs in an assortment of sizes and frames sat atop the dressers.

I was correct in assuming that the fireplace in the great room was also in this room, although not as predominant. It was raised about eighteen inches above the floor and also had a mesh grill in front.

Again, tribal rugs had been placed strategically on the clay-tiled floors, and framed photographs of both landscapes and family adorned the walls. Above the bed was an intricately carved and inlaid cross, undoubtedly the gift of native admirers.

To the left of the hallway was the little girl's bedroom. In keeping with the general motif of the house, her twin-size bed (also made with a wood frame) was covered with a blanket resplendent with pictures of animals done in a cartoon style.

Pink curtains covered the niched windows. The walls boasted pictures that the child herself must have drawn with colored pencils. Above her bed, as in her parents' room, was a small cross fashioned of stamped tin and mounted on wood.

More rugs and niche closets completed her retreat.

To finish: a small, but well-designed washroom nestled between the two bedrooms. A glass-enclosed shower and a whirlpool tub stood out as two of the most luxurious items in the house.

I noticed one thing immediately: no pet dog, cat, or any other creature was included in the family group. I missed my friend Fenton, the basset hound with an attitude problem, who was an integral part of the Granlin family, my previous hosts. He had entertained me when things were quiet and my guidance was not immediately required.

Based upon my many years of experience, a child needed a pet to be a recipient of her love and to receive, in return, the dedicated love and protection that the creature could offer.

It also provided a vessel for me to inhabit.

I stayed around while the family had their dinner and then prepared for sleep.

It was during dinner that the child stopped eating for a moment and stared at me while a smile formed on her small mouth.

She knows that I am here, I thought, *but she isn't sure of what I am. A good first step.*

"What are you smiling at, sweetheart? Did you remember something that happened today?"

Patch turned to her mother with the same smile still on her face and said in her childlike voice, "No, Mommy. I smiled at the nice spirit who has visited us. Don't you see him?"

Maeve turned to her husband with a quizzical look on her face and said to the girl, "No, sweetie, but if you see him, and he is a good spirit, then it's okay. But finish your dinner now, because it's almost bedtime."

Quiet reigned at the table while mother and father exchanged quick, puzzled looks at each other and ended with a shrug and a smile.

I'm sure that they believed the child had created an invisible friend, as many children tend to do. In a way, it replaces the companionship of a pet and affords the child the benefit of being able to say what she pleases without receiving any adverse judgment in return.

I restrained myself from saying anything to Patch. It wasn't time yet.

CHAPTER 46

From what I had gathered, Maeve worked at a souvenir/crafts gallery in Taos and brought the child to work with her every day. It seemed the little girl had the gift of bringing smiles to the customers and, in fact, knew the stories behind many of the handicrafts displayed.

What I also learned, during conversation between the minister and his wife prior to their retiring for the night, was that Patch had been left in Maeve's car about four years ago. A note left with the child, which they kept in a locked box, read,

> *Our child was born from love, but we cannot offer her anything more than that. We are poor, have no jobs, and are too young. Please: she is our gift to the world, and we know that you will give her a good home. God bless.*

They read this almost every night to remind them of the gift they believed had come from God, for they were not able to conceive themselves.

It was at this time that I took my leave and waited outside for Leader to return.

My first impression of the household: good people, nice home, and much love; not wealthy, but rich in other ways. I wanted to become familiar with their daily routines and get a better feel for the relationships among themselves, as well with other people in their circle. Then it would be my time.

I also wanted to understand their religious beliefs. It was none of my business what faith they practiced, but I had seen the results that zealots could generate in the innocent minds of children, and I would attempt to interfere if that was the case here, though it seemed unlikely.

Leader was certainly taking his time getting back—probably found a bar fight or two to enjoy. What a character he was: good natured, but with a glint of mischief. He made for a lively companion.

I'll bet he has some very lively stories to tell. In fact, he probably has some that I wouldn't appreciate hearing ... or would I?

CHAPTER 47

Rather late at night, as I waited outside for Leader, I sensed movement in the great room. Wondering who it was at this time of night, I took it upon myself to investigate—covertly, of course.

It was the minister, dressed in pajama bottoms and a dark blue terrycloth robe. He was walking quietly, his footsteps muffled by a pair of soft leather slippers on his feet.

He opened one of the drawers in his desk, removed a bottle, and proceeded to pour himself half a glass of an amber liquid.

Quietly closing the drawer, he sat down on the couch and took a good sip of the contents. Then he leaned back and sighed with a sound I could only identify as, perhaps, sadness?

His wife came in a few minutes later, sat down beside him, and rested her head on his shoulder.

"What is it, love? I thought you had given up on the sip."

He placed the glass on the table and put his arm around Maeve.

"I know I did, honey, but there are times I feel I haven't accomplished what I was put on this earth to do.

"The congregation hasn't grown as much as I had envisioned, and its income can't keep pace with its expenses. I guess I get down on myself sometimes, and a sip of the good stuff tends to ease me."

"Hey, foolish man, we aren't starving, and we have a fine roof over our heads. Give it time, and the people will come to you."

Sighing, the Reverend Bill replied, "I hope so, but I don't have much confidence. They seem to refuse to give up the old ways. I know that the old Spanish missionaries tried to change their heathen ways hundreds of years ago, but the natives' paying lip service to them doesn't count as success. So we have people of two faiths, either of which they choose to follow when the opportunity presents itself.

"I'm almost tempted, and I know it's totally wrong, to allow Anna to spread the word that Patch is indeed the chosen one, just to garnish an increase in attendance."

"Bill, you of all people should know that would be a grave sin in God's eyes. You cannot exploit our little girl just to add a bit of luxury to our lives. We are rich enough."

"I know ... I know; hence the sip. I hate to say it, but it does help to put my mind straight ... and yes, I do remember my promise to you, and I have been fine all these years."

Sadly, Maeve asked "... and have you been sneaking off for a bit now and then? We have a child now, and there would be no excuse for you to ride the wagon again!"

"I open the drawer now and then, when I feel the need to relax my mind. It's of no real concern to me, and it shouldn't be to you. You have my word."

With that, they got up, and Bill put the glass in the sink before he and his wife retired once more to their room.

That had been a very interesting moment. You would think that being a man of God would elevate a minister—or a priest, a rabbi, an imam, or what have you—above the needs of the average person and render all desire for mind-altering substances null and void. The only answer I can comprehend is that they are as human as the next person, and although they answer to a higher authority, they still enter their pants one leg at a time.

I've heard it told that some practitioners are able to elevate themselves onto another level of consciousness, thus alleviating the need for mind-enhancing drugs, by availing themselves of deep fervent prayer.

My guess is that man's mind has not evolved as readily as his body. He is able to control the obvious—that being the five senses augmented by his physical accoutrements: eyes, nose, mouth, ears, and skin. But again, it is the complexity of the mind that finds him mired in its infancy. I wonder what his body will have evolved into by the time his brain has progressed to an even status with his physical presence?

Hmmm ... all of this just because the Reverend Bill took a sip.

CHAPTER 48

Leader still hadn't returned. *Okay, I'll search him out and drag him back to this site of dynamic tedium, as he will undoubtedly describe it.*

Zipping to the town of Taos was accomplished in a nanosecond. Leader was right; it was a quaint town with a definite Western feel to it. That being the situation, I headed for the largest and loudest saloon I could find … and there was Leader, having a conversation with an obviously inebriated cowboy. To the casual observer, the unfortunate man seemed to be having a serious discussion with a large, artificial potted cactus. It doesn't matter what the subject of the chat was, suffice it to know that Leader was egging him on and having a fine old time. I would guess that this was a harmless alternative to out-and-out warfare.

"Leader, if you're finished tormenting that poor man, let's get going. We have to decide what our next step will be.

"I have to tell you what occurred between the minister and his wife. There appears to be a little glitch in paradise: nothing to be overly concerned about, but also something to keep an eye on.

"The Reverend seems to be possessed by a few demons and reverts to a nip once in a while to ease his thoughts of failure. From what I deduced from a short conversation between him and his wife, there must have been a time when a nip wasn't enough, and he did indeed have a serious problem.

"We have to make sure that it doesn't happen again, and that could mean my introduction into his life. I think I will follow him closely for a while and see when and if I can achieve contact. My one fear is that he might confuse my intervention with a visit from his god. The

result of that could be very harmful to a man looking for some kind of salvation."

"What do you intend to do about his daughter? When are you going to meet with her?"

"As of now, she's doing fine, as is her mother; the main concern is the father."

"Again, what do you want me to do? It seems as if you have everything in control for the time being.

"Would you mind if I spent some time just observing the area? I am getting interested in the lives of the native people. Perhaps whatever knowledge I can ingest will be of use to us later on."

"Sounds like a plan to me. There is one thing I would ask you to do, and that is to respect their desire for secrecy when it comes to their religious rites.

"It's obvious they will never know you are there, but it's the ethical thing to do."

"Ahh, Bean. The temptation will be great, but I yield to your wishes."

"Actually, they are a very spiritual people, and there's always the possibility that they will sense your presence ... and again, as with the minister, they might misinterpret your existence as being godlike in substance."

"I just might like that. I could be a Leader in more than name alone."

"Don't even go there.

"I have enough on my mind with thoughts of the Demonic Duo—I can't worry about you, too!"

"Bean, you should really learn to relax. Your sense of humor is definitely on the ebb."

"So go already. If I need you, I'll get hold of you one way or another. But please, behave yourself. I'd surely hate to see human sacrifices being performed in your name."

CHAPTER 49

By very early morning, the temperature had dropped significantly. The sky was alive with the signs of a million universes broadcasting their presence to the world in a coal black sky. The earth, in turn, was alight with a hard, ethereal glow reflecting the intense illumination from a moon traversing across the heavens, altering the color of the landscape and creating a scene from a horror movie. The sound track was punctuated by the screech of owls searching for rodents and lizards to fill their bellies; the high-pitched squeaks of bats on the lookout for their evening meal of insects; and the occasional "yip-yip-ahoooo" of the coyote on the prowl for his feast.

And the Fellows family slept soundly.

I'm sure that more than one of you has wondered how I, as nothing more than a cloud of electromagnetic energy, retire for the night. Well, I don't go to sleep as you recognize sleep. I sort of create an envelope of ions which floats in the air, subject to the capriciousness of the wind. As for my thoughts; I just turn them off, just as one would silence a TV or extinguish a light.

Although I am in a period of rest, I'm still fully aware of my surroundings and can react immediately, if necessary, to any interruption that may affect either me or any life form currently within my realm of concern.

The sunlight rising over the New Mexico desert was a wonder to behold. It was as if all life resided in a world fashioned of adobe, for the earth and its multi-textured surface appeared to merge with the man-made structures dotting the ground. The one exception was the mission, whose whitewashed facade glowed bright orange, as if it were announcing itself as a special place—a place of reverence.

To demonstrate the holiness of the scene, Father Bill stood motionless in the garden of his house of worship, stared eastward and, awed by the view, recited his morning prayers. It was a scene reminiscent of the far-distant past, when primitive peoples gathered in reverence to their gods and greeted each day as a renewal of life.

Could his faith, then, be that much removed from the faith practiced by his neighbors?

The Reverend Bill failed to notice Anna Walks With Grace standing off to the side, watching him. Her wrinkled face smiled faintly, and she nodded gently as she took in the scene. I could sense that Anna understood fully what he was experiencing, for within her was the wisdom of her ancestors and the knowledge of the conflict that was within her minister. *Patience,* she thought. *Patience will be the teacher, and he the student.*

Anna knew of the conflict within his soul, but she also knew that he would soon be given the guidance necessary for him to achieve harmony with life.

The emergence of his wife and child from the house snapped the minister out of his reverie. They were off to work, and he walked toward them to say his good-byes. Patch met him halfway and, in a vision of innocence and joy, threw herself into her father's arms for a hug.

"Have a wonderful day, sweetheart, and take care of your mommy."

"I will, Daddy, I promise."

With that, he gently put her down and replaced her with his wife in his arms.

"Are you okay, Bill? I'm concerned about you after last night."

He smiled and replied, "Maeve, my love, fear not, for the demons have flown off to their lairs, and I am off to mine. They dare not show their faces in my house!"

"Oh, Mommy, there's Aunt Anna. Can I thank her for my new necklace?"

"Sure, honey, but make it fast—we have to get going."

After the child had thanked her, Anna placed her hands on Patch's face, stared into her eyes, and spoke a few words in her language. It was as if she bestowed a blessing of sorts upon the child. Patch smiled as if she understood Anna's meaning; somehow, she did.

"Leaving a little early today, aren't you, love?" Bill asked.

"Today is our turn to open the gallery," Maeve answered as she entered the car. "We should be home early this afternoon. Maybe we can have a cookout? I'll pick up some steaks at the mart. What do you think?"

"Do you have to ask? Sounds great."

"Later … love you."

With that, they left for town, and the Reverend Bill retraced his steps to the mission.

"What brings you here so early this morning, Anna? Come inside— we'll talk."

He didn't notice what looked like a convoy of cars and pickups heading toward them down on Route 64, from the direction of Tres Piedras. It wasn't until they started to pull into the parking area and the dust from their tires blew across the field did the minister finally take heed and respond.

"What is this, Anna? What's going on?"

She declined to answer, waiting instead for the group to gather. There must have been twenty or more vehicles sitting like a covey of lawn cars in front of the mission. As the people gathered, a hush came over them when a man, bent over with the weight of countless years, appeared. A path opened, and the people bowed their heads in veneration as the ancient one approached Bob and Anna.

My God, I could hear the minister thinking. *I've heard of him, but I thought he was just a legend. It must be the sachem that the people refer to as* Giver of the Word.

What could he possibly want here?

The old one, with the support of two husky men, stopped in front of Bill and Anna.

Quietly, so that Bill had to bend down to hear, the sachem greeted him.

"*Buenos dias, padre. Es un dia agradable para que finalmente nos encontremos. Debemos entrar su casa y hablar.*"[23]

"*Mil perdones, Viejo. No soy un buen speaker del espanol.* Do you habla en ingles?"[24]

The old man nodded. "*Si,* I will talk in English. Let us go inside."

---

23 Spanish: "Good day, Father. It is a fine day for us to finally meet. We should go into your house and speak."

24 Spanish: "A thousands pardons, Grandfather. I do not speak Spanish very well. Do you speak English?"

The group of men and women, dressed in colorful combinations of both native and Western attire, quietly took their seats on the wooden benches in front of the altar, where Bill now took his place.

"I am surprised and honored by your presence here in the mission. Pray tell me, what it is that you wish of me?"

Anna Walks With Grace stood up and approached the altar. "If the good father permits, I will aid you in understanding what will be said here today."

"As you wish; it is my privilege to receive your help. Now please proceed with your talk."

The old one, with the aid of his two helpers, stood in respect to the Reverend Bill and proceeded to speak. Aside from his voice, silence descended upon the room, and not even the hum of an errant insect dared to interrupt what was to follow.

"I have come here to tell you a tale that has been passed down to our people from before we arrived at this spot on holy Mother Earth. Our history is not written on paper or on the skins of animals. It is a spoken one and must be learned by those chosen to do so. They in turn pass the words on to the people for all to hear. It is not written because it is ours and ours alone and not to be shared by outsiders.

"Today, I will share something with you, because I have been told that you are a good man and a man of God."

"I am honored, Sachem. Please continue; I will not interrupt again."

"It is said that there will come a dark time and that man will engage in a great final battle between good and evil. Disease and starvation will precede the conflict, and the outcome will be a costly one. The earth will be profaned by the blood of the warrior as well as by the blood of the innocent.

"In the days before this mortal combat, the world will suffer from many conflicts that no country will be able to avoid. The air we breathe and the water we drink will be poisoned, and the sun's rays will be dimmed by what is called pollution."

At this point, the old one sat down to rest a moment.

"*Por favor alcalde*, please stay in your seat and continue," Bill entreated. "I greatly appreciate the respect you show to this unworthy man, but if you agree, I, too, will seat myself. It grows warm, and we will be more comfortable sitting. Perhaps you would want some water to quench your thirst?"

"*Gracias*; it will be a good thing."

Bill went to the cooler he kept to the side of the altar and passed out bottles of water to those who requested them.

The old one continued:

"From across the seas will come a force of evil such as the world has never seen. This blasphemer has one goal, and that is the destruction of man as we know him today. She will reign over the souls who give themselves to her—yes, to her, for this evil is garbed in the guise of a female, as our stories tell ... and if I am not mistaken, your ancient stories also tell of such a person."

The minister interrupted again with a note of humility and asked, "If this is indeed so, then what does your history tell you will happen? Is man to disappear for good, or is there a chance he will be able to fight back and defeat this abhorrent evil?"

The old one paused for a moment and then answered, "The stories also tell of a force for good who was conceived at the same time as the evil one was spawned. As they are opposite in spirit, they entered our world at opposite ends of the earth. They are destined to meet, and this gathering will end with the termination of one of the spirits and predict the future of man, if he is to have one.

"The most excellent result of this summit would be for good to destroy evil, and then the desert will once again bloom with life, and man's hope for peace will be fulfilled.

"The alternative would be for the two combatants to destroy each other, and man will be left in the same confused state he was in at the beginning of his time."

"When do your stories tell us that this event will present itself?" the Reverend Bill inquired.

"It has started already. She has been born in darkness and at this moment is being tutored in the evil ways. When she shall emerge from the darkness and claw her way into the world of man is not known, but be advised: it will not be long before we start to feel her power, and history will record the consequences.

"Wars of hate and suspicion have already broken out in all corners of the earth, and the days of bows and arrows have been replaced with those of bullets and bombs; the increased threat of lethal man-made diseases permeates the fear of scientists; Mother Earth has inundated the world with severe storms, earthquakes, floods, volcanic eruptions, and other manifestations of her anger. All this and more forecasts increasing episodes of what will be occurring in the near future. Combine nature's fury with the potential of the evil one, and the time for concern has arrived."

Confused, the minister asked the old one, "You have mentioned the evil one, but you have also neglected to mention the force for good. Has this entity been born yet ... and where, if it has been born, does it live?"

A strange look crossed Bill's face as he started to comprehend where this discussion was headed.

Not wanting to announce his growing concern to the group in front of him, Bill waited for the sachem to carry on with his oration.

"I believe that you know deep down what I am going to say, but I will say it nevertheless.

"Will you tell us the reason you named your beloved daughter Patch?"

Looking around from face to face, Bill replied, "When she was left with us, by God's grace, she emitted such an aura of tranquility that we named her Pax, which in the Latin language means Peace. Patch became her common name."

A silence fell upon the room once more, and all eyes were on the minister; his eyes were on the old one.

Bill, starting to get a bit edgy and turning to Anna, declared, "I'm not sure I like where this discussion is going. My daughter is just a little girl, and there is nothing supernatural about her!

"I don't know where, or whom, this idea sprouted from, but I ask you to leave it alone ... to forget it."

Turning once more to the old one, Bill said as calmly as possible, "I think this meeting is over. I do not want to offend anyone, but I have work to do, and if there is nothing more, I will take my leave of you. You may remain in the mission if you desire. It is always open to all people of all faiths."

With that, he returned to the house and sat at his desk, fully intending to prepare his sermon for the following Sunday service; the words did not come. What did come were thoughts of the sachem. He refused to acknowledge even the remote—and he did mean remote—possibility that the old one was correct in his assumption about Patch.

How could any parent in their right mind believe that their child was the savior of mankind, the second coming of God's charge? It's all just primitive superstition with no reference to reality. Let the tribe believe what it will. This is the twenty-first century, not thousands of years ago!

No ... not my Patch!

Doubt grew in his mind. Bill sincerely believed that there would come a time when Jesus shall return and grant the peace of his father to all who followed his tenets. If this was so—and to Bill there were no doubts—why couldn't the messenger be in the form of a little girl?

Hence ... if a little girl ... why not Patch?

The headache started then and prompted him to open the drawer. Guilt and the memory of a sincere promise stopped him. Suffering a throbbing in his head would be less painful then suffering the remorse of lying to his wife, so he just sat there with his thoughts.

CHAPTER 50

At the mission, no one stood to leave. They were prepared to remain until the sachem felt that his undertaking had been accomplished to his satisfaction. Judging by the response from the minister, the opposite had occurred, and they were primed to stay put—for what eventuality, they didn't know, but the Giver of the Word was intent in his duty.

And so it remained for the rest of the day: an impasse of wills, with nobody offering to concede defeat.

Maeve and Patch returned home later on in the afternoon.

As Maeve left the car, she looked at all the cars parked in front of the mission with a puzzled expression. *I wonder what that's all about,* she thought.

After unbuckling Patch, Maeve opened the rear door and removed a large object covered with a piece of dark fabric from the backseat.

The little girl ran to the front door, shouting, "Daddy, Daddy, look at what we have! Can we keep it? Please, Daddy?"

My curiosity was aroused, and I followed them into the house.

"Daddy, Daddy, see Virgil? Can we keep him? Mommy says it will be okay if you want to."

I was sure that this would prove to be a humorous diversion from the intense event of this morning.

"If it isn't my favorite girls. How was your day and what in heaven is that huge thing Mommy is carrying?"

"It's a Virgil, Daddy," Patch said, jumping up and down.

"Pray tell, what is a Virgil?"

With that, Maeve removed the cloth cover and presented Virgil, the cockatoo, to the Reverend Bill.

Not usually at a loss for words, this time he was stunned.

"And what do we owe the honor of inviting this Virgil bird into our house?"

"Someone placed the bird in our car today and asked us to take care of him," Maeve explained. "I'll tell you all about it later. Meanwhile, I don't think it would be a bad thing to keep him. Patch has already fallen madly in love with it, and it, in turn, has adopted her. They really do get along quite well."

The Reverend Bill laughed and answered, "Why not? It just makes this day even weirder than it already has been."

"Talking about weird," Maeve asked, "what are all those cars doing at the mission and with you here with me?"

Bill gave his wife a quick rundown of what had transpired earlier in the day. He didn't touch upon his doubts; he would leave it for later ... perhaps.

While he and Maeve were talking about the morning's activities, Bill heard the front door closing. Looking around, he didn't see Patch anywhere. The bird, yes, but no Patch.

Going to the window, he saw the girl walking to the mission, no longer hopping and skipping as she usually did. It appeared as if she were involved with a personal task he couldn't understand.

By the time he reacted, she had already entered the mission and closed the door.

Both Bill and Maeve walked quickly to the church and went inside. What they saw stopped them in their tracks. The people were now standing and with bowed heads were facing the altar, where Patch was standing in a great pool of light with such a look of calm on her face as to have been painted by a great master.

Tears streamed down the faces of many of the people, while others murmured softly to themselves.

Giver of the Word approached the girl with great reverence and greeted her: "My daughter; we have waited many, many years for you, and I thank the maker for allowing me to greet you in his name before he called me to his side. The time is slowly approaching when the world will require your powers to put an end to the evil one. It is your task to return to holy Mother Earth, the means to bear the fruit of peace once more.

"As for me, it is now my time to join my ancestors. Anna Walks With Grace will take my place here on earth.

"Take care, my child, for your task is a hard one, but love will give you the strength to prevail—and you are indeed loved."

Patch reached up and touched the sachem on his shoulder, and as if by magic, he was transformed into a handsome young warrior. It was in this visage that he rose slowly into the brightness above the altar and gradually disappeared.

Now tears filled the eyes of everyone in the assemblage, for they had lost a great person.

Patch turned to Anna and motioned her to come forward; she addressed the congregation. "You have all seen Giver of the Word start his voyage to the maker. Be not sad, for it was his reward for being true to the words of the ancient ones. Look now to Anna Walks With Grace; she has been chosen to walk in his shoes. She is a wise and strong leader, and you can follow her without fear."

It was Anna's turn to speak to her people, and she spoke in English in deference to Patch who, unbeknownst to the group, spoke and understood all languages of the people.

"It has come to pass that our daughter has arrived. The stories tell us that she will combat the evil that will be forthcoming. It is our obligation to protect her, so I ask you to pledge your allegiance to her and to keep her presence in utmost secrecy. To alert the world of her being will weaken her and strengthen the evil one. Are we agreed?"

To a man and woman, an oath was declared.

At that, the light above faded, and a little girl stood by herself in front of her daddy's church while the assemblage filed out of the mission—but not before bowing their heads to Patch, who didn't understand why.

Everyone bowed, that is, but Bill and Maeve, who stood at the rear of the mission, frozen in disbelief.

Maeve was the first to snap out of her trance. "Did I ... no, did *we* just see what I think I just saw? Our little girl is a goddess of some kind? What? How? I don't know the first thing about raising a goddess, do you?"

Staring at the front of the mission, Bill replied, still stunned, "Err ... no, I don't think so. She looks like a little girl now, so we treat her that way and face the goddess when she visits. Let's not mention what we have seen to her and wait to see if she does. Okay?"

"Yeah, sure, okay with me. This is so weird ... our daughter is going to save the world? That little girl? Pinch me, love, and say it ain't so!"

"If we pinch each other, we'll be black and blue for days. Shhh ... here she comes."

"Mommy and Daddy, let's go and play with Virgil. I want to hear him talk."

With that, off she ran to the house, just another little girl doing what all little girls do.

Hands clasped tightly, her parents followed, each immersed within his or her own thoughts—chief among which was the fear of losing their daughter. They both resolved that they would do all they could to keep that evil from harming her, even if it caused injury to themselves.

Bill and Maeve had known what was occurring in the world, and that was a prime reason for their relocation many years ago. Although childless at the time, they had been convinced that their presence in this seemingly remote area could allay some of the misery that they felt the world was wallowing in. Unselfish and true to their values, they had managed to achieve a modicum of harmony amongst the indigenous people.

And Patch was their reward.

CHAPTER 51

When they arrived back at the house, they saw Patch trying to talk to the bird, but he just stood there in his cage, as if he were the lord of the manor, not saying a word.

He remained mute all throughout the meal and afterward.

"I thought parrots are supposed to talk," stated Bill. "It would be our fate that we have one who is either mute or simply a snob."

"Give him time," Maeve said. "I'll bet that he's looking us over and deciding whether we are worthy of his attention."

"Worthy of his attention, indeed! I tell you, love, after what has gone on here today, I'll believe almost anything. Why don't the three of us go outside for a breath of fresh air? I know I could use a draft of God's breath."

The sky was exceptionally clear that evening, and Bill, pointing at the billions of stars in the sky, asked Patch to recite the Twinkle rhyme. So together, they started: "Twinkle, twinkle, little star, how I wonder what you are. Up above—"

Suddenly, from inside the house, in a loud, almost stentorian voice, the following ditty was heard:

**Scintillate, scintillate, globule vivific,
fain how I fathom thy nature specific.
Distantly poised in the ether capacious,
closely resembling a gem, carbonaceous.**[25]

---

25 Latinate version of "Twinkle, Twinkle, Little Star."

"What in heaven was that?" Bill asked.

"It's Virgil, Mommy and Daddy—he's talking to us! Let's go inside and talk to him."

There he was, in all his magnificence: strutting around his cage, his head bobbing up and down, reciting his own version of the famous old limerick over and over again.

"I think we have a little problem," Maeve said as she turned to her husband. "How do we shut him up now that he has decided to honor us with his babble?"

"I don't know, but I think if we cover the cage with that cloth, he might go to sleep. I know I'm tired, and I wish I had a cloth to cover myself with now."

Patch said good night to Virgil as her father placed the cloth over the cage and silence was gifted to them once more.

"This was certainly a day to remember," Maeve declared, walking toward the bedrooms while holding Patch's hand.

"Amen to that," Bill intoned almost religiously.

With their daughter snuggled in her bed and their evening ablutions concluded, Bill turned to Maeve and asked her about the bird.

The question brought a few tears to her eyes as she reached into her pocketbook and produced a sheet of notebook paper. Maeve handed it to Bill, who read it aloud.

You've done a wonderful job with our daughter. She is a happy, loving little creature. We couldn't have asked for better parents. Our lives have turned around now, and we have started a new family—one with substance and a promise for a successful future. It would prove to be harmful to your child—who, by the way, was named Helen at birth— and to your family if we made claim to her now. So please, be good to her, and someday, if you feel so inclined, you might tell her about us and why we did what we had to. If you do decide to do so, please emphasize the fact that we loved her so very much, and it was for that reason that we left her with you.

Also, please accept Virgil as a companion for your daughter ... Patch, isn't it? He entered our lives at about the same time as Helen did, and he developed an affinity for the child. Perhaps they can renew their relationship. He has somehow absorbed the ability to quote excerpts from the classics, and that's why we named him Virgil. He'll be a wonderful companion for Patch and for you.

Thank you, and bless you

Now they looked at each other, both with tears in their eyes.

"Did you see who it was that gave you the bird?"

"No," she said while giving him a dirty look. "The gallery was especially crowded today, and I didn't recognize anyone. They must have changed over the years, and even if they hadn't, I don't think I could have remembered them.

"I can't keep asking myself, why us of all people? There must be countless couples out there who wanted a child to love but couldn't have one of their own."

"One doesn't question the forces; to do so refutes their power over us, and it is our duty to accept and fulfill their wishes," Bill said, sounding as if he were intoning a sermon to his congregation and imitating, in kind, the stentorian voice that had materialized from Virgil.

Maeve turned to him with an impish look on her face. "Ommmmm, waddy waddy ommmm ..."

"Ahh, go button your lip, girl; 'tis the truth I speak, and being a man of God, I speak only the truth!"

"Ommmmmm, waddy waddy, ommmmm."

"Respect: I don't get no respect," Bill complained, mimicking the late comedian Rodney Dangerfield and his famous lamentation. "Turn the light off now; sleep beckons, and lord knows I need it."

Light outs, a kiss, and sleep.

CHAPTER 52

So many questions were answered today that I have acquired a sense of relief. The girl has been exposed as an entity conceived in righteousness, and her destiny has been declared. In addition, a vehicle has been offered for me to inhabit. What better creature than a talking bird? And, I may add, a seemingly intelligent one at that.

All of this without any input from me ... amazing! I am still incognito for all intents and purposes until I opt to change it.

The one person who will need input from me as soon as possible—and it will have to be done delicately—is the minister himself. I don't believe that he seriously accepts the choice of his daughter as the savior of humanity; in fact, I'm not sure that even he accepts the entire concept of the threatening battle that has been preordained by the old one and his followers.

His thoughts, which I have admittedly continued to pry into, are that the rationale for the coming conflagration—earthquakes, hurricanes, volcanic eruptions, and so on—merely involves natural phenomena that have been recurring for centuries. Even the various conflicts, which have been recorded in history books and biblical texts as taking place thousands of years ago, are common place to man. Why are they any more significant today than, say, one hundred years ago?

These questions require answers from me. I'll await my chance, and Virgil will then commence his rhetoric.

I'm glad that Leader has taken his leave for the time being. He would prove to be a distraction while I get the ball rolling here. Of course, his assistance will prove to very welcome at a later date, but now … I don't think so. Although I'm sure that his anecdotes about the people and places in the area will no doubt prove to be enlightening and humorous, they will have to wait.

CHAPTER 53

The next day arrived with no mention of the previous day's events.

Maeve and Patch left for the gallery; Virgil was fed, and his papers were changed; and the Reverend Bill sat at his desk to continue working on Sunday's sermon.

As usual, he tended to talk to himself in a quiet tone.

"Hmmm ... yesterday's incident has brought the subject of good versus evil to the forefront once more. Wonder what approach I'll take this time, considering what happened yesterday.

"I just can't bring Patch's involvement into the discussion, because I will not encourage the parishioners in their conviction that she is the embodiment of their righteous daughter and the redeemer of mankind. It's just primitive superstition. The very thought is against everything I have been brought up to believe all my life."

Ah ha—here is my opening! Hold on, it should be quite an awakening.

"*Arrkkk! Not so different, Bill. The image of good as defined by various cultures is unimportant as compared to the ultimate purpose; arrkkkk!*"

"No ... no. Is that bird actually talking to me? This is too much! First my daughter is a goddess, and now I'm having a conversation with a damn parrot."

"*I am not a damn parrot; I am an intelligent cockatoo. What's so wrong with having words with a cockatoo? Do you really think I can pose a problem for you? Just feed me and change my papers, and you have a friend forever. Arrkkk!*"

"Are you going to tell me that you are a part of this conspiracy to place Patch in the forefront of the clash between good and evil? I have to believe that all this craziness is somehow tied together."

"Arrkkk! What if I have been sent to forge her latent powers into a weapon powerful enough to thwart the objectives of Lili-It and her guardian, Whoever? Arrkkk!"

"What are you talking about? Who is Lili-It; and who is Whoever? Good grief, I sound like an owl! Am I going to meet them also? Should I plan dinner or something—maybe a few steaks?"

"Arrkkk! You do not want them for dinner. The only steaks they're interested in are protruding from the chests of their adversaries. They are the evil that is forming in the jungles of Africa, and when they are ready, they will make their presence known to us, as well as to the world. Arrkkk!"

"You are serious about this, eh? When will this malevolence take place, and how will Patch be prepared to, as everyone says, do battle? Were you sent here by Giver of the Word and his followers? Who are you?"

"You know something, Virge, I am having a hard time with all this stuff. I'm also having a hard time trying to figure out how I will pass all this information on to my wife."

"Arrkkk! First of all, my name is Virgil, not Virge. Please remember that!

"Now I will attempt to answer your questions.

"Yes, I am quite serious about the oncoming conflict, and yes, I have met both Lili-It and Whoever. Believe me, we'll all have problems once they start their voyage to hell.

"Third: no, I don't know when this will take place, but it's never too early to begin her training. She will need all the help I can give her. Be confident that she will have help both from me and a compatriot of mine, as well as from the power of prayer from the people.

"Fourth: I was not sent here by anyone ... at least, I don't think I was. It is my destiny to guide mankind onto the path of righteousness— or morality, as you wish—and Patch has become my charge. Like it or not!

"Fifth: as to who I am ... you're not ready for that yet. You've got enough on your plate already; you don't need to cope with that insight.

"So tell your wife what you please, and be prepared for a few slaps from her to snap you out of your blathering. And leave that drawer closed! Arrkkk!"

I took my leave of Virgil following our conversation and snooped around the outside area again. However, I was never too far away to hear sounds coming from the house.

Virgil started with his "Scintillate" recital and nearly drove the minister out of his mind. Every time he asked the bird if he knew another poem, Virgil would stop, take a deep breath, and recite "Scintillate" all over again.

I could imagine Bill saying to himself, "Why did he stop talking to me? Or did I imagine the whole episode? This bird is definitely nuts, and if he continues, he'll have company in that cage of his!"

CHAPTER 54

It wasn't long before the Reverend Bill came out, slammed the door, and headed for the mission for some peace and quiet. Notes in his hand, he fully expected to complete his sermon in the silence of the chapel.

He got his wish ... at least for a little while. His refuge was interrupted by the arrival of Anna Walks With Grace. I'm sure that cheered him up immensely.

"Anna, it is with much humility that I greet the new sachem. What is it that you wish of me? Are you here to confuse me more than I am already?"

Anna chuckled and then replied to Bill, "Confuse you? Never. I have come to pay my respects to the father of our holy daughter. Did you not witness the miracle that took place yesterday? You must trust me when I say that we had no hand in it; no magic was used, no hypnotism. Giver of the Word has indeed gone to the sacred place to sit beside the maker, and Patch was the messenger sent to channel his spirit on the path to his ancestors.

"Do not deny what you saw, and do not mock us for what we said will surely come to pass."

"Anna, what do you know about a talking cockatoo who recites Latin ditties? We have one in the house who also warned me about the evil ones and claimed that he had met them in a faraway place called Africa."

"I know nothing about such a creature, Reverend Bill. I should like to see this talking bird, if you will allow me."

"Sure, go on to the house; you can't miss him. He's the only one home who sings in Latin."

CHAPTER 55

I let her study Virgil for a while and suffered her to listen to what just might become his final dirge. Just when she had given up any hope of conversing with him, I stepped in.

"... *fain how I—ah, good day, Anna Walks With Grace. I feel privileged to meet you. We have gathered to meld this special child into a virtuous and moral supremacy to confront the evil that will force itself upon the world. I look forward to my absorbing the power of your prayers, for they will certainly add strength to my ability and help build the necessary defenses to defeat Lili-It and Whoever.*"

"You are not the bird, are you? What matter of entity are you? It is spoken in whispers about the ancient ones who commingled with the spirits of the natural things. They were helpful in allowing us to live in harmony with Mother Earth. They have long since gone to their place; however, we still revere them and try to practice their preachings."

"*You are wise, Anna Walks With Grace, and to answer you, yes, I am called Bean, and yes, I am of that race that your ancients shared existence with. The bird is just a vehicle; it is easier to assume a physical identity than to startle people with a noncorporeal voice, and a talking cockatoo seems to fit the bill.*

"*I am older than old but have not retired to the place, as you refer to it, for I have a mission to perform—one that I have been performing since your ancient ones lived among us. But first I must tell you that they were good people and praised the bounty that your Mother Earth furnished to her children back when the world was fertile and the crops grew bountiful.*"

185

Her sudden realization that she had come face to face (figuratively speaking of course) with an entity such as me proved to be rather emotional for her. It took a few minutes for her to recover and continue with our dialogue.

"What powers do you possess, Bean? I would imagine that speaking through a parrot doesn't approach your true abilities."

"Cockatoo, please. The powers that I possess now are greater than they were yesterday and will be tame compared to what I will possess tomorrow. I have no idea what I will be capable of, but however strong such powers will be, they are a force for good and cannot be used to harm or destroy an enemy.

"You will learn of them as our relationship grows, but, as you requested from your followers concerning the little girl, I must ask you to keep my presence secret.

"The Reverend Bill knows me only as a precocious bird, and I would like to keep it that way, at least for a while. He has gone through a lot in a very short time, and the company of a faerie imp residing in his home would surely push him over the edge."

"You have told the minister about the evil ones coming out of Africa. I only have an idea where that place is, but I imagine that it is far away. I do not know when they will make their entrance, but the words tell me that there will be great destruction in their path and that suffering will be most terrible."

"Yes, that is what I believe also. I envision a final encounter between good and evil; in the course of this great conflict, many, many innocents will perish, as well as an equal number of the followers of hell. We can only wish that your holy daughter, Patch, will prevail, and mankind will be able to once again sleep the sleep of peace.

"My wish is to avoid that conflagration from the fires of hell and meet that evil on neutral ground. I believe we can stop her without encouraging the destruction as we envision it."

"Well said, Bean. You may be confident in knowing that I, as well as my people, will give you whatever support we are capable of. However, I'm afraid that our help will be mainly in the form of prayer."

"Do not underestimate the power of prayers from the devout. I have seen the results of such religious fervor, and they are not to be taken lightly.

"I think we should end our discussion now. The Reverend Bill will get suspicious if you spend too much time here.

"*We will meet many times in the coming days, Anna Walks With Grace, and we will have much to talk about.*

"*If you need me, just concentrate, and I will be with you wherever and whenever you need me to be.*

"*It is one of my powers, if you may.*"

"I will go now. My blessings be with you."

CHAPTER 56

As I had guessed, Bill had gotten a bit suspicious, judging by the fact that he was slowly approaching the house and arrived just as Anna was taking her leave.

"So, Anna Walks With Grace, what did you learn from Virgil? Did he offer you any gems of wisdom?"

She paused on her return to the parking lot, turned to face the minister, and said in a singsong manner, "Scintillate, scintillate, globule vivific, fain how I fathom your nature specific ..."

"Very funny, Anna. I'm glad that your new position hasn't reduced your sense of humor."

"Be well, my friend. We will meet again soon. And please remember me to your wonderful family."

Bill stood by the door and watched Anna drive away. *Why did she spend so much time in the house?* he thought. *No normal human being could tolerate Virgil's poetry for more than a minute, and she was there for about thirty minutes.*

Out of curiosity, he went inside and confronted the bird. This time the bird was silent and just gazed at Bill. It was almost as if Virgil were humoring the minister.

This prompted a staring contest, which Bill was fated to lose ... and, of course, he did.

"Crazy darn bird," he murmured.

I just couldn't help but answer him. *"Arrkkk! Crazy Bill! Arrkkk!"*

"That's enough of that nonsense!"

"Arrkkk! Nonsense. Arrkkk!"

"I've had it with this feathered fiend! Where's my shotgun? Squab for dinner!"

"Arrkkk! Bill for dinner! Ha ha! Arrkkk!"

"I won't get drawn into another dialogue with you. The whole thing is a scene out of the cuckoo's nest—or, should I say, the parrot's cage? I should call Dr. Mobish and get a prescription for some antipsychotic preparation. I have no doubt that I'm ready for the padded room."

"Arrkkk! Stop being so melodramatic, Bill. You've got a long ways to go before they strap you down. Arrkkk!"

Exasperated, Bill asked Virgil, "What do you want from me? Lately it seems that everybody wants something from me.

"Would it help if I started reciting your little scintillation?"

"Arrkkk! I don't think that even I could stand that.

"What I want is for you to stop your protestations and equate the past day's events with the possibility, just the possibility, that what transpired had some validity to it.

"Accept the fact that there are more truths in this world than you have been taught to believe. Why is it that there are so many religious alternatives for man to choose from, if not for the attention paid to the individual tenets of various religious convictions?

"Many well-established religions are based on metaphysical spiritualism. Take yours, for example: can you see or touch your God or the metaphysical image of his Son? So why not believe that a common parrot can converse with you in an intelligent manner? At the least, you can see me, and—heaven forbid—you can touch me.

"I don't claim to be a god—far from it: I'm just your average busybody spirit whose goal is to provide a guide for man to achieve his true destiny, which I—and it seems I might be alone in my conviction— deem to be an eternity of peaceful coexistence with all manner of life.

"Is that too complicated for you to comprehend? Arrkkk!"

"Why a cockatoo? If you presented yourself in the guise of, let's see, a holy man, perhaps one could find more legitimacy in your proclamations."

"Arrkkk! Bill, open your mind, and let the fresh air in; it can be so invigorating! Besides there are already too many holy folk around here, and if you look, there aren't very many cockatoos. Arrkkk!"

"Something tells me that your 'arrkkk'-ing has been constructed just to annoy the dickens out of me.

"Why don't we disperse with the introductory throat-clearing and converse like two normal—omigod, did I say normal?—whatchamicallits? "

"As you wish ... arrkkk! Sorry—I just had to do it one more time.

"How can I help you in further understanding the situation? I can't create images of the forthcoming apocalypse on your adobe wall; I can only guarantee that it will be shattering in its commission.

"Your daughter has been selected by the forces to be the vessel, the conduit, imbued with the ability to counteract that horror. From what I can gather, the control that overcomes her is not permanent. It seems to arrive at times when its presence is required and departs when the situation has been alleviated. In the interim, she is just your little girl again and has no memory of the episode.

"I can well imagine that you will have difficulty in bowing to her leadership when those periods of spiritual control are in effect, but you'll have no choice if you are sincere about your true feelings.

"Another thing to consider, and I have no hesitation in alerting you to the possibility, is that she will ultimately understand what has become of her, and it is then that she will need all the support you can give her. In the interim, I will become her friend and guide through Virgil but gradually wean her off that situation. She will have to learn to control her powers and call upon them as needed.

"Why has she been blessed? Why was she chosen? I can't answer those questions. In fact, I can't even agree that it has been a blessing. The responsibility is so awesome that to instill it in a mere child cannot be referred to as a holy sanction. But you must accept it as reality and learn to deal with it.

"She will need your support, as well as the support of your native parishioners—especially Anna Walks With Grace—as the time grows closer to that inevitable summit.

"The spiritual world has been around longer than time immemorial; you just have to trust that it still exists and place your confidence in it.

"You should be able to separate the two belief systems and continue your own religious philosophy. In time you might even acknowledge that they aren't so far apart."

"So, correct me if I'm wrong, but your vision for the future is formatted around the potential demise of man as a viable entity? That's kind of a bleak prospectus, isn't it?"

"For the foreseeable future, perhaps; beyond that, I see a rebirth of energy based upon a fundamental concept grounded in a natural order. Man will have to reinvent himself and utilize the remaining technology to work for him ... and not vice versa."

"Natural order? What about technology and the progress it promises to make man's burden easier?"

"Technology? You ask about technology. It's against all that nature has endowed us with.

"Technology has provided man with the means to bastardize and simulate that which has been provided and replace it with false commodities emitting nothing but poisonous discharges. You have been afflicted with all sorts of maladies that have no known cures.

"At least whatever ills nature has caused, she has a cure for. That is her responsibility. Such cures just take time and effort to locate.

"I firmly believe that technology, allowed to run unchecked, has been the curse in preventing humanity's effort to evolve to a higher plane. It has also fueled its inexorable and almost insatiable greed.

"As man's existence becomes more complex and puts a strain on his present mental capacity to deal with the new stresses that technology fosters upon him, it appears that he becomes more aggressive in his actions.

"As the runaway advancements in technology strain his ability to understand and control it, he becomes more and more frustrated due to the very speed of that advancement and the frustration produced in not fully keeping pace with it. That frustration could be the impetus for his increased violent behavior.

"The schism formed between modern civilized man and his uneducated competition grows greater as technology forces him to increase the complexity of his mind, utilize areas of his brain that until now have been dormant, and question age-old beliefs and tenets.

"I feel that technology will suffer during the approaching storm, and much of it will be lost.

"I am partial to a dictum of the late Walt Kelly: 'We have met the enemy, and he is us!'"

"So we must first slide backward, perhaps at a great loss of lives, before we can go forward—is that it?"

"That's it."

"And Patch is our salvation—is *that* it?"

"That's it."

"I still have difficulty talking to a bird."

"That's it ... at least for now."

"If you'll excuse me, I need to take a walk; I feel another headache coming on."

"One question before you leave: if you would want me to assume another identity, who or what would you prefer?"

"A good question, Virgil. Let me think about that one."

And with that, the minister left. I could see that he was in turmoil, and I felt sorry for him. Everything that has happened has been against all that he has learned and practiced most of his adult years.

If you noticed I purposely did not emphasize Leader's role in all this. The less one knows of him, the stronger the surprise will be. What with his newly acquired emotions, I hope he won't feel slighted. It will give him more time to do his thing.

CHAPTER 57

To avoid too much confusion, I chose not to inhabit Virgil unless the situation called for it. Therefore, when Maeve and Patch returned home, the bird was standing on his perch and, believe it or not, whistling Dixie—and in tune. Not the most requested tune, but miles ahead of his previous scintillating oration.

Patch ran over to the cage and greeted Virgil with an exuberant "Hello, Virgil. What did you do today?"

"Arrkkk! Hello. Virgil scintillates. Arrkkk!"

Oh, no, thought Bill, *not again!* Out loud, Bill asked, "Isn't there anything else you have to say for yourself?"

"Arrkkk!" Virgil said, "to be or not to be: *that* is the question."

"Wise guy! I'm sorry I asked."

Bill retreated to his desk and Maeve to the kitchen to prepare dinner.

Patch went over to the birdcage, but before she got there, Virgil let loose with another gem.

"Arrkkk! Dinner for two, my dear? Some wine? Arrkkk!"

"Virgil, you are a silly bird!" Patch stated while giggling to herself. She pulled a kitchen chair over to the cage, and it looked as if she were preparing to have a conversation with him.

So, I thought, this was as good a time as any to begin my contact with the child, now that her parents were busy with their own thing.

"Virgil, let's play a game. I'll say a word, and you can say it back to me, okay?"

"Okay, sounds like a plan to me."

"Virgil, you silly; I didn't say that."

"No, you didn't—I did."

'That's not the game I wanted to play. Now behave yourself!"

"Instead of playing a game, why don't we just talk? I could be your best friend, and we can say things to each other that nobody else would know. How would you like that?"

"You mean like secrets?"

"Yes, like secrets. What do you say?"

"I'd like that. Do you have any secrets to tell me?"

Boy, do I have secrets to tell her!

"Do you know that you are very special girl and that you can do very special things?"

"Can I really? Like what? Tell me!"

Uh-oh, did I ask for that one! What do I say now?

"Like now: you're talking to a bird, and he is talking to you. How many people do you know who can do that? I'll bet not many.

"And how many people have a bird who's their best friend?"

Phew! Did I get out of that one?

"I bet I'm the only one … right, Virgil?"

"Absolutely! Tell me, Patch, what do you like to do?"

"Well, I do like to talk to people at Mommy's store. Some of them are very nice, and I like to help them find special things in the store.

"Sometimes I see a person who looks sad, and I go over and try to cheer them up. I like it when they start to smile. It's like I make them all better.

"Yesterday, there was a boy who was in a chair with wheels, and he looked sad also. His mommy and daddy were looking at some rugs, so I went to him and took his hand. It got very warm, and a few minutes later, he stood up and looked at me kind of funny and walked to his parents.

"They were so surprised that they dropped the rug they were holding and hugged the little boy. It seemed that he had been very sick when he came in, but now he was better. He tried to tell them that I held his hand, but they didn't hear him, because they were laughing and crying. Kind of strange!

"He couldn't a'been very sick, could he, Virgil?"

"You didn't tell anyone what happened, did you? What you did was very, very special, and it should be a very big secret between us. Do you understand?"

"No. Why can't I tell Mommy and Daddy? They'll be happy that I made the boy better."

"It's such a special thing that people won't believe you and will say it's just your imagination or an exaggeration. Either that or they will call you a liar, and we know that you aren't a liar. It could also be a coincidence; maybe his medicine was working, and he felt better from it.

"So you see, Patch, it has to be a secret between us."

"Do you believe I helped that boy, Virgil?"

"Yes, I do; that's because I know you're special.

"Did you see a bright light when you touched the boy?"

"No, but I thought that I heard the old Native American man tell me what to do. I looked around, but he wasn't there. Maybe it was just my imagination again."

It was about that time that I felt Bill and Maeve staring at us. Although they couldn't hear us, they sure were interested.

"I think we should say good-bye for now. I can see that Mommy has dinner ready, and it looks like spaghetti. I'll bet you like spaghetti, don't you?"

"It's my favoritest food. Good-bye, Virgil; see you later."

I really enjoy children, but having a discussion with them is tough on the mind—probably tough on the reader also, I guess. It has to be done to add some reality to the tale.

CHAPTER 58

Things were moving faster than I had thought they would. It had been only a couple of days, and already the girl had performed incidents that were far and away beyond anything I had thought possible. The amazing part was that they had been accomplished without any guidance from me.

I want to explain things further to Patch, but to proceed, I feel I should have permission from her parents. To achieve that next step, the minister would have to speak to his wife, and the both of them, in turn, would have to establish a dialogue with me. The only fly in the ointment would be if one of them were hesitant about my actual presence, my abilities, my commitment, what I hoped to gain from my intervention, my personal agenda, whether the entire scenario about the oncoming conflict is real, and so on. I wouldn't pit one parent against the other; it would only harm Patch, and that isn't in the cards.

I'll give them a few days to discuss it, and if no accord is forthcoming, I'll step in and see what I can do. Meanwhile, I won't eavesdrop, and I'll continue my interaction with the child when the situation presents itself.

So, back to the breezes while I await Leader's return. I could sure use a little diversion about now.

I find my thoughts a bit jumbled as to what has occurred and the primary source of power behind the accomplishment of the acts. I have many questions, and intervention into Patch's mind is of the utmost importance in gaining the answers.

If I'm unable to gain that access, and if I don't receive permission from her parents, I will have to act externally in the capacity of an independent contactor. This could possibly form the basis for a confused and disjointed alliance, as well as greatly reducing our efficiency and strength.

Now you see why I want to fold up and drift with the zephyrs. Everybody should try it at least once: just fold up and float, sort of like returning to the womb while gliding in a helium-filled balloon.

CHAPTER 59

"*Hola*, Bean!"
Hola? Now what?
Oh, well. So much for my zephyrizing. It was a good idea while it lasted.
"I have returned."
"Obviously—and not very quietly, either. What misery have you caused?"
"Is that the warm welcome I've become accustomed to receiving from my fellow traveler?
"It is not, and I am hurt!"
"Ah, pain becomes you."
"Do I note a bit of sarcasm in your tone of voice?"
"No more than usual, I suppose."
I proceeded to recount all that had transpired in the past few days.
At first Leader was a bit flippant, but he calmed down when I told him about the disembodiment of Giver of the Word and the fact that the girl had no recollection of the entire event.
His first concern was the same one that had piqued my curiosity.
"It's obvious that someone or something has assumed control of the child. I'm afraid that if you decide to meld with her, and there is indeed another presence inhabiting her mind, the consequences could be disastrous for her."
"I agree with you wholeheartedly, but I have a feeling that the entity is a good one and means no harm to her. In fact, during our little discussion before dinner, she mentioned that she had heard the voice

of Giver of the Word. Intellectually, that would be an impossibility, but spiritually, I have to give it credence.

"The old man was there when that ethereal beam of light was evident by the altar and before he assumed the guise of a young warrior and rose to his maker.

"I tell you, Leader, I think his god is using him as her guardian, and he has assumed the same task as we have. My feeling is that somehow, he will contact us and suggest that we join forces in our mission to combat the iniquity soon emerging from the east. The key word here is soon."

"Have you done anything like that before—I mean, work with another spiritual being not related to our kind?

"That sounds pretty dicey, if you ask me."

"To answer your question, no, I haven't; this will be the first time. But until he makes an appearance, I'll continue my association with her and see if she will permit me to leave the bird and be with her at all times. That might force his hand and entice him to a meeting of the minds. Now tell me what you have been inciting."

"Is that the esteem you hold me in? You really know how to hurt an ion, don't you?

"Well, I'll ignore your insults and give you a rundown of my latest exploits.

"After surveying the area known as North Central New Mexico—I got that name from a pamphlet some elderly tourist lady was reading in downtown Taos— what interested me was a reference to a place called Española.

"Why, you ask me, did that place, out of the rest of the area, attract me? Go ahead, ask me."

"Come on, Leader. Please ... just tell me."

"Okay, just because you asked me politely. It's listed as the first European capital in this country, established somewhere near the year 1598. Before that this was land belonged to the indigenous people, the original Native Americans.

"For your information, I witnessed the Spanish conquistadores overpowering and enslaving the Native Americans back then. Blame it on my fascination for the human's penchant for aggression. It was bloody and quick: a combination of fear, strength, weaponry, and disease to which the natives had no immunity.

"I never realized that this was indeed the first European-contrived capital in the so-called New World.

"What I found particularly interesting is the fact that at the same time, Europe itself was undergoing a renaissance of art, music, and religion—the basis of what humanity refers to as civilization.

"But what would civilization be if not for war, religious heresy, diabolic conspiracies, and the omnipresent disease?

"I suppose that the Spaniards, in their pretentious view of things, wanted to introduce civilization, as they practiced it, to the Native Americans. It looks as if they succeeded, judging by the end result.

"And what did they gain by their tried-and-true civilized methods? Nothing but a decimated group of slaves and lots of sand.

"I left the area before the natives rebelled and were ultimately defeated."

"By any chance, did you run into any native religious leaders—Anna Walks With Grace, for instance?"

"I'm sorry, no. I spent most of the time flitting from one place to another and just observing the people and the changes that have occurred since I was last here five hundred years ago. It's funny that except for the small towns that have sprung up, the land hasn't changed ... but the population has. The majority of the people are white, while the native population is only about two or three percent.

"I suppose the conquistadores achieved a degree of success in their effort to alter the world as they saw fit. The Catholic religion is at the forefront of faiths, while the practitioners of the Taos religion are diminishing. The same holds true for the languages spoken. While the majority speaks English, the older people still speak Spanish, and as the population gets younger, even Spanish is being fazed out."

"What about the Taos language?"

"Fewer and fewer natives speak that tongue. It's a shame, because their history is bound up in the spoken word, and it has more meaning if spoken in the original Tewa. But that's progress, isn't it?"

"Progress, eh? What I've learned throughout the millennia is that progress just provides the increased knowledge for man to better enslave his fellow man by spiritual, intellectual, and physical means.

"Lili-It and Whoever will make good use of this so-called progress in their distorted march toward a new chapter in the evolution of man.

"Back in the 1930s, I was monitoring a gentleman named H. G. Wells while he wrote a screenplay for a movie based on one of his stories, 'The Shape of Things to Come.' This film, by the way, proved to be prophetic as to the start of World War II—you do remember that one, don't you?

"Well, in the script, he had a character named Cabal intone the following statement concerning progress and the search for knowledge as he spoke to Horrie Passworthy, a character prepared to launch into space:

"And if we're no more than animals, we must snatch each little scrap of happiness, and live, and suffer, and pass, mattering no more that all the other animals do or have done. It is this, or that. All the universe or nothing. Which shall it be, Passworthy? Which shall it be?"[26]

"I believe that Wells blames the downfall of man, at least in his movie, on the uncontrollability of progress, and I seem to recall another quote, although I'm not sure whether it came from the same film. I'll paraphrase it: 'Can't we stop progress? At least for a while, so man can catch up to himself?'

"Maybe Wells wasn't that far off."

---

26   H.G. Wells, "The Shape of Things to Come" (1933).

CHAPTER 60

"We've discussed progress before and man's losing effort to either keep pace with it or catch up to it. It will reach a point where there is nothing concrete to base progress upon due to a complete lack of techno-comprehension. His new future will be governed by a cabal of theoretical pundits whose promises for a carefree future will become a new faith-based religion."

"You're hatching another scenario for disaster. Let's deal with one at a time, if you don't mind."

"So shall it be done.

"What's your next step?"

"My next step?

"The Reverend Fellows, I think. There are three major points I have to realize from him. Once they have been clarified, we can proceed.

"But before I begin my involvement with the minister, I have to face the one bee in the bonnet, and that is the acknowledgment of who the guardian is. Somehow I feel that the old one is just a vessel—albeit recognizable and one that is familiar and sympathetic to the child—for a greater force ... a force that reigns supreme over our intervention and our abilities to combat the malevolent ones.

"First, I have to get the minister to believe in me, or at least instill in him the possibility that I could be telling the truth in my estimation of the certain clash of moralities that is forthcoming.

"Second, I have to know what he and his wife have decided as to my participation in their child's spiritual education, and ...

"Third, will they allow me to insert myself, if need be, into the mind of the little girl?

Some people might consider this child abuse, and in reality, I don't blame them. It could be interpreted as interfering with the natural growth and maturation of the mind of an innocent and impressionable organism. The power to slant her thoughts and moral principles is an effective weapon for the dedicated blasphemer. Those alterations could conceivably affect a change in her very soul.

"Cult leaders and political despots have misused those methods for centuries in order to build a power base to serve their personal agendas.

"It is a very solemn responsibility, and her parents do not have any reference as to our goodwill. Trust is a very difficult gift to offer a stranger. Food and shelter is not the same as trust.

"What would you do in this situation?"

"The truth? I would tell you to bug off and leave us alone: 'You don't exist and you're just an hysterical aberration brought on by the conflict with the old ways of my native congregation,' et cetera, et cetera.

"But remember, I am an inveterate cynic, so don't judge my reactions to those of emotional humans.

"In retrospect, I believe that they will eventually go along with you, but not after a great deal of soul-searching ... and also with the proviso that they monitor the proceedings."

"That would be agreeable to me. Once they see that my only concern is for the well-being of Patch, I'm sure that I will be able to rely on their cooperation.

"I do have anxieties about the time situation. We both know that Lili-It and her bodiless servant aren't wasting any time in their preparations, so it's imperative that we get a move on.

"Leader, I have a request of you, and I won't hold it against you if you refuse."

"Sounds rather ominous, Bean. What is it?"

"Would you retrace our trek back to village where Lili-It and Whoever reside and keep track of their actions?"

"Wow! That came out of left field, didn't it?

"You mean I'll have to give up monitoring bar fights? I don't know, Bean. You're asking too much of me."

"It's okay if you refuse. I'm sure that there are things for you to do here ... even if I have to create some."

"Bean ... Bean. There's that sense of humor again. Of course I'll go. Sure beats watching sand grow."

"I thought you would.

"There is one very important proviso, and that is for you to remain hidden. I can't stress it enough. And be especially careful when it comes to Lili-It; she is more powerful and more perceptive than Whoever."

"Gotcha! Anything else?"

"As soon as you feel that they are on the move, and as soon as you are able to get a feel for their plan of action, come back and alert us.

"I'm sure that by then, some indication of their potential will be forthcoming, and we can follow their exploits in the news media.

"While you're gone, I'll continue to provide my assistance to all involved parties here. My goal is to combine them into a formidable group of determined warriors."

"When do you want me to leave? I'll have to pack a few things first."

"Very funny. How about as soon as possible? I'm beginning to have trepidations about our future."

"But Lili-It and Patch are so young. What can you expect them to achieve?"

"Their lack of contact with the forces that direct the shortcomings of mankind, combined with Patch's innocence and desire to help others, will produce in each an energy that will be concentrated on their goals. There will be no interference from outside societal influences.

"In fact there is the strong possibility that the final conflict will occur much sooner than we originally considered. I only hope that we'll be prepared for it.

"So, be gone with you: be off, and be wary, and be safe, and behave."

"I'll be off now, and be alert to all matters that be."

CHAPTER 61

With Leader's departure, I found myself once more in the living room, where the minister was engrossed in writing what I deduced to be his next sermon.

I observed him for a while, marveling at his powers of concentration—that is, until I decided to induce a moment of jocularity into the proceedings.

"Arrkkk! Feed me; put down your pen and feed me! Arrkkk!"

"What? Who's there?" the Reverend Bill said, startled, as he dropped his pen. "Oh, it's only you, bird."

Can't you see that I'm busy and definitely not in the mood for more nonsensical verbal sparring with you? And stop with that irritating 'arrkkk'-ing!"

"Whoa, we are in a nasty mood today, aren't we?"

"I guess so.

"When we decided to relocate here, I was looking forward to a life filled with ministrations to my flock amid an air of calm and nonviolence as compared to the life we left in the big city. Although I was faced with a conflict of belief structures—namely Christianity versus totemic idolatry—I felt that the two religions shared many similarities upon which to base my teachings.

"For all intents and purposes, I truly believed I had achieved that goal … that is, until you arrived with your fantastic prophesy of doom and with the totally implausible declaration of my child's powers and responsibilities.

"Now I find myself unable to concentrate on my work and instead find myself chasing your words around in my head, attempting to reach some understanding and acceptance of your trepidations. You have reopened an old wound and poured chili sauce on it!"

"You're absolutely right. I came uninvited with an obnoxious mixture of wise-guy humor and implausible statements. If I had the time, and if your daughter weren't who she is, you might still be immersed in your cocoon. But I don't, and she is, so I had no other choice.

"It is imperative that you and your wife reach some understanding and allow us to implement my—our—plans for the future in the race for humanity's salvation.

"You must believe that I am sincere in my vision for the future!"

"Your sincerity doesn't afford me much solace. We are still debating my daughter's future health and well-being. It's your very sincerity that causes my turmoil. My angst is that I do believe you, but the sacrifice we might have to endure is, as you can well accept, very difficult to concede.

"If you don't mind, I need a break from these clashes of thought. There's a TV program I wanted to see, and it'll be on any minute now."

"Sure ... if I may, I'll watch it also. What is it about, if I might ask?"

"From what I gather, it's about DNA and its origin in man. Perhaps a discussion of evolution and religion will surface. I'm very interested in the subject, being a minister myself."

With a sigh of fatigue, the Reverend Bill walked across the room to the television and turned it on. Once he had arrived at the correct channel, he plopped himself down on the couch, poured a glass of wine for himself, and waited for the program to begin.

The TV took a while to warm up; it being an old tube model working from a rabbit-eared antenna.

The first image that appeared was that of a man screaming about some kind of rag that absorbed gallons of liquid and never wore out. Seems that all you need, then, is one piece for the rest of your life: interesting. Where's the profit in an item that lasts for all eternity?

They should make clothing from it, so you can do away with the incredible amount of stores out there: one suit, one shirt, one color, and so on.

The next image projected was of another man, also seeming to shout about his program, called "Drop Back Ten and Punt"—why did all TV personalities have to go hysterical to make a point? At first I thought it was about sports, but then I realized it was a quasi-news program that centered on controversial topics. Today's subject was, as the minister noted, about DNA and its hypothetical origin, or something like that. One thing I am positive about: it wasn't going to be a deep, scientific treatise on the subject, owing to the fact that the viewers had a short span of attention.

I know that you are sitting on the edge of your seat, just dying to hear what was discussed, so I'll insert a piece of what was brought out by the esteemed guest.

The invited guest du jour was the renowned expert on DNA, Dr. Heinz Seibenundfunfzig, author of the best seller titled *Ten to the Umpteenth* (seems that the number ten is significant?). The doctor's focus is to investigate the origin of DNA and its effect on the belief system of mankind.

Dr. Seibenundfunfzig asked the moderator—who, I forgot to mention, was named Matt Christmas—to call him Heinie.

That Christmas character constantly interrupted his guest, Heinie, with questions and then proceeded to answer them himself, not allowing his guest to interject anything except a few words—that is until Heinie put his foot down and told Christmas (and I paraphrase, as is my prerogative) to stuff a stocking and let him speak.

Now to the substance of the matter: the point to be made is that DNA is so complex—more so than the largest supercomputer in the world—that the chances for it to have appeared through spontaneous generation (a theory that has been expunged from the scientific community for many years) is, as the title of the book states, *Ten to the Umpteenth* power. Not enough ink or paper existed to depict the true number.

And the good doctor marched on:

> *"If the theory of spontaneous generation has been pooh-poohed by the scientific community, the door is open wide for Creationists to look to DNA as an instrument of God's grand design. How else could such a concept have appeared without any scientific explanation beyond that of absolute conjecture? That must have really been some Big Bang.*

Aha! Now comes the part that the Reverend Bill was anticipating.

"Science has yet to arrive at a rational explanation
for its conception. Can it say that man's DNA, using that
as the penultimate combination of genes, had truly been
derived from some primordial, and seemingly offensive,
puddle of ooze?

"What if that seed was nothing more than a very
sophisticated program, not unlike a computer program,
which was allowed to germinate in the primordial ooze by
an alien power? What if such germination transformed that
seed into a viable life form and, throughout millennia upon
millennia of mutations, ultimately formed what we know as
modern man? Hence DNA is nothing but a supercomputer
with the power to reproduce and constantly learn from its
mistakes ... although, in man, that function appears to
have incurred a fatal glitch: his inability to learn from his
mistakes and his tendency to incessantly repeat his errors,
albeit in many guises, throughout his history.

"Can we then accept the hypotheses that God is but an
overseer and not the all-powerful spiritual being perceived
by various religions to exist? He or she was sent here to
supervise an experiment to create a life form that would
exist in a new world and be given the powers of creation
and destruction, but answerable only to the originator. His
introduction of the DNA program was the seed planted to
create that life. To continue this train of thought, might he or
she have varied the seeds in diverse areas of the earth, thus
creating a multiplicity of species in an experiment to observe
which one of them would be able to adapt and survive?

"Man, the survivor that he is, has now been endowed
with the intellectual capacity to accomplish his ultimate goal
of creating a mechanical facsimile of that program outside
of his body. But he is centuries away from accomplishing
it. And if he does achieve his goal, can humanity look
forward to a future, à la **Terminator**, where machines have
replaced the skin and bones of man? Another question
would make itself known, and that is 'What happens to
the soul?' Is the soul just a segment of the DNA, and is
that reproducible in an artificial mode? Is the soul and
its shadow, emotion, the one major obstruction to man's
achievement of physical autonomy from the evolution of
the machine? Can data be a future relative of mankind—
indestructible, self-repairable, and constantly hungry for

knowledge ... without, perhaps, the need for aggressive behavior?

"Man's ingenuity to man will replace his inhumanity to man.

Oops, I don't think that the good minister expected this train of thought. It should go a long way to add fuel to his already steaming mood.

"I am afraid that each question I have presented to your audience is in itself the prelude to lengthy discussions of their own.

"At the present time, I believe no absolute answers to my queries exist, and as a scientist, I am loath to acknowledge this. As to the question that separates society in a most emotional manner—that being the controversy between the theories of evolution and intelligent design—both premises are enmeshed in a belief system based upon their adaptation and classification of faith. I fear that without intervention from without, and with no definitive answer to that penultimate of questions, those belief systems will remain an integral part of man's internal and external conflict, forever fueling his aggressive nature."

With that final statement, Heinie faded into a commercial featuring a cartoon character babbling monotonically about some technical device that every human obviously needed in order to add meaning to his lifestyle.

The Reverend Bill launched himself off the couch and turned the TV off just as the image of Matt Christmas started his high-pitched monograph, thanking his now-good friend Heinie and inviting him back at a later date.

"Yeah, right—like I'll watch him at a later date," Bill muttered. "Darn atheist!"

"Calm down, Rev; differences of opinion make for intelligent discussion, and intelligent discussion leads to an increase in knowledge. An open mind, sir—that's all that is required!"

"Not now, Virgil. I am not in the mood for an intelligent discussion with a bird. We'll talk later."

CHAPTER 62

"Stop!
"Cease!
"Desist!"

"Have I again earned your ire? We were doing so well for so long that I finally began to relax."

"I just can't understand your fascination with religion. You appear to be totally consumed by it; totally preoccupied almost to the point of neglecting the story. What is it with you?"

"Can't you see it? Everywhere I look, there is a reference, either directly or indirectly, to religion. Every conflict—whether an aggressive physical demonstration resulting in human and material destruction; political and judicial disparity manifesting itself in seemingly unsolvable divergences of belief and practice; or simply everyday communication between man and man, man and woman, adult and child, media and society—has as its roots religion!

"I am driven, almost to the point of lunacy, to make sense of the cause of the unquenchable fire that burns in humanity, ignited by their need to place their trust in an almighty entity."

"My not being human and not being tormented by your rabbinical forays into the meaning of meanings doesn't preclude me from trying to understand your needs. But aside from your complexities, we have a story to tell, and I will not allow you and your hauntings to interfere with it!"

"Ah, Bean, don't you see that even your tale is submerged in religious undertones? Good versus evil: the basic tenet of all religions. How can you deny it? Even your thoughts of evolution versus intelligent design are nothing but the contemporary appearance of a century-old concept: science versus religion, in which *The Book of Bones* is opposed to the book of Genesis and the global gathering of mythological explanations as to the origin of earth and its minions."

"If morality, truth, and righteousness are nothing but religious issues, you are correct in your assumption. But we have discussed previously whether those qualities can be inherent in humanity without the subjects having to base them on some religious ideology. I believe that is so, and I will persist with the story, keeping that theory in mind.

"So if you will kindly clear your mind of those spider webs, we will continue with my *story!"*

"I bow to your wishes, and I promise that I'll try to tell *your* story.

"Proceed … or rather, I'll proceed."

CHAPTER 63

**"It is whispered in the darkest of dark;
In the deepest of deep;
That He himself fears the wraith called,
Total."**[27]

Taking an obvious hint from the minister's gray disposition, I departed from the scene, not wanting to further exacerbate the situation. So I took refuge in the mission for what I hoped would be a period of retrospection and calm. That was not to be, for sitting in the front aisle with her hands covering her face in deep meditation was Anna Walks With Grace.

For the first time in my recollection, a human initiated contact with me. This was, as you can well understand, quite a shock.

"I know you're here," she said, "and although I do not know who you are, I must believe that you are a spirit sent to me from the world beyond. Would you be Giver of the Word?"

How did I answer her without giving myself away?

As in response to my conundrum, the same beam of light that had served as the vehicle to bear Giver of the Word to his reward presented itself once more on the altar in front of the sachem. Using that as my conveyance, I answered her.

"I am here, Anna Walks With Grace."

---

27 Stephen Stuart, *Rantings* (2009).

Anna, still keeping her face covered, asked, "Am I allowed to see you?"

Utilizing the power of suggestion, I replied, "No, you may not see me, for I am the light of lights, and the briefest vision would be cause for your eyes to cease offering their gift of sight."

This revelation triggered a series of tremors that racked her body for a brief period of time.

"Do not be alarmed, Anna Walks With Grace, for it is the anxiety and fear for your people that has summoned me."

This was going to get very complicated with all the roles that I was playing. I supposed that the intricacy of the situation compelled me to assume the various characterizations. *We'll see.*

"Are you the speaker from the bird?"

"I am indeed he; you remember when I told you that the bird was just a vehicle so as not to alarm you. For now, I have chosen a ray of light, since you are familiar with it as the path that Giver of the Word rode to his reward in the great beyond.

"We have much to talk about and not much time for action. Your fears are well founded, and I will enlighten you on the approaching maelstrom."

"Yes, it is fear that fills my heart. I see a darkness coming, within which a vast pit will open, swallowing the souls of humanity's charges. This will inaugurate a period of an apocalyptic reign of terror wherein the horseman will ride unfettered throughout the land.

"However, through this darkness I see—or do I feel?—a spark of light flickering in the shadows, much like the wick of a taper as it gasps its final ration of fuel … and that spark takes the shape of a little girl.

"Am I not wrong that this childlike figure is the form of little Patch?"

This was starting to sound like a pontifical dialogue between two elderly princes of the church.

Here we go again.

"You are correct in your vision, Anna Walks With Grace. A great darkness approaches from across the seas, and it promises to envelop much of the world as you know it.

"And yes, you are also correct in identifying that spark of light as the spirit of Patch. We both remember when she stood in front of the congregation and transformed Giver of the Word into a young warrior prior to his ascension.

"You must also recall her curing your nephew Justin. There is one other event you are unfamiliar with, and that is her restoring to health a lad she encountered at her mother's gallery. That boy was confined to a wheelchair until Patch touched him gently. She had moved on before he stood and walked to his parents, so there were no eyewitnesses."

"Yes, yes, I remember, of course. But I do not recollect the story about the boy."

"I learned that fact from Patch herself in as innocent a manner as any child could relate. She was a bit confused by the event and wanted to tell her parents about it, but I insisted she keep it a secret between us for the time being.

"Can you imagine the chaos if it became known that she is a healer?"

"Tell me then, what is the meaning of her image as it struggles to remain a bright light surrounded by the insatiable, all-consuming blackness?

"Am I to believe that she holds within her essence, the capability to thwart the oncoming evil?"

"Not as an individual warrior, but more like a general directing her forces to engage the enemy while utilizing her assets to their best advantage."

Anna seemed to ponder that statement for a while before resuming her questions. It gave me the time to engage in a visual reconnaissance of the small chapel.

I was wrong in assuming that Anna and I were the only inhabitants, for scrunched down in a corner seat at the rear of the room was an individual appearing to be in a stupor—drunk or asleep, I wasn't sure. I was sure, however, that he was alive, due to his labored breathing and the subtle tooting of his nasal flute. Why I hadn't perceived his presence before, I couldn't answer, but I would have to be especially careful that he didn't bolt out of there screaming about voices and visions.

"How do I call you?"

"I have assumed the identity of Virgil for the Reverend Bill and his family, so you may address me the same."

"It is a noble name, and I shall do so, thank you."

"You spoke of Patch utilizing her forces—you spoke in the plural. Would you consider it discourteous if I asked you to expand on that statement?"

Keeping the tooter in the rear in sight, I replied to Anna. *"Well, first of all, before I answer your question, the forces for evil are very powerful and increasing in influence and strength every day. The specter whose goal is world annihilation is called Lili-It, and she is aided by a presence that has existed since time immemorial."*

"This presence, as you call it—you are personally familiar with it?"

"I am, yes. He is referred to as Whoever because he has not discovered the ability to transform himself into the physical manifestation of an identifiable image. Therefore, who is he? Whoever."

"I understand. Your ancestry and his are, perhaps, similar in nature?"

The tooter had begun to stir in his less-than-pleasant garments, arousing my curiosity as to how he would react to Anna addressing a beam of light.

"It is, yes. However, I had no knowledge of his presence at the time of the origin.

"Now, to continue with your question as to the plural, as you refer to it: yes, there are forces for good that will gather at the necessary time and will add to Patch's might. You have been chosen by those who guide as one, whose influence and respect can command a cadre of souls who follow a credo of virtue, morality, and decency."

"Tell me, Virgil: what can I do to help?"

Suddenly, a voice blared out from the rear of the room, "Help? I don't need no damn help. Nobody asked for no damn help!"

Now was as good a time as ever for me to excise myself from the scene. And, as a matter of fact, the sun had moved enough so that the beam of light I had hitched my Virgil persona onto was gradually diminishing.

"Hey, lady, I'm talking to you. I said that I don't need no damn help.

"What are you doing, ignoring me?"

"We shall speak again soon, Anna Walks With Grace. Until then, gather your charges, and be prepared to align yourselves into a viable force for good."

"I will do my best."

With that, I ended my conversation with Anna and awaited the play between her and the pile of rags in the rear.

"Hey, lady, who in hell are you talking to? Are you nuts or something?"

Rising slowly, with the dignity that only a leader of her stature could command, she turned to face the object of her disruption.

"There is no need to shout, my son. What is it that you require?"

"Listen, lady: let's get something straight. First of all, I don't need no damn help; second, if you really want to help, how's about a few bucks for my daily swig of elixir; and third, and this is the most important thing, *I am not your son!*

"Let's get something else straight, my son. First of all, every man is my son; second, I was talking to my spirits, and I am not nuts as you so colorfully inquired; and third, and *this* is the important thing: *you will not be getting a few bucks for your daily swig!*"

Anna started walking down the aisle to confront the interloper on a more personal basis. She didn't feel a bit threatened by his brash and unkempt countenance.

"Whoa there, princess! Don't come any closer to my bubble. There's no way that our bubbles can occupy the same space."

"Not knowing what you mean by your bubble, and judging by the effluvia surrounding your aura, I don't think I would want my bubble to come anywhere near your bubble anyhow!" Anna snapped back.

Hmmm; good retort, Anna. I didn't know you had it in you, Bean mused.

This definitely had the potential for a popular sitcom. How about *Sachem and the Sot* or, perhaps, *Pow Wow and the Bow Wow?*

"Ouch, lady, and touche," he replied, rising to a sitting position and changing his demeanor. "You sure got me that time. I must apologize for my apparent lack of civility. Permit me to bow in reverence."

… and he did—and most nobly, I confess.

"There is no need to prostrate yourself to me, nor to apologize, sir. I accept you as you are … tasteless as it may be.

"Oops," she added. "That was uncalled for. It is my turn to beg forgiveness for a most uncalled-for repartee."

A grin began to form on the face of the stranger, and he almost appeared to be human.

"Madam," he said. "Rather than refer to me as your son, you may call me Dr. Crank. In all modesty, that is the nomenclature that has been fostered upon me by my few contemporaries, due in part to my most genteel nature and to my obvious high intellect."

"Dr. Crank it shall be, and I am in awe of your modesty."

Just about that time, who should arrive amid a slamming of the door and a thumping of boots but the good Reverend William Fellows?

Not noticing the two individuals at the rear of the chapel, he started to walk to the front of the room.

I counted about four steps before he abruptly stopped and said aloud, "What in God's name is that smell?"

"This is really starting to get interesting. What a first episode this will make on the sitcom!" Bean thought.

That was about the time Bill spotted Anna Walks With Grace and the pile of rags now called Dr. Crank.

"Good day, Reverend," Anna said, completely unaffected by his outburst. "And it is indeed a good day, is it not? Allow me to present to you a new member of our congregation: the esteemed Dr. Crank; a most genteel and modest individual of outstanding intellect."

"Umm, a pleasure I'm sure." Well, maybe not. "I am the Reverend William Fellows, the pastor of this house of worship, and I bid you welcome, as all those who seek solace in the Lord are.

"And a good day to you, Anna Walks With Grace. 'Tis truly a wonderful day and getting better now that you have chosen to honor me with your company."

Struggling to hide his apparent distaste, Bill turned again to the disheveled apparition, who bowed and started to address him.

"Pleased to meet you, sir, but I beg you not to come too close, as our bubbles will not be allowed to merge. Allow me to express my sincere gratitude for your most gracious acceptance of my company.

"I neither wish anyone harm nor displeasure; I desire instead to seek refuge in the peace and solitude of your house. I also beg your forgiveness if my attire and unmistakable effluvia, if you please, causes you discomfit.

"Due to circumstances beyond my control, I have not been able to attend to my daily ablutions, as is usually my habit."

Perhaps there was something to his modest claim to intellect.

And the first episode continued …

"Not to worry, Dr. Crank. You may, if you wish, use the washroom in the corner and attend to your ablutions, was the word I believe you used. I may also offer, if it is not insulting to you, some articles of clothing that I have outgrown."

"I see that charity is still alive in this world of avarice and suspicion.

"I thank you, sir, for your kindness and willingly accept your benevolence."

Turning to Anna, Dr. Crank again bowed and said, "Madam, my thanks also to you for your poise in accepting me, not as I physically present myself, but as a fellow human being.

"You have taken a giant step forward in restoring my faith in mankind."

I sort of missed Crank's opening brashness; there had been an explosion of extemporaneous color to it. Now, I'm afraid he sounds like a Victorian con man out to seduce a rich widow.

Well, dear reader, we shall keep watch on this knave, and woe to him who besmirches the beauty that is Anna Walks With Grace.

… Thought I'd try to ham it up a little there. Sorry!

Anna and the minister backed up a skosh as Doctor Crank uncoiled himself from the pew (or was it the pee-yew?). Taller than originally thought, he moved with an elegance of movement that described, perhaps, a dancer or an athlete. As he glided toward the washroom, one could almost envision a large, predatory bird floating on the wind while it scanned the earth for its next meal.

CHAPTER 64

"And now, Anna," Bill asked, "What brings you to the chapel at this hour? I would think that you had chores to do at the res."[28]

Anna appeared uncertain as how to proceed.

"You look troubled," Bill tried again. "Is there anything I can do?"

"I have been having a premonition," she said, "of an immense darkness, and I can't seem to rid my mind of it. I see a world in perpetual night ... and a great deal of suffering ... and much, much death.

When I arrived at the mission, I was visited by a spirit dressed in a great brightness, and his name was Virgil."

"Virgil?" the Reverend Bill exclaimed. "Virgil the cockatoo?"

Anna nodded. "He said that the bird was just a physical manifestation of his spiritual being. He assumed that form so as not to alarm people. He approached me in the form of a great, white light—the same light as that which Giver of the Word ascended into the hereafter."

Judging from his reaction, the pastor was not having a good day.

First of all, he was faced with my presence and all that I had told him about Patch and the coming conflict; second, he was not very pleased with the TV program about DNA; third, he endured an introduction to the apparition named Dr. Crank; and finally, he received the revelation from Anna Walks With Grace about her meeting with me, alias Virgil.

I could almost feel his need for a drop of his special pick-me-up. Maybe he and Doc Crank could share a bit of the elixir?

Nah ... bad idea.

---

28 Slang for reservation.

"And what did Virgil communicate to you? Let me guess: how about a force of malevolence coming this way and an epic battle between good and evil that will shape the future of mankind for all eternity? Do you really believe all that negativity coming from a bird—or, in your case, from a light beam?"

Anna lifted her head up and gazed into the Reverend Bill's eyes "Did you not speak to him yourself, and did he not convince you of his fears?"

"Yes … yes he did, and I am trying to believe his pronouncements, but claiming that Patch, my little girl, is to be the guiding force in this so-called epic … now that's hard to accept, especially for a father. How can I accept that this child is the vessel for some kind of supernatural force?"

"I can't answer that question for you, Reverend Bill," Anna replied. "And I do appreciate the turmoil you must be undergoing, but I believe it to be so; I base that assumption on my own personal experience."

"Be that as it may, Anna, it is still one large lump to swallow.

"Walk with me back to the house, if you please, while I dig up some clothes for Dr. Crank. We've got to bury those rags he's wearing now. Perhaps Virgil will honor us with some conversation without the materialization of mysterious light beams?"

As Anna and the Reverend departed, I asked myself if I should meet them or add to his frustration by having Virgil be himself: an ordinary cockatoo.

Just then I heard Dr. Crank in the washroom. Gone was the civility demonstrated previously, and it was replaced by his original brashness.

"Damn it: where in hell is the %$@&*#% soap? How in hell do they expect me to wash properly? And they call this a towel?

"Hey, out there: answer me. Where in hell is the damn soap?"

The last expletive was punctuated by the washroom door swinging open and banging against the wall.

"Hey, out there: didn't you hear me?

"Hey! There ain't nobody out here! Wonder where in hell they all went?"

With that final outburst, Dr. Crank proceeded to stretch himself out on a bench and take a nap—albeit quite a sonorous one.

Now back to my problem.

Actually, I reasoned, this would be a good time for me to start a dialogue with both Anna and the Reverend Bill. The Prophet, his acolyte, and the preacher—and not to forget, a bird: this was the stuff that legends were made of.

CHAPTER 65

"Let's see now," the Reverend Bill muttered to himself. "Those old jeans and these shirts that Maeve really dislikes ... calls them Farmer John shirts. She says that they don't befit a man of my position. They should fit Doc Crank, however. Even if they don't fit like custom clothes, beggars can't be choosers."

"Hmmm," he added a moment later. "I think I just made a pun".

"ARRKKK! At least your mood has gotten a little brighter since this morning. If you ask me, it couldn't have gotten any worse ... but I'm sure you won't ask me. Arrkkk!"

"Welcome, Virgil," Anna said in a most respectful tone. "I must admit that your earlier appearance as a beam of sunlight was quite awesome.

"I don't know what or who you are or whether you are a messenger from the gods or indeed God himself ... although that thought conveys an overwhelming wave of emotion within me."

"Anna Walks With Grace, I am neither God nor his messenger. I am instead the embodiment of what was once an uncomplicated existence within nature's bounteous endowment, which was provided to all who worshipped her simple order. My race existed within that world since its birth and was free to exercise a credo of respect for all living things."

"Ahhh. And where are your people now, Virgil? Why have they not joined together and faced down that evil you so fervently describe?"

That question ignited a spark in the minister.

"Yes, if you claim that you are so righteous and are just one member of an entire race of related entities," he chimed in, "why would you

222

need the aid of a little girl whose very existence could be threatened by you?"

"My people, as you so succinctly describe them, have retired to the forests or wherever they may be isolated from your species. They do not understand your need for self-destruction and your penchant for sheer evil. Evil was never a part of our existence and was in no way part nor parcel of our vernacular.

"It was the human race that invented that term, and it was the human race that elevated it to the lofty position it now holds.

"Your history is resplendent with evil, and your race doesn't strive for its removal. It seems to need a homecoming, and I believe that's what it truly is, to recall a sincere reason to exist."

At that statement, Anna interjected her voice.

"Virgil, you cannot sincerely believe that the entire human race is innately evil. There is goodness and morality out there. Even you will have to admit that fact."

"Absolutely," the minister added. "I could not hope to convene a congregation such as the one I have assembled without sincerely believing that morality survives and that there are enough souls desiring to share that tenet."

"Aye, but the numbers are receding, and it is time again for evil to return and reclaim its inheritance. It has surfaced countless times in the past, only to have receded, much as an epidemic will recede on its own. It is never completely eradicated, but instead waits in the wings for a replenishment of its power, almost as if it succeeds in completing its assignment and withdraws until, according to Malthusian concepts, a reckoning has been reached whereupon human reproduction has surpassed the ability to feed itself."

"Come on, Virgil," the minister said in a condescending tone. "Even you don't believe that nonsense. The plague was delivered to man as a segment of God's great plan, as are all events that humanity must endure to ultimately reach the forgiveness and love that God bestows on all who practice his ideology."

"Come on yourself, Reverend," I counterattacked. *"Are you telling me that your God sanctioned the Holocaust and the killing fields of Cambodia to be an integral part of his great plan for humanity?*

"And the Black Death ... did your God create the filth and deprivation of humanity to welcome the infestation of disease-ridden rats to kill off almost sixty percent of the existing world's population?

"I don't think I would ever have the desire to fully comprehend the final plan he has in store for your species."

"That is a topic we could debate for all eternity. It revolves around an austere belief system and one's definition of faith."

"Agreed ... and perhaps we can address that debate at length sometime in the future?

"We have more important matters at hand.

"If I had the necessary proof and were able to observe it firsthand, I would be able to project oncoming terror to you. As it turns out, a compatriot of mine has traveled to Africa to view the scene for me. When he returns, I'll have a better idea myself of the devastation we can expect and the timeline for its arrival."

Anna responded to that statement by asking, "You never mentioned a compatriot, Virgil. Is he also one of your kind?"

"He is, and Leader is his name. He and I had been separated for many, many years and only recently recommenced our relationship. He is a bit more animated, as well as more adventurous, than I am, but he has a good heart and will do all in his power to aid us in our cause. His experiences, as well as mine, would fill innumerable volumes of historical relevance, and I have no doubt that our tales would, in no small manner, alter the course of written and accepted history.

"But, as in our future discourse of your God's plan, I'll have to put off another discussion on many of history's misconceptions.

"All I ask now is for the Reverend Bill to allow himself to give serious thought to what you and I have accepted as fact, Anna.

"What say you, Reverend?"

"As you wish. But I do want to hear what your ally, Leader, reports as soon as he returns, if that is agreeable to you."

"It is, and if I may suggest it, you should return to the mission soon. I think Doc Crank is off and running again. He was ranting and raving about soap and his new clothes.

"I hate to say it, but he's definitely one egg short of a dozen."

"He is one of God's children," the minister declared. "And he is part of his plan. But, as promised, we won't go into that at the present time."

It was at this point that Anna said, "I must disagree with you, Virgil. I do not accept your prophesy as fact ... yet.

"I will admit, however, that you do paint a rather convincing picture. I am relying upon my faith and visions as well as your declarations, so be comforted in the knowledge that I am taking this matter very seriously."

"*I appreciate your honesty very much, and as soon as Leader returns, I'm sure that all of your hesitancy will be alleviated—yours as well as the Reverend Bill's.*

"*Until then, I would strongly suggest that the two of you return to the chapel and tend to the good Dr. Crank. But wear kid gloves; he's off and running on a different level than most humans do.*"

CHAPTER 66

"He is a most interesting person, this Dr. Crank," Anna said. "I'm curious as to what his story is.

"I feel a serious conflict within his psyche ... perhaps the possession of an obvious cultured background that, for some inexplicable reason, is being deprived of personal worth when he realizes its emerging presence in discourse with others?"

"Anna, don't you have enough to deal with without taking on another cause?"

"He is a lost soul. How can I not offer whatever solace and guidance is within my power to tender?"

"You are indeed an image of hope in a scenario of despair. We shall make a formidable alliance when it comes time to confront our nemesis from across the sea."

Just then, the Revered Bill returned with his shopping bags of fashion outcasts.

"I've prepared a wardrobe fit for a man of his unique and questionable stature—a king of the road; a most genteel rapscallion, and so on and so forth.

"Anna, will you accompany me to the chapel and see to the garbing of our guest?"

I was beginning to like this man. He may have been opinionated and stubborn, but he did possess a refreshing sense of humor, and that was one of the most important traits that man could claim as his own.

I would follow them shortly, but until then, I had to confront this uneasiness I was finding myself mired in.

Unfamiliar territory.

CHAPTER 67

At times in the past, my relationship with an individual occasionally reached a point where I would question my own choices. *"Have I said the right thing?"* "Is my advice directed toward the most advantageous conclusion?" *"Am I protecting my charge to the best of my ability?"* Those doubts were but fleeting thoughts in an existence of heartfelt truth and compassion.

I've never really felt it necessary to seriously question my actions. I don't think that I have ever indulged in a sense of false bravado, for I've always believed that my intentions were sincere, and although I might not have been successful 100 percent of the time, my efforts were without an iota of malice.

Maybe I was flip or mischievous, but only as an attempt to alleviate a more serious situation and to escape the solemnity of the moment.

I could not recollect a time when my direct involvement in a situation would affect such a multitude of humans. One person, one soul, yes. But millions and possibility billions of souls? Never! The very future of a species could ultimately be decided by my assessment of the state of affairs that would present itself.

My belief that I could absent myself for an interval and frolic with the squirrels was always available to me. Unless my charge was experiencing a life-altering situation, my absence wouldn't be felt; at least for the moment.

My existence was ideal. I could dispense a bit of peace and compassion for an entity in need, and I could innocently cavort within a circle of tranquility at my discretion.

All that innocence, while still contained within a sphere of purity, had now been most rudely infected with a sense of insecurity ... and yes, possibly, fear. In fact I may have been more human that previously considered and, until now, that was not a bad gift. Somehow, I had the premonition that I would no longer be able to cavort with my squirrel friends, because I feared that I would not possess the innocence that was so prevalent in their social order.

I fully recognized the infestation, for lack of a better term, of emotions and feelings that have been the primary motivation for actions and inactions among individuals and societies in general. These forces have provided the impetus for second thought and hindsight brought to life by the many decisions and objectives of everyday human existence.

I was not human; so why was I suddenly endowed with this assignment—which, in turn, birthed this unfamiliar agitation in my thoughts?

Who, or what, entity had provoked my interference in a trial of such magnitude that the smallest mistake in judgment could spell the ultimate extinction of a life force otherwise endowed with the unique potential for a most rewarding future? I was sorely tempted to effect a human response by screaming, "*Why me?*"

I would soon be directly involved in the decimation of countless lives. Whether those lives were innocent or culpable of unheard of horrors is insignificant; this had never been my credo, and I had never considered such blame to be a factor. It was never my distinction to make, nor one that I coveted.

I would gladly absorb many of man's qualities, especially when they presented themselves in deeds of selfless expression: humor, love, and sensitivity, all possessing a proclivity for righteousness. However, I could not and would not be endowed with hate, aggression, greed, and self-aggrandizement at the cost of a complete absorption of human traits.

What my evolutionary path promised me in the future was too abstract to comprehend, nor did I want to recognize it. For all intent and purposes, I could very well be the seed of a new life form that could conceivably be the creation of a society both industrious and benevolent, whose goal would be the betterment of all life ... another responsibility that would someday be the origin of great conjecture. But for now, more serious problems awaited consideration.

The first step will be to gather a list of the forces that I consider to be on the side of radiant goodness and then to organize them into an armada of might, by which the upcoming conflict will be met and hopefully shattered for the foreseeable future. Hear me, for I am under no false assumption that whatever victory we achieve—if that be our destiny—will be a permanent one or that another and more potent force won't present itself at a later date. The present can only affect the future as long as the subjects allow it to; but history has proven time and time again that it will repeat itself, utilizing bigger and more efficient weapons of catastrophic proportions.

Maeve and Patch will obviously be brought into the scheme of things, with emphasis on the glossing over of the severity of the scenario for the benefit of the young child. However, methinks that Patch is smarter and more astute then I give her credit for, and she will soon discover for herself what the threat encompasses.

For now, I am compelled to await Leader's return and get a firsthand account of the shrike's progress. That will afford me the knowledge necessary for me to implement my strategy for the upcoming conflict.

CHAPTER 68

I attempted to push my thoughts aside and join my fellow do-gooders as they attempted the beautification of a perennial weed garden. I feared it would take a spreading of a concentrated dose of fertilizer to alter that blight.

The Reverend Bill was quietly addressing Doc Crank in an attempt to awaken him.

"Hey, Doc? I've got some new clothes for you. Why don't you wake up now and try them on?"

"What the hell do you want? Can't you see you're disturbing my sleep? Where the hell are your manners?

"Ahh, Reverend, and good sister Anna; it is so good to once again bathe in your most perfect company.

"Please accept my apology for my rude repose in your home. I am duly embarrassed for taking advantage of your generosity and sincerely beg your forgiveness."

"No need for apologies, Doc. You were obviously in need of a well-deserved rest, and Anna and I ask your forgiveness for disturbing you.

"I've prepared a wardrobe of clothes that I hope you will accept as our display of friendship."

"What can I say but thank you? You have touched my heart in a manner that has not been accomplished in many a year.

"My present circumstance has tended to repel such outgivings of kindness. I accept, in all humility, your gift and would like to offer my services in return.

"What can I do for you to extend my gratitude?

"I am a whiz with a mop and have been known to hammer a nail and saw a plank or two."

This guy could surely pile it on, although I didn't think it was an act; he still retained the refinement and sophistication of a bygone time

I was curious, as I believe both the minister and Anna were, as to the cause of his collapse into the despair he found himself in at the present. He might be crude and antagonistic at times, but he was also a gentleman and most sociable at other times.

"Anna, what do you think? Can we find a place for the doctor in our group?"

The smile that enveloped her face answered that question.

"Reverend Bill, you old softie, I'm sure he will be a valuable asset to the congregation. So I answer yes to your question."

"Doc," said Bill. "Why don't you go and try on your new clothes? I also brought you some towels and a bar of soap to refresh yourself."

Upon the closing of the door to the back room, Anna turned to the Reverend Bill and asked him, "What are you going to say to your wife and Patch about the new man? Are you sure that he won't pose a threat to them?"

"Are we ever sure of anything, Anna?" he replied. "I believe that he was sent here for a reason, and he wouldn't have been if there were any possibility of harm to either myself or to my family."

… and from the back room, a tirade: "God damn it! I can't get these damn pants off. Damn things must be glued on my damn legs! Need a damn hose to get 'em off! Damn it!"

"Are you sure you want him around Patch?" Anna asked. "He's apt to scare her to death. I'm not concerned about Maeve; her Irish temper ought to keep him in line. It's the little one I'm concerned about.

"Dr. Crank, eh? I wonder what his real name is."

"I share your concern, Anna, but again, I feel he's here to serve a purpose, and that purpose is not to cause injury to us."

"I hope your assessment is correct; with that, I am off to the res. There are tribal needs to address, and I feel this is the time for me to meditate and seek guidance from they who speak in whispers."

"Adios, Anna; a safe trip to you, and may the gods look after you ... and I mean all of our gods."

"... and to you, Reverend Bill. *Vaya con Dios.*"

CHAPTER 69

SLAM! SLAM!

"Daddy, we're home, and we just saw Anna Walks With Grace. Where are you?"

"I'm here, sweetheart," he answered through an open window.

A hurricane blew through the door as little Patch stormed in. "Daddy, Daddy, we're home! Did you miss us? We missed you!"

"Does the monkey miss his tail? Can the elephant miss his trunk?"

"Daddy, you're so silly!" she said as she leaped into his arms.

The look on his face was most assuredly the envy of all creatures. Humans have such a capacity for love that one cannot imagine the dichotomy of love versus hate that so permeates their world. It has been said that it takes less effort to smile than to frown, and I must be smiling … somehow.

"Hi, sweetie. Did you have fun today with Mommy at the gallery?"

"We sure did," said Maeve as she shut the door behind her. "Tell Daddy about the funny man who was there this morning."

"Okeydokey. Daddy, there was this funny man dressed in old smelly clothes who walked around the gallery, singing silly songs. Mommy was going to ask him to leave, because she was afraid that he would scare the other customers away."

"… and what happened then?" Bill asked.

"Well … he really liked the art and the jewelry and the rugs, and when he wasn't singing, he was very polite to the other people and even described the stuff to them."

"He did, eh? Did he give you his name, by any chance?" the minister inquired.

"He had such a silly name, Daddy. He said his name was Dr. Crunch or something like that."

"Dr. Crank, honey," added Maeve.

Trying not to act shocked, Bill asked, "... and what happened to your Dr. Crank?"

"Well, he stayed there for a while, and then he just ... disappeared."

"Disappeared? He just disappeared?"

Maeve sort of shrugged and answered him. "He just disappeared. It was the strangest thing. First he was there, entertaining the visitors with his knowledge of the native art and singing the most ridiculous songs, and the next thing we knew, he was gone, much to the chagrin of the customers. 'Twas very strange indeed."

"Hmmmm ... very strange indeed, eh?"

Just then, as if someone had called for a segue, a song burst forth from the back room in the most powerful basso profundo the chapel had ever contained.

♪ ♫ ♪ ♪

"Hey, Jolly Molly, how're you, my little Dolly?

Awash in yer 'tire of pink, by golly.

♫

Did ya ... did ya dance today,

on the first of May?

♫

Or did ya sing a song to your Polly?" [29]

♪ ♫ ♪ ♫

"It's Dr. Crank, Daddy!" Patch cried as she ran to the back of the room just as the hobo virtuoso entered the chapel attired in his newly acquired sartorial splendor.

Crank to you, but that idiot song sounds vaguely familiar, Bean pondered.

"Away, away we fly, little princess, into the arms of your Prince Charming; only he has the power to keep you from the evildoers that this world is rife with."

"Prince Charming? You?" Bill sputtered. "Will someone please tell me what in blazes is going on here?"

"Shhhh, Bill, it's all right," Maeve soothed him. "Patch is in no danger from him. There is a sort of connection between them that is almost spiritual—even eerie, if you ask me. They seem to converse without speaking."

Dragging the wayward wretch by the hand, Patch came face-to-face with her father and begged, "Can he stay, Daddy? Please, can he stay?"

Bill glanced over to his wife, who nodded affirmatively. "Well, Mommy seems to think it will be all right. But he has to promise to behave himself and make himself useful around the place. Agreed?"

"Most assuredly, my liege. I am yours but to command, and 'tis mine but to obey. Cast all your doubts asunder, for I will prove to be a most worthy chattel."

"Good grief, what have I gotten myself into this time? First an orphan bird who prophesizes doom, and now a homeless poet with a dual personality! Maybe I should lock the two of you in the house from now on?"

"Pshaw, me love; everything has a purpose under heaven. I'm sure that it will all prove to be a fortunate happenstance," Reverend Bill said to Maeve.

"As you wish; let's all head to the house. I'm starved, and I'm sure that the good doctor also suffers from a growling belly. What say you, Crank?"

"Aye, a morsel or two of a tasty repast would be most agreeable at this time.

"But first, I would like to straighten my facade a bit and arrive at your abode in a manner best suited to your kind and generous hearts."

CHAPTER 70

Something was not right here. I know that I had seen him before, but somehow, his identity evaded me. Know that this phenomena doesn't occur very often, especially with my extensive experience and memory.

"*Hola*, Bean, my compadre. It's not your memory that eludes you; it's just an expansion of my—or should I say our—powers."

"Leader! Is that really you? How did you ever accomplish that? You actually became a visible entity and were able to have a physical substance. Will I be able to create that effect? When did you learn to do that? When did you return from Africa? Were you able to glean any information about Lili-It? My God, man—man?—speak up!"

"Whoa, and slow down with the questions. There is plenty of time for us to converse and for me to ease your anxieties. We'll have a sit-down after I dine with the Fellows family. You're most welcome to join us in your Virgil-ness."

"You can bet your ions I'll be there, complete with preened feathers and a squawking excitement."

"Let's proceed then to our—or should I say, my—place at the dinner table. It's time to *crank* up the situation."

CHAPTER 71

"I have arrived, my newfound friends, and I bring you greetings from this time-worn example of a life besotted with woe. I would cautiously suspect that my fortunes have changed and, with the anticipation of the upcoming feast at your table, I am certain that the emptiness in my stomach will now be sated, as will the emptiness in my soul. Huzzah!'

"Huzzah, indeed!" spake—oops, I mean *spoke* the Reverend William Fellows. "Let's see if we can enjoy a quiet meal tonight. I really don't think that I can take any more weirdness today."

"Oh, hush up, Bill! If it weren't for the excitement that each moment provides, we might as well be slugs."

"Yes, Daddy, hush up!"

"Oh, no! Not you, too?"

"I am afraid I might have introduced a bit of tension into the calm of this house. If you wish, I will retire to my sanctum sanctorum and leave a most excellent family to the enjoyment of this fine meal."

"Please ignore him, Doctor," Maeve said. "He's being a bit of a grouch this evening. I'm not sure what it is that's irking him, but I have a good idea, and it has very little to do with your presence."

*"Aarrrk! For want of a fork, the pea shall fall. *[29]* Aarrrk!"*

---

29   Stephen Stuart, *Rantings* (2009).

"Virgil! Will you please shut up!"

"Aarrrk! For want of a word, the fool shall be silent. [30] *Aarrrk!"*

"Will someone tape his beak shut?" Bill asked the room. "There is no more room in my head for this cacophony of absurdities."

"Virgil, Daddy wants this to be a quiet meal. You and I can talk later, okay?"

"Arrkkk! Your wish is my command, me love. Arrkkk!"

"Omigod, he's mimicking you now, Maeve. Do we have any recipes for cockatoo stew in that old cookbook of yours?"

"However," I added, "I shall resign myself to your wishes—or should I say, demands—and behave myself."

Suddenly, the minister started laughing, and pretty soon, everybody was laughing. The tension had broken, and they ate, albeit with brief interruptions of grins, titters, and out-and-out hilarity.

"Tell me, Doctor: what brings you here to this peaceful dot on the planet? It would appear to me that residence in a large, populated area would be more to your advantage than a field of sand and cactus."

"Ah, my good religioso, 'tis a fair question and deserves an answer that I will attempt to enlighten you to.

"I have wandered this world for many a year and have seen much unhappiness and despair. I have been invisible to most people, as they were wont to stroll through me. I have pleaded for alms and have received naught but a penny's worth. I have reposed in doorways; under bridges; and when the opportunity arose, under the joyous celebration of a billion universes.

"My path led me here for what, I do not know, but I do believe in the wonder of a future day wherein we shall all reminisce that it was indeed an advent of hope for one and all. It is as if I were directed here by an invisible entity with an agenda that will become evident in the upcoming days."

"Well said, Doc," Bill said. "Perhaps your arrival is a good omen, as you seem to believe. But for now, I think we should bow our heads in silent gratitude for the bounty that has been placed before us and then lift our forks and partake of that most delicious bounty.'

"Aarrrk! A tear from a bloodshot eye has emerged. Aarrrk!"

---

30   Stephen Stuart, *Rantings* (2009).

"Yonder image of avian beauty has the mouth of a poet coiffed in a visage of fine plumage. And yet, the caged one should be seen and not heard. Perhaps a fricassee of parrot served upon a bed of wild-rice pilaf?"

"I couldn't have said it better myself," intoned the minister.

"Aarrrk! Bitter words! Bitter men should be seen and not heard. Aarrrk!"

The glance I received from Reverend Bill would turn coal dust white. "Later my feathered friend", his expression said. "Later".

"Tell me, Doc, what's the cause of your apparent personality changes? You bounce from a rash, truly outspoken scoundrel to a most cultured genteel image of civility. I am curious as to whether or not you are aware of the altered states."

"Ah, you've noticed? ... and I thought that those changes were imperceptible to all but a chosen few. Congratulations! You must be chosen."

"Chosen? By whom?"

"By whom? That's a fine query, my most excellent religioso. Actually, I have no idea.

"But 'Why?' is another question and one deserving of a true and righteous answer.

"Hmmm, where shall I begin my saga ... and how brief be the telling? Stop me, my newfound friends, if my tale imposes numbness to your minds."

"What have I gotten us into?" mused Bill. "Go ahead, Doc and be certain that I will interrupt you if dullness reigns supreme or if you become akin to an ice-cream headache."

"A fair and most descriptive statement.

"As I stated before, I have traveled much over a great deal of this earth during the many, many years of my existence, and in doing so, I have been in contact with an extremely wide slice of humanity. Be they of gentle persuasion or be they aggressive, all were the image of man's, pardon me, fair damsel, it is but a generic term from a widely traveled and varied soul.

"I am but a simple person," "*Simple, my sparks!*"—"and am dismayed at the turbulence exacted by those of a belligerent and destructive nature. My attraction is drawn to the more gentle and kind societies, and it is those cultures that I chose to emulate. Thus you see before you my presentation of their spirit."

"How noble," said Maeve. "I couldn't have said it better. You have an Irish spirit, Doctor. Perhaps your lineage goes back to the auld sod?"

"Old sot, perhaps," Bill said. "The only sod in his background is the sod he has tainted with his body when he chose it to be his mattress."

"Bill, don't you think it's time for you to stop with the sarcasm? Dr. Crank is our guest, and if I am not mistaken, he will be for a while."

"Again I bow to your sensibility, my love.

"… and to you, Doc, my apologies. Please continue with your tale. Despite my obvious derision, I'll admit that I'm a bit intrigued by your background. Can you be more explicit about the people and places that you have visited?"

I beg you not to apologize for I am unworthy of it.

"As far as people, places, and things are concerned ... all in good time.

"I request forgiveness, for I have sidetracked us diners from the enjoyment of this most glorious feast long enough, and I must abandon myself now to a relief of my exhaustion. So to bed I go, with the expectation of the peaceable slumber long missing for this man.

"'Twas a strange, but a sincerely rewarding day for this errant child of the misbegotten; so I beg your forgiveness as I take leave of your presence, and I harbor an acute anticipation to a new day filled with new surprises and splendid rewards."

"'Night, Doc."

"A good night to you, Doctor Crank."

"Sleep tight, and don't let the bedbugs bite."

"*Aarrrk! Behold, for the air is cleansed once more. Aarrrk!*"

I've never seen a person move so quickly as when the minister flung his napkin at poor Virgil's cage. The terrified squawking that resulted from that sudden attack did not emanate from yours truly; it was instead a response from the prisoner himself.

"It's okay, Virgil; Daddy didn't mean anything bad. He was just playing with you. It's just his way of saying hello.

"Here is piece of lettuce for you. I'll come over and visit with you after dinner. Okay?"

What a sensitive child she is. The fates sure have a predisposition for choosing worthy subjects for their work.

It was at this juncture that I decided to extricate myself from this venue and rely upon Virgil's terror as my excuse for not communicating with Patch. I had more important things to do, such as berating my "friend" Leader. He had a lot of explaining to do.

CHAPTER 72

"It's good to see you, Leader. I was going to say, "again", but did I ever actually see you?

"No matter; what I want to know is, to put it briefly ... everything!"

"First of all, we—our species, that is—have the power to transmit via sight and thought any image we choose. But having the ability doesn't mean that all of us have the knowledge of its existence. Perhaps it's a good thing, because in the wrong hands (a human colloquialism), the potential for catastrophe is enormous. I will confess, however, that I have never utilized it until now, although I have attempted to in the privacy of my surroundings.

"Nevertheless, I felt that introducing myself into the situation at this juncture would accomplish two things: first and foremost, I could develop a relationship with the child without fomenting any suspicion that I am nothing more than a strange man; and second, I could induce her—unbeknownst to her, of course—to become aware of her abilities and of her future responsibilities."

"I was expecting to achieve that myself."

"But if you give the matter some thought, how seriously could she consider your profundities if they emanated from a ... and I don't mean to be facetious ... a bird?

"To put it more bluntly, my lord, you 'aarrrk' too much!"

"To be serious for a moment, Leader, I am beginning to have trepidations about the entire situation. I'm just a simple imp with no experience with matters of this complexity. I've never organized

anything beyond my own interventions, and they required no one but myself to achieve their end goal.

"Now I find myself with the awesome responsibility of managing a potential cadre of warriors to engage in an impending conflict wherein the outcome could be disastrous to humanity.

"This is not who I am, nor is it what I am! How can I consciously arrange an act of aggression that could conceivably cost the lives of countless people?

"No, I'm not the right entity for this adventure. I don't even know if what I believe to be a serious threat isn't just my imagination."

"The potential threat is not your imagination! I repeat, it is not your imagination! The danger is real and is more insidious than we first realized. Not only that, but it is progressing at a very alarming rate!"

"The question of my responsibility in the matter can be debated ad infinitum, but I'm afraid that due to the total absurdity of its premise, the veracity of my musings would be distorted until there will be no chance that it could be accepted.

"One can take a question, no matter how it is supported by fact—if indeed there is fact—and distort it beyond all recognition, as if it were trash strewn upon an ocean of rhetoric, by using subterfuge, lies, misquotes, and out-and-out crocodile emotion.

The chance of an intelligent debate, whereupon ideas and hypotheses are presented intellectually and with no ulterior motive other than to reach a conclusion acceptable to all, is nigh onto impossible. If one remembers the furious and emotional debates that occurred in 2009 and 2010 concerning health reform in the United States, then my 'preposterous' warning of a potential conflict of heroic proportions is not so off the wall.

"Crocodile sincerity has become a very marketable trait, because the people want to believe that all is well with the world, and anyone who dispels that dictum is nothing more than a kook wallowing in paranoia.

"So, Leader, what chance do I have of convincing anyone that a potential conflict of heroic proportions is inevitable?"

"If you put it that way? No chance whatsoever.

"I have witnessed destruction such as I have never seen before, and as you know, I have been an observer of a great many scenes of devastation throughout history. This Lili-It and her aide-de-camp, Whoever, as you refer to him, have created a small but auspicious black

hole of total obliteration with her birth village at its epicenter, and it doesn't appear to encounter any obstacles to its sinister advance.

"The trees were devoid of bark and foliage, the loss of which left the branches resembling grotesque stick figures out of a children's horror story.

"The ground was a mixture of brown and gray, as you would expect the surface of the moon to be. If I looked closely, I could make out the carapaces of insects and the skeletal remains of birds and beasts as they slowly turned to dust, leaving nothing behind except memories of what was and what will never be again. And mingled with the fading imprint of life, I was able to differentiate what had once been the understructure of those unfortunate humans who had not escaped the debauching of their world.

"If I were able to realize the sense of smell, I'd distinguish, perhaps, an indescribable miasma of noxious odors. Being unfamiliar with the experience, I would venture to say that it was the smell of death.

"In fact, I would expect the various media to begin reporting on this 'anomaly that seems to spreading in Central Africa.'"

"Are you including all manner of life—animal as well as plant life?"

"Total annihilation of all life forms: a veritable black hole!

"Bean, I have seen wars of indescribable brutality; I have seen men and women do things to their fellows as would be festive in hell; but I have never seen devastation on such grand scale as I witnessed in Lili-It's wake."

"What can she possibly hope to achieve from a dead world? She would rule a world devoid of souls over which to rule. I don't get it!"

"What about the preparation for a repopulation of the earth by an alien species?"

"I think we should stop right there. It's probably just an intervention of pure evil committed by an agent of pure evil. There is no other explanation. Can't you accept evil for the sake of evil?"

"Too simple, Bean; there must at least be an irrational—at least for us rational folk—explanation for their obscene actions."

"If you discover that explanation, I trust you will enlighten me?

"Now I think it's time we formulated a workable plan. However, I have no idea how to proceed!"

CHAPTER 73

"Okay," Leader said, "this is what we're going to do. You are going to attend a meeting of those whom you believe to be possible allies. It will be undoubtedly be at a service of sorts in the chapel.

"You will then concentrate very hard on an individual who will be absent from the meeting and who you feel that the congregation will pay heed to.

"If you do this successfully and are able to withstand any and all distractions, you will project that individual's image for all to see.

"Once that feat is accomplished, I will transmit the images I was party to while observing Lili-It.

"If that doesn't persuade the group, we might as well return to the forest and hide under a large rock!"

"I don't know, Leader. It sounds rather far-fetched to me. Now I have to become a projector introducing a three-dimensional image of the man who isn't there? What next, an original music score? This isn't a blockbuster media event, my friend."

"Actually, in a manner of speaking, it is nothing more than a media event of acute sensitivity.

"This is as good a time as any for you to try out your ability to project the image of an individual from your memory. Just relax, and erase those fears from your mind. Now choose a memorable character from the millions in your past and concentrate on him or her. I'll be quiet for a change ... at least I'll try to be."

Pick someone from my past, eh? How do you select one grain of rice from a bowl when they all tend to clump together?

"Come on, Bean—you have to concentrate!"

"It's like a wheel of fortune spinning and spinning, and where it stops, nobody knows."

"Now you're a carnie? One person ... just one person. It isn't that difficult, is it?"

Aha! I had one. I had spoken to Ghost about him a while ago, so he was still fresh in my memory.

Let's see ... eyes (that's very important) ... hair, height, voice ... hmmm ...

"That's it; I can see a faint shape emerging. Keep trying ... you're doing it!"

I wished he would shut up and stop interrupting my train of thought.

Interestingly, it was not as difficult as I had thought it would be. The more I focused on him, the more I remembered the nuances that were the essence of his being. *It's those eyes; I've got to capture those eyes.*

"You're almost there. I can see him as if he were standing behind molten glass.

"There you go. I knew you could do it. He's as clear and sharp as if he were standing next to us ...

"Wait a minute! It can't be!

"Omigod, Bean—it's Adolf Hitler!

"I can't believe you produced Adolf Hitler! Of all the millions of people from your past ... good people; benefactors of society; fun-loving, talented, beautiful people ... you produced Adolf Hitler?"

"Let's get something straight. I don't remember any restrictions on the type of individual I could experiment on, do you? Good. See, I had discussed him with Ghost a while ago as one of the subjects I had failed to influence ... and, well, he was still on my mind, especially now that we're arming against another evil persona.

"Don't worry. I won't produce him in front of the congregation. I've got someone else I'm thinking of.

"Actually, I think it would be quite humorous if Hitler tried to convince the Reverend Bill and Anna to fight evil. Just picture the looks on their faces."

"I have to admit it. You really had me going for a minute, and I actually thought you would introduce him to the cadre of this house of worship. Judging by your past protestations of insecurity, this would be a surefire way to put the royal kibosh on the entire project."

"Don't think I haven't given it a bit of a thought.

"But fear not, my brave and errant knight; we will band together as a well-oiled unit and defeat the minions of darkness. Huzzah ... huzzah!"

"I hear voices coming. It's time for **Dr. Crank** to reappear and for kindly ol' Adolf to vanish.

"Bean, did you hear me? Adolf ... vanish ... now!"

"Err ... you never told me how to erase an image once it appeared."

"Just stop thinking about him, you dolt!

"Congratulations: after spending a thousand years with those bloodsucking friends of mine, I must admit that you have surpassed them in your confoundedness!"

"I'm never too humble to accept a compliment. Thank you, Leader, and off to hell he goes."

CHAPTER 74

"... I don't know what to believe anymore, Maeve. Am I the only one who won't accept that the world is coming to an end and that our daughter is the only person capable of saving it?

"Talking about Patch, are you sure it's all right to leave her alone in the house?"

"She'll be fine. Virgil will keep her company, and she has the TV if she wants. We won't be gone long."

"I'm just a bundle of nerves, Maeve. Too much, too soon. Whatever happened to peace and quiet?"

"Take it easy, Bill. Come—sit down and relax. Sometimes the strangest and most unbelievable events have a basis in the reality we already knew.

"We both accept," Maeve continued, "the fact that Patch is an extraordinary child. We saw what happened when Giver of the Word passed and took leave of his physical presence. Why not then admit the possibility that perhaps, just perhaps, she might have the capability to perform what Anna says she can and must do?"

Maeve rested her head on Bill's shoulder and gently massaged his hand.

He remained pensive as she slowly raised it to her lips.

"What are you thinking now, me love?"

The minister straightened up, kissed his wife on her forehead, and started, rather hesitatingly, to finally expound on his true thoughts.

"I can acknowledge Anna's premonitions; she is a spiritual person and possesses certain primitive powers passed down to her in her role as shaman. Although as a Christian, I have a certain hesitation in acknowledging them, I won't deny her beliefs, as they are righteous in theory.

"Now," he continued with a gesture of disbelief, "comes a bird, reciting colloquies of similar prophesies of impending doom while intoning snippets of literary gems.

"On top of this mélange there is the mysterious appearance of a rather odious fellow wallowing in a seemingly confused state of mind. To add a touch of perplexity to the scenario, he also hints at an upcoming event.

"Granted, he hasn't mentioned Patch's involvement in this mysterious occurrence, but I'll wager that he will."

"Aye, and he will. But I must first mull over the preponderance of thoughts that are running unfettered through my cranial cavity. So be patient, my liege, it will become evident shortly. The truth will be told."

Startled, Bill turned toward the rear of the chapel and spied the object of his discourse lying on a bench with his arm raised in greeting.

"What the … I forgot he was here!

"I'm sorry if I woke you, Doc. My wife and I were just discussing some personal family matters. We'll leave now and permit you to catch up on your sleep.

"See you tomorrow."

"No need for you to depart on my account, sir and madam; I was enjoying your agitation and your decidedly confused state of mind.

"Be advised, sir, that your wife has espoused certain viewpoints that should be accepted for their wisdom and veracity.

"However, I can tell you that, without any doubt and without any further accounting to detail, you and your family will participate in a future event that will have a great impact on the destiny of your world.

"And now, without any further bandying of words, I wish you both peace and add: get the hell out of here and let me sleep!"

Not wanting to press the issue, Bill and Maeve shot the doctor a serious stare and took leave of the chapel and its peculiar inhabitant, closed the door, and headed home for what I believed would be a night of agitated sleep and much head-scratching—for the minister, anyway; his wife seemed to have accepted the possibility that all the predictions had the potential to become reality, especially those concerning the role her daughter would play in this modern tragedy. Chalk it up to a mother's absolute (some might refer to it as blind) love for her child no matter what it may entail and a father's natural instinct for the protection of his family. However, it has been said, and has been portrayed in books and film, that a mother's defense of her child—physical, verbal, or what have you—can overpower the strength of an assault on her child by man, woman, or beast.

The protection aspect runs the gamut from an immediate aggressive reaction to danger to the tortured reasoning of an intellectual approach to the crisis. There is much to say about each of the responses, and I'll leave it to you to mull it over and say either "Who gives a damn?" or "I wonder if what he said is true? Hmm ... gotta give it some thought."

CHAPTER 75

I took my leave of Leader and followed the Fellows as they followed their dreams[31] for Patch and returned to their house. I wanted to see if they continued the discussion or whether they felt that enough had been said for the time being.

"Shh," said Maeve, motioning to her daughter fast asleep on the couch. "She must have been exhausted; 'twas a long day."

"Bill, look at the peaceful expression on her face. It's almost as if she exists in a perfect world, awash in serenity, with nary a care to furrow her brow. What is it that they say about the innocence of youth—and when and from whom do the wee ones learn to fear and to hate? I wonder if there was ever a time when innocence was the way of all things."

"Eden," he answered.

"Aye," she answered, "but in Eden, there was no thought given to the propagation of the species. They just were; 'twas a further example of the Poof Factor; here one moment and gone another. There would be no Patch … and to take it a step further, no us. But there would also be no hate, no war, no bigotry—none of the sins that are said to be inherent in man. Could be called … boring?"

"Do I detect a theological slippage here?"

"Just tired, and more than a bit concerned for Patch's future."

"'Nuff said," he replied as he lifted his daughter from the couch and carried her off to her room.

---

31 A slight play on words from "Look to the Rainbow" from the musical *Finian's Rainbow* (1947); lyrics by E.Y. Harburg and music by Burton Lane.

It was at this time that I departed, feeling as if there would be no further dialogue, and returned to the chapel to bask in the company of Leader the Crank and his basket of surprises.

CHAPTER 76

"Well, Leader, I'm back. The family has retired for the night without any additional discussion of the pictures that were created so audaciously by us in their minds.

"I think that enough doubt has been planted in the minister's mind for us to be confident that he will slowly accept much of what we advocate."

"Do you really believe that, Bean?

"We don't have the luxury of expending a great deal of time and effort to alter the thinking of a stubborn mule."

"True, but a mule will bray and bray until he ultimately relinquishes his obstinacy and allows himself to be led forward."

"I don't know; we can urge him just so much with the lash of reality until he has formed impenetrable calluses and loses his sensitivity to its touch."

"We have no other choice at this moment. Patience is required, and we will afford him the respect he deserves.

"Now, did you learn anything useful on your trip to Africa? Did you figure out a timeline or location for our interception of Lili-It and Whoever—and, more important, do we have a chance to defeat them?"

"Questions, questions. Is that all you have to say to me after I've returned from such a harrowing trip?

"No 'Good to have you back' or 'Really missed you, Leader'?

"Are you quite finished yet?"

"All right, already; it's just my usual inane banter. I lose control periodically and submerge myself in an air of obnoxious revelry.

"When I arrived back at the village, I enveloped myself in a cloak of invisibility and was prepared to survey the situation. However, I was not ready for the scene of complete devastation that awaited me.

"No sensitivity toward the village's inhabitants was apparent in the remains; no compassion had been given to the community into which she had been born and in which she was raised. The village had been was thoroughly decimated.

"Her progress can be compared to the placing of a lit cigarette along the bottom edge of a sheet of paper. First the paper turns brown as it slowly heats up. Then the brown darkens to black before the paper ignites in a flame, which expands outward, generating an ever-increasing hole of total destruction.

"Despite the potential she encompasses and the area of waste she is accumulating, the spot is just a dark brown at the present. But be advised: it is on the verge of combustion, and once that happens, it will get progressively more and more difficult to extinguish.

"I do have to add one point that shocked me as well as it will astonish you: she knew I was there. Protected as I thought I was, it was not enough to avoid detection by that thing of evil, for I was assaulted by her voice injected into my mind.

"She spoke clearly in a sweet and seductive tongue, at first acknowledging my presence and then delivering a message undeniably meant for you."

"And what was that message?"

"In as sweet a voice as one can imagine, she said, 'Tell your impotent comrade to retreat into the background and avoid any conflict with me, or I will destroy him, you, and your little heroine, and I will track down all of the remaining members of your race and incinerate them. There will be no room left on this earth for any entity in opposition to me."

"Good God, Leader: has she truly been able to neutralize one of our most potent defenses? I shudder to think what additional power she will be able to employ against us!"

"I fear that as the hole of devastation increases, so will her strength, and our ability to combat her relentless advance will be weakened.

"If I'm not mistaken, her strength multiplies as she absorbs the souls of her victims, much as a vampire's influence is fortified by the blood of its subjects."

"What are you intimating?"

"As of now, the only souls she has managed to absorb are those of simple, primitive beings with very few aggressive tendencies; their essences instead encompassed the basic skills of survival. What scares me the most is the notion that as her sphere of influence grows, she will ultimately engorge herself with the sustenance provided by the characteristics perfected by the so-called enlightened world— and by that I mean the utilization of all the sophisticated methods of subjugation and aggression developed by modern civilized man, as well the facility to think outside the box and formulate new approaches to her achieving her goal.

"She is like a siphon slowly draining the tank of resistance and incorporating its fuel to increase the ease with which her engine will function."

"The picture just gets bleaker and bleaker. This affair d'morte strengthens my belief that Homo sapiens traces its ancestry to the African continent and that this same birthing place will be the cause of its extinction."

"What comes around goes around, eh? However, we also discussed that the notion of man's beginning taking hold in only one tiny spot on this entire globe is intellectually unbelievable. It is tantamount to saying that in the entire universe, with its myriad of solar systems, stars, and planets, only one orb encouraged life. The vast differences in physical characteristics between societies cannot be blamed on environment only.

"To substantiate that claim, a report was issued a few years ago that the remains of a forty-seven-million-year-old proto-human specimen were found in Europe.[32] If this is true, and anthropology is just a science built on theory and conjecture, as well as on bits and pieces of physical evidence, how did that simian—if indeed the proto-human was apelike in stature—manage to relocate thousands of miles away from his supposed place of birth? I'm sure the grass wasn't greener in some cave in Central Europe; I doubt he was

---

32   Author's note: This theory has since been disproved. The remains have been ascribed to that of a primitive mammal. Interesting; so was man at one time. Interestingly enough, the matter is still disputed.

lured there by an enticing path of peanuts or carried there by an errant kayak. To further strengthen my hypothesis, Peking Man supposedly arrived in China as a result of the 'great migration of Homo erectus' from the African continent only two million years ago.

"What is interesting is the conjecture that various species originated in diverse areas of the earth. Now the questions present themselves: Was it a random event that caused man to evolve in Africa and dinosaurs in places as varied as the isolated Patagonia or the fertile-soiled New Mexico? What in the ooze contained the specific ingredients for this motley banquet of life—or was it the result of an experiment initiated by an entity not of this earth to see which invention would ultimately survive?

"Assuming the migration theory is correct, why would man leave the warm, fertile, and bounteous continent of Africa and head to the freezing climate of the north countries? Perhaps one can put the blame on his underdeveloped brain?

"I suspect that the evolutionary/migration concept that places Africa at its nexus has, as its roots, the fact that more proto-human bones have been unearthed in Africa than in any other region on earth, because the weather is warmer and the ground softer."

"Judging by your take on the situation, what can we possibly do to counteract this malevolent force? How can we possibly endow Patch with power substantial enough to neutralize Lili-It?"

"Questions, questions, and with no answers to satisfy. The only advice I can offer is to take one step at a time."

"And the first step is ... ?"

"... Another query, and another bit of advice; you'll know when the time is ripe.

"Bean, I don't know if you realize it or not, but you are becoming more and more human, with your emotions controlling more and more of your thoughts."

"I've tried to avoid thinking about the potential evolution occurring within me. Your inherent powers and my newfound ability to project images in virtual reality combined with the apparent growth of human emotion in my mental structure leaves much to contemplate. But this is neither the time nor place to submerge myself in a distraction from our common cause.

So for now, I think I'll hover under the stars and recharge. As the good minister said, 'Too much, too soon.'"

"Go: hover away. I'll just stretch these rickety bones of Crank on the bench and snore myself into oblivion.

"Until tomorrow."

CHAPTER 77

I decided to return to Virgil the first thing in the morning. Inquisitiveness motivated my judgment, owing to a continuing curiosity as to whether any additional discussion would occur about our dilemma. On second thought, I decided to blend in with the environment, rather than unite with Virgil. Let him have his fifteen seconds of fame; all I wanted to do was listen.

"G'morning, Virgil," Patch said to her avian compadre.

"Arrkkk! The dawn brings forth a huzzah to life, and you are the light that shines brightest. Arrkkk!"

"Daddy, what did he say? Is he being silly?"

"Well, sweetheart," Bill said, "he is being silly, but he is undoubtedly quoting some epic poem from an obscure poet. That's why he was named Virgil."

That bird sure didn't need me to project profundities; he did well enough on his own.

"Arrkkk! *Obscuro ... obscuras ... obscuramos ... obscuran ...* arrkkk!"

"Is he speaking Spanish now?" Bill asked as he twisted in his seat and peered at the bird.

"Either he is a feathered savant, which I sincerely question, or some very lonely individual with an incredible amount of patience imbued in him a vast knowledge base. Just imagine the quantity of verbal triggers that must have been stored in his birdseed brain to enable him to respond as he does. Simply amazing!

"Hey, Virgil," Bill asked, "what's the name of the poet whose work you just quoted?

"Let's see if can answer that," Bill whispered to his wife.

Without batting a pinfeather, the whitewashed cockatoo replied in a deep, cultured voice and with a pure Castilian accent, "Arrkkk! *El poeta eth Ethteban. Un poeta muy obthcuro.*[33] Arrkkk!"

That set Maeve off in uncontrolled teary laughter, resulting in a spurting of orange juice onto the table.

Pretty soon, everyone was laughing, including me—which, I may add, is quite a feat. To top it off, Virgil himself started squawking in a facsimile of laughter, which only added fuel to an already hysterical situation.

The sound must have carried to the chapel, for who should arrive but Dr. Crank, resplendent in his new duds and with a calico handkerchief stuffed in his shirt front.

"What ho! Have I missed a performance from the family jester? Although I might appear to all as a miscreant, I do thoroughly enjoy a moment of levity. From whence comes the objet d' mirth?"

I had thought nothing could further incite the already unrestrained laughter, but I had been mistaken. The sight of Crank, with his hair slicked down in a spiffy comb-over, wearing a bright plaid shirt stuffed haphazardly into a pair of Farmer Johns that had been two sizes too small for him to begin with, not to mention the aforementioned bib, provided the stimulus for a new round of hilarity.

It was Maeve who appeared to be affected the most, for she left the table holding her stomach and rushing, I believe, to the restroom to relieve the sudden pressure instigated by the moment.

"Enough already," choked Bill. "Crank, sit down and eat your breakfast. My wife and daughter have to go to the gallery, and I have writing to do. This silliness must come to an end, and the serious nature of life must continue."

"Arrkkk! Horse puckies! Arrkkk!"

"Yon winged philosopher has indeed a way with words. The truth to man's existence lies somewhere within his proclamations; that is, if one spends a lifetime on the mountain."

---

33   "The poet is Esteban [Stephen]. A very obscure poet."

At that moment, Maeve returned, jackets in hand, car keys jingling, and lunch boxes filled with the day's comestibles.

"It's getting late, Patch," she said. "Hurry up and brush your teeth; we have to be at the gallery soon. Say good-bye to Virgil, and give Daddy a kiss. Don't forget Dr. Crank. He is our guest, and you should be polite to him also."

With a good-bye to the bird, a kiss to her dad, and a curtsy to the doctor, Patch ran off to prepare for her day.

Maeve duplicated her daughter's actions, including an exaggerated curtsy to the doctor, and was off to work with Patch.

"Doc; when you're finished with breakfast, I have some work for you to do at the chapel. The grounds need some cleaning up, and the plants could use some watering. See what you can do about that section of garden at the back of the house. I can't seem to grow anything there. You can also continue painting the interior walls of the chapel. I started to do it myself a while ago, but interruptions put the kibosh on it."

"Twill be my pleasure, good preacher. It is said that honest toil is one step nearer to heaven."

"Well said, Doctor. And if it is heaven you desire, you have arrived at the correct venue. I am the resident expert."

"Then we have a subject for extensive discussion at a later date, my robeless monk."

Leader the Crank left shortly after polishing off his breakfast plate, as well as everything else not consumed by the family.

With a robust belch, he closed the door behind him, and all was quiet once again.

It was time for me to initiate contact with Virgil and ease into a conversation with the minister.

CHAPTER 78

Bill cleared the breakfast table and prepared to do his daily paperwork at his desk.

I waited until he got comfortable before I addressed him. It was best for him to be a little rested ere I upset him again.

"Arrkkk! 'Tis a foine marning ta ya, Reverend Fellows. How be ya?"

"So now it's a brogue with you, eh? What's next, Pashto?"

"I would speak Pashto if I had any computer knowledge; sadly, I don't. Nevertheless, we must talk. Tempus fugit and all that stuff, you know?"

"*Tempus fugit* for you, maybe, but I don't have the time to spend on your theories of the coming apocalypse. I have the business of running my congregation, as well as the necessary upkeep of the chapel.

"People are in need of my ministrations, and the poor await my assistance."

"What if there came a time when that was gone, and survival was the all-consuming project? What if you had it within your power to truly aid those in need and provide them with a future, rather than just subsistence? Could you turn your back on them and ignore the fact that you had the prior wherewithal to prevent the coming upheaval?

"Not you, Reverend Bill. You are too benevolent to hide in the sand. So what is it that prevents you from facing the truth? Stubbornness? A conflicted belief system? Tell me, please. What can I say or do to win you over?"

"Proof. I need proof. Not just the rantings of a seed eater or the superstitions of a witch doctor. It's proof!"

"Other than transporting you to Africa, what is there?"

"You tell me. You're the one who bears the responsibility of convince me, aren't you?

"Enough for now, it's time for the news and then for Matt Christmas."

"I thought you had had enough of that character and his pretentious guests."

"I was pretty upset, wasn't I? You can't blame Christmas for the views of his guests now, can you?"

"Quiet now, the news is on!"

"... and fall has come early to the Arctic this year. It promises to be a very colorful one, and the tourists are flocking there in great numbers to admire the changing of the leaves. The hotels are filling up fast.

"From Africa comes an interesting story. It seems that the astronauts in the International Space Station have noticed a strange abnormality in the center of the continent. A definite black spot has made itself present, and after comparisons with previous passes over the area, the astronauts believe it is slowly enlarging.

"Scientists are baffled as to the cause and nature of the incongruity in an erstwhile verdant territory. The general agreement is that it is not the result of fire.

"That does it for this morning. Stay tuned for Matt Christmas and *Drop Back Ten and Punt*. His guest today is the esteemed futurist L. Forrest Greene.

"Remember: tomorrow is another day, and the news will definitely be new."

"Er, excuse me, Reverend. What did he say about Africa? ... Something about a black spot?"

"Coincidence, I'm sure".

"I'm sure."

"Shh ... my program is starting!"

"I'm Matt Christmas, and this is *Drop Back Ten and Punt*."

"Today's guest is the esteemed futurist and theoretical author L. Forrest Greene. Mr. Greene will talk today about absolutes in nature."

"But first, a word from our sponsor."

But first, some slick-looking character in a white jacket had to smoothly extol the virtues of a balm to grow hair. Couldn't see the need for such a thing myself.

"Dr. Greene, aren't absolutes necessary in the chaotic world we live in?" Matt Christmas asked upon the program's return. "Don't they offer a bit of constraint in the exploding social divergence that is captivating our society?"

"Interesting question, Matt. However, the only absolute is absolutely nothing.

"What, then, you ask, is the definition of nothing? If indeed the universe were created by a big bang, where did the elements that created the big bang come from if there had been nothing to begin with? We have to redefine absolutes ... or do absolutes exist at all? The only absolutes, as scientists tell us, are the absolutes of the speed of light and absolute zero; both are measured in an absolute, controlled environment, if they are measured at all.

"How do we know that space is an absolute vacuum? Scientists can only speak in generalities and conjecture, as their experiences in space are extremely limited. What exists just around the bend?

"The same would apply to absolute zero: is all of space subjected to the identical environment wherein absolute zero is not accessible? Is the lowest temperate recorded, that being −400°F on the moon, the closest measurement to absolute zero the scientists have discovered?

Absolutes, again, are based upon unknowns, with the exception of the conditions created in the lab—and yet even the lab hasn't been able to physically reach absolute zero. Therefore, the results of the achievement of that magic number remain hypothetical, based upon mathematical projections and assumptions.

"Scientists base absolute zero upon the following ratings: −459°F, −273°C, and 0°K. But here is a question that should scratch a few itches: if absolute zero is ever attained, what exists beyond it? Nothing? Or will it be a true absolute?

"We judge spatial distance based upon the time it takes for light to travel from one point to another. But does this widely accepted speed represent a true measurement, considering that light has to first travel through our

atmosphere, which in itself is not a pure vacuum? Perhaps the extraterrestrial object being determined has, as a shield, an atmosphere of its own, which would also tend to affect a precise calculation. What about the myriad of known and unknown anomalies that abound in the vastness of space? Would such things as the gravitational attraction of planets, asteroids, comets, asteroid belts, gaseous abnormalities, black holes, and so on and so forth corrupt the absolute of the speed of light?

"To measure the distance from one point to another, absolutes must come into play. For our calculations to be effective, a straight line must exist between the objects in question. I question the existence of a pure straight line; that, too, is an absolute. If the straightest line that man is able to produce is that of a laser, could not the beam be altered by its passing through various gaseous clouds or be distorted by the prismatic distortions of ethereal ice crystals?

"So what happens, then, to our concept of absolutes when calculations are inhibited by any number of unknowns? It appears that both 'nothing' and 'absolute' become abstract terms measurable solely in a rigorously controlled environment and in calculations based upon theoretical musings chalked on a slab of slate."

"Food for thought indeed, Forrest. And now, a word from our sponsor."

This time, it was a scantily dressed woman extolling the virtues of a balm that would remove unsightly hair. *Would somebody please make up their mind?*

"Enough of that drivel," Bill said as turned the TV off. "I wonder where Christmas finds these quacks. Does he choose his guests just to confound and entertain his listeners—or perhaps to provide a platform to demonstrate the inherent sincerity of false prophets? Ooops ... sorry, no personal slight intended. These guests' credibility leaves much to be desired, if you allow yourself to actually examine the drivel these purveyors of sour pickles dispense.

"Well, I've got more important things to mess up my mind with than the exhortations of some weirdo!

"You appear to be more distressed than usual, Reverend. May I be of any assistance?"

"I see that you do not inhabit your alter ego this morning. What do I owe this honor to?"

"No need for sarcasm; I have concerns for you. Don't consider it an honor, just ... one friend approaching another."

"You're my friend now, eh? After all this turmoil you created, I'm suddenly your friend? Wow! Friends like you, I don't need!"

"Are you finished yet? Let me know when your arm is exhausted from the self-flagellation you are so determined to inflict. Then perhaps we can talk?"

He was quiet for a while and just stared out the window at nothing in particular. His thoughts overpowered his ability to focus on anything visually. It was if he were in a trance.

After a few minutes, he seemed to snap out of his stupor and turned around to face the room. He wasn't able to see me, obviously, but this was of no importance; he knew I was there.

It was then I noticed that his eyes were filled with tears, and I observed tiny rivulets of liquid wending their way slowly down his face. This was a time for silence from me; words would have been most insensitive.

"I had a dream last night ... at least I think it was a dream. It was so real ...

"In it, Patch came to me first as a little girl—actually as she really is. 'Don't be concerned for me, Daddy ... I'll be fine,' she said to me.

"She then proceeded to enlighten me as to the same prophesies that both you and Anna have informed me about and that Crank alluded to. She started out with the voice of a child.

"Patch tried to convince me to accept the warnings and use whatever authority or influence I might conjure up in support of the efforts that you, Anna, and the powers that be control. As she spoke, her voice slowly matured, and as the scenario morphed into a vision of horror and devastation, Patch seemed to age. The visions became almost unbearable, and as her appearance shifted to that of a girl of about ten or twelve, she was suddenly consumed by flames and was transformed into a pile of ashes that dispersed as if a great wind had intruded upon her space."

"That must have been horrible for you. Please continue; it wasn't the end of the dream, was it?"

"She reappeared again as a little girl. But this time, she painted a different picture. In this setting, Patch, me, you, Anna, a legion of spiritual entities, and the souls of countless warriors enveloped in a brightness that was impossible for mortals to endure met and engaged in combating the evil that had been preordained as a test for man's destiny."

"And then what?"

"Now here is the strange part—as if the entire dream wasn't strange enough: as the story progressed, and as the confrontation tended to tilt toward our side, Patch again slowly aged. However, this time, she was transformed into a beautiful young woman, became a loving mother, and entered her older years content and secure in the knowledge that we had all done the right thing. Even stranger: her children were miniature versions of Maeve and me."

"That's not a bad alternative to the first part, now is it?"

"No, you're right. But there was one thing that troubled me, and that was the fact that neither Maeve nor I appeared as adults. Does that signify that we will not survive the conflict—hence our rebirth as infants—or am I reading more into the dream than is necessary?"

"I'm not a trained therapist, so I can't interpret the dream in psychoanalytical terms; but speaking as a layman, it would appear to me that the dream is a subconscious representation of the forces working in opposition within you. Right, wrong: good, evil: all would seem generate an untenable situation, given the parameters you have been blessed with. But remember—and this is most important—you are a man who sincerely believes in right and good. There should be no clash of ideals for you to agonize over.

"The depiction of Patch's destiny and the fact that you and your wife were not included as adults in the dream are of no consequence. It was just a dream, and nothing more! Perhaps—and I just may be stretching this pseudo analysis a little—Patch recognizes her powers and feels that she must protect you two from harm; hence the symbolic image of a mother and her children. What greater demonstration of protection and love is there?

"Remember, a dream is just a compilation of thoughts, images, experiences, and countless other stimuli. It is not reality, just a version of a fantasy conjured up in your mind. That fantasy may aid you in arriving at a solution to your personal indecision—to perhaps explain past events—or you may write it off as just that: a fantasy.

"No one but you can decipher it."

"It's just ... well, you know. It's against all I have been taught and believe in. However, if I believe in a God who in himself is just a manifestation of all that is good in man, why not trust in an alien spirit who professes to preach the same credo?

"You see, that is my dilemma: if I give you credence, have I slighted my God?"

"First of all, I am not a god, nor am I an alien, so erase those thoughts from your mind."

"Then what are you, if not some pagan deity?"

"The best way I can describe what I am is that I am an elemental entity endowed with the knowledge and powers that millennia of existence within a natural world have instilled within me.

"I am not to be worshipped, just heeded or ignored as desired. My powers far exceed the capability of mortal man to grasp, but be assured that they are used only for good and not to further any desire for supremacy over any natural species."

"Then accepting you does not in any way affect my faith in God?"

"Absolutely not! Your belief is so strong that your faith will never be tested—no sacrifice on the mount for you."

"I see. Give me some time to digest your latest reflections.

"To tell you the truth, I feel a bit relieved now. We'll continue this discussion later."

"Always a pleasure; feel free to discuss anything with me".

"There was another thing I was tentative about approaching you with."

"And what, pray, would that be?"

"Maeve had the same dream last night."

"But she didn't show any outward signs of anxiety this morning."

"That's because she's accepted the situation and feels secure in the knowledge that Patch will achieve the objective given to her and that she will ultimately come to no harm. Maeve sincerely believes that Patch will be the salvation of mankind, and that's the reason she was willed to us."

"... and you weren't going to tell me about that, eh?"

"Probably sometime, when and if I felt the time was ripe for such an assertion."

"... and how do you feel about it now?"

"Go now, and leave me to my work. Go ... scram ... skidoo!"

CHAPTER 79

"Where did you ever get the idea for that getup? You are the epitome of a cartoonist's depiction of a country bumpkin. And that comb-over ... that was a masterful finishing touch!"

"Methinks, O Invisible One, that you are pleased..."

"Cut that out, Leader! We have more serious things to discuss than your tonsorial masterpiece."

"We should take a minute or two and attempt to recover your errant sense of humor."

"ENOUGH!"

"Enough it is," Leader said, shedding his Dr. Crank persona.

"What've you learned since we last spoke?"

"Well, it appears that the minister is coming around. His daughter is developing her abilities swiftly and was able to insert herself into her parents' dreams. It proved to be a catharsis of sorts for both parties.

"I think that this Sunday's services might be a convenient time to make our first attempt at contacting the congregation. What think you?

"Sounds good to me, if you feel the time is right."

"How do we go about achieving it?"

"I'm not completely sure yet, but I believe that Patch will play a role in it.

"What I would like to accomplish is to produce the image of a respected individual and have you describe the situation in Africa as

you witnessed it. But before you do that, I will initiate the contact in order to attract the attention of the group.

"Once that is accomplished, you will take over and, using my same voice, you will proceed to do your bit. When you feel that you have related enough of your knowledge, I will again take over and bring the entire scene to a conclusion."

"Sounds like a plan."

"What I would like to achieve, ultimately, is the use of the same identity as our foil, if you understand what I mean—our spokesman. The congregants will believe him without question.

"My only reservation will be the Reverend Bill. He must accept what we are trying to do. Without his cooperation, the entire plan will fold no matter what Patch, Maeve, Anna, and her people feel.

"Sunday will be the telling moment."

"Not to worry, Bean. We'll put on an Oscar-worthy performance guaranteed to bring even a Sphinx to tears. There won't be a dry eye in the joint! I was a captivated student of the immortal Sarah Bernhardt."

"That's what I'm afraid of. I would prefer maybe the stoic Winston Churchill.

"No matter; it'll work out fine."

I was going to end our meeting when I remembered one last thing.

"Leader, when you were in Africa, did you attempt at any time to create a shield around Lili-It and Whoever?"

"No; I wasn't sure whether it would work, and I sure as heck didn't want them to know we had that ability, at least for the time being. It was enough for my presence to be sensed by her. Enough … and scary, if you know what I mean."

"Somewhere along the line, we will have to attempt it. But I'm not convinced that between the two of us, we have enough power to achieve a force field strong enough to contain the both of them for any prolonged period of time."

"Are you thinking the same thing I am? It will take an immense effort for us to convince the congregation to join us. I don't know if we have enough time to turn over every rock and leaf and convince our brethren that it is in their benefit to assist us—not only that, but to keep our allies shielded enough so that Whoever and Lili-It will not become aware of our unity."

"Agreed; so maybe you should leave now and start your trek to locate and enlist as many of the folks as possible? Convincing one will double your chances, and so on and so forth. It's just simple mathematics, and within a short time, we should have a good idea of our prospective strength."

"What about the disappearance of Crank? He's slowly gaining a reputation around here, you know."

"I'll take care of that; don't worry. Just hop on your stick and get going. If you can find a way to keep me apprised of your progress, I would appreciate it. Try to be back for Sunday's service. You can return to your efforts afterward."

"Will do.

"Roger ... Wilco ... and out."

I think this will be a good time for me to hibernate and spend some prime time in contemplation. Let everyone work out their uncertainties by themselves. Sunday will be the telling point as to whether we proceed with as much strength as possible.

My curiosity as to Patch's growing supremacy over the natural order is tickling my fancy.

One idea that has been bouncing around my ions—and one that has been fueled by Leader's revelations—is the possibility that she is one of us and has used her abilities to project the image of young child. What better way to achieve an appearance of innocence and trust than project the identity of a beautiful, loving little girl?

If my theory is true, she has developed well beyond Leader and myself, and if not, she is a true healer of bodies and souls. We'll find out soon enough.

CHAPTER 80

Sunday arrived, bestowing upon Leader and me a bright, clear stage for the first act in our production. The audience arrived soon after the main characters. Leader made his presence known to me a few minutes before the Fellows family made their debut in the chapel, but I wasn't able to question him on his quest—not enough time.

Everybody was curious as to where Crank had disappeared to. He had been gone for only a few days, and although the place was quiet once more, he had instilled a bit of levity in the everyday lives of the family that was markedly missed. I decided to remain mute as to the mystery of the missing miscreant; as he described himself. Knowing him, he would make his reappearance into a major production.

The Reverend Bill made his way to the altar as the congregants slowly took their seats. Maeve and Patch took their seats on benches in front of the minister, hands on their laps, and awaited his sermon.

Once the room had quieted down and the people finished greeting each other, Bill commenced his homily.

"I see that we are blessed with a fine and glorious day, and I bid you all welcome. A day such as this should make us all believe in God's love and realize that the aches and pains in our bodies and minds are the itch of a minor mosquito bite when basking in his magnificence."

For a while, he went on about the usual topic of right versus wrong.

"Who is right, and who is wrong? What is right, and what is wrong? Is a slap on the face more productive than reasoning when hysteria or overreaction presents itself? Is a physical confrontation called for when one does not possess the ability for deductive reasoning? Is physical confrontation a manifestation of man's brutal inheritance, as some scientists state?"

... and on and on. Unfortunately, I had heard this discussion time and time again. I was disappointed in his choice of topics; I had been hoping for a more thought-provoking subject. But, in reality, the focus area would provide a decent segue for our intervention.

Just as he was getting warmed up, Patch arose from her seat and approached the altar. Startled, the minister halted his speech and stared at his daughter. Maeve made an attempt to restrain her daughter, but failed.

Patch looked up at her father, and the look in her eyes caused him to retreat a few steps; in doing so, he unconsciously offered her his place at the lectern.

As before, a bright beam of light came cascading down from the ceiling above the altar and bathed the girl in its warmth. This caused the audience to gasp in wonderment, and they lowered their eyes in deference to the brightness of the ethereal light.

She smiled at the audience, turned to where I was in attendance, and nodded slightly in my direction. I was again amazed at her cognizance of my presence.

I took this recognition as my cue to begin the show.

I slowly created the image of the one individual that I knew would capture the attention of the people in attendance: Giver of the Word. As the people realized what was happening, they began to cry out, and tears began to flow; for this was the image of man beloved by the tribe.

I suppose you would say that I took advantage of their superstitions to suit my timetable, but it was the only way I was confident I could capture their attention ... and capture it I did. In fact, I was more successful than I could have ever imagined.

Upon my total transformation, the group became silent. I looked around, and my gaze rested on Patch. She acknowledged the recognition with a bow of her head.

To avoid any confusion, I'll continue the narrative from Giver of the Word's persona. However, I'll continue in English, because the Taos language is extremely difficult to write and is just as difficult to pronounce.

"Greetings, my people. I have returned to you for a short time at the behest of the Great Spirit. I bring to you his love and his request that you continue your adherence to the old ways, but also learn to adjust to the new ways, for assimilation is the true path to enlightenment, and the Reverend Bill is a fine and sympathetic teacher, and one worthy of your trust."

I hoped I wasn't being too irreverent in taking advantage of their religious fervor to attain my objectives.

I had thrown that "fine and sympathetic" bit in for Bill's benefit. I didn't want him to react with too much disbelief at this presentation of mine.

"A darkness is threatening to cover the land, and I fear that you are in serious danger. Due to the changes in the belief structure of the people and the lack of concern for the old ways by the young among you, the Great Spirit has lost some of his force over evil.

"I was sent here to ask for your help.

"You must gather those who you feel are true to him and would offer themselves to carry out his bidding. It may be a dangerous endeavor, and some of you may not survive. But do not fear, for he will welcome you with open arms, and you will sit by his side for all eternity and sing the songs of the old ways. Your names will be revered by those yet to come.

"There are some here today who will lead you and do their utmost to protect you as you march into this maelstrom of evil. Look to Anna Walks With Grace; look to my angel, Patch—she is young, but she has within her the strength and will to achieve prominence in the forthcoming mission; and look to the Reverend Bill, who will rise to a leadership he has yet to acknowledge."

Was I carrying it a bit far? Was my act kind of hokey? Well, it was about time for Leader to make his entrance anyhow.

"Close your eyes, my people, and heed my voice, for I will send to you images from the horror itself. Be not fooled by the depraved perpetrator of wickedness, for while she too is but a young girl in visage, but she is also ancient in her pollution and depravity. This crone is called Lili-It, which is the name given to the exiled one from the garden of purity back in the earliest of times."

Leader took over and transmitted images from his observation of the destruction following in Lili-It's path. He left nothing out, no matter how horrendous it was … and the people quaked in shock at the total devastation. Leader added sound to his presentation: the screams of pain and death from the beasts as well as those of the humans caught in the vortex of the debacle.

Maeve shook her head in disbelief as her body seemed racked with tremors, for the images were obscene.

The Reverend Bill stood almost catatonic and unconsciously dropped his notes for the sermon.

Anna Walks With Grace stood there mesmerized by both the icon that was Giver of the Word and the pictures she was receiving from him.

The faithful in the chapel moaned and rocked as if they were weeds snapped by a fierce wind whose currents played a dissonant howl though the stalks.

And Patch stood there in that bright sunbeam with a look of wisdom greatly belying her age.

Leader completed his presentation, and we were both silent for a moment, letting the information sink in. Then I spoke up once again through the old one.

"Look to those who will be your protectors and leaders. Gather as many of my people who are the true believers, bring them forth to this holy place, and make ready."

From the center of the congregation, a voice inquired whether Giver of the Word would appear another time.

I replied that I would if the Great Spirit thought it of importance.

With that, I faded the likeness of Giver of the Word, and a great silence prevailed throughout the building. I was concerned that Crank would decide to make an entrance at that time and befoul the mood, but Leader held himself back. I must say, I had had my doubts.

The beam of sunlight that bathed Patch had also grown fainter, and it continued to do so until it also vanished and she became a little girl once more.

Bill recovered from his stupor and, returning to the altar, dismissed the congregation. I don't believe he had anything of relevance to pronounce to the people at that time.

Soon all that remained were the Fellows family and Anna Walks With Grace.

"Are you a believer now, Reverend?" Anna asked the preacher. "Patch is indeed an angel, as Giver of the Word has decreed. What she will become after the battle has waned, I do not know; but I do know that she will be venerated as a true goddess by our people for all time.

"We will talk."

And with those final words, Anna Walks With Grace took her leave from the group.

Maeve took her daughter in her arms as if she was protecting her from whatever lurked in the darkness.

"What's the matter, Mommy? Why are you squeezing me so hard? Let's go outside and go for a walk. It's a pretty day, isn't it?"

"Sure it is, sweetheart," Maeve answered as she relaxed her hold on Patch. "Come on, we'll pick some flowers from the garden. Daddy will meet us later. I'm sure he has some finishing up to do here."

"I'll catch up to you guys later. Have fun."

CHAPTER 81

"ALL RIGHT ... ALL RIGHT ALREADY!" Bill screamed. "All right, damn it! What do you want from me? I give up! You've proven your point, and I bow to your superior knowledge.

"How can I continue preaching from my pulpit of the goodness and redemption of lost souls when I am now a part of a cadre of war? You have included me in your army of what you claim is a righteous endeavor, and yet you have promised casualties galore. It's an oxymoron! Are you telling me that I must first cause death before I can preach life? I am not God inducing death as the payment for a rebirth of existence. It's not as if a victory against your evil beings will affect any major change in man's morality. All that I can hope to achieve as a participant in your crusade is a return to yesterday. Who will know what we have achieved and what can we feel, except guilt that we have contributed to the demise of fellow humans? Does your end truly justify the means?

"Damn it, are you here? Answer me!"

It was my decision to remain silent. He had endured quite a shock that morning and had a lot of emotion to vent as his stream of consciousness depicted. Any interaction with me would have exacerbated the situation. It was enough that he had accepted the situation, so I decided to let him calm down and mull it over for awhile.

Just then something caught my eye from the rear of the room. Crank was slowly materializing—that is, until he caught a stern look from me. This wasn't the time for his wisecracks. Our discussion of such important matters would be difficult enough without his enflaming the present state of affairs.

"So, did we perform an Oscar-winning play? I rather thought it was quite convincing, didn't you?"

"Stop patting yourself on the back"—a human phrase that had no meaning to us, of course—*"and tell me what you've accomplished."*

"It wasn't easy to locate our fellow faeries. There are so many rocks to overturn and caves and small holes to spelunk and if they don't want to be found, they won't! In addition to those hiding places, do you realize how many forests there are on this darn planet?"

"Are you quite finished with your introduction? How about getting to the heart of the matter?"

"Bean ... sense of humor again.

"Okay, I located a few of our brethren and related the seriousness of our plight. I tried to convince them that the outcome would definitely influence them and would undoubtedly impinge upon and alter their sedentary existence.

"I did manage to persuade enough of them, who in turn agreed to spread out and convey our message to the others. If everything works out the way I planned, as more and more are swayed, they themselves will spread the word, and so on. We could eventually end up with quite a formidable militia."

"How long do you anticipate it will take before you have a good idea of the size of our horde?"

The Reverend Bill continued with his tirade: "On top of it all, who will guarantee the safety of my daughter; of Maeve; of Anna; indeed, of my entire congregation? Can you accept the responsibility for their well-being? How do I know that you will really participate in the actual conflagration? How do I know that you really exist and that you're not just a figment of my disintegrating mind? Dear God, am I just talking to myself here?"

"Can't we shut that guy up? I think he's lost his marbles."

"Leave him be. He just experienced quite a shock to his belief system and needs time to recuperate and regain his senses. I'll deal with him later, once he completes his spewing.

"What's next on your agenda?"

"I'll be returning to a predetermined meeting place, and at that time, I'll have a good idea of the size of our reinforcements, and I will devise a means to contact them when the moment presents itself.

I'll also have to allot time in order for them to relearn the old powers that have been forgotten all these years."

"A good plan, Leader. You should go now, and I'll look forward to your return; thanks for your help with the intervention here."

"And good luck to you with your Reverend Looney."

Leader nodded at Bill, who continued to rant: "... and how do I convince people to follow me, and how do I know I'm doing the right thing? What do I know from battlefield strategies? I lead parishioners, not soldiers! I do not have the skill of a Joan d'Arc, nor do I desire it!"

... and on and on and on ...

CHAPTER 82

It was a lovely day, so I lingered around outside and quietly watched Maeve and Patch in the garden. Patch was very proud of the small bouquet of desert flowers she had gathered. She giggled as any normal little girl would giggle while she chased a butterfly round and round the blossoms. And when it landed on her mother's nose, she laughed as though it were the funniest thing she had ever seen—and perhaps it was. Who would have guessed that this was the same young one who had mesmerized a congregation of Native Americans just a few minutes ago? Who would have guessed that this young one would hold the future of mankind in her little hands?

If her mother gave it any thought, she never let it be known. Patch was just a happy child without a care in the world, playing with her mother; nothing more, nothing less.

The door to the chapel opened and closed without much fanfare as Bill emerged. This idyllic scene could change abruptly if he continued his rantings, but it appeared as if he was ranted out. He waved at the little group and walked toward them slowly, with a wrinkled brow and an incongruous smile on his face. When he arrived at their picking place, he stood there and just stared at his daughter.

"Why are you looking so serious, Daddy? Come help Mommy and me snip some flowers."

"I'm staring at the two most beautiful girls in the world and thinking how lucky I am to be a part of their lives," he answered Patch. "I want to remember this picture for the rest of my life."

"Daddy, you are almost as silly as Virgil and Dr. Crank. Daddy, where did Dr. Crank go? Doesn't he like us anymore?"

"You know something, honey? I was asking myself the same question. Didn't you tell me that he disappeared from the gallery when you first met him?"

"Aye," Maeve interjected. "He was entertaining the visitors, and the next thing we knew, he vanished."

"Like a magician, Daddy. Maybe he is one."

"I can see the billboard now: 'The Amazing Dr. Crank and his Suitcase of Wondrous Rags.'"

"Bill, you're being facetious again."

"What's fassyteeshus, Mommy?"

"That's your father, sweetheart, when he says ridiculous things like that."

"Okay, let's just chalk it up to his being a strange hombre—or, as the locals would say, *un hombre muy loco*," said Bill. "I'm sure he'll come back in due time and when he gets hungry enough."

As Patch wandered off to another area in the garden, Maeve cozied up to her husband. "Are you okay?" she asked. "You look a bit haggard."

"I guess I am kind of exhausted after experiencing something I can't explain. Tell me, hon, did all that really happen, or was I daydreaming?"

He seemed to reconsider, tilting his head, before he continued. "No ... don't say anything. I'm afraid of your answer. I don't know if you heard my tirade in the chapel. It was as if someone had opened the valve on a pressure cooker before the pressure had been bled off, and the cherries exploded, covering the walls with a viscous coating of hot, uncooked sludge!"

Taking his hand, Maeve responded sympathetically: "I take it by your colorful description that you accepted the assertion that has been offered to us?"

"I'm loath to admit it, but ... yes, I believe so. Although it stretches my imagination, I find myself in accordance with the doomsday scenario. But Patch? I still can't comprehend the role she is expected to play."

"Maeve, she stood there like an angel bathed in a glow of celestial intensity and offered up the image of a man who passed on our very dais ... and the people held her in such awe that it brought tears to my eyes. I had to fight the desire to bow my own head in reverence. She's just a little girl ... just a little girl."

"Shh, me love," she said as she cradled his head in her hands. "It will be all right—you'll see. I myself don't understand all that has occurred, but I do trust Anna, and somehow I feel that our Dr. Crank is involved in this play also. Don't ask why I feel that way, but nobody comes and goes without some evidence of his being."

"Are you insinuating that he is some kind of ghost, or perhaps a spectral manifestation? If you believe that, I have a confession to make that will make as much sense as your declaration."

"And what is that, m'love?"

Taking a deep breath, Bill replied rather sheepishly, "Err, Virgil isn't what he seems to be."

"You mean he's not a bird? He sure looks like one—feathers and 'arrkkk' and all that."

"No, no, he does look like a bird, silly. But it's just a front for some kind of spiritual entity. Those quotations he spouts are programmed to divert your attention from his true identity."

A strange glint appeared in Maeve's eye as she probed her husband for more of his interesting prattle. "Aye ... and what, pray, is that? Who do you think he is if not a cuckoo cockatoo? Hmm ... I thought that was quite clever, didn't you?"

"You're patronizing me now, aren't you? However, I must admit that there are times when he is just an intelligent bird. But there are also times when he and I have long discussions about the prophesies of doom that are slowly approaching.

"Stop that tsking, and ask Anna if you don't believe me. She's also conversed with him about the very same topic. I'm sure that religion, as we practice it, isn't the paramount force behind the necessity of repelling the darkness that is gaining on us, but nevertheless it is spiritual in nature."

"What is it you're trying to say, Bill?"

"'There's more in heaven and earth than are dreamt of ...'[34] 'Beware the whispers that call out in the grayness of our half sleep.'"[35]

"Bill, stop with the Virgilisms. I might start to believe that you are possessed!"

---

34   William Shakespeare, *Hamlet*.
35   Stephen Stuart, *Rantings* (2009).

"Who knows? Maybe I am, or perhaps nothing is real, and perhaps this is nothing more than a fantasy introduced into our minds by a preponderance of hallucinogenic matter in the air.

"Hey ... we're all stoned!" Bill announced with an impish grin on his face.

"Mommy, Mommy!" shouted an excited Patch. "Look at these new flowers I just picked. Aren't they the prettiest flowers you ever saw?"

"Where did you find them, sweetheart? I don't remember seeing them before."

"In the garden by the back of the house. There are all kinds of pretty flowers there. Did you plant them, Daddy, so you could surprise me?"

"I ... I guess I did, honey. I've been so busy that I forgot all about it."

"I'm going to pick some more. Can I put them in my room, Daddy?"

"Of course you can. We'll find a nice vase later, okay?"

With that, she ran off, happy as only a little girl can be: no cares and no thoughts aside from her revelry in the simplicity of adding a bit of beauty to her world.

"Maeve, that garden was dead this morning. I could never get anything to grow there."

"I know ..."

CHAPTER 83

It was dinnertime, and the family sat around a table gaily decorated with a ceramic vase in which a bouquet of desert blossoms rose skyward, a triumph of color designed by mother and daughter.

I took a position in a corner and became one with the décor, not intending to interrupt the group's integrity.

"Arrkkk! If I was a bird in a gilded cage," Virgil sang. "Arrkkk!"

"You are! Look around you, my feathered itch, and tell me what you see," Bill responded with a bit of sarcasm.

"Arrkkk! A prisoner doomed to a life of humdrum captivity, sayeth the convict. Arrkkk!"

"And if you don't be quiet, doomed you shall be!"

"Arrkkk! Bitter words gush forth and fuel the fool. Arrkkk!"

"Daddy, why are you teasing Virgil? He's just a silly bird being silly."

"Out of the mouths of babes, et cetera, et cetera ..." Maeve murmured.

"I know when I'm outnumbered," Bill said. "I surrender."

At that moment, Patch turned toward me and said, "Mommy and Daddy, there's my spirit friend."

Immediately, her demeanor changed, and Patch assumed the same persona she had taken at the altar.

"Honey, I don't see anyone. Do you, Bill?"

"Not at all. Patch, what do you see? What does your spirit friend look like?"

At that, Patch stood up and walked over to me. "Greetings, Bean. I wanted to thank you for your assistance this morning—that is, yours and Leader's, if that what he is called? I am who you think I am;

you are not alone. You do not follow a solitary path on your way to achieving a future that is proving to be unattainable, but it is noble nonetheless. There are other paths and other dreamers walking uphill on very slippery slopes.

"You may speak through the bird, if you wish."

"Patch, what's h-happening?" Maeve sputtered. "Are you all right? I'm scared, honey; you're talking very strangely." She grasped Bill's hand and implored him to say something, anything, to alleviate her sudden fear. "Bill? Please say something! I think I'm going crazy."

Bill looked as if had been pole-axed. He stared first at his daughter and then at the bird and back again.

Patch returned to the table and regained her seat, but gone was the little girl. In her place sat a figure projecting an image of infinite intelligence and immeasurable warmth clothed in the body of a young girl.

She spoke: "Maeve and Bill, you will soon know what has occurred. Above all, do not fear for your little Patch; absolutely no harm will befall her. She is still here and will return shortly with absolutely no memory of what has transpired. Her health and innocence will be as before."

"You're not going crazy, sweetheart," Bill stated. "We both are. There must be an overabundance of mushroom dust in the atmosphere. This can't be real ... can it?"

"It is real," the Patch creature said. "The final battle of good versus evil was preordained to occur at this time in man's existence—the battle, but not the outcome, as that is yet to be established. This battle is the reason we have all been brought together at this instant. Some might call it fate, and some might call it coincidence; however you wish to describe the situation, we are here. Each of us is but a part of the whole; when joined, we will form a formidable force in opposition to the forces of darkness."

"If you want me to be a part of this conversation—or confrontation, if you prefer—unlock this cage and place me alongside all of you at the table. I don't think I will be taken seriously as a disembodied voice."

Patch nodded in agreement, slid her chair back, and walked to Virgil's enclosure. Upon unlocking the cage, she held her arm out, and taking that action as an invitation, I transferred my perch to that limb.

Virgil was uncharacteristically quiet as I took over his character. No "arrkkk" this time—just me being myself, but a bewildered me. The quiet continued as I assumed my position with the group on the armrest of Bill's chair at the head of the table.

A period of retrospection followed, permeating the atmosphere and giving impetus to many different facial expressions: suspicion, indecision, wariness, confusion, discovery, introspection, and so forth. Imagine the students of the Acting 101 course, and you have a good idea of the scene at that moment.

I was thinking that the only people missing were Leader and Anna Walks With Grace.

No sooner had that thought was ended than a knock was heard at the door. Without waiting for a proper invitation, in walked the subjects of my reflection, with Crank bowing in deference to the sachem of the Taos people.

"Behold: 'tis but two wanderers in the night requesting shelter and sustenance from this bounteous table.

"Why, prithee, are you so solemn? This should be a place of joy and gratitude to the giver of life!"

Anna added, "I was driving by after visiting two of my people needing counseling in a family problem when I saw the lights on in your home. I was taking it upon myself to make an uninvited visit when I was accosted by this apparition clothed in a jester's garb also intending to thrust himself into your company. I am not intruding in anything private, am I? If so, I will take my leave and extend my sincere apology."

"Come on in, you two, and find some chairs," said Bill. "You might as well become a member of this circus. Act one has already begun, and I'm sure that two and three will be just as unbelievable as the first."

With that, Crank and Anna took their palaces at the table: Anna in a soft side chair and Crank on a step stool, as befitting his rank.

"Bill," Maeve said, "I'm going to get a glass of water. Would any of you like something? I have a feeling that this is going to take some time, and I'm getting awfully thirsty. I think I'll spike it with some aspirin."

"A double shot of Sterno would be more like it," Bill replied, trying to inject a bit of humor into the surroundings.

"A man after my own heart; a double Sterno with a twist, if you would be so kind?"

"You'll be satisfied with a glass of water also," Maeve replied to Crank, "and the only twist you'll get is to your ear if you don't behave yourself!"

"I bow to your generosity, fair lady."

Looking around at this future command center, I was bemused by the motley appearance of its content. Try to imagine the sight that presented itself: a beautiful young girl with the countenance of a soul blessed with eternal wisdom; her mother, a normal and loving person; the girl's father, a learned, spiritual man with a skeptical nature and a somewhat excitable temper; a magnificent cockatoo with the mouth of a poet imbued with arcane profundities; a Native American woman, spiritual leader of her people, and a follower of the old ways; and last— and this is where it gets a bit complicated—a fellow faerie in the guise of an outspoken and sometimes crude object of derision and puzzlement who was nevertheless a generous and honest fellow (I speak, of course, of the good Dr. Crank).

This group, this gathering of a most unlikely liaison, would form the basis of our campaign against an antagonist that, within herself, blended all of the evil that could be attained from this world. She needed no other reinforcements other than Whoever, her guide and advisor.

If you think I had trepidations, you win the jackpot.

My curiosity had been piqued concerning the entity that had appeared in the guise of young Patch. If she were indeed a member of our society, why hadn't I felt her presence?

"Later, Bean," she said in a voice no one else could hear as she intruded into my thoughts. "There will be time for us—that is, the three of us—to familiarize ourselves with each other. All your questions will be answered, I assure you."

"Do you have a name, or should I refer to you as Patch?" My response was equally undetectable by our comrades.

"Patch will do for the time being, if you don't mind. I, like you, have assumed many personalities and many names. But names only depict the physical image of an entity and not the soul within; so Patch will suffice."

"I—or should I say we—are at a disadvantage here. You seem to know of us, but we have no idea who you are. Actually, the Fellows—Bill and Maeve—have no idea who I am, but I'm sure that will all change in a few minutes."

"Anna," Patch said out loud, "you are a true believer and a welcome adjunct to our group. I have no doubts as to your faith in my assertions and to your unselfish assistance when it is required.

"Dr. Crank, we will talk later. Meanwhile, I am confident that you will control yourself and remain silent."

"I am your servant, my lady of mystery."

"That will do, Doctor."

More curiosity: why hadn't this "Patch" person identified Leader as one of us? His glance at my Virgil persona reflected my curiosity. Her decision not to out Leader was another point for later clarification.

"I am, as Dr. Crank has asserted, an object of mystery—at least I am to most of you, with the exception of Bean, who temporarily inhabits your Virgil. He and I are of the same world."

Well, that answered my first question: she was indeed from the realm of faeriedom. But again, who was "she," and why hadn't I heard of "her" in my many travels? To paraphrase one of man's great heroes, she was a riddle, wrapped in a mystery, inside an enigma.[36]

"It would be simpler for you to think of me as a benevolent spirit rather than for me to describe in reality what I truly am or what Bean—or Virgil, as you know him—is."

"Okay," Bill said. "So you're some wondrous spirit who apparently has great powers but—and this is our main question—why have you chosen *our* daughter to be your puppet? There are millions of youngsters in this world. Why Patch?"

The Patch object continued, ignoring Bill's insistent attitude. "I can attempt to understand your deep concern for your daughter and your desire to protect your family," she said. "To fully comprehend the reasons for recruiting Patch, you would have to allow yourselves to believe in forces that may contradict the very ideology upon which you have based your entire belief system.

"While most religious precepts tend to focus their attention on one series of tenets, forgoing any theories that might initiate diverse thinking, there are in existence countless forces working their magic in ways that are not susceptible to human detection.

"These forces have been around since before man's ancestral microbe was accidentally nourished. Ancient man, in his simplicity and naïveté,

---

36 Winston Churchill, in a radio speech describing the Soviet Union delivered
    October 1, 1939.

accepted their presence and, in a manner of speaking, worshipped them as godlike beings in an innocent attempt to show gratitude for the gifts that nature had bestowed upon them. We weren't gods in any sense of the word but instead a derivative of nature evolving in a parallel corridor. We derived much of our power from nature's continued grasping for a fulfillment of purpose—or at least that was true in the beginning of earth's origin. However, we continued to expand our powers much more quickly than nature, for each new creation increased our influence ... and while a great number of those natural creations expired due to cosmic changes, we never relinquished our abilities, but developed further, compounding our authority."

"But ..." Bill managed.

"More buts?"

"Quiet, birdbrain!" Bill shot back.

"Ouch! You really know how to hurt a member of the flock."

"To continue what I was saying," said Bill, "before I was so rudely interrupted: but nature can be enjoyed by the exercising of one's senses, while the forces you describe can only be ascertained by utilizing a belief system employing knowledge of the supernatural."

"Supernatural? Not really. We are not in competition with nature; we are more symbiotically attuned to it. What affects the natural order affects us as well, and while what affects us has no bearing on nature, we can, if so desired, affect nature's world. You see, we have prospered more significantly than nature has."

A moment of silence transpired, as if the Patch vessel were in thought.

"However, in reflection," she continued, "I might tend to agree with you. We are in fact supernatural elemental inhabitants of nature. Now that should confuse you more than you already are."

"To the contrary," answered Bill, "I can accept the supernatural aspect of your existence more than some esoteric definition you might employ."

"Now that that's settled, we'll go on," Patch said, demonstrating a bit of exasperation. "Your daughter, Patch—the name you so affectionately bestowed upon her—exhibited many unique traits upon her birth. Again, to put it in simplistic terms, she seemed to have inherited both human characteristics as well as those of our faerie brethren. How that happened, we cannot explain. Therefore, we were curious as to what she would accomplish with those gifts, so a decision was made to observe her periodically as she matured.

"Meanwhile, on the other side of the world, another child was also born with combined traits. This time, in addition to human features, she had inherited traits from the evil side of our society. That child absorbed all of her power from the extinction of life forces that disappeared from nature—and there were a very great many of those doomed designs. Those forces disappeared by natural selection as well as via humanity's need for self-destruction. That being the case, you can well imagine what the constantly increasing devastation of all life forms has accomplished in reinforcing her abilities."

Maeve was so completely enthralled by the narrative that she had hardly touched her drink, while Bill alternately scratched his head and cracked his knuckles.

Anna unconsciously rubbed a beaded tribal talisman that dangled from a rawhide thong around her neck.

Crank, on the other hand, seemed entranced with a deposit in his handkerchief. He wasn't demonstrating any overt interest in what Patch was saying. Much to his credit, he did remain silent, as ordered by the young lady's (now admittedly supernatural) guide.

"Your Patch has demonstrated abilities that up until now were considered faerie gifts—namely, the ability to heal and to bring life to erstwhile unfertile areas. Those traits, combined with her joy of life and her ability to give and receive love, have fashioned her into a force to be reckoned with. In your vernacular, she might be considered a saint; however, she is but a gifted one who requires great care and understanding, lest she be branded a freak, a heretic ... or, more disquieting, a god. Humans are so starved for figureheads to love or loathe that a hint of a societal anomaly could be the germ that encourages a growth of emotion that would then feed a seemingly uncontrollable response. Patch must not be allowed to become an object of public scrutiny.

"These are some of the qualities that have elicited special attention from my world. It is also why she has been chosen to be the leading force in the upcoming clash of ideologies.

"Patch is the only human being with a chance at defeating her opposite number and allowing humanity to continue its existence, at least for a while longer.

"Although time is of the essence, she must be eased into the knowledge of her inherent powers and her acceptance of them as—and I shudder at the term—a weapon. She will be faced with the possibility that her powers could be utilized to cause the loss of life that is anticipated in the final conflict. Of paramount concern is her acceptance of that scenario.

"We will talk more of that later. It's time for me to take leave of you. You have much to occupy yourselves with for now.

"Bean, I trust we will be engaged in discussion shortly, so why don't we excuse ourselves?"

"Methinks I will gather my marbles and remove myself from this circle of abnormalities," Dr. Crank offered. "You see, I am the only normal denizen in attendance."

"Yeah, good night, Crank, and good night to whoever you are," said Bill. "It's been a pleasure, I'm sure."

"Arrkkk! ... and to all a good night from Virgil. Close the door on your way out. Arrkkk!"

"I'll take him back to his cage," Maeve offered. She offered me her arm, which I accepted immediately, and placed me back in Virgil's wire-framed abode.

"Mommy and Daddy, I think I'll go to bed now. I'm tired."

"Okay, sweetheart," Maeve answered, a look of amazement on her face as she once again held her daughter in her arms. "Come on, then. We'll brush up, and then I'll read a story to you. Daddy will come along soon, won't you, Daddy?"

"Huh? Oh, sure," Bill managed to reply as he stared blankly at the spot where Patch had sat, obviously trying to absorb the night's events. He rose from his seat and, as though in a trance, cleared the table and put the soiled dishes in the sink. Then, shaking the cobwebs from his head—or at least making a vain attempt at it—he made his way to his daughter's room to join his family.

CHAPTER 84

I'd have given anything to be present when Bill and Maeve discussed the evening's events. Unfortunately I had business elsewhere, and nothing was going to keep me—or Leader—from attending that meeting.

It was a strange and somewhat sobering feeling to suddenly be made aware that others like me were marching to the same piper. Had I only known of their existence ... had they known of mine ... how much we could have accomplished? Or if they had been aware of me, as the Patch had let on, why hadn't they identified themselves?

Imps had once belonged to a loose society who reveled in each other's company. Although we were admittedly mischievous, we were not aggressive, and the thought of harming one another was not part of our belief structure.

Man and his total lack of respect for that which nature provided, including his relentless urge to possess and destroy it, had forced us to retreat to the deep forests and fjords, to the high mountains, and to the vast emptiness of earth's wastelands in order to avoid further contact with them.

In our rush to escape further torment, we had strained our own relationships to the point where we chose to isolate ourselves from our own communities in an effort to remain hidden from those callous and greedy spoilers.

Some of us had chosen to ally themselves with the human race and participate in their self-destruction. Man was a willing subject, and aid was given to him while becoming intoxicated with the ability they possessed to foment the very behavior for which they had been exiled from Eden. (I note, for example, both Whatever and Whoever, imps of less than honorable morality.)

No longer were we able to trust our brethren, so those who chose to remain hidden went off alone and avoided any further contact. I don't know how many of those anti-entities actually made contact with man, but judging by the mayhem that has occurred throughout human history, I would venture to say quite a few imps made themselves available.

Perhaps that was the explanation for my oblivion to Patch and the others she spoke of.

The very fact that Leader and I had remained comrades was anathema to what had transpired in the world of the faeries.

"Bean," Patch's imp said, "your inquisitive nature, your compassion for the less than fortunate, and your ability to reason logically are the mainstays of my decision to enlist your help against the hostilities that will soon consume us, as well as a large segment of humanity."

"I have to admit that your intruding into my thoughts is most disconcerting. I'd prefer an immediate cessation of that rather nasty trait. If I am to be of any help to you, I must be free to think for myself without interference. Agreed?"

"That goes for me also. I require a certain degree of privacy to mull over my own deep thoughts."

"Deep? You, Leader? Deep?"

"Bean, you shame me. Just for that, I won't say another word, and you will not be able to partake of my most profound opinions. It will definitely be your loss."

"Agreed."

"Agreed. I will respect your privacy. Your thoughts are your thoughts alone—unless, of course, you choose to share them," Patch said.

I was a bit uneasy about her quick response to our demand; indeed, I didn't feel secure that she would honor her promise.

"There is a quiet spot not too far from here that would make an ideal meeting place for us to get to know each other. I suggest we retire there and begin our dialogue," the Patch thing suggested.

CHAPTER 85

It was a barren spot, devoid of any vegetation but populated by scorpions and rattlesnakes luxuriating on rocks that were quickly losing their daily allotment of the sun's heat.

My apprehension was being reinforced by her choice of conference locales.

What was it about her that disquieted me so much? It was as if I was constantly on alert, balancing her mollifying human connection, as well as her praise of me, with her ability to intrude into our minds ... and, again, her strange and questionable option of so desolate an area.

These thoughts must be placed on hold until I had the security of knowing that they would not be compromised. I wonder how Leader was faring with this new turn of events. *Actually, he should be okay, not being the most profound of thinkers.*

"Who am I?" she began. "I am as you are. I, too, have chosen a path designed to salvage the human species from its incomprehensible—and seemingly relentless—voyage to obliteration. And yet," she continued, "I am different in some respects."

"And, pray tell, where do we differ, if we both have the same aspirations? Hasn't that been my goal? And, if I may interject, where have you been? Why haven't I heard of you throughout the millennia?"

I felt as if she were smiling at my naïveté, perhaps even humoring me.

"We had the same basic objectives, but that's where the similarity ended."

She felt my puzzlement at her repeated patronization of me. I was beginning to resent being treated like an immature imp.

"I'm truly sorry, Bean; I don't want to insult you, and I apologize if my attitude projects that treatment."

"I thought we had an agreement about mind intrusion?"

"Ouch! You're right ... again, my apologies. It won't happen again."

Either she is keeping to her promise, or she's hiding it pretty well. We'll see.

"To continue," she said, "while you concentrated on the individual in need of assistance as your contribution to humanity, I, in turn, concentrated on the confrontation with the most evil of evils. It was my assignment—and one adopted entirely by me—to either defeat or to slow down the advancement of their malicious inception. In doing so, I was able to absorb, or possibly reacquire, powers I had never given thought to. I needed to either adapt to the situation and fight back or resign myself to failure and withdraw."

"And what are those powers you speak of? Are we able to acquire them ourselves, or are we to just follow behind you and dispose of the remains?"

"Bean, you and Leader have within your essence the same abilities I have been forced to attain. It's just a matter of reacting accordingly to circumstances that present themselves. It's more of a reflexive attitude than a learned one. From what I am able to ascertain, those powers are limitless ... and if I am not mistaken, beyond our belief system."

Leader, who until then had reclined, as Crank, on a large rock, carefully displacing a rattlesnake of abnormal size, looked up in response to Patch's description of her acquired powers.

"If I might ask, what are those powers you speak of? I've learned a few of them myself and in turn instructed Bean on their usage. If there are more, I would love to know."

"Easy, Leader; I'm sure that when the time comes, she'll let us in on her secrets—won't you, Patch?"

"When the time comes, you'll find them yourselves. Wasting time trying to obtain them now is fruitless."

"You've spent a lot of time combating evil; so what have you learned about it? Does man indeed have a subconscious attraction to darkness? What of his God and that God's tenets of morality? Why was nature conceived with such delicate beauty, if not to counteract the horror of human dissonance?"

After a few moments of introspection, the Patch thing spoke.

"Bean, you ask too many questions that can only be discussed hypothetically, and we don't have the time now to lose ourselves in the abstract. But I admit that those issues have inhabited a niche within my mind also."

"The subject of religion has also been foremost in the mind of my ghost. He has reverted back to that topic many times in our collaboration."

"Ghost? What ghost? Is there an apparition that has been inserted into our midst?"

"No. He is the penman of my memoirs, and I rely upon his imagination and rhetoric to carry my tale.

"He will not interfere with our business but instead will offer our story for the world's amusement and critique.

"So, please continue ..."

"As you wish ...

"So, Bean: which came first, nature or God? Did their God create nature, or did nature create God? If God appeared first, who existed to worship the creator? It's the 'tree in the forest' question. If nature appeared first and continued its evolution when man made his appearance, did his admiration of the beauty and majesty of nature elicit a feeling of such intensity—they would refer to it later as a religious intervention—that his search for its meaning and understanding led to the creation of a mystical entity responsible for the ultimate presentation of the world's decisive gift? Or did God create man for the sole purpose of receiving praise for his fashioning of the flora and fauna?

"It seems a stretch of the imagination to believe that the soup that provided the nourishment for man also provided the nourishment for the millions upon millions of species as diverse as the bedbug, T. Rex, eohippus, and the fruit bat. How busy was that errant microbe spreading his seed like an oversexed Casanova risking permanent prostate damage? It was definitely a four-hour Viagra moment, and not a doctor in sight!"

And from Leader: "A most marvelous sense of humor, madam. Perhaps you can share that power with Bean. It seems he has lost his along the way."

CHAPTER 86

"Stop!
"Cease!
"Desist!"

"Ah, Bean. I was anxiously awaiting your intervention into the narrative. All I had to do was approach the subject of religion again, and there you were. You are getting to be a creature of Pavlovian responsiveness."

"Sadly, you're correct in your assumption. But in a more optimistic vein, I am beginning to accept your assumption that religion provides impetus and guidance for man's false sense of reality."

"Bean, you don't get it at all. In fact, you are falling into a quagmire of cynicism and pessimism. Religion is necessary for man to carry on. By placing his insecurities and frailties in the bosom of a mystical being—a being that he holds in the highest esteem—he is able to accept a position of repentance and reverence while exulting in forgiveness. It's the forgiveness that alleviates the feeling of guilt that would destroy his ambition and desire to go forward with his evolution."

"I bow to your superior intellect once more. I also would like to offer my gratitude for not making me appear too simplistic in my approach to life. You do show respect to me, and for that, you may continue without much ado.

"Later."

CHAPTER 87

Apologizing for the interruption, I continued my dialogue with Patch.

"Would you then say that all life was merely an arbitrary toss of the coin—sort of the right seed mating with the right egg?

"That concept would tend to describe the plethora of mutant species that appeared and the extinction of those that weren't able to survive the tribulations of an evolving world."

"I would definitely agree with your observations.

"Those seeds were imbued with one of two characteristics: one being the inability to survive and the other with the ability to reproduce and evolve haphazardly into whatever organism would eventually reign supreme and prosper. However—and this is a doomsday hypothesis—I believe that the surviving classes were instilled with a preprogrammed destiny designed to eventually eradicate said life form. In other words, would that life form have the ability to cope with the end result of its progress, or would that same progress provide the impetus of its eventual destruction?"

"I've attempted to insert a positive feeling into my story, taking into consideration that the contemporary world is projecting a very serious pessimistic aura.

"It's evident to me that, although you claim to fight the most evil of evils, you are resigned to a very bleak future ... and yet you choose to continue to nimbly avoid the blades of the windmills."

"Have I become so transparent, Bean?

298

"I'll admit that my encounters have taken their toll on me, and as much as I have been able to emerge triumphant in the past, another more powerful state of affairs always arises from the horizon, and I am obligated to face that issue.

"So you see, as the encounters progress, they will eventually reach a point where I am no longer equipped to extend my influence over the most evil of evils. That timing mechanism will finally attain its point of ignition, resulting in the final conflagration."

"I have to say that you have, without doubt, fallen into an abysmal pit. Don't you see any glint of redemption in your torrid vision of the future?"

"Redemption, you ask? Just open your eyes, Bean—metaphorically speaking, of course—and see the worldwide growth of hate and violence ... assisted—most ably, I must add—by weapons capable of inflicting cataclysmic destruction, with no evident design or plan to avoid total annihilation.

"I fear that man has become too complicated to survive. The only survivors, and the only original inhabitants from the primeval Petri dish, will be the simplest of organisms: bacteria, viruses, and cockroaches. It will be a fit ending to an experiment that was initiated in violence and evolved haphazardly."

"Phew!"

"Phew from me also," added Leader.

"You want optimism? You are my optimism," countered Patch. "You two, the little girl Patch, Anna, and our bashful brethren provide my optimism. Neutralizing my overt pessimism is a belief that a glimmer of hope can always be found somewhere, if one searches for it. I'm certain that I will be unable to resist that gray and gritty cloud of ill-inspired pollution alone. The question is, then, who will I be able to rely upon when the need arises? Fewer and fewer sources of morality and decency survive out there, and fewer and fewer of those sources are willing and able to join forces when possible annihilation is offered as a reward. I can't promise an afterlife of glory or the ministrations of countless virgins."

"All right, then; we agree that there is optimism. Although I, too, believe that darkness looms just outside the reach of humanity, I also strongly believe that, with some effort, we can keep it at bay. Defeating it ... that is another issue.

"If that effort is defined as our contribution, so be it. I have the feeling that if we are able to demonstrate some success, more will come to their senses and join us. How, then, can we lose?"

"Ever the optimist, eh, Bean?

"And what do you have to say, Leader? Are you willing to exert every effort that you can bear to join our crusade? You seem overwhelmed by the thought of accessing new powers rather than the idealism of counteracting evil."

Crank stood up, brushed an errant scorpion from his shirt front, and spoke clearly. This time, he spoke without the exaggerated tone of his pompous image of the clown.

"I've learned much from Bean in the years that we have traveled together. I have grown to understand feelings and emotions from all life sources, especially from the human element, and I will admit that I can understand that race a bit more realistically now.

"They should be given the chance to continue their evolution as preconceived by whatever power granted it … unless, of course, the power that grants is also the power that taketh away.

"So yes, I'm with you, and I'll do whatever it is that's demanded of me."

With that final statement, Crank faded and joined us in a charged cloud of ionic energy.

I'm still wondering why the Patch entity chose to conceal Leader's identity from the mortals. I'm sure that the girl knows the truth, but she is also keeping it to herself.

CHAPTER 88

The night passed with much introspection into the personal philosophies of the three of us. Some we agreed upon, with while others were more controversial. All in all, it was a very informative time well spent.

Have I changed my opinion of the new arrival? Perhaps, but something is still bothering me, and I can't seem grasp it. There has been no reference to any suspicion by Leader. Perhaps I'm imagining things?

So, after our faerie summit, night gave way to dawn, and dawn eased its way into day. The daily routine commenced with breakfast for the Fellows family, followed by Maeve and Patch scooting off to the gallery. And as usual, the Reverend Bill retired to his desk to prepare the day's business.

I chose to remain invisible for a time while Leader and our new compatriot departed on a trek to locate whatever faeries had committed themselves to our cause. They could be gone for a few days, so it was up to me to maintain some sort of sanity here.

"Arrkkk! What a night it was ... it was! Arrkkk!"

"Is that you, Virgil, or is it really Virgil?"

"Arrkkk! Is it me you desire, or is it me? That is the question! Arrkkk!"

"Is it me or is it me? We're getting kind of metaphysical now, aren't we? For a caged beast, that is."

I guessed it was time for my appearance. Bill had suffered enough since last night.

"We're all in a cage of one sort or another, Reverend. Mine happens to be made of wire."

301

"Are we now going to wax philosophic?" Bill asked without a shred of humor. "To tell you the truth, Virgil—or whoever you truly are—I'm not in the mood. Last night was a rude awakening for me. Patch, on the other hand, was totally unaffected by the night's revelations. I felt that she was part of the scene, rather than an outsider like me."

"...And your wife, Maeve? How did she react? I don't recall any adverse reaction emanating from her corner, other than a little dig at Crank."

"We didn't talk much after we put Patch to bed. I guess there were no words that could describe our feelings at the time. I know that I myself was ... how can I put it ... befuddled? So many questions spun around in a maelstrom of thoughts in my mind; mere words would prove to be a disjointed cacophony of atonal sound."

"Did sleep provide a catharsis of sorts for you?"

"Sleep, you say? Maybe in a year or two, but definitely not in the near future.

"Maeve is so much calmer than I am, if her external persona is any indication. At first I could see that she was troubled and perhaps puzzled by the evening's activities, but as she prepared for bed, she became noticeably calmer, as if she understood what was to be. Not just understood, but accepted it.

"Her strength is the cornerstone of the family, yet here I am: a man of God who has accepted the responsibility of guiding my flock through the various tests that he has placed in the path toward righteousness.

"She should be the leader of the congregation, not me."

"... and if I had a tail and long ears, I, too, could be an ass!"

"I am being an ass, aren't I? It's just the fear of a relapse into a past I would like to forget. Unfortunately I don't have the ability to endure a profusion of stress-related situations. That's one of the main reasons I have immersed myself into a life given over to my God.

"Perhaps my commitment to the church is being tested?"

"Perhaps ... or perhaps we're all being tested in one way or another by forces beyond our comprehension. You wish to call it God; I call it the forces of destiny. But either way, it's a progression of events that seem to follow a preternatural order.

"Think of it this way: of all the cars in the world, why was yours chosen to receive the gift of a little girl who is destined to become a symbol of morality and a savior of humanity? Perhaps fate or

perhaps your god—who can rightly say? But something designed that intervention; it didn't just happen!

"Or it could be divine intervention.

"Is it also divine intervention when an automobile jumps a curb and takes the life of a young child, or when a musical virtuoso loses the mobility of her fingers?"

"So that's your forces of fate?

"Be it as it may, there is a plan, and I prefer to call it divine."

"Perhaps when our voyage is complete and man has been granted a respite, we might garner the knowledge that we are fated to seek. But do we really want to know the answer?"

"The search is what keeps us—the 'religiosos,' as Crank refers to us, going, and the faith of the inaccessible answer is indeed our faith.

"What would the Hebrews do if their Messiah actually made his appearance? On second thought, would they sincerely believe that the individual presented to them is indeed the promised one?

"So you ask whether man really wants to know the answer; he couldn't cope with it!"

"What you are insinuating is that man fashions answers to suit his present condition, ignoring the hunt and creating his own belief structure. It's a sad treatise on a sad existence."

"Well, it surely beats waiting by the bus stop for Godot,[37] doesn't it?"

"Excuse the change of subject, but isn't it time for your Matt Christmas program to air?"

"You know something, Virgil? That would be good a reprieve for me ... clear my mind or something."

I didn't reply to that but remained in the vicinity. I guess that I was getting used to the absurd rhetoric broadcasted by Christmas's guests.

Bill turned the TV on just as a commercial for an attorney pleading for the souls of man's best friends injured by a mysterious element present in a certain popular brand of dog food. There actually was a slobbering bulldog (cute, wasn't he?) talking with a British accent. I wonder who trained it? Amazing!

The program started with Matt Christmas sitting at his ersatz office desk with a mug of what I supposed was coffee in his hand.

---

37 "Waiting for Godot" is a play written in 1948–1949 by Samuel Beckett.

"Ladies and gentlemen, tonight's guest is Cecil Malcome-Malcome, the author of a treatise just emerging from obscurity, titled *Too Young to Be Born*. I'm sure that you will find it very interesting."

The apparition now on the screen was resplendent with a head of unruly crimson hair atop a rather round head punctuated by the smallest eyes I had ever seen on a human being. Forget his bulbous, veined nose and thin lips; it was his BB eyes that got my attention. Porcine would closely describe his countenance.

"Good evening." It speaks *"What I have to say might change your concept of man's future, so I beg you to stay tuned.*

"Man was destined to be an awkward moment in the evolution of life on the planet Earth and no more. He was not designed to evolve into the alpha beast he brazenly believes he is. While other species rely on the defeat of the weak in order to propagate the fittest of their respective order, man does not. By allowing himself only a brief span of years in which to safely reproduce, he fails to take into consideration the potential for physical ailments and disabilities to make themselves known. That predetermined allotment of time generally falls between puberty, commonly accepted to be about twelve years of age, and approximately thirty-five years of age, the most fertile period."

"What I have to say might change your concept of man's future, so I beg you to stay tuned.

"I wonder where he's going with this?" Bill exclaimed.

"With the advancement of medical technology and the invention of medicinal preparations, he has been given the ability to live longer than necessary. However, the advent of medical science is a false indication of the viability of true bodily health and natural fitness.

"Thus, if man were indeed meant to be a lasting force on earth, and if the survival of the fittest came into play, he should have been designed to incur the period of fertility in his middle to late middle years—say, fifty-five to sixty-five years of age. This would allow the fittest of the species to reproduce and weed out the weakest.

"But what about those who have been aided by external support and have achieved a modicum of health at the age of fertility you ask?" I do? *"Well, unnatural substances in the molecular makeup of the body would greatly reduce*

the ability of the body to reproduce. The body would recognize abnormalities and reject normal fertilization of the ovaries. Hence it would guarantee that only the fittest would reproduce, and ultimately man would attain his position as the superior life force on the planet."

"Where on earth does Christmas find these beauts?" mused Bill.

"You will, of course, say that he would be unable to care for a child at that late age. This is true if judged by factors that are prevalent in our species at the present time. But if he were capable of reproduction at the age suggested, he would also have been designed to live longer than he is expected to live now and therefore be fully capable to offer the care and nurture necessary for the infant to grow, mature, and prosper.

"What of wars, disease, famine, and other means of unnatural demise, you ask?"

I do? *"I do not consider these a viable method of population control. Good question, though. While disease devastates those who have failed to produce the natural antibodies necessary to combat the deadly infections and would signify a weakness of body, both war and famine are external elements that affect the weak as well as the healthy. This is unfortunate, obviously, but there would still remain enough able-bodied and healthy subjects to maintain and cause the species to flourish."*

With a gracious, (and most gratitude-inducing, at least for Bill and me) interruption, Christmas segued into a commercial featuring a bunch of youngsters looking as if they had just awakened, hopping around like marionettes controlled by a spastic puppeteer. The soundtrack, based on a score by a DJ Master Drek, consisted of unintelligible chanting with an accompaniment of mesmeric drums, screeching guitars (I think they were guitars), and flatulence—all this for a new soft drink. What ever happened to pretty people dancing around a maypole?

"I feel better already," Bill declared as he turned the TV off. "It's amazing what pseudoscientific double talk can achieve, isn't it, Virgil? However, I can do without that commercial.

"It's almost as if modern music is going the way of modern writing, or vice versa. What with texting, hip-hop, and primeval hand gesturing, we are allowing ourselves to evolve into an alien culture. I say that because it sure is alienating me!"

"With that bit of profundity, I'll leave you to your work. I'm waiting for the Patch spirit to return from an important meeting, which should give us a handle on the amount of help we can expect to fortify our defenses with."

I departed Virgil and made my exit. The bird showed no ill effects from my intrusion. In fact he preened his crown feathers and extolled, "Arrkkk! Woe is us; woe is me; woe is you; and woe, woe, woe your boat. Arrkkk!"

I wondered if a lobotomy was called for.

CHAPTER 89

"Woe is me" is right. I find myself facing a conundrum. I was drawn to this family, especially the Patch child, in an effort to combat the horror called Lili-It. Now I find that I have been used as a pawn in a much larger scenario.

Do I continue my nurturing of the girl, or do I relinquish that obligation to this new player, whose qualifications I do not recognize, whose history I do not recall, and whose goals appear to be a carbon copy of mine?

I suppose that in all fairness, I should allow her a fair amount of time to prove to us that her intentions are legitimate and that her leadership in this venture will be accepted by all involved, especially me.

So, for the moment, instead of keeping watch over the youngster, I will investigate the area known as New Mexico.

At first appearance, a certain dichotomy presents itself. You have on one side a barren expanse of heat and sand—a most unforgiving and unfriendly land. On the other hand, you have the cool of high altitudes. In the desert, you are stimulated by the sheer beauty of countless wildflowers making their appearance in what appears to be a haphazard manner brought to fruition by the periodic rains that nourish the seared and sandy soil; that abstract canvas of line and hue draws the attention of birds, insects, and a varied assortment of wildlife, whether winged or legged or serpentine.

There is history here.

Pass by the arroyos; walk through the canyons; step through the brush and over the rocks and sand. Listen to the wind: "Hey … ay … ay … ay … ai …oh!"

Listen to the rattle of the serpent, the "screee" of the raptor, the plaintive siren of the coyote; song of the night.

There is history here, from the shuffling of moccasins to the ringing of spurs, from the clang of swords to the thunderous blast of cannons, from the screams of countless clusters of innocents to the subjugation of a people … to the rebirth of a nation and a rekindling of pride.

There is history here.

Thousands of years of history.

As in the history of the civilized world as we know it (including religion, violence, and the renaissance of art and music … and more violence), there is also history here of religion based upon a renaissance of the soul, portrayed by art and music dedicated to the gods of what is and what was, of violence wrought by the capriciousness of nature, the ambition of brothers, and the greed of the civilized world.

History is relative as perceived by diverse societies … but it is history. If you listen hard enough, you will hear it, and perhaps join in its song.

"Hey … ay … ay … ay … ai … oh!"

Daytime is a time for avoiding the oppressive heat of the desert. The cold-blooded denizens thrive in the sun's warmth by replacing the cold of the previous night.

The warm-blooded ones dart here and there from the ever-changing shade of a rock or a cactus or the meager protection afforded by the tendril-like projections of the desert flora. Constant movement makes them a difficult target for the snake, the spider, the hawk.

Nighttime is their time for foraging. It is then that they become the predator and not the prey. What was once a dinner now becomes the diner.

This desert offers a microcosm of nature's grand theme: big fish eats little fish. The eternal food chain thrives here, with man at the apex as the prime predator with only himself as his worst enemy. He is not a consumer of body but a cannibal of the soul.

The desert is but one climatic variation in this New Mexico country. One can slowly climb through many different areas where desert flora and fauna change into magnificent trees, like oak and pine and spruce; and continue upward, through pine forests; and climb still higher—

where, finally, only wildflowers and algae exist. Along the way, the traveler might run into (if they aren't careful, that is) bears, mountain lions, and the less predatory deer and antelope. Looking up, one may spot eagles, hawks, owls, and a multitude of songbirds.

This almost mystical site seems to epitomize what gifts nature has bestowed for all life to enjoy. Without man; it is a Garden of Eden meant to exist in an aura of peace and complacency—an ideal locale for the emergence of the angelic Patch. Irony, perhaps, but I am wont to believe that it is an endowment of fate … which, I'm sure, the minister would find immensely debatable.

Primitive man drew much of his strength from the mysteries of the natural world; perhaps that strength still exists, and we will be allowed to draw from it ourselves. Anna would have more knowledge of that prospect than I would.

CHAPTER 90

Late into the night, I still had heard no word from Leader or from the Patch entity. I really needed to find a different name for her; "the Patch entity" was really ridiculous.

The church interior afforded me a haven in which to relax my thoughts and achieve a feeling of serenity. I can't call it a religious epiphany, so I'll just refer to it as a man-made refuge in a world of impending chaos. Don't even think of calling it rationalization!

I guess I wasn't chosen to be allowed peace and quiet. The opening of the chapel door roused me from my stupor as the Reverend Bill sauntered in, dressed in his bedclothes.

He quietly approached the front of the building and sat himself down on one of the benches facing the altar. He sat there for a while, staring but not seeing the image of his deity positioned on the wall in front of him.

I left him that way for a while before I decided to accost him in as calm a manner as I could conjure up.

"It's late, Bill. What brings you here—a physical or spiritual ache?"

"Is that you, Virgil? You seem to be everywhere."

"Not really everywhere, but when I'm needed, I do seem to be available."

"I'm concerned that we might not have the necessary alliances needed to be successful in our future conflict with the so-called evil of all evils. If she is as powerful as you and the new entity describe, perhaps we should try to entice as much of the public as we can to join with us? Or am I being simpleminded?"

"Try to understand; it's not sheer numbers that will turn the tide in our favor. It's more of an attitude; a sincerity of purpose; a true belief in a tenet of morality and ethics—what you would call godliness. It is the only weapon that could defeat Lili-It.

"I don't believe that you could ever enlist an army of your people to agree on any course of action."

"What do you mean by that? Surely if they agreed on a definite course of action, they would flock to our side?"

"In reply to your suggestion of enlisting the people's aid in confronting our dilemma, Reverend, let me remind you of a most memorable speech by your president as he addressed the Union many years ago.

"Please don't let his speech mirror any opinions I might privately hold, but instead accept it as a reflection of the futility of your election process and the fickleness of your fellow humans."

His answer was, as I expected, "I'm anxious as to where you're going with this, Virgil. Please proceed."

"This is as close to verbatim as I remember. It was quite a raucous occasion; I was there in the body of a female observer seated in the balcony. No need for me to explain why I had chosen her as a subject; suffice it to say that I was there.

"Here goes ..."

"My fellow Americans, I come before you this evening not to mollify you with platitudes or rhetorical words of optimism. Instead I am here to enlighten you as to the true condition of our beloved country.

Our government, the government which you have duly elected to serve both you and the future generations of Americans, has lost its way. Your children and grandchildren are in danger of inheriting a land that has been seriously divided by a concerted effort promulgated by your elected officials who have become mired in negativism.

No longer are they able to think for themselves and review the many public-interest questions that are presented to them by the voices of the people; they are instead blindly following the dictates of party solidarity.

We have become a government no longer of the people by the people and for the people, but a government embattled in the most insipid form of partisan politics.

Abraham Lincoln, in his Gettysburg Address, spoke of a great civil war testing "whether this nation or any nation so conceived and so dedicated can long endure."

My fellow citizens, we are once again involved in the midst of a great civil war. Only this time it is not fought on a theater of physical aggression; it is fought in a field of rhetorical combat. This is our battlefield; a hall of a hundred souls that have become so caught up in opposition to each other that progress, and the ultimate salvation of our way of life, is threatened.

A new leadership has been unanimously elected by you, the people, as a rebuke of the policies driven by the previous administration. Yet the wishes of the people have been ignored by the disciples of the past in a concerted effort to detract from our attempts to heal the malignant sores that manifested themselves in unmitigated aggression against sovereign nations; economic high jinks; budgetary irresponsibility; fiscal favoritism to the wealthy; and the manipulation, dissolution, and destruction of our credit-based society.

For every beneficial program designed for the public interest, the opposition has voted an unequivocal no.

The irony is that you the people, most affected by the policies of the past, have expressed their feelings in favor of our programs while your elected officials continue to ignore your wishes and disparage the spirit of recovery.

This is indeed a nation divided unto itself.

Lincoln said, "The world will little note, nor long remember what we say here, but it can never forget what they did here."

The world may not remember what is said here, but you must remember if we are to succeed and endure as Mr. Lincoln stated.

You have been told that taxes are an evil thing devised and encouraged by the "spend, spend, spend" policies of the newly elected government.

Let me enlighten you as to what those taxes have provided: Social Security ["Yeah!" by the left], Medicare and Medicaid ["Yeah!"], minimum wage ["Yeah!"], unemployment insurance ["Yeah!"], FDIC ["Yeah!"], and many, many more programs that have made life for the working class more comfortable and offered to them the potential for improving their standard of living. It has provided the means for their children to achieve a higher education and contribute to the betterment of society.

Each and every one of those programs, plus countless others, have been denigrated by a cabal of naysayers. Now those same purveyors of elitism are plodding ahead once more on a predestined plan of obstructionism.

We cannot let that happen!'"

"It was at this time that the members of the other side began rising from their seats and storming out of the hall. They were shouting unbelievably vicious epithets, such as, "liar," "demagogue," "socialist," and whatever else they could come up with in order to inflame and distract the listeners.

"Their very response accomplished nothing less than proving the viability of the strong and unprecedented charges leveled by the president."

"Our Judeo-Christian ethic demands that we give aid to those less fortunate than ourselves; for everyone of us faces the possibility of falling into a temporary pit of despair and need. I will emphasize 'every one of us'; therefore we must prepare for that eventuality by contributing our fair share of whatever wealth we might accumulate into a pool of magnanimity. It is the basis of morality and the salvation of our way of life!

Taxes are the most important requisites for the continuation and growth of an altruistic, compassionate, and service-oriented society!'"

"Well, he went on for some time, berating the now sparsely inhabited right-leaning side of the great hall.

"The speech, the likes of which had never been heard before in the history of your government, incited condemnation and ire, as well as cheers and exultation, amid the portals of politicos nationwide.

"It served as a rude awakening among the populace, but with a superhuman effort, the beleaguered opposition did what they seem to do the best, and that was the injection of bumper-sticker slogans and emotional buzzwords into the media and minds of America. And as usual, that propaganda blitz accomplished an ebbing of the emotion caused by your president's fiery rhetoric.

"So don't think that appealing to the people for aid in our imminent conflict with the evil of Lili-It will accomplish any more than the threat of global warming elicited at the same time. Nothing has changed. Your government is still mired in a tar pit of partisanship, and there have been no noticeable, albeit perhaps negative, changes in the perception of life. Global warming has been relegated to a minor position in the unending rhetoric of political banalities, and your earth—our earth—is slowly becoming uninhabitable. Your politicians, and I must emphasize my non-partisanship, concentrate on plotting the destruction of the presidency and have forgotten the plight of its citizens. I can assure you that after spending time with the architects of your government, this is not what they had in mind!

"I have withstood the temptation of involving myself in national and international politics to control despotism, inequality, and other means of depravity toward human society. Therefore, I don't condone, nor do I condemn, the policies of your government. I chose to recount that speech solely for what I believe would be an example of futility in your desire to enlist the aid of society and its leaders."

The Reverend Bill remained silent for a while, digesting my treatise on nonparticipation. I could sense his uncertainty as to the soundness of my logic.

"Don't you think that if the people understood the danger that apathy could foster among the world's population, they would band together in a supreme effort to counteract the danger? I just can't believe that they would turn their back on almost sure annihilation."

"The people have become totally apathetic toward anything that occurs outside their personal sphere of influence. They have become so inured to government's failure to accomplish anything beneficial for society that they have banded together in small groups in a last-ditch effort for their salvation. Politician's promises have been given numbers, and the people have resigned themselves to ignoring the proffered hackneyed discharges and referring to them, sarcastically, as 'Promise Number 3' or 'Policy Number 18.'

"Sadly, it has become a laughing matter, and I fear that the end result of this indifference will be devoid of humor ... and will be catastrophic."

"Virgil, you are exhibiting an excess of pessimism. We can't proceed against

Lili-It while being led by a commander submerged in defeatism. Snap out of it!"

"I guess you're right, Bill. But I can't overlook the fact that that stalemate war in Afghanistan has been going on for almost twenty years already and has only proven to be a game board for stale tactics and the training ground for aggressors and aggressees. It has also become the testing ground for new and vastly improved weaponry. There is no finality to that absurd situation, so how can we expect a decision of any value to be forthcoming?

"It will be entirely up to us to save their backsides, and the ironic part is that they will never know what we have done."

"I didn't know that fame is that important to you."

"Fame? No, not fame, but the realization that we have banded together and acted in a positive manner with only one goal in mind and that there was no bickering back and forth and no attempt at assigning a number to our policy. That is what is important to me: involvement and decision making by and for the group."

"Mr. Lincoln's beliefs, Virgil?"

"Mr. Lincoln's words will become prophetic, Reverend, once we have convened on that great battlefield of a war that we are fated to engage in. It is no longer a choice, but our destiny."

"My reason for coming to the chapel this late was to infuse some serenity into my psyche, but all that you accomplished was the accumulation of additional anxiety. I hate to complain too much, but you seem to have inherited my sanctuary. We'll have to work something out; I need this place for my own peace of mind."

"And so it shall be. However, if you need to talk to me, I'll always be nearby; agreed? I'll leave you to your solitude now."

CHAPTER 91

… and that's what I fully intended to do: grant him the solitude he demanded and deserved. But that was not to be, for the Patch entity returned and, to her credit, expressed a sincere degree of concern for Bill's condition.

"What are you doing?"

"The minister is in turmoil, Bean. He needs reassurance that what he will be called upon to do won't open the door to purgatory."

"What do you intend to do about it? He's teetering on the edge of collapse, and I wouldn't want him to have a breakdown."

"What I am going to attempt might not sit right with you, but you have to trust me. I believe that it will be a positive solution. I need your word that you will not interfere, no matter what you think. It is important to me … and to the minister."

"I don't know. Somehow I feel responsible for his present condition, as well as for the stresses that the family is caught up in."

"I give you my word that what he finally decides will be his own decision."

"If I believe that you have overstepped your interference, I will cut in and put an end to it. So go ahead; I'll be in the background, watching you."

Bill sat on the bench facing the altar, which had become his favorite spot in the past few days. He seemed to find solace in the symbolism that the podium and the totem of his belief provided.

It was at this juncture that the Patch surrogate made her move.

"Reverend, why do you torture yourself so? Is not the cause a righteous one?

Bill looked up, startled. "Virgil is that you? I thought we had agreed that I would be given the courtesy of privacy?"

A misty image of a man in coarse robes appeared in front of the minister. He was tall and with a sunburned face. His hair was long and somewhat matted, and it seemed to be bleached from countless days in the sun. He had a peaceful countenance about him, but his eyes held a look of both sorrow and strength, of compassion and of hope. He appeared to be carrying a heavy load, but his arms were empty.

"Who are you? Am I finally cracking up?" Bill asked.

"You are the same man as you were yesterday and will be tomorrow," the entity said. *"As to who I am, I am whomever you wish me to be."*

"Why are you here? If you are who I think you are, why have you chosen me to honor with your presence? I'm just a simple country preacher doing my best to offer guidance to whatever souls need consolation.

"Wait a minute! What am I doing talking to a ghost? What's next, howling like a coyote?"

"Howl if you may, but simple you are not. You do what you do without seeking reward, Reverend Bill, for your reward is the knowledge that you have given aid to your fellow man. That, Reverend, is the noblest of gifts, but you cannot deny that you are also seeking guidance and solace yourself. And you search for it in the truth of your scriptures."

"The scriptures ... are they your words? Are you ...? Nah, my imagination just short-circuited!"

"Shhh; do not trouble yourself with a needless search for the identity of who stands before you. Let us talk instead about what it is truly upsetting you."

Bill sat there, entranced by the figure before him. Finally, resigning himself to the moment, he started speaking, more to himself than to his visitor.

"I have always believed in a peaceful approach to conflict: *'Accipere quam facere praestat injuriam.'*[38]

---

38   kk Latin: "It is better to suffer an injustice than to do an injustice."

"Turning the other cheek," he continued, "is a strong weapon in demonstrating one's ability to withstand an assault of both verbal and physical abuse.

"A bruised face is a small price to pay for the advent of harmony.

"But now I find myself in a demanding situation that a raw cheek is incapable of preventing. I find myself in circumstances whereupon I shall be called upon to commit physical violence upon my fellow man. This is against all that I believe and all that I have been preaching for these many years.

"How can that be right? Is not peace what you have advocated in your sermons?"

The robed entity smiled at Bill's recitation of a Latin phrase as he placed his hands on Bill's shoulders. It was with a look of sympathy and concern for the man that the entity addressed him.

"My sermons: have you not yet given up on the search for who I am? My true identity is not important, but the words we share are.

"I will attempt to convey a story to you," **the entity continued.** *"Perhaps they will provide or initiate a possible resolving of your quandary."*

I became enthralled with the play being enacted before me. Any thoughts of interfering with the actors dissolved with the anticipation of what would emerge from this conference of two. *I think that I'm beginning to see where she is going with this scenario. Very interesting ...*

"It was a dark time for my people when I was born. After many years existing in a land replete with tribal authorities, they came together and gave themselves over to the worship of one God. This extraordinary concept was not welcomed by the powers that be, so they were castigated and enslaved.

"Their deity was a harsh one who demanded strict observance to his edicts, with no room for forgiveness. My people had lost all hope for redemption and freedom.

"I felt that we deserved more than the fear of our God, so after many years of wandering through foreign nations, observing their beliefs and spending many more years in contemplation, I arrived at a new concept, combining old beliefs with new ideas.

"My ideology, while based upon the original commandments, stressed brotherly love, aid to the needy, and redemption for our sins. I believed that if we followed those objectives, upon our deaths, we

would be reborn in a heavenly place where peace and love would reign throughout all eternity."

"But didn't you find yourself feeling anger and resentment at the rulers of your land?" Bill interrupted.

"Once, when I felt that my people were employing usury against those unfortunates who were unable to provide for themselves, I resorted to violence and ejected them from our temple."

"You are who I think you are. Why do you avoid my reciting your name?"

"It is not necessary for names to be praised; just words and the messages that they convey. May I continue?

"I must apologize to you for drawing this story out too long. I guess that I don't have the opportunity to interact with people much anymore.

"After I ejected those hypocritical Pharisees, the people turned against me, and I was sacrificed for their sins.

"I was a simple man with no other goal than to give spiritual aid and the promise of an afterlife filled with love, as do you, to my fellow man. What threat could I have been guilty of? I guess the notion of equality and the sharing of substance with love for our brothers were considered dangerous concepts. Since when has love become such an ominous threat to the survival of society?

"I did not anticipate, nor did I promote, the formation of a movement in my name. I shudder to think what has occurred. Furthermore, words that I had never uttered but were attributed to me had become gospel to the new faith."

"But those words," interrupted Bill. "Those words have formed the basis for one of the world's great religions. Even if, as you say, they weren't your words, what could you possibly have against them? It's not as if they incite people to foment anything but peaceful thoughts."

"In truth, they are as you say—the words are pure, that is. But those very same words have been used to enslave billions of people, and due to their selective use by ambitious leaders, they have, in fact, been used to incite a vast number of inconceivably aggressive actions.

"That movement, based upon those very expressions, has became an organized religion, and with it have come conflicts for power and the amassing of enormous riches not intended for the needy but instead for the powerful elite.

"... and all in my name.

"I was just a simple man with a simple desire, not a symbol of wanton greed and aggression—and, most important, not a preacher of intolerance toward others. Out of all of man's misdeeds, I find that intolerance most repugnant of all.

"All has been accomplished in my name!"

"And what of the faith of your fathers?" Bill asked. "Did you not cast dispersion upon those who followed the tenets of that 'harsh God'?"

"No, no, no! Just because I no longer felt a connection with that belief system, I felt that every man should be able to follow the dictates of his own soul.

"Because their faith promoted learning above all, they became ostracized for their success in their societies and especially in the trades. In every organization from petty governments to full-sized nations, due to their own greed and gluttony, all turned to the learned ones for loans to salvage their own existence. When it came time to repay those debts, they themselves accused the lenders of excess greed and proceeded to further condemn them.

"If it wasn't loans they coveted, it was excessive taxation. It was an unbearable situation that constantly forced those subjects of brutality to seek new horizons to settle in.

"So what we have is anger, fear of a monotheistic belief system, and jealousy arising from their success in the business venue. So we end up with a denunciation of an entire race. They were forced to continuously escape the tribulations forced upon them and, in a concerted attempt at survival, dispersed to the four corners of the earth."

Again a question from Bill: "You disparaged the harshness of their deity, and yet you seem to show, for lack of a better word, pride."

"It was the faith of my fathers, and it was my faith for many years. It was the foundation for my beliefs, so how could I not respect it?

"There is one aspect of their religion that I want to emphasize to you, and it is the fact that the only thing that kept the followers enveloped in the sanctity of their convictions as they wandered the earth was the strict adherence to the tenets of their God. No matter what land, what government, what trials they encountered, their devotion kept them as one people. They knew that someday, they would come together once again in their own land and be joyous once more."

"So," Bill asked, "what is it you're trying to tell me? Am I to continue to suffer the contradictions in my mind without any chance of relief? Is there no answer?"

"Just this: no matter what hardships or adversity one might face, the right to defend yourself against injustice is your entitlement ... even if, God forbid, it involves violence. A strict adherence to your fundamental beliefs, if they are righteous in nature, is your inherent strength.

"*So when you find yourself facing your maker and feel that you must beg forgiveness and ask for penance, be prepared instead to bask in his praise, for in your case, the end will justify the means, and you will be blessed."*

"And finally, do not feel sorrow for those souls who were sacrificed in your battle against evil, for they will be your congregation in heaven. Remember, 'Amat Victoria curam.'"[39]

"I realize that I may be a bit self-centered," Bill said, "but will I survive the encounter?"

The image smiled and answered, *"I cannot foretell the future; nor do I want to. You will know the answer to your question when it presents itself. Just bear in mind that you combat evil 'Ad maiorem dei gloriam.'"*[40]

"Will I ever see you again?"

"Do you see me now?"

With that reply, the image faded as if the light had slowly been dimmed at the final curtain of a highly reflective performance of one— in this case, perhaps, a virtual reality recital worthy of the highest plaudits.

Bill collapsed on his knees, and tears fell unashamedly down his cheeks. I believed that a tremendous weight had been lifted from his shoulders and that he finally had arrived at a decision which he could live with.

---

39 Latin: "Victory favors those who take pains."
40 Latin: "For the greater glory of God."

CHAPTER 92

"Stop!
"Cease!
"Desist!"

"I was waiting for you to come charging in again.

"It's the religious thing again, isn't it? I thought we had it covered the last time you interrupted the story: as long as man puts his beliefs above and beyond his physical being, religion will in the forefront of thoughts.

"We have talked about this countless times, Bean. What I want, for the umpteenth time, is for my wayward race to think for themselves. I have nothing against religion, but I fear that we have become enslaved to words preached to us by unscrupulous leaders, both in the religious arena as well as in almost every aspect of our lives, especially politics.

"We blindly follow whatever tenets appeal to us, whether or not they excite unconscious bias or bigotry in our minds. Those words, declared in a most deceitful manner, have formed the basis of a society split into so many divisions and subdivisions that the only way for us to come together would be for a major catastrophe to threaten our very existence; that is a horrible solution for the salvation of a once-proud nation.

"Think of our mysterious character. To paraphrase her dictum, it's the words—think of the words and not the uses that have been debased.

"I am afraid, Bean, that we—man, that is, are reverting to our tribal origins. These divisions and subdivisions I speak of are causing us to merge into an excess of societies within our social order out of a necessity propelled by an emotional need for self-preservation."

"I guess I didn't have to say anything this time. You've expressed your feelings in a thoughtful and passionate manner, and I respect them. The only thing I fear is that you might turn this story into a condemnation of religion. Sometimes I fear that you are walking a tightrope there."

"Just the opposite, Bean. Religion is the mainstay of society and the glue that prevents it from falling into chaos. But when it is used as a tool to achieve ends which are in contradiction to its original purpose, I must speak out. While I do not subscribe to nor do I promote any one religion, I myself follow the dictates of a self-imbued aura of morality in as pure a form as I can consciously permit myself to. It might not be recognized as a formal religious articulation, but it is a sincere sentiment."

"I believe you; that's why I chose you to write my stories.

"I'm sure we will converse many times in the future, but for now, continue with your words."

"As you wish."

CHAPTER 93

The Patch entity and I quietly left Bill to his reverie and convened in a region only accessible to our kind.

"That was quite a performance. You almost had me believing that you were a reconstructed image of him. How did you know what was in his mind ... or was it just a bunch of words designed to placate the minister?"

"Do you recall when I said that I wandered the earth for many years? Well, I was his companion in the wilderness, as well as his sounding board as he searched for his answers to the complexities of faith."

"Those were his words, then?"

"In a manner of speaking—maybe not verbatim, but the general substance of his thoughts and beliefs, yes."

"I am very impressed by your obvious attachment to history. It's just a matter of fate that we had never met during our journeys."

"Perhaps we did meet on separate occasions, but it wasn't the correct time to become acquainted?"

"Perhaps."

"Help me clear something up, if you will."

"If I am able to, it will be my pleasure."

"It's getting sort of ridiculous referring to you as the Patch thing or the Patch entity. What name would you be willing to call yourself for the sake of simplicity?"

"Hmmm ... I never gave it a thought before. I have never had a name, with the exception of 'Him Or Her Of No Name,' so how about something that signifies that? How about Jaindeaux? Kind of romantic, eh? However, you can call me Jain."

"I like it! Jaindeaux ... Jain. Good, Jain it shall be. I even think that Leader will like it.

"Well, Jaindeaux, what's our next step?"

"It's late, at least for humans. Maybe we should also call it a night and withdraw. Tomorrow will bring new life to the world, and we should be ready to welcome it."

CHAPTER 94

The sound of a child's laughter brought me back from my venture into the realm of introspection to the practical reality of life. Below me, seated on a bench in the garden, was Patch and, of all people, the good Dr. Crank. They were having a fine old time, with Crank reciting a few of his ridiculous ditties and Patch laughing and clapping her hands in time to his tunes.

♫♫♪♫
"Hey! I once knew a flea.
♪♫♪♪
He was a he-flea, not a she-flea,
♫♪♪♫
but a flea was he, and not a bee.
♪♫♪♪
Tra-la-la-la-la, tee hee!

This is an imp of many talents; however, I've yet to find a talent that is more useful than his ability to make a child laugh. I know that behind his absurdities, there lurks a faerie of a most serious and—although he might conceal it—a most sentimental nature.

Patch and Crank were having such a good time holding hands and dancing to his ditties that I decided to leave them to their repartee. What I truly wanted was to confront Jaindeaux and finally get a grasp on her timely appearance and interjection into our cadre of evil fighters.

I waited awhile before conducting a quick search of the area. She was gone without a trace—not even a ripple in the ozone. Crank and Jaindeaux had seemed to be getting along fine, and I was sure he knew where she had vanished to.

Now I was forced to wait for Leader to finish his playtime, so I could question him.

CHAPTER 95

The coughing and sputtering of an old—I believe it was actually a Hudson Hornet—car approaching the chapel caused Patch to look up.

"Oh, look, Dr. Crank: it's Anna Walks With Grace!" shouted the little girl. "I'll bet she'd like to play with us."

Before Crank could say anything, Patch dropped his hand and ran to greet her friend.

"Anna, Anna, come play with us. We're having such a fun time!"

Anna's face lit up as if the sun had burned its way through the grayness of a desert storm.

"Come, child; give Anna a hug. It is such a joy to see you. What are you doing out here by yourself?"

"Oh, silly, I'm not alone," she replied. "I'm playing with that silly Dr. Crank, and Virgil is there, too. He's not singing with us; he's just sitting there watching us."

Turning toward Patch, Anna said with a puzzled look on her face, "Where are they, child? I don't see them."

Crank chose that moment to materialize and called out to Anna, "Hey hey sacred sachem, come join us for a bit of terpsichorean reverie and a song."

Anna looked up and was startled by Crank's sudden appearance. Not trusting her eyesight, she blinked a couple of times before responding to his invitation.

"It will be my pleasure, Doctor," she said with a furrowed brow and a voice tempered with suspicion.

"Child," she said to Patch. "Where is Virgil? I thought you said that he was there also?"

Anna looked around as if she half expected me to poof into view, as Crank had done. Without answering, Patch took Anna's hand and gently pulled her toward the bench where Crank was now sitting.

"Please, child, don't pull me too hard. I woke up this morning with a bad pain in my back, and I have a little trouble walking fast."

Patch stopped immediately upon hearing Anna's plea and peered into the woman's eyes.

The girl's expression changed to a more somber one; she clearly felt the pain in Anna's body. Without further hesitation, she placed her hands on the area that was causing Anna discomfort.

"What are you doing, child? Aiee—your hands are so hot!"

Within a few moments, Patch stepped back, enveloped in what could only be described as a heavenly glow. As the glow dissipated, Anna straightened up in surprise.

"I don't know what you have done, child, but you have the hands of the gods. Come, let's go and join your friends. I could use a little cheering up.

"Dr. Crank," Anna addressed the errant boulevardier, "how lovely to see you again. I must say that your irreverent witticisms have been sorely missed. May I ask where you have been—or perhaps I shouldn't really want to know? And where is the ubiquitous Virgil? Patch mentioned that he was sitting with you."

"Virgil? Am I not enough of a presence to satisfy one and all? What could you possibly want with that dour blanket of civility? He is as much fun as a carbuncle on the end of one's nose.

"So come join us, and give yourself to a moment of worry-free frivolity."

"Indeed I shall," said Anna with a grin on her face and a light step in her walk. It was as if her troubled thoughts had evaporated, and a few minutes of nonsense would be more than welcome.

"Come, Anna, and sit on the bench with us," Patch beseeched, still holding on to the sachem's hand. "Dr. Crank might even sing another song for us."

As Anna Walks With Grace sat on that old garden bench, a calmness such as the moment before night gives way to dawn enveloped the area.

"Good morning, Anna," I said in a quiet voice, so as not to alarm her.

Looking around and seeing nothing but Dr. Crank and Patch, Anna replied, "Virgil! It's true: you are here. Would it be presumptuous of me to ask if you could present yourself in a manner to which I could identify more realistically?"

"If you mean a physical presence, yes, I will bow to your request. Is there any image that would be acceptable to you, or should I choose one at random?"

"Beware my spiritual companion, for this imp has a very limited imagination, and what you get might not be what you want. He is apt to morph into a squirrel and, if I may interject a bit of seriousness into this discussion, conversing with a rodent could be quite disconcerting."

So much for the tranquility of the moment.

"Crank, is there no end to your outlandish outpourings? Why, a squirrel would offer a bit of a novelty, as well as a cuddly object to caress."

"Enough from the two of you," scolded Anna. "Virgil, you may be anyone you wish to be … and Doctor, stop chiding Virgil!"

At that moment, Patch jumped up and clapped her hands. "Could you be a butterfly? I think butterflies are so pretty."

"Ahh, a butterfly! 'Tis a most clever solution to a most absurd situation, my dear … although I might have chosen a large feral moth myself."

With that snide remark, I transformed myself into a colorful butterfly and landed on Patch's outstretched hand.

"Thank you, Virgil," she said, with as happy an air as only a child can convey.

The mood changed almost immediately upon my materialization; Patch lost the innocence of youth and assumed the air of a mature person.

Alarmed, Anna spoke in a voice filled with confusion. "What has happened here?" she asked. "I was looking forward to a simple encounter with a few friends, and now I find myself caught up in some kind of bizarre symposium.

"My God," she exclaimed, "how on earth can I participate in a serious discussion—if that is the proposal—when I am faced with a child who is an adult; a ridiculous buffoon who appears and disappears at will; and a talking butterfly? If this is what I will be accosted with in my position of sachem, I had better give it much thought!"

"It's the words, Anna—just the words, and not the messenger."

"Where have I heard that before?" Anna muttered.

"My friends," Patch started. "My comrades in harmony, my crusaders against evil, ye defenders of morality: I would like to offer a little more enlightenment as to the malevolence of our adversary."

Good grief, she's been hanging around Crank too much.

Patch spoke to us as if we were sitting at her feet, and she was lecturing to a team of disciples.

"This harpy called Lili-It leads an army of one fueled by the fear and panic of the dying, and her battle cry is a symphony of the death knells of her victims. As the numbers of her victims grow, so does her strength and her area of influence, from the confines of a small village in the wilderness to towns, cities, and nations. As long she gives birth to suffering and death, she will cultivate larger and larger fields of ash.

"Her path is northward, the same direction man's supposed ancestors took as they proceeded in their evolutionary trek. There is no army left behind; there is no viable existence, for as she consumes the life force of her victims, they in turn revert, in kind, to the ashes of an extinct conflagration that desecrates the land as they slowly disintegrate and merge with the barren soil.

"Dear Anna, think of the remains of a ceremonial fire in your village the day after your rituals were consummated. What is left in the pit after eons and eons of religious rites? Ashes and the charred remains of a once-fertile square of land. This is what has commenced in Lili-It's path of hellish endeavor.

"Once the essence of her victims is absorbed, she must create new victims to replenish the lost ones, and she does that by constantly moving forward. There is no 'retreat' in her vocabulary, for retreat would spell failure. Without those new bodies and their souls, her strength would fail; ashes offer no sustenance for her. She may ultimately become too weak, without the nourishment of death, to offer any decisive opposition, but she can never die. She can only lie in wait for a new awakening of man's propensity for evil.

"There might, however, be a chance for holding her in abeyance if the three major religions joined together and used their power of righteousness and morality against her, for they have an inheritance of similar ancestry and have but to accept their commonality.

"But the antipathy and hate toward each other's beliefs and presence in the lands holy to each respective religion defeats the chance for the mutual coalescence necessary to augment a permanent halt to her advance. In fact, that very animosity may actually reinforce her sense of invulnerability; she thrives on discord and aggression."

We were so silent after that impassioned narrative that the mere dropping of a pin would have stampeded a herd of bison feeding in a valley many miles away.

Anna was the first to break the silence. "This is not the way I expected to spend my day," she said. "I think I have joined you under some misguided circumstances."

"Fright not, lady, for the happenstances young Patch has spoken of are occurring many leagues from us and do not affect our well-being at the present time."

"At the present time, you say? What do I take that to mean? That it is only a matter of time before we partake of the confrontation? And what, if I may ask, is our plan of action?"

I remained silent and just observed the debate going on around me. Butterflies should be seen and not heard.

Patch took Anna's hand once more and in a soothing tone said, "My dear Anna, please do not fret. Events are being set in motion at this very time. We must await the return of Jaindeaux, and then we will all convene and finalize the battle plan."

"And who, pray tell, is Jaindeaux? Is she another member of your spirit patrol that seems to be enmeshed in this cadre of improbability? And what about you, Virgil, if you are here at all? Silence does you an injustice; do you have anything to add to this black comedy?"

"I am truly at a loss for words, Sachem. Give me a moment to digest Patch's account of the oncoming melee, and I will stir my profound thoughts into the simmering casserole."

"My breath is short, and my ears await your wise and deep deliberations. I beseech ye to be prompt in your counsel."

I suddenly became the center of attention—figuratively, speaking of course; I was still invisible, excepting the image of a solitary butterfly, but my presence was felt by all but Anna Walks With Grace, as she hadn't developed the necessary sensitivity to see beyond the obvious as of yet. The conversation was unexpectedly put on hold in the hope that I would impart weighty words of wisdom.

"What Patch has said is most definitely dire in its meaning. I have no pretensions as to how to formulate a successful battle plan; I'll leave that up to the so-called experts. However, the scenario she paints of the aftermath of Lili-It's diabolical march and the incineration she leaves behind brings to mind an insightful bit of poetic license from my ghost. Unless we are successful in our endeavors, his words will wax prophetic and could very well be words incised on the final monument to man's failed habitation of this earth."

**"The dust has blown away
and only the pebble survives;
no longer
able to skip the waves."**[41]

Unbeknownst to us, the Reverend Bill had quietly joined the group. "Virgil," he said, acknowledging my heretofore indiscernible physicality, "you never cease to amaze me with your ability to switch personas—and, if I may add, the variety in your choices of likeness. But ... a butterfly?"

"I no longer have any doubt," he continued as if he were delivering a sermon, "of the eventual success of our mission, and I have accepted it; I have also accepted you and your ethereal brethren as allies. I must say that your words—or should I say the words of your ghost, as you call him—are quite glum, but they should become the seeds of our battle cry. Let the future of the words they portend endow us with the strength and fortitude necessary to defeat this godless entity."

"Amen," said Anna.

"I'll Toot my horn and rata-tat-tat my drum to the rhythm of the meter," sang the troubadour of the absurd.

"'Tis a foine thought indeed, Father," added Patch in her mother's Gaelic lilt.

"'Tis indeed," said Bill, smiling as he gently kissed his daughter's head.

---

41   Stephen Stuart, *Rantings* (2009).

"Virgil," Anna interjected, "does your ghost have any further words with which we can reinforce our commitment? His outpourings of gloom serve to instill in us a feeling of rejection for his pessimism; it is fodder for our optimism."

"I believe his take on evolution might suit your query. If I can remember, it goes something like this ..."

Evolution
(à la Ghost, as he penned it)

T he ...

First step is the hardest: it is the rising up from the primordial dust.

Second step is hesitation: it is the uncertainty of remaining upright.

Third step is confidence: it is the knowledge that there will be yet another step.

Fourth step is excitement: it is the ability to run.

Fifth step is the total rejection of common sense: it is the desire to scamper untamed and liberated in uncharted directions.

Sixth step is retribution and the crippling of the body and soul when the rationale for attaining an end to the journey is lost.

Seventh step is the return to the primordial dust.

Eighth step...there is no eighth step.

The Reverend Bill, still reciting in his sermon voice, added, "I can't accept that the entire race of man will, in one cataclysmic episode, revert to the lifeless dust that, for all eternity, will swirl through the endless vacuum of space with no definitive destination in mind. It is almost similar to purgatory, where the souls of the lost bide their time until a place is defined for them.

"I wonder if within that seemingly lifeless swirl of dust, there resides a microscopic grain of being that can form the basis of existence for another day?"

"We are drifting from the topic at hand, Bill. Maybe your Matt Christmas and one of his guests will debate your theory? Until then, we have to await Jaindeaux's return. I suggest that we take leave of this microconvention and tend to our chores."

"Daddy," Patch called out, once again a little girl. "I hear Mommy calling us for breakfast. I think she's going to make waffles today— yummy, my favorite! I'll race you to the house!" And off she ran, giggling all the way.

"You're all welcome to have breakfast with us, if you so desire," the minister told Anna. "There's always plenty to go around."

Anna stood up slowly and shook her head slightly, as if trying to tune static out of her mind. "I'll take you up on the invite if you don't mind, Reverend. All this has left me a bit dazed. A cup of Maeve's coffee would hit the spot about now.

"I'll say one thing, Bill: if it weren't for your presence, I would swear that I was encased in a Victorian cabinet of oddities alongside shrunken heads and viscera from a midget unicorn."

"My sentiments exactly," Bill replied.

"I extend my heartfelt gratitude for your most gracious invitation, but famished I am not," Crank announced. "My butterfly amigo and I have to attend to faerie matters and, unfortunately, they do not include sustenance. I wish you all a most glorious feast." Under his breath, he muttered, "Bean, where in hell are you"?

"I'm coming ... I'm coming. Do you think it's easy trying to fly against the wind? Give me a second!"

There is a fuzzy line between privacy and curiosity. I would enjoy being a fly on the wall in the kitchen and listening to the conversation that I was sure was going on right about then. It would take little effort to re-inhabit the caged one, but propriety won out, and I remained with Leader, abandoning my guise of a butterfly.

There was, in all reality, nothing further to do except wait for Jaindeaux to return. Where she had gone and what she had accomplished is open for conjecture, but it would be a waste of time to attempt enlightenment.

Patch, on the other hand, was improving the ability to alter her personality from a young child into a mature entity. I don't believe that she has developed far enough to do it at will or to assume the identity of a clairvoyant on a permanent basis. My hope is that it will be a temporary manifestation and one that will either disappear when all this has been completed or put into some sort of limbo to re-emerge when needed. If, however, her gift matures with her years, she will be placed in the unpleasant role of either a freak of nature or a wondrous symbol of religious fervor. Either position would undoubtedly result in a degree of infamy that could endanger her very existence. Man, although reveling in the technological excitement of progress, is still superstitious, suspicious, and immature and will let emotion overrule acceptance. Whatever the end result will be, the journey toward it promises to be a fantastic voyage.

Leader went off to who knows where, and I assumed my usual escape into the realm of introspection. Peace and quiet was the rule there, and I relished the thought.

CHAPTER 96

I let my mind wander back to a time when the earth hadn't been as overpopulated with humans as it is now—a time when nature was the ultimate sovereign ruler over its domain. Back then, the natural order was the normal means, and man, in his infancy, was but an insignificant actor.

How I had relished those days. There wasn't much for me to do in my role of do-gooder at the time, but it didn't matter, because innocence and simplicity blanketed all living subjects.

I lived the carefree life of a faerie along with countless constituents of our various orders. It was as close to the Eden of your scriptures as your prophets could describe ... but far more than that. You don't have the words or the language to accurately describe the prevailing attitude.

Now it was there that I retreated, in an effort to rid myself, at least temporarily, of the enormous responsibility that had befallen me. You would call it meditation, and in a way it was, but without the requisite "ommm."

Patch's butterfly best embodied the carefree mood I attempted to envelop myself in. Gossamer wings of brilliant color floating weightless on the whimsical attitude of the breezes, I drank the nectar of the blooms displayed in a masterpiece of impressionism while I exulted in the serene warmth of a sun bestowing the gift of life to all.

These are your words in a language that you could understand: simple, but no way as descriptive as our tongue.

As completely lost in my reverie as I would have desired to be, I still found myself thinking of Patch and what the future held in store for her. Although I was imbibing the nectar that was so graciously placed before me, I could still hear her voice calling, "Bean ... Virgil ..." I guess that my mind was unable to rid itself of the complexities it found itself mired in.

"Bean ...Virgil ... can we talk?"

I suddenly realized that my mind was not playing tricks on me, nor had I become intoxicated by the blossom's offering. Patch herself was communicating with me—not in the physical sense, but through the teleportation of thought. She has matured further than I had first imagined.

It was more of a plea than a request. "Bean ... Virgil ... I am confused and scared. I need support and perhaps an understanding of what's happening to me. I feel as if the words that appear to be coming from my mouth are emanating from another individual ... and yet, there is no one else in close proximity. They are not the words of the child I am ... I was ... I was ... I am.

"Who am I? Or, more specifically, what am I?"

Why was it that I was always the recipient of these esoteric inquiries? *"Who am I? What am I?"* Heck, I was beginning to question my own self—even my own sanity! *Who in their right mind would offer a noncorporeal entity with supposedly no human emotions sympathy? But those same people have no qualms about demanding deep philosophical answers from one. Where is the justice in that?*

I should position myself on an outcropping of barren rock situated upon some isolated windy mountain and set office hours for the discharging of mindless profundities. Maybe I can arrange an hour with the Reverend Bill's Matt Christmas?

Now that I had submerged myself in self-pity, an emotion totally alien to us faeries, what could I offer Patch in the way of encouragement?

"I'm here, Patch, although I don't know if I can answer your questions.

"Who, what, and why are the most common questions asked by your species. There are no absolute answers to questions seeking the reasons for your being. In fact I find asking myself those very same questions.

"With the exception of the lower forms of life, who just accept the who, what, and why they are, we the so-called higher examples, are more inquisitive and, perhaps, more insecure in ourselves as to the who, what, and why.

"Environment, evolution, and genetics all combine to form the random physicality that we project to the world. One can even include the position of the stars; the time of the day; and the day of the week, month, and year. Was it raining, or was the sun shining? Which way you were facing when you were born? Was music playing? What kind of music? And on and on.

"We are all a potpourri of chance, a repository of ingredients I choose to call fate.

"Some people are preordained to be carpenters; others ... scientists, artists, ne'er-do-wells, religious leaders like your father, and so forth."

"But ... then we don't have any choice at all? Do I have to accept the fact that I may be a freak of nature? One instant, I am a little girl, happy and living with a family I love and who loves me. And then, suddenly, I am this schizoid example of nature's arbitrary design.

"Look—here I am conversing with you as if I was some mature academic carrying on a philosophic debate with an ancient spirit, and I'm only a mere child!"

"Your father would probably say that you were touched by God and endowed with divine abilities to be utilized in the furtherance of his grand design for mankind ..."

"And that's your answer? I'm touched!"

"In simplistic terms ... yes. But touched by whom? Or what? Aha! That's the question."

"People who are described as crazy are also described as touched. What you're saying, in fact, is that you think I'm crazy. Wonderful: so now I'm to believe that the chosen one, the one who is expected to lead the righteous in a final battle of good against evil, is crazy? What does that say to the rank and file who must put their faith in a leader you describe as mad?

"Perhaps we should empty the hospitals for the insane and enlist the inmates in our cause. What greater recipe for success can be found than the loony leading the loony?"

"Aren't you exaggerating just a bit? I don't know what lies ahead in your future, and if I did, I couldn't very well alert you to it. I don't know how you'll control the constant shifting back and forth from child to adult, and I don't know what the culmination of your powers will achieve; but I do know that you are not crazy, as you so vividly put it. I also know that as you become more comfortable and as you learn more

about those powers, you have to exert extreme caution as to how you utilize them. Millions of lost souls could very easily latch on to your facilities and consider you a godlike figure. Before you realize what has occurred, you will have an immense following, and a new religion will be presented to the world with you as its leader."

"Is that so wrong? With what I believe in, combined with those powers you speak of, I could in fact cultivate a revolution of morality and doom immorality to its rightful position in the core of the misbegotten. I could achieve in a few years what has yet to be attained by man even after thousands of years."

"But you are not a god, however seductive or tempting the notion might be."

"If it takes a god for the world to realize that the way to survival is the path that I choose to follow, then a god I'll be!"

"Consider, if you may, that the words of past prophets have been bastardized beyond reality and that the original tenets have been lost forever. What you hear now are the convoluted precepts of countless false prophets and fanatics passed down century to century as the words of their respective divine beings. Not only have they been convoluted, but their meanings have been interpreted to fill whatever void is present and whatever end is desired."

"Consider if you may that they didn't have the benefit of the modern communication facilities we have now. My words will be my words only, spoken in person to those who wish to hear them. My deeds will be You-tubed, Facebooked, Googled, cabled, prime-timed, satellited, DVR'd, and taped for posterity. I will have no fear of what you refer to as bastardization. Perhaps that is what I have been chosen to accomplish? I envision a ministry of the air whereupon my actual presence is not required but instead beamed to the world at a location of my choosing and at a random time."

"How can I respond to that except to say that maybe, just maybe, you're right, but you will join a long list of TV and radio evangelists who preach their messages daily, weekly, and at all hours of the day and night. What will make you any different?

"Anna Walks With Grace has said that you are chosen: again, chosen by whom ... or what? How would you utilize your powers without exposing yourself to the constant demands of the hordes of the needy and selfish society following you not because of your words, but because of what you can do for them personally?

"Let's get something straight: I—we—have no idea of what those so-called powers will evolve into. They very well might offer a means of salvation to a paranoid, suspicious, self-involved, aggressive world that would like nothing more than to live in peace and love thy neighbor.

"Patch, you suffer from the immaturity of youth. Your words might suggest maturity, but your lack of life experience suggests naïveté. I'd say that although you foresee a human race yearning for a world as you envision, you can't be so sure that's what they want. Your hope for mankind is not necessarily man's hope. Do you intend to sway the masses, utilizing your metaphysical facilities—if that is what they are—to believe that you alone are the embodiment of brotherhood and that your dream is for a future devoid of fear and want?

"You might achieve your goal, but your aspirations would prove to be short-lived. the demise of the prophets of history and myth gave birth to movements that benefited not the whole of society, but of the few who assumed the mantle of leadership by nefarious means and altered their words for self-aggrandizement."

"What if my so-called powers granted me eternal life? That would solve the problem of my words being altered to fit the selfish ambitions of the few."

"You're beginning to scare me, Patch.

"If indeed a seed has been planted, extreme care must be utilized to fertilize it with great concern, so it grows straight and tall, and its blossom is one of beauty. If, however, it is planted in polluted soil and nourished with poisonous fare, the end result would be ugliness and a shoot to avoid."

"'Tis an interesting concept and one to ponder at length … at another time".

"And now what will you do?"

"Now what? Now I think I will play with Virgil, he of the preening; and help Mommy with dinner. I find myself in desperate need of a few 'arrkkk's."

CHAPTER 97

**"The shadows of despair; of rejection
and depression
need but a scintilla of the sun's radiance
to deliver hope; and it always appears
after the mightiest of tempests."**[42]

Phew! I quake at the thought of yet another soul elevating herself to the loftiness of a godhead—another *diviner du jour*. In the past, the number of individuals professing to preach a message of sincerity coupled with a desire to minister to those in need, while at the same time avoiding a rise to a self-proclaimed position of celestial authority, were few and far between.

Yet history is filled with false prophets yearning for the adoration and the power that that lofty site grants. How many of those diviners of morality started out innocent but fell victim to the adulation that inadvertently goes along with that filling of the niche in the psyche of the lost and despairing?

It is a very tempting aphrodisiac of the spirit, a snorting of the drug of delusion and dreams … and an addiction not easily cured.

My deepest concern is that Patch might not be able to survive such enticement. If she were indeed immortal, would her sheer physicality be enough to arrest any debasement of her ideology? That visible presence would be in contrast to the spiritual immortality of past prophets and

---

42   Stephen Stuart, *Rantings* (2009).

the altering, in kind, of their precepts. Does society prefer a spiritual essence to that of a physical entity? Would the presence of a living, easily accessible, and visible prophet be an impediment to her veracity? It would cause man to ponder the possibility that man indeed created his god in his own image and not vice versa. Maybe man himself is God, after all, for isn't he the master of his own destiny? Your history is replete with leaders of society and religion who aspired to be gods. Look upon the grandeur of the pharaohs, the reverence of the Dalai Lama, and the mystique of Hirohito: all were gods in their own right and in human visage. Furthermore, you cannot overlook the miscreants, the leaders of baseless sects who professed to be the voice of God, also in human form.

Either way, Patch faces decisions that could ultimately alter the course of humanity. Phew!

"Stop!
"Cease!
"Desist!
"Hold up!
"Whoa!"

"What is with that impassioned plea, Bean? 'Stop! Cease! Desist!' would have been sufficient. Actually, in all reality, I half expected you to interrupt."

"That's good; I wouldn't want to disappoint you.

"I've given you a great deal of latitude in your obsession with religion, but I think you might have exceeded the boundaries this time. You seem to be offering a conclusion when you talk about man himself being God instead of the spiritual representation that has been the accepted norm throughout the ages.

"I'm a little uneasy about the direction this dialogue is taking."

"I believe that the inclusion of the word 'maybe' would have been enough to offset your expected apprehension. It was just a question. It was almost as if I were asking myself, 'What if?'

"I'm sure that your readers are intelligent enough to put it in the correct perspective, aren't you?"

"Touché; I will bow to your explanation as usual. But I'm still a bit wary. So humor me, and in the future, maybe you can discuss your controversial thoughts prior to your including them in the narrative?"

"If I did that, we would never complete this consortium of pages. You have to trust me to follow the parameters we have agreed upon, both in the original novel as well as in this one."

"Sometimes you appear to taunt me with your attempts to infuriate the reader. No ... infuriate is not the correct term. 'Raise the hackles of' might be a better phrasing.

"Nevertheless, please continue ... but remember that I am always watching you."

"How can I ever forget?

"Now, if you'll excuse me ..."

CHAPTER 98

Where is Jaindeaux? In the brief time since she made her first appearance, I've become quite dependent upon her; although I should know better.

Leader seems to have accepted her and has no trepidation about following her lead in our odyssey. Maybe I'm just a bit piqued about her taking charge after all that I have done?

How about a little humanism: if our journey fails, I can identify her guidance as the impetus of our collapse.

Wrong! It's not who I am. Jealousy is not an impish quality!

"Bean." The voice resonated in my ions.

"Jaindeaux, is that you?"

"It is," she replied. "I will return shortly, as soon as I complete a few more errands. Just keep watch on everything. We'll have much to discuss when I get back."

"That's an understatement. Wait until I introduce you to our future God."

"What are you talking about? We don't have time for such nonsense."

"It might not be as nonsensical as you think. We'll talk later."

CHAPTER 99

The normal household routine returned for the time being, with Maeve and Patch in town doing the week's shopping and the Reverend Bill at his usual position at the living-room desk.

For once Virgil was subdued and concentrated instead on preening and eating his seeds.

It was an idyllic scene, as if nothing of any portent had interrupted the lives of an average family concerned with simple, everyday chores.

The temptation to interrupt this storybook facade was too great to ignore, so I shamelessly entered Virgil and prepared to confront the good Reverend Bill Fellows.

"Arrkkk! The pen scratches, and the words appear: just temporary marks on a temporary surface meant to serve as tinder for a bonfire of futility. Arrkkk!"

Looking up from his daily ritual, the minister, with unmasked exasperation, asked, "Is that you, Virgil the avian, or is it Virgil the alien? Either identity, I have work to do and a discourse with you, whoever you might be and however stimulating it might be, is not commensurate with my pious obligations."

"Virgil the alien?"

"We're getting a bit uppity now, aren't we, Reverend? I thought I would offer my sensitive side to you in the remote event you needed to unload some of your conflicted soul-searching. I guess I was wrong, so I won't barge in on your religious reverie."

"I'm sorry, Virgil, but writing is one way to put aside what you refer to as 'conflicted soul-searching.' I know we'll have to face it much sooner than later, but I can't relinquish my missionary responsibilities for something that has yet to arrive."

"You have something there, Bill. I should have more definitive news in a day or so; so try to keep your sanity until then. You'll have sufficient opportunity to rant and rave at that time."

"Thanks for the encouraging words, Virgil; it really helps!"

Should I mention Patch's latest contemplation about becoming the future savior of humanity, or should I leave well enough alone?

Leave well enough alone? Right. Thanks, reader.

"There is always one sure way to forget your pressures, and that is, of course, another brain drain from Matt Christmas and his bevy of boneheads. Isn't it time for his latest guest to pollute the airwaves?"

"It's kind of late, but we might still catch some preposterous rhetoric," the minister suggested. "Let's see now; I've been having a little problem with the TV set lately. It takes longer and longer to warm up, and when it finally does, I'm greeted by flickering and snow. It'll make Christmas's guests appear as if transmitted from outer space. Kind of fitting, don't you think?"

As predicted, it took a while for the picture to arrive, and when it did, we were greeted by a bespeckeled female orator, complete with a straight hairdo; sunken cheeks; pronounced chin; a nose that Virgil would envy (except for a strange bluish growth on her left nostril), and a low, almost masculine voice.

> *"If births were to stop instantaneously and man became immortal, would progress continue to forge ahead, or would society ultimately become stagnant and eventually just fritter away? Would war be an eternal game with no winner and no loser and—in a positive vein—no casualties? And yet, would there be any reason for war at all? Furthermore, would there be any reason for reason?"*

It was at that profundity that Matt Christmas interrupted.

"I would like to thank Professor Sigrid Lokisdotter for her thought-provoking talk.

"On our next broadcast, we will have the noted astrophysicist Saito Bokchoy from the esteemed University of Bensonhurst. He will talk on the theory of bubble universes, a topic that will undoubtedly excite our interest. He has received some critical notoriety with this hypothesis, which concerns man's true identity."

The show cut to a clip of Dr. Bokchoy speaking:

"Perhaps each human being is a universe unto himself. He or she consists of atoms, molecules, bacteria, viruses and electrical impulses, much like an organic solar system controlled by a central element, like a sunlike entity, circulating life around and around, almost as if in an astral configuration. Is the external form of the body just the bubble containment of his personal universe? Could the extraterrestrial universe be the embodiment of a live entity of which man is but an atom or bacteria or even a virus in its containment?"

"I know that you are as excited as I am in meeting Dr. Bokchoy.

"But first, a word from our sponsor ..."

Would you have ever thought that toilet bowls extolling the benefit of a wondrous cleaning and disinfecting solution would be so happy? I believed that the minister's face flushed from my question.

What kind of stories your commode would relate? On second thought, I'd rather not become (a) privy to that information.

"My goodness, Virgil—is the world's academia truly stocked with grants for mindless research like Dr. Bokchoy's? I just cannot believe that universities would endow their faculty for research like that.

"Christmas seems to outdo himself every day. Interesting, though: didn't Crank rant about bubbles when he first entered the scene? I wonder if it's a coincidence.

"But you're right: I feel better already. Now leave me alone, and grant me peace!"

"Arrkkk! ... and so to sleep the sleep of the lost and discarded. Arrkkk!"

"Well spoken, bird."

Well spoken, perhaps, but is was time for me to be silent. Of course, I can't speak for the true bird. He's free to babble at will unless Bill decides to cover his cage.

As for me ... well, I might just hang out for a while—unobtrusively, of course. I'd like to see what, if any, dialogue commences when the family returns from their errands.

As the minister prepared to turn the TV off, he stopped in midstride as the latest news briefs emerged on the screen. The main topic was a report of a strange malady that had started as a small anomaly originating in the center of the African continent and had since grown in size and direction.

"Satellite observations show that this manifestation appears to be moving at a slow pace north and east toward what scientists believe could be a possible intrusion into the lands of the Middle East.

As of this report, no eyewitness description of this potential devastation has been available, but from what we have gathered, its spread could be best described as similar to the insipid growth of a malignant cancer.

Interviews with local inhabitants have been hampered by the unbelievable fact that there appears to be no survivors.

From what the cameras aboard the space lab report, a large migration of animal life away from the incoming conflagration seems to be in effect. Humans, on the other hand, appear to be totally unaware of the danger heading their way. The only life, if could be referred to in that manner, is the multitude of black dust devils randomly swirling across the barren wasteland.

Meteorologists, environmentalists, and other scientists, as well as astronauts in the space lab, are keeping a close watch on this never before seen phenomenon, utilizing the most sophisticated instrumentation available.

Preliminary investigation describes the scene as appearing to have been scorched by extremely high temperatures, but sensor readings contradict that theory. The land appears to be totally devoid of life and has temperature readings hovering around the freezing point.

The United States has requested an emergency meeting of the Security Council and, it is whispered, will put the blame on fundamental radicals.

Meanwhile, minority congressional members will put the onus on the president for his failure to combat terrorism.

We will strive to keep our listeners informed about this developing story."

"Virgil, if you are still here, I think it would be safe to say that the time is slowly approaching for our intervention, if any, to commence.

And yet I haven't seen a viable plan presented by any of your cohorts to instill confidence in me as to the future success of that mission. What say you?"

"I say, as I said before, in a day or two. Patience, Bill, patience."

"I sincerely hope so," he said as he extinguished the TV image. "My stress level is slowly elevating."

I kept my own trepidations to myself, not wanting to further excite the gentleman.

To pass the time, I decided, mainly out of curiosity, as I am wont to do, to reside for a few minutes in the mind of the garrulous cockatoo. Is he an avian savant or just a repository of mimic? There are some examples of the feathered species that are quite adept at mimic.

Point of reference: I once inhabited the psyche of a professional photographer. His name, although I pride myself on my memory, escapes me at the present and isn't important to my reminiscence. He was married at the time to a rather frivolous fashion model and was in the throes of initiating his entry into the world of glamour and fame.

Their rather intimate apartment, located in what was considered an artsy part of the city, was also home to a winged creature. This time it was in the countenance of a large black raven who, as it was, resided in a grimy monkey cage, a gift from the local pet store. This feathered aper had mastered the ability to recreate the voices of numerous humans and would enter into conversations with itself utilizing the intonations of those same individuals. In addition, due to the time spent residing in that same pet shop, it had managed to retain the sounds of the various denizens of said animal repository. So Raven spent the day deep in conversation with his many personalities while interjecting dog barks, sirens, and bits and pieces of popular songs—a true and motley community of one.

As for the photographer ...it's not important at the present, but perhaps the subject of a future revisit or a tale of its own. I might even recall his name.

When I entered his brain and examined his thoughts more closely, I discovered that Virgil was older than previously considered. I gathered that he must have lived for at least fifty years and had been the pet, or mascot, of either a classical repertory theater or of a university faculty cafeteria. Whatever his background, he has amassed a vast encyclopedia of literary bons mots and incomplete phrases and quotations from varied profound intellects as well as those of Matt Christmas's ilk. His ability to recall those absurd passages at what appeared to be the proper time is probably coincidental ... at least I think it is ... at least I hope it is!

Oh, well. I saw nothing more there, so I took my leave of that cranial cave of rhetorical splendor and retreated to a corner to await the return of Maeve and Patch.

CHAPTER 100

How long I hung there, I couldn't accurately inform you, but I was snapped out of my reverie by the sound of a car door slamming. Footsteps on the walkway halted as the door opened.

"... and you will have to be very careful what you do in the future, sweetheart," Maeve was saying. "There are some people who would take advantage of your God-given healing ability, and they could harm you."

The Reverend Bill looked up from his desk and asked his wife what the problem was.

"Arrkkk! It is the return of light and life to the stillness of this cave. Arrkkk!"

"Hi, Virgil. We bought you some birdseed and some fresh fruit," Patch said excitedly as she ran toward the bird. "Here, have a grape."

Bill smiled at her exuberance and for a moment felt a chill as he thought of the possibility that her childhood would be a fleeting moment to be replaced by a metamorphosis—not into an object of beauty, but into a creature of unknown substance.

He turned toward his wife and noticed a frown that had formed on her face.

"What is it Maeve, me love? Why the sad look?" he asked her.

"It's Patch, Bill," she replied softly.

"What ... is something wrong with her? Is she hurt?"

Maeve smiled a forlorn smile. "No, there's nothing wrong with the little angel. In fact, it's just the opposite. I'm afraid she's too good, and for that I fear for her."

Bill walked over to his wife and took her hand. "Tell me, love, what's causing you to be so disturbed?"

Looking toward the birdcage where Patch was talking to Virgil, he said, "She looks fine, Maeve—the same happy little girl that she's always been."

Maeve squeezed Bill's hand, took a deep breath, and began to relate an episode that had just transpired.

"We were at the food market … you know, the big one right outside town? Well, we were both pushing the cart and talking nonsense when Patch stopped and pointed down the aisle. We were in the cereal lane and were reaching for her box of Oatie O's when she stood up. Her face suddenly became very serious.

"Mommy," she said, "what's wrong with that man?"

I followed her vision and saw the old mayor, Sam Stilt Walker. You remember old Sam, don't you? You and he used to have such wonderful discussions about current events. For some reason—I think it was on purpose—you who were always on opposite sides. They would get pretty vocal at times, but the conversations were good-natured, followed by a cup of tea and a good laugh.

"Bill, he was bent over and appeared to have great difficulty walking. He shuffled as if in great pain while holding on to a walker. It was so sad. People tried not to stare at him and made an obvious attempt to avoid any contact with him."

She paused for a moment before continuing with her story.

"It was about this time that I felt a hand on my shoulder. It was Jeanette Felton, Ben's wife. I turned around to say hello, and we got sort of involved in catching up on the latest gossip. You know me when it comes to gossip!

"Did you know that there is a rumor going around that our drinking water might—"

"Maeve, please continue with the story about Patch."

"Sorry, me love. I was so involved with Jeanette that I failed to notice our Patch had wandered down the aisle and approached old Sam. When I realized she was gone, I looked up and saw her with him. She seemed to be involved in a serious dialogue with Sam. Passersby turned to look at the two of them. It seemed they were praising Patch for her obvious concern."

Bill was slowly getting anxious listening to Maeve's drawn-out version of the incident that so affected her, but he managed to hold off saying anything. He projected the patience of a saint … which, for him, was a major effort.

"Do you remember—of course you do—that sort of glow that surrounded her at the chapel? Well … there it was again, as Patch reached down and put her little hands on Sam's arm.

"Now, this is the interesting part: nobody else appeared to notice it. 'Twas very strange.

"Here's where it gets a bit sticky. Sam raised his head and gazed at her in wonderment as he slowly stood up; the pain apparently gone. His back straightened, and he gazed at the walker as if he couldn't comprehend what it was doing there.

"Meanwhile, the shoppers just stood there in silence and wonderment as they stared back and forth between Sam and Patch.

"Then it happened. An elderly woman cried out, 'It's a miracle!' and tried to touch Patch. Pretty soon, the rest of the shoppers were tearfully joining in.

"Patch was not aware of the devotion being paid to her. Instead she stood up on her tiptoes, kissed Sam on his cheek, turned, and skipped back to us as if nothing had happened.

"I quickly paid the bill and left the market before a riot happened.

"I'm afraid that the story of Sam's apparent healing will be around town in an instant. You know: it's a small town, and anything out of the ordinary is fuel for the fire!"

Maeve was quite upset, so Bill took her in his arms and gently hugged her.

"We'll deal with the public when and if the time comes. We can call it a spontaneous healing, or maybe a hysterical regeneration … which, unfortunately, will be short-lived, as most of those things are. We cannot refer to it as a true healing!

"We must keep the word 'miracle' out of our minds. It's too dangerous!"

Patch, meanwhile, was teasing Virgil with a grape, and the bird was having a good old time babbling to her.

"Arrkkk! A bit of the grape, my dear. 'Tis a fine vintage! Arrkkk!"

Patch was laughing in a most carefree way. There was nothing more on her mind than toying with her bird friend. It was almost as if the family were living in two separate worlds but were cognizant of the fact that both worlds could come together suddenly and cause great trouble.

And it happened soon afterward with the honking of horns and a knocking on the front door.

With a quizzical expression on his face, Bill looked out the window and saw six or seven cars parked on the lawn and by the mission. Prominent among the autos was a white van with the call letters of the local TV station blazoned across the side panel.

The knocking on the door was the result of a reporter's insistence in gaining entrance to the house.

The stylishly dressed blonde woman with perfect makeup pleaded with the Fellows to allow her in and answer a few questions about the report of a supposed miracle at the supermarket.

Glancing at Maeve, Bill shrugged, as if surrendering to the obvious.

"This might be the only way to put this chaos to rest," he said to his wife as he opened the door and invited the reporter and her cameraman into the living room.

"Reverend and Mrs. Fellows, I'm Taffi Thyme with station WOYE. Is it all right if I ask you some questions? I promise I'll be out of your hair quickly."

Maeve stepped forward. "It will be our pleasure," she said with a slight curtsy. "Can I get you something to drink? Some water, perhaps?"

"No, thank you," the coiffed cutie replied. A nudge from her cameraman prompted her to ask Maeve for a drink of water for him.

"No problem," Maeve answered. She went to the kitchen, pulled a bottle from the fridge, and handed it to Ms. Thyme's assistant.

"Well, what can we do for you?" Bill asked. "Wait a minute ... isn't your station the one that televises Matt Christmas's program?"

Taffi Thyme replied with a smile, "Yes. Are you a fan?"

I could sense a feeling of mild revulsion emanating from her as she realized that this rural preacher was a follower of that nut and his cadre of pseudoscientific cronies.

"I wouldn't go so far as to say a fan. Tell me: is he serious, and where does he get those brain-injured talking heads? I watch his program when I am in dire need for transportation from reality or to clear my mind in preparation for a sermon or two. Believe it or not, that nonsense provides me with a deep well of subject matter."

A look of relief swept across her face as she realized that this small-town minister was more than a simple rube.

"Reverend, I must admit that I ask myself those very same questions. However, Matt is truly a very bright man, albeit one possessed of a weird sense of humor. I had the honor of meeting him in person at a station function awhile ago, and I have to say, we had a very interesting discussion about various topics."

I myself was pleasantly surprised that beneath that carefully manicured symbol of reportage lurked a mind much less similar to that of Virgil's than I had previously guessed.

"I'm sorry for the interruption," Bill said to the reporter. "Please, continue with your questions."

"Mr. and Mrs. Fellows, there was a report that your little daughter was the dispenser of some sort of a miracle this morning at the supermarket in town. Eyewitnesses stated that she cured an elderly crippled man by the name of Sam Stilt Walker, or something like that? What can you tell me about that rumor?"

"Well," Bill said, "I was at home at the time, working on Sunday's sermon, so I'm not sure what it is that you mean. Perhaps my wife can help you?"

Maeve stepped forward and pointed at Patch, who was still feeding the bird and having a wonderful time talking to it. "Virgil, you're going to get so fat eating all those grapes that you won't be able to stand up," her daughter said, giggling.

"Now, Ms. Thyme, do you honestly believe that that little girl is capable of performing a miracle in a supermarket, of all places? If indeed Mr. Stilt Walker did appear to stand up and, to all appearances, be 'cured,' I would guess that it was a delayed reaction to his medication and not, as some would proclaim, a miracle. I'm sure that once his medication loses some of its potency, he will revert, unfortunately, to his previous nature.

"Miracles are the domain of the devout in need of an optimistic boost in a life of spiritual need. Perhaps today's shoppers fit that bill; I don't pretend to acknowledge that possibility. My husband would be the person to debate that issue, not me. All I can add is that Patch was in the wrong place at the wrong time and was the recipient, unfortunately, of a misperception of reality. Phew, did I say all that?" Maeve complained.

"Well said, m'love," Bill responded. "I couldn't have explained it better."

Turning to the reporter, he added, "Now, Ms. Thyme, what do you intend to relay to your listeners: a miracle or a miscalculation of truth?

The last thing we need around here is a riot of hopeless souls seeking salvation from their physical and mental ills by terrorizing a little girl. Am I correct in my belief that you will do the right thing?"

Ms. Thyme stood up and turned off her microphone. "You see, Reverend, I am in a quandary. Stations rely upon ratings to attract advertisers, and controversial stories draw listeners, who in turn affect ratings. If you give me your word as a minister and refuse any further interviews, I'll write this one off as a false lead. Your daughter doesn't deserve the consequences that a sensational story would cause.

"I'm sorry, but I can't do anything about the people out front. I suppose that they will eventually go away as the story dies down. I'll do my best to convince them that it was just a mistake in perception and that your Patch is nothing more than an innocent little girl caught up in some sort of religious fervor."

"Madam, you have a deal!" Bill responded.

"'Deed you do," Maeve added. "Tell you what," she continued, "if you're finished for the day, we'd love to have you join us for dinner. I was going to make some pasta and salad—nothing fancy, I'm afraid."

"That's the best offer I've had all day," Taffi Thyme answered. "I'd be honored. But first I have to append an ending to the story, which I'll do outside. I need a background for my on-camera voice-over, and those cars on your lawn will suffice nicely.

When I'm through, I'll send Carter back to the station with the tape, and I'll return. Pasta and salad sounds great!"

With that, Taffi and Carter packed up the equipment and left the house.

"I wonder," Maeve thought out loud, "is she what she appears to be, or is it a ruse in order to get a better story?"

"We shall see what we shall see," the minister proposed. "But until something suspicious occurs, she is still our guest, and we'll treat her in that manner."

Maeve nodded and turned to go to the kitchen and start preparing dinner.

"Patch, honey, say good-bye to Virgil for now and help me prepare dinner. We have a guest joining us, and I want to show her how good a cook you are."

CHAPTER 101

The reporter returned about fifteen minutes later.

"You can use the washroom if you'd like," Maeve suggested. "It's just down the hall."

"I can surely use it right now. I'm really a cold-weather gal, and this heat gets to me sometimes. If you'll excuse me, a splash of cool water on my face would be more than welcome about now."

While she was gone, Bill quietly asked Patch not to talk about the episode in the supermarket too much. "We don't want to create a panic," he said.

"Okay, Daddy. But wasn't it funny how Mr. Stilt Walker just stood up? Maybe he wasn't as sick as he thought he was?"

"Maybe so, maybe so," Bill said almost to himself.

"Do you feel better now, Ms. Thyme?" Maeve asked Taffi.

"Absolutely, and please call me Taffi. Ms. Thyme tends to age me, and I hope I don't look as old as the name makes me feel!"

Everyone seemed to relax, especially after the introduction between Patch and Taffi went smoothly. Perhaps a few friendships would evolve from this rather strange meeting?

"First of all, we'd like to thank you for your report," Bill stated. "It will go a long way to dispel any rumors that could arise from the incident. We live a quiet existence here, and the thought of hordes of people imploring Patch to cure them is totally unacceptable."

"It was my pleasure. Actually, I don't believe that your daughter is some kind of wonder worker. But I think I should warn you that the station sent out another reporter to get the story from Mr. Stilt Walker himself. In fact, Norm should be at the reservation about now."

Sudden quiet descended upon the table. Maeve and Bill glanced at each other for a brief second, and I felt a little panic in their silent communication.

Bill spoke. "I've known Sam for many years, and I can trust him to tell the truth. He's been known to tell some whoppers in his life, but if"—he turned to Virgil"—the spirit presents itself, we won't have to worry. He'll do the right thing."

For a second, I just hung there and then I got the hint. *If the spirit ... that's me!*

I was out of there is an instant and shot straight to the reservation. It was easy to spot his home: another white WOYE van was pulling up to it. Before Norm could leave the vehicle and get his equipment out, I entered the building.

Sam was standing up in his living room and doing a little jig. I'd bet that he hadn't done that since his illness.

No time to waste. I entered his mind immediately and took control with as little pressure as possible.

By the time the reporter knocked on the door, I had the old gentleman sitting quietly in an overstuffed rocker, bent over and humming to himself.

Luck was on my side. It seemed the story hadn't reached the reservation, so there were no crowds to contend with ... yet!

"Come on in; the door's always open," I yelled with a quivering voice. I had put that inflection in as a last-second thought. If I could make the reporter think that Sam was nothing more than a doddering old man, it would be fine.

"Excuse me, sir, are you Mr. Sam Stilt Walker? I'm Norm Filsch with station WOYE. I'd like to ask you some questions if you don't mind?"

"Speak up, young man. These ears of mine have seen better days ... at least I think they have. Can't remember much anymore.

"Station WOYE, eh? What's that mean? Is it another one of those trading posts that sell that authentic made-in-China 'Indian jewelry'? They seem to pop up like locusts on a cornstalk."

"No, sir. Station WOYE is a TV station. If you don't mind, I'd like to talk to you about what happened at the market this morning."

"TB? Does someone have TB? Nasty thing, that TB. My wife, Pigeon Beak, joined the Great Spirit many years ago; had the TB. Terrible, terrible ..."

"TV as in television!" Norm said with a little exasperation in his voice.

He looked around the small living room and realized that there was no set to be seen. "You do know what a television set is, sir?" he asked the old man.

"That's probably one of those picture boxes that the young look at all day. I suppose that they like those stories better than the ones the elders speak of. Maybe you can tell your people about that?"

"Please, sir ... about the supermarket."

"Supermarket? Oh, yes, I was there in the morning. Had to buy some tick spray for my sheep. The feed store is closed on Sundays, so I had to get a ride to the market. Do you have any sheep? You'd better have some if you want to get hitched up someday!"

Turning to his cameraman, Norm quietly asked him if the old man was nuts or something.

"Did a little girl cure you of your pain in the supermarket this morning?" Norm pressed.

"Little girl had pain in the supermarket? Tsk, tsk, poor little thing. How is she now? You know, I have some herbs here that could help her."

Norm turned off his microphone and whispered to Gnute, his assistant, "That's it! I'm finished here. This guy's as nutty as a fruitcake. Why do I get these assignments? There has to be a real story somewhere around this desert!"

"Eh, young man? Leaving so soon? Sit down and have some yucca juice. I don't get many visitors anymore."

"Yucca juice?" he murmured. "I'm out of here!"

... and with that oath, he was gone.

I waited until the van had sprayed dust in its hurry to leave the "crazy old man" behind before I returned him to his true self and his little jig.

Although a bit dazed, Sam would have no memory of his encounter with the flummoxed reporter from WOYE.

CHAPTER 102

I returned to the Fellows household as quickly as I could. Just as I resumed my place in the corner, a ringing sound emanated from Taffy's pocketbook.

"Excuse me," she said. "I have to get this call; it's from my partner, Norm. He was the reporter who interviewed Mr. Stilt Walker."

"Hey, Norm. How did it go? What? Calm down ... take it easy. What happened? He's what? Nuts? No story? Yucca juice? Okay, okay ... take it easy. Go home and have a beer; I'll talk to you later. No, there is no story. It was just an emotional reaction to a natural thing. Ciao."

After ending the call, Taffi turned to Maeve and Bill. "Poor Norm! Seems that his interview didn't go very well. Claims that the old man was a bit strange. Believes that his mind is slightly out of tune with reality."

With a smile of relief, Maeve said, "We could have warned your Norm about Sam. Since his wife passed, he hasn't been quite the same. Tends to wander a bit. Kind of sad, really; he was a good friend of Bill's."

"Yeah, I miss the old curmudgeon," Bill added as he sneaked a wink at Virgil.

"Arrkkk! To ignore the raving of a madman, one must be mad himself. For madness is but a short step from sanity. Arrkkk!"

Startled, Taffi asked, "Who said that?"

Grinning, Patch answered their guest. "Oh, it's only Virgil. He says the silliest things sometimes."

"Virgil, say hello to the nice lady."

"Arrkkk!"

"Just ignore him, Taffi," Maeve suggested. "Otherwise, he will regale us with imperial nonsense all night."

"Amazing," Taffi said. "Where did he learn such profound mutterings?"

"'Tis a long story," Maeve answered. "Perhaps later."

As if on cue, the front door opened, and we were greeted by a vision of a mismatched and rather colorful wardrobe. "Aha! The table was set with care, and I have arrived to take my place among the celebrators and partake of the morsels of fare. Prithee, tell me who is that most lovely damsel daintily forking a slice of carrot?"

Startled yet again, Taffi asked "Okay, who said *that*?"

Still grinning, Patch answered again, "Oh, it's just Dr. Crank. He is just as silly as Virgil sometimes."

"Come on in, Crank," Bill invited. "Say hello to Ms. Taffi Thyme. She's a new friend of ours and, I'm sure, would love to make your acquaintance."

"Thyme as in the très delicate of spices?"

Crank approached Taffi, gave a most formal bow, and, taking her hand in his, gave it a sensuous kiss.

Taffi blushed and stammered a reply. "I am very pleased to meet you, Doctor."

"Have a seat, Doc. You might as well join us, inasmuch as a spot of drool has emerged on your chin."

Meanwhile, Taffi leaned toward Maeve and quietly asked her, "Who is that man?"

"'Tis another long story," she whispered. "Perhaps later still?"

An air of comfortable relaxation settled over the dinner party as preliminary overtures evoked the beginning of a new friendship.

The discussion of the whos, whats, whens, and wheres of life experience formed the necessary thread to bind the individual to the group.

Even Crank behaved himself as only Crank could. He proved to be quite chivalrous in his treatment of their guest, and it appeared that he had won her over completely.

With an "It's getting late, and I should be heading home," Taffi stood up from the table and hugged everyone—even Crank, who, I must add, attained a slight crimson flush on his cheeks. He really took pleasure in the minutia of his role.

"It was a most enjoyable and educational evening, and I thank you very much for your generosity," she added.

"Taffi, me love, the honor was ours. We look forward to seeing you again soon. You are always welcome at our table."

With a wave, she was gone, and a hush permeated the air.

"I liked her, Mommy. She's very nice. I think even Virgil liked her."

"That's very important, sweetheart. If Virgil gives his approval, Ms. Thyme must be okay."

"Aye, a true beauty. Love beckons me once again. Behold the beating of my heart! It is racing pell-mell to the recesses of my mind, which itself is filled with the attar of red roses."

Leader never ceased to amaze me with his clowning. He must have really reveled in his impersonation of a human being; he had everyone taken in. But no harm was done, and he did insert a little humor into the air.

"Good night, Crank," Bill said as he ushered the good doctor to the door. "We'll talk tomorrow."

"As you wish ... so shall it be. Adieu to you all, and a bon nuit to all."

Maeve pushed her chair back, stretched, and got up from her seat. She took Patch's hand in hers, and they started walking away. "Time for a little girl to go to sleep. It's been a long evening, and she must be very tired. I know her Mommy is."

"I'll start to clean up," Bill volunteered. "'Twas a foine meal as always, love."

"Relax, my good man. We'll do the dishes together when I get back. Meanwhile, give your daughter a kiss good night."

"'Night, Daddy. I love you."

"Love you bunches, sweetheart."

Retiring to his favorite chair, Bill did as his wife suggested: he relaxed ... and promptly dozed off.

I remained quiet so as not to disturb him and, as if sensing Bill's demeanor, Virgil also ventured into silence.

CHAPTER 103

"Well, what do you think?" Maeve asked Bill after she had gently awakened him. "I liked her, and I do believe she is sincere in assuring us that the 'miracle' matter is closed."

With a yawn, Bill replied, "I hope so, hon. The thought of the stampede of a healing crusade at our front door is frightening. But yes, I also think she's sincere. In fact she might prove to be a great help when we finally start our trek into infamy."

"Trek into infamy? Isn't that a bit of the corn, William?"

"Aye, I guess so."

"There is one thing that continues to bother me. What if someone else follows up on Sam Stilt Walker and finds that he really is cured? With a little serious research, a good reporter just might come to the conclusion that he isn't as crazy as he appeared."

"That's a chance we'll have to take," Maeve said. "Maybe with some help from Taffi, the story will blow over. It's those few shoppers at the market that I worry about. Maybe they'll go the way of those UFO people up in the hills? Who knows?"

"Take me to your kitchen, Earth Woman!"

With a kiss on his cheek and a smile on her face, they headed to the kitchen to clean up.

"I've been watching the news," Bill said. "They're starting to get serious about that 'anomaly,' as they call it in Africa. Some very important people are expressing concern about its continued growth.

"I think it's slowly approaching the time—well, not slowly enough, unfortunately—when we'll make the final commitment to engage that effluvia from hell. In fact I have the feeling that it could come any day now."

"I won't deny it: it occupies mind every waking moment of the day." Maeve nodded in agreement. "It's not us I fear for; it's our little girl. If she is indeed an angel, the stress of battle could harm her forever, and I don't think that I could live with that."

"If indeed she is an angel, as you believe," Bill returned, "I'm sure she will be protected from any injury despite the delicate nature of her mortal being. Somehow I trust Virgil and his people to afford her the protection she might require."

"Virgil and his people?" What did he think that we would be able to do? I suspected we were far less equipped than Bill realized—unless, of course, Jaindeaux possessed knowledge that she hadn't enlightened Leader and myself with. We had never engaged humans in any physical confrontation before. Observed, perhaps, but not actually engaged.

Something told me that Jaindeaux wasn't a novice in these matters. Be that so, I was uneasy about my participation in any mission that could incur human fatalities. War is a blasphemy against the natural order of things. The role of life is not meant to induce death … and yet there I was, on the threshold of committing that horror!

If I were human, I would have been completely bald by then, with strands of my golden locks snagged in the sharp jags of my serrated fingernails.

It was time for me to go also.

… and I did, to a quiet place.

CHAPTER 104

The sun rising over the morning desert is a wondrous sight. It is almost as if a celestial film director is inserting one magnificent color filter after another in order to improve upon reality, except that those colors are themselves the manifestation of reality.

Witnessing such a vivid demonstration of nature's indomitable creative powers, I couldn't help but question the rationality of its destruction by the powers of darkness.

Is ugliness more desirable than beauty, or is ugliness itself representative of its own beauty? I wonder what Lili-It and Whoever saw in the shards of the mirrors fragmented by the sheer repulsiveness of their image?

"Knock, knock; hello there. Are you awake? Can Bean come out and play?"

Leader. I couldn't think of a less welcome arousal from one's thoughts.

"Go away, and let me be. I want to be alone! Isn't there an innocent soul for Crank to haunt? You have successfully interrupted my appreciation of the morning's essence and replaced it with a nightmare ... daymare? ... morningmare? I don't know ... look what you've done! Feh on you and the mag-wave you rode in on!"

"That's the gratitude I get for being your only friend. Insults ... all I get are insults. Maybe I'll just find a new friend who appreciates me!"

"I should be so lucky.

"Okay, now that you're here, what can I do for you?

"By the way, have you heard from Jaindeaux yet?"

366

"No. I was hoping that you might have by now. She has so seduced us into her fold that I'm not sure whether we can proceed on our own. I resent being put in that position!"

I almost feel powerless without her leadership. How did we allow her to exert such influence over us?

"Do you ever think—and I don't mean that facetiously—that there is a supreme imp overseeing our existence? Maybe Jaindeaux was sent by that entity to give us guidance and encouragement, because we are an anathema to the direction man appears to be marching in, trancelike in his unwavering progress toward the River Styx and the underworld beyond."

"Been there, and I'm positive that man won't be pleased by the heat and overcrowding. Sort of like visiting Miami Beach under the influence of steroids while imbibing sulfuric acid instead of Cuba Libres."

"I love your colorful description of the netherworld. Perhaps we should suspend posters depicting your experiences in various areas of the world ... although I think that there are people who would actually look forward to a visit under the misconception that it is, in fact, heaven. Judging by some of the living conditions I have seen around the world, I could see why some would feel that way, while others would believe that they were already there."

"Too early for such profundities, Bean.

"By the way, what was all that chaos about Sam What's-His-Name and the supermarket? What'd he do, steal some peaches or something?"

"I wish that's all he did. Seems that Patch did one of her healing sessions on him at the local market while a few shoppers witnessed the exchange. Created somewhat of an undesirable scene. I had to perform a little prestidigitation and throw off the media hounds. You probably would have enjoyed it."

"Sounds like it was right up my alley. Did it work out all right?"

"So far.

"Ah, here comes Anna Walks With Grace. Wonder what she wants so early?

"Time for me to do some peeping. Why don't you stick around and keep looking for Jaindeaux? Give me a buzz when she returns, okay?"

"Aye-aye, sir. Roger, Wilco, et cetera."

Anna parked the old Hudson in front of the house and knocked gently on the door. It was opened by Maeve and Patch as they were leaving for the gallery.

Pleasantries were offered back and forth as they passed each other.

"Go on in, Anna," Maeve offered. "Bill is at his desk as usual. Bill," she yelled. "Anna is here to see you."

"Tell her to come in," he answered.

"Thank you, Reverend," Anna said. "I won't take up too much of your time."

"Always an honor to see you, Anna. What brings you out so early? Nothing wrong, is there?"

I followed her in quietly and assumed my place in the corner.

Anna took her jacket and hat off and placed them on the couch. Bill put his work aside and took the chair facing her.

"Some tea or a cold drink, perhaps?" he asked Anna.

"No, thanks, Reverend. I'm fine."

"So, is there something I can help you with today? Always a pleasure."

Anna cleared her throat and started. "You know, of course, about Patch and Sam Stilt Walker, I'm sure? Well, the story began its relentless march around the res and the outlying areas."

"We know all about the incident," Bill replied. "In fact we had a reporter here for dinner last night, and she assured us that the story would fade away … depending, of course, on whether Sam could restrain himself from proclaiming a miracle."

"I thought that would be a problem," Anna offered. "So I had his nephew pack him up and drive him to his sister's hogan in the area you call the badlands. There's no phone and no TV, so we shouldn't have any trouble from him until the whole thing blows over."

"Well done, Anna. You don't know what a load you took off my mind. We had this horrible vision of a line of invalids, deformed bodies, and other poor souls queued up like a soup-kitchen procession, waiting for the sainted angel of mercy to cure them."

"Reverend, do I denote a bit of sarcasm in your voice? We must not criticize the ill fortunes of others, you know."

"Aye … you're right as always, Anna. It's just that the stress is getting to me, and the uncertainty of our strategy is weighing on my mind. Virgil promised some relief shortly. He's waiting for the return of one of his fellow entities and the news it will provide."

"You will keep me informed, I expect?" Anna asked as she stood up and reached for her hat and jacket.

"Definitely," Bill said while walking Anna to the door. "You are a significant member of our squad. Thanks again for your help with Sam Stilt Walker."

Bill glanced at his watch as he closed the door. "Darn," he said, rushing to the old television. "I almost missed Matt Christmas again. That's the second time in a week—must be an omen or something. Come on, come on. Warm up, already!"

"... so if I understand correctly," Matt was asking his guest, "your atheistic point of view runs counter to the biblical description of Genesis."

"What puzzles me," replied his guest, *"is the claim that your god created you in his image. The question I have is this: the image of what? His physical bearing or his mental sway—or perhaps both? If indeed it was this descriptive being, then was he not just a man initially, or had he in mind a species of godlike potential?*

"Consider what has been accomplished in his name, and you have to wonder about his so-called image. He had to create an entity who would be able to deal with the passionate conflicts in the minds of his conception—the fashioning of a valve for the release of the psychological pressures that he introduced. If you are a mirror image of your god, what does your future have in store for you besides continued despair and ultimate extinction?

"Perhaps he was a bit inexperienced in world building, considering he had to start from scratch. Point of fact is his failure to create a species that could survive positively and thus evolve and endure throughout the eons of their existence. They were but experiments that were allowed to evolve on their own, without a definitive plan for their survival. Perhaps, then, he tired of them and left their creation unfinished to concentrate on some other venture.

"Boredom?

"If that indeed were the case, what did he leave unfinished in man? Had he become bored with him also, leaving his creation as a work in progress put temporarily on hold ... or bored due to the species reaching a point where progressive evolution had ceased to occur?

*"Another thought has punctured the balloon of
rationality: if your god created you in his image, whose
image was the subject for, say, the warthog, the safari
ant, or perhaps the three-toed sloth? Here's one: who was
the model for the dinosaurs, or was it the collective
endeavor of exiled model makers? It was as if the
earth were a design project for a freshman year in art
school. Inexperience is the father of failure. Need I
say more?"*

"I'm afraid that if you say more, I will be bombarded by irate
listeners whose very basic faith you have just trampled upon.

"Why don't we leave it there? Maybe we can continue our dialogue
privately at another time," Matt offered. He turned toward the camera.
"I would like to thank—at least I think I would like to thank—my
guest, Ethelbert Grimely, the leader of the Philosophical Institute of
Conceptual Thought, with headquarters in northern California, for his
most interesting and controversial take on the basic tenets of religion.

"Mr. Grimely kindly agreed to be our guest today due to the last-
minute cancellation of Professor Saito Bokchoy, who was unfortunately
delayed due to a scheduling conflict. However, he will be here tomorrow
to discuss his concept of bubble universes, which is very close, I'm sure,
to the minds of many of you.

"Now, a word from our sponsor."

More dancing ensued; this time, three pieces of colorful candy of
some kind were singing about the health aspects of sugar and its affect
on the skin of children's faces. It took a while before I realized the
product so fervently pushed was an anti-acne potion.

Is man so inherently barbaric that he must always perform a dance
when emotion presents itself? The intense beat of the drums and
amplified instrumentation; the trancelike attitude; the chants of a captive
audience; the colorful attire; and the loss of control all seem to contribute
to the obliteration of civilized thought. Mix this with the scream of
sirens, the honking of automobile horns, the screeching of brakes, and
the roar of jet planes—all products of contemporary society—and what
do you end up with? Lucy, the supposed missing link, on the walk with
backward-facing caps; with miniskirts and high boots; with suits and

ties; with notebook computers and cell phones and miniscule music boxes. It is nothing more than the Planet of the Apes![43]

"Heresy!" Bill shouted. "It's nothing but heresy! Christmas has sunk to a new low in his choice of guests! That's it; no more; I've had it with him!"

"Until tomorrow," I interjected. *"You know you're addicted to his brand of nonsense."*

"Never again! Heretics, quacks, loonies: it isn't my world, and I hope the influence on the minds of his listeners is not too great."

"Bill, that's just it. It isn't to be taken seriously. Christmas understands the human animal and its need for escape from the depressing world situation; that's why he enlists those weirdoes as guests. Just look at the reaction he attained from you. Think of the thousands of other listeners who have similar reactions and you then comprehend his approach to entertainment."

"Bah! We cannot allow humanity to question what God has ..."

It took a moment for me to realize that although the minister was still ranting and raving, and his lips were still moving, no sound was coming from his mouth.

It took another second or two before he realized it also, and puzzlement replaced ire on his face.

We were immersed in a silence so profound that one could question whether or not we actually existed in reality.

"It is time, my friends," said a voice, so sweet and yet so resolute, emanating from a place of no place. We were tuned into an energy source beyond any rational description.

"Jaindeaux."

"Yes, Bean. I've returned."

"Is it time?"

"I'm afraid so".

Bill seemed to recover his wits and blurted out, "Virgil, what's going on?"

"Be calm and have no fear, Reverend. I am called Jaindeaux, and I am the one who spoke for your daughter.

---

43 "Planet of the Apes" refers to the motion picture of the same name, first screened in 1968 and directed by Franklin J. Schaffner. "Planet of the Apes" is based upon a novel by Pierre Boulle, "La Planete des Singes".

"The time has come for us to prepare to engage the menace that is inexorably approaching. Gather your allies, and we shall meet this evening at your chapel. I have much to say."

It was an infection so intense as to be almost biblical in nature. I half expected a nearby bush to catch fire and start speaking to me as well.

With the conclusion of that pronouncement, we were once again united with the sounds of life.

Virgil was off on a tirade with no one in particular, and the TV was still offering useless and needless bits of sound and picture before Bill finally stumbled over and turned it off.

"Virgil … or is it Bean? Since you first appeared, I find myself constantly asking, 'What just happened?' Does this finally mean we'll be preparing to march into the who-knows-what-and-where?

"It's funny, but I've been agitated over the lack of information and planning, and now that it has finally arrived, I am asking myself, 'Why so soon?'

"When will this be over, and when can we return to the peace and serenity that was?"

"I don't want to sound pontifical, but it will be over when it is.

"As for returning to life as it was, I'm afraid that will never happen. Society will undergo a transformation such as never existed before, which it will have to accept and learn to coexist with, or Lili-It will have won, and your past will be just that: past."

"And what of Patch and Maeve and Anna and the rest of our family? Are they to survive, or will our lives up to now have been nothing more than the hypotheses of future explorers? Was our brief attempt at happiness just a tease? Was it too brief? Was it worth it?"

"I truly wish I could answer your questions, Bill, but I can't see, nor can I forecast, the future. Let's try to remain calm for now. I'm sure that Jaindeaux will provide some insight for your concerns. As for me, I have to go and meet with my people[44] in preparation for this evening's meeting.

44　A Bean note: I keep referring to my fellow faeries and imps as comrades and people in order to introduce a bit of familiarity to the reader. Any esoteric descriptions of 'they of my ilk' would be confusing and prey upon your limited imagination.

"My only advice for you, again, would be to remain calm. Maybe there'll be a rebroadcast of Matt Christmas's show, so you can numb your mind."

"Yeah, right; out of the ions of imps comes wisdom. Later, Bean or Virgil, although I'm not looking forward to it."

"Later."

CHAPTER 105

Well, here we are, as motley a cabal as have ever been joined together. You know them all: Bill, the minister; Maeve, the wife; Patch, the changeling; Anna Walks With Grace, the Native American sachem; Dr. Crank, aka Leader, a psychic image of a wayward troubadour; and two as-yet-invisible faeries, united all in a brave and slightly irresponsible force with one thought in mind: to defeat evil on the field of battle.

Senor Cervantes, where are you now that we really need you?

The visible members of our group sat themselves upon benches in the front of the chapel, as if awaiting the featured speaker. I, in turn, just hung back, not sure if I should assume the image of a familiar human or not. However my question was answered shortly afterward, when Jaindeaux affected the image of Giver of the Word and appeared at the podium.

I decided to affect the likeness of a person well-known to all. A voice entered my mind as Leader turned toward me.

"Don't you dare materialize Adolf Hitler again," he warned me.

"Don't be absurd," I answered. *"I was thinking of Don Quixote. More fitting, don't you think?"*

And so the image of a tall, bearded gentleman stood erect and attentive behind the assemblage, replete with sword and deformed lance.

Now our cabal of brave warriors was complete. To the uninformed eye, we were inhabitants of the social hall in the cuckoo's nest.

"Aieee!" wailed Anna Walks With Grace. "Is it really you, Father? Have you returned to lead us once more?"

"Perhaps I should have chosen the features of one not so recognizable," Jaindeaux replied sympathetically. "I am very sorry if I caused you to react in such a manner. If you so desire, I could manage to assume the identity of one more agreeable to you?"

Anna, recovering from her shock, spoke up. "Please don't change; I would deem it an honor to have Giver of the Word in my presence once again, even though he is but a false image. He was a great man, and I know deep down that you'll not soil his memory."

Jaindeaux peered down at Anna and nodded. Then she slowly examined the faces of all who were present; pausing for a moment at Don Quixote. "Most appropriate, Bean," she said as the entourage turned and grasped the significance of my selection.

I had to explain who I really was before they were comfortable with me. I half expected Crank to utter some inane remark, but he remained silent for once.

"The time has come," Jaindeaux finally began. "I have been very busy during the past few days, as you will soon see. Due to the complexities of my duties, I was obliged, unfortunately, to work alone. I was charged to create a myriad of unrelated situations and somehow bring them all together into a cohesive and viable whole.

"I am going to inform you of what I have achieved ... or hoped to achieve. Unfortunately, it will take some time, so make yourself as comfortable as you can on those hard benches. If anyone wants to take a break, please let me know, and I will pause in my discourse."

Crank stood up and announced, "To prevent any future interruption of your anxiously awaited homily, I should like to retreat to the little room in the back and tend to some private matter. Would anyone like to join me?"

With a crack on his head from the don and a stern reproach from Jaindeaux, Crank regained his seat and looked sheepishly at the gathering while affecting a rather exaggerated bow of forgiveness.

"Now, unless there are any further interruptions, I will continue," Jaindeaux said, seeming rather annoyed.

"The strategy that has been decided upon, and the one that will save the most human lives, is one that has never before been attempted on this scale. The use of man in his physical appearance will be replaced by the spiritual fervor of his soul.

"Now, I can understand your confusion as to how something like that would be accomplished, and I will try to simplify the explanation.

"Numerous studies have been conducted on the effects of group prayer. On some occasions, it has been noted that certain beneficial results have been recorded, although skepticism from the scientific community and a large segment of the medical world is widespread.[45] We believe that the power of prayer is a controlling factor in the healing of body and soul. Accepting that theory, we have taken it much further. We now believe that the power of prayer can defeat the insipid forces of evil if, and only if, it is conducted in concert with vast numbers of the devout and at the same exact instant."

Bill then spoke up, expressing doubt as to how this seemingly impossible feat would be accomplished. "How do you intend to amass such a vast number of people to pray—if that is even the correct term— at the same precise moment, considering the multitude of time zones? In fact, what religious faction are you concentrating on? In fact, how do you intend to contact those very people and convince them to offer their prayers? Furthermore, prayers to what and to whom?"

"Bill," Jaindeaux said. "You are jumping ahead, but your questions are valid and must be answered.

"Within a week, all human beings who have deep respect for their religion and who offer their prayers in the most devout supplication to their god will be made aware of the demand placed upon them. They will, of course, be offered the choice of submitting to the necessity of offering their prayers unselfishly or being excused from that responsibility and having no memory of our request."

Bill repeated his question, obviously still unsatisfied: "I ask you again: who will you notify, and most important, how will you reach them?"

"You really must learn to control your impatience, Reverend.

"All right, then: I spent a considerable amount of time both researching and observing the many religions that comprise within their fold the majority of followers.

"I then contacted—and this was no easy matter—as many of our imps and faeries as I was able to locate. With help from an increasing number of them, I was able to spread the word and convince many of

---

45   Howard Eisenberg, "Paranormal Medicine: Mind Over Matter in the Genesis and Cure of Disease." More information on this article is available in the addendum. http://www.ncbi.nlm.nih.gov/pmc/articles/PMC2379031/ pdf/canfamphys00309-0072.pdf

the seriousness of the state of affairs. Once they had been enlisted, I then enlightened them as to the unlimited powers that they possessed but had lost the memories of.

"It is impossible for me to tell you the precise number of my people I have recruited, for even I don't know. Suffice it to say that the membership is enormous.

"They were sent to all four corners of the globe and were able to induce thoughts in the minds of the devout that they should all congregate in the temples, churches, and other venues of devotion on a certain day at a certain time."

Again, Bill spoke: "Isn't that a stretch of the imagination? How in the world could they single out the just from the rest of the population? Seems far-fetched to me!"

Jaindeaux took a deep breath and replied, "Think of a computer and how you type in a keyword and poof: out comes dozens of Web sites and links. Well, thought patterns are electrical impulses themselves. So if—and remember, we are nothing but electromagnetic impulses ourselves—we are able to weed out those significant electrical patterns, what is there to stop us from tying onto them and restructuring them a bit? It was just a theory until we were able to prove it attainable. And then it was just a matter of a ping here and a zap there until we achieved our goal.

"Do you understand now, or is it still too complicated?"

"I understand, but the potential for misuse of that power is frightening ... and yet very thrilling, in a positive vein, to contemplate. What, then, is to stop you from inducing a sense of peace and brotherhood into the minds of those whose goal is to foment anarchy, distrust, and— more pointedly—sheer hate and the inevitable war? It seems logical to me that if you can accomplish one, you can create the other. Or am I reading it wrong?"

Sighing, Jaindeaux admitted that the possibility of going that route had been debated, but the sheer amount of adverse conditions was much greater than time would allow.

"Think," she said. "It isn't just man who is trapped in this ordeal; it is nature herself who is also rebelling. Melting ice caps; increased instances of earthquakes, such as the horror that hit Haiti in 2010; the proliferation of stronger and stronger tornadoes, floods, drought, and atmospheric incongruities; and the introduction of drug-resistant bacteria and viruses and other influences that, combined with man's degradation of his very soul, are the cause of the effect we must now combat. The amalgamation of man's fostering of international terrorism, his insatiable greed, the proliferation of nuclear weapons, the advanced research on biological weaponry, the insipid mass introduction of pollution into the very substances that form your bodies, and, again, the apparent disregard for human life all have come together at one time to form, once again, the perfect storm.

"The greatest threat of the time being is that of Lili-It, who, by her very nature, is assimilating those obscene negative forces and constituting a seemingly indomitable aura of destruction. She is slowly moving north, absorbing more and more poor souls to be converted, first to fuel for her engine and then to ash destined to be dispersed aimlessly by the wind, deposited on a lifeless plateau and then blown around for time immemorial, never to find peace. It is a reminder of the frivolity and fragility of life itself: the biblical 'dust to dust,' with the exception that this finality of purpose is not natural, but induced."

"So, Giver of the Word, my father, is that the future you envision for your children?" questioned Anna. "Have you appointed us as the sole saviors of humanity? You have always been the most learned and revered of the people, so I bow to your wisdom. We shall do as you demand."

Jaindeaux decided to pause in her discourse for a few moments to let her audience catch their breath. It was a good idea, as her words depicted a dark time ahead with no guarantee for survival.

Patch, on the other hand, had dozed off in her mother's lap, an innocent whose childhood was slowly drawing to a close. With the demise of the child and her rebirth to maturity would come the dawn of a new age of hope.

The main question seemed to be what Jaindeaux had in store for each of the members. Inasmuch as she had said that no mortals would be on the front lines, what could they be expected to do?

"Could anyone use a drink of water?" asked Maeve quietly, so as not to awaken her daughter.

Both Anna and Bill nodded, so she gently placed Patch on the bench, covered her daughter with her coat, and went back to the house for refreshments.

Jaindeaux remained quiet while the others murmured among themselves.

Crank sat silently, deep in thought, while I asked her what my part would be, insofar as she had already enlisted the help of our kind.

Another "Be patient, Bean" was sent back to me, and I was quiet again. I was being patient again … and again!

CHAPTER 106

**"When a spiritual union of the
virtuous merge with the warriors of light;
Can the darkness of evil and its minions
of death
trust any hope for survival?
Aye: 'Tis only relative as to
the degree of the morality of the soul:
if indeed there be one.**[46]

After the break, Bill once again queried Jaindeaux. "If this anomaly in Africa is so threatening, why haven't other countries expressed concern? Why hasn't the United Nations called for an emergency session? I don't understand why a few people here in New Mexico have the responsibility of addressing what should be a major concern for the world."

"Once more," replied Jaindeaux., ""You have gone right to the head of the class for insight. As you know from history, countries cannot act on the spur of the moment. Even in the case of disasters, formulating a plan of action takes research; days of committee meetings; discussions between advocates and antagonists; organizing material and logistics; et cetera. To put it simply, there isn't that much time left for an organized response to a catastrophe of this magnitude. And if they were able to respond, they would find themselves facing an enemy more powerful

---

46   Stephen Stuart, *Rantings* (2009).

then they could have imagined who is not susceptible to the most modern of weapons. How do you attack a metaphysical adversary? The most you could hope for is the effect of a sprinkling of water on an inferno of cataclysmic proportions.

"I was going to wait until later before handing out individual responsibilities, but your constant striving for detail has pre-empted that plan ... especially in your case, Reverend.

"Your area of responsibility requires that you be the only physical presence at the scene of the final conflict. Your sole weapon will be the written word. It will be your task to record the event, much as you would inscribe your thoughts into a diary."

Startled, Bill asked, "You expect me to be at the forefront of the action without any protection? Where is the logic there? By all rights, I should last a few seconds, if even that long, before I become nothing more than an indistinct particle of dust. What kind of record would that provide to future historians?"

Jaindeaux nodded her acknowledgment of his concerns and stated, "That's where Leader—or Dr. Crank, as you know him—enters the picture. He has the power to cloak you in a blanket of invulnerability. You will be able to witness everything that occurs in your vicinity without any impediment to your vision. You will be protected from any harm whatsoever, and it will also provide you with the gift of invisibility at the same time. In other words, you will be there and yet not be there.

"Leader will also be able to provide additional insight and observation, which should add to your accounting. Who knows? He might be able to inject some humor into an erstwhile solemn situation."

"I don't anticipate this being a laughing matter, but I nevertheless accept your request, and I will do my best."

"I had no doubt," she added.

"Ah, my esteemed religioso, you recall that the pen is mightier than the sword, so it is imperative that you to stick it into the ear of the evil one con mucha frueza,48 eh, Senor Quixote? Words of wisdom from your protector." An inane, or insane, interjection that only Crank could administer.

"Anna, yours will be the responsibility of gathering those men and women in your nation who profess a deep religious fervor both for humanity and for the love and respect that is the true spirit of Mother

Nature. You will bring them to this chapel at the given time, where they will bear witness to a sight so profound and so splendid as to change your life and theirs forever. You will have the authority—temporarily, I'm afraid—to influence the countless clans of Native Americans and their various factions to join with us. They, too, will congregate in their own prayer sites, again at the correct time.

"As for now, I think you should take leave of this assemblage. There is much for you to do, and the sooner you start, the more you will accomplish."

Anna stood up and wrapped her shawl around her shoulders, but not before bowing her head in reverence to Giver of the Word (or at least to his image). "It was an honor to be in front of you once more, my father. You are remembered by all who are righteous and true to the faith. May he who is the giver of all life grant you eternal peace. Farewell."

As soon as Anna had left the chapel, Jaindeaux turned toward Patch, who had awakened. It was as if the little girl had known that her time had come and was prepared for whatever responsibility Jaindeaux would assign her. Her eyes were not the eyes of a child any longer.

The two of them stared at each other for what seemed an endless time until Patch nodded and smiled, and contact was broken.

"Patch, you were chosen many years ago and endowed with certain powers and with the ability to employ them when and if the situation presented itself. Who was responsible for the granting of those powers, I am not at liberty to reveal. Was it a gift or a curse? I do not know, but what I do know is that the time is rapidly approaching when those powers will be required to be employed."

"Why?" Patch asked. "Why was I chosen and not some other child? What was it about me that garnered such special attention?"

"Again, I am not at liberty to tell you, but what I can say is that it was not a random selection.

"At the gathering of the righteous, and at the time preordained, you will send out a message describing the situation and the possible sacrifice they will be called upon to offer. The message itself will be transmitted through your thoughts and relayed and amplified by my fellow faeries scattered around the globe. All will hear and understand the significance of your words, as there will be no language barrier to overcome. The physical image you will convey will be ethereal in form, almost angelic in appearance, while your voice will project sincerity and tenderness, as is commensurate with your position of leadership.

"Be prepared, however, that you will be worshipped as almost godlike in stature, and because of that, you will be followed without hesitation."

Jaindeaux continued, "I accept the fact that there will be those who will not willingly give of themselves. They in turn will be excused and will forfeit any memory of the proceedings. As for the remaining congregants, they will be told that you, and you alone, will be the controlling force behind the expedition to the outer fringe of hell ... and perhaps further.

"Priests, ministers, rabbis, imams, chiefs, spiritual figureheads, and other leaders of religious convention will identify you as a messenger in their discipline and not as some generic entity to be viewed with suspicion.

"The process of thought projection has been incorporated into religions throughout the ages via the mind's surrender to deep meditation. To accomplish change to any degree, the subject had to rid his or her mind of any impure thoughts and concentrate solely on the object of its devotion. Your projected image will be the object of devout concentration.

"Group meditation has also shown success in effecting the healing of the body and mind, as well as physical change at a distance. What we hope to accomplish is the very same, but on a scale never before attempted.

"Patch will project an image of the confrontation and again, through the amplification of vast imp brigades, it will enter the minds of our congregants. They in turn will concentrate all of their awareness on the messages that she will convey to them. If recorded trials[47] have shown positive results utilizing but a few dedicated and pious practitioners, the inclusion of millions—or perhaps billions—of minds concentrating on the efficacy of one thought could move the earth. Think of the construction of the pyramids in Egypt. According to some concepts—and judging by the sheer number of blocks of granite and the labor force needed to place those blocks in an exact plan—it would have taken

---

47   See http://www.noeticscience.com; see also Debra Williams, "Scientific Research of Prayer: Can the Power of Prayer Be Proven," 1999 PLIM Report, Vol 8, No. 4, http://www.plim.org/PrayerDeb.htm; see also the reference to Dr. Daniel Benor in Dr. Laurance Johnston's "The Science of Prayer and Healing," http://www.healingtherapies.info/prayer_and_ healing.htm.

hundreds of years to complete the construction. But envision thousands of minds in complete harmony, concentrating on the raising of block after block, and you have the power of thought projection and mind over matter ... and so it was.

"All that is required is a sincere belief that their prayers—or, indeed, their own heartfelt and honest thoughts—can affect their subject and bring about a cure to a disease or a change in the course of an event, and almost anything is feasible.

"Perhaps the thoughts of even the nonbelievers, if they are pure of mind, can achieve similar results. Unfortunately, we do not have the time to investigate that theory in any depth. Instead of utilizing just the religious arm of humanity, if we can convey the message to all souls, we might be able to increase our power a thousand-fold. But how do we accomplish that, and where do they amass to practice that perception? I cannot stop time to allow those supplicants to fulfill their obligation. Time is not a luxury for us to benefit from.

"Lili-It, on the other hand, consumes the souls of her victims at will and with an insatiable appetite and then disposes of the bodies as if they were some sort of repugnant flotsam. So instead of an army of maligned thoughts, she must rely upon the constant accumulation of new unfortunates.

"If we can put a hold on her progress, she will no longer be able to replenish or add to her strength. In that event, she will be vulnerable to our defensive strategy, and we will be able to turn the tide on her."

Patch, in the voice and demeanor of a mature adult, asked Jaindeaux if the lives of her followers would be endangered in any way.

"You will impress upon them that their souls will be the combatants in the skirmish, but their corporeal beings will remain in their holy places. However, if the sheer strain utilized in the endeavor proves to be too much for them to bear, and severe damage to their mind is incurred, their bodies will indeed suffer irreparable damage. As I mentioned previously, and as reward for their sacrifice, they will be transported to a place of peace and enlightenment for all eternity.

"You will know what to say at the time designated. Fret not."

Maeve held on to her daughter's hand as if fearing that the girl would take leave of her body and become the angel that Jaindeaux had described.

"Maeve," Jaindeaux continued, "you will remain here in the chapel, and it will be your responsibility to provide the anchor that will be necessary for your daughter's connection to mortality. Without your strength, she will rise above man and become, for all eternity, the reality of the image she will project, and you will lose her forever.

"As for me, I will serve as her connection to the spiritual world and provide the strength and guidance essential for her to complete her mission. That obligation will be overwhelming in its complexity due to the fact that not only will she be the spiritual leader of her followers, but she will be the driving force and supreme leader in the confrontation with Lili-It."

It was Bill's turn again to interrupt. "Am I to believe that the approach to Armageddon will be manned only by those devout subjects of humanity and not by those people who do not profess membership in an organized faith? Don't they have a say in their future?"

"An excellent question, Reverend, and I will attempt to answer it to the best of my ability.

"Consider what I said about this being a battle of souls. In a confrontation of good versus evil, it is the soul of the individual that conveys the passion and adherence to the tenets of their belief system. The nonbeliever—and I do not relish that term, but it will suffice at the moment—in comparison practices a belief system that relates to himself and, although his premise is exemplary, it has the force of one, as compared to the fervor and commitment of the group. And it is the sheer number of souls joined together in a community of common structure that we require, for in numbers resides the strength of purpose we will need.

"Man is an island unto himself; we require a continent of souls instead of an archipelago of scattered atolls.

"There's another fact to take into consideration, and that is that this is a scenario of a war of souls and not battalions of men under arms. Who are they to face? Who are they to fire their weapons at? It is best to fight for our cause with the strength of congregation rather than the disorder of leaderless hordes of confusion."

I waited patiently for word of my participation, but none was forthcoming. I wondered what my role would be. What assignment was left in the grand scheme that required my help?

The meeting broke up, and the principals departed before my name was called.

Both Leader and Jaindeaux vanished without a farewell.

Left alone with my thoughts, I puzzled over my obvious lack of responsibility.

Don Quixote also vanished, not having any further purpose and without nary a windmill to tilt at.

I then took my leave of the chapel and decided to seek out the minister and ask him if he had any idea as to what my duties might entail.

CHAPTER 107

The Fellows household seemed to be in turmoil, with the family engaged in some familiar ritual.

I decided to approach Bill while Maeve and Patch were out of the room.

"Er ... Bill. If you have a minute, I'd like to ask you something. It's pretty important."

"Is that you, Virgil? Ooops, I mean Bean. Can't it wait until tomorrow? It's pretty late, and we're kind of exhausted."

"I realize that, but it won't take long."

"Were you talking to me, love?" Maeve asked as she entered the room.

"No, honey. I was talking to Bean ... I think."

Just then another voice entered the conversation.

"Mommy and Daddy, aren't you going to tuck me in?" asked Patch, clutching a stuffed animal and wearing her favorite pajamas, with the tiny animals emblazoned on them.

When Patch detected my presence, the little girl suddenly disappeared, replaced by her alter ego.

"Bean, I know why you are here. You feel as if you were ignored; but please don't despair. You will be advised as to your role in due time. But for now, it is late and time for all of us to go to bed."

"Err ..."

"Good night, Bean."

"Good night, Bean."

"Nighty night, Bean."

... and I was alone again.

Maybe Virgil will have a kind word for me, I thought.

As if on cue, his voice burst forth in the empty room.

"Arrkkk! Close the door on your way out! Arrkkk!"

Now I was really depressed, and that was difficult for an imp who supposedly suffered no human emotions. I had just been given the bird—and by a bird, no less!

CHAPTER 108

Feeling sorry for myself was a new sensation for me. Was it a learned trait garnered from all those years of contact with my subject, or was it just an aping of man's self-pity? I didn't know, but I felt lousy!

From my position floating above the ground, I allowed myself to reach out and let wave after wave of human need pass over me. Here indeed were causes that cried out for my help. I was needed and, although the causes did not appeal to me personally, they left no doubt that they would benefit from my intervention.

If I remained there, I would continue to be an outcast, and I could not bear that stigma. The least that I could do was to go out in the field with my other faeries and contribute whatever I could to aid in the impending debacle.

Time is a relative matter, and I don't know how long I wallowed in self-pity. All I know is that my internal conflict had a direct result on my ions, and I glowed like a child's jar of lightening bugs.

I decided to pay one last visit to the Reverend Bill and seek his advice. The master had need for the thoughts of his student. This demonstrated how low I had sunk!

The sun had already risen by the time I entered Bill's home, and he was seated, as usual, in front of his desk, busy writing what I supposed was another sermon. I had never seen him as involved with his work as he was now, so I decided to wait a while. Perhaps he would take a break soon.

My patience wore thin and I had to do one of two things: either I left the scene and went on my way to find a new subject to guide, or I interrupted his labor and sought his assistance in alleviating my agitation.

Virgil had the eerie ability to sense certain vibrations in the air, and he appreciated my discomfort. He stopped his incessant bobbing up and down and looked in my direction.

"Arrkkk!" he said quietly, as if conversing with himself. "Arrkkk! Pity is akin to a lobster not really needing a bath but intrigued by the color red. Arrkkk!"

I had no idea what he meant by that, but he did manage to interrupt Bill from his concentration.

"What did you say, Virgil? What lobster?"

"Arrkkk?"

"Good morning, Bill," I said, hoping he wouldn't be annoyed at my disruption of his dailies. *"I don't mean to disturb you, but I need your input into a matter that is very important to me personally and one that could conceivably affect the cohesiveness of our group."*

"No problem, Bean; I needed a break anyhow.

"Jaindeaux managed to arouse my interest in this diary she wants me to keep, and she was here earlier to answer a few of my questions. I had no idea how involved I would get into putting my thoughts down in this notebook I found in the bottom drawer. That's what I have been doing all morning.

"What can I help you with?"

"I am in a quandary. In the past, I have always known exactly where I stood and, in most cases, I was in control of the situation. However—and again, this is a new situation for me—I have no idea where I fit into this state of affairs."

"Continue," he said as he put his pen down and leaned back in his chair.

"It seems as if everyone has been assigned an area of responsibility except me, and I can't figure out why I have been ignored. The only reason I can think of is that my contribution has been completed, and any further service is not required. I've never been fired before; in fact, I was always the one who ended relationships."

"Oh ho!" exclaimed Bill. "Do I detect a wave of self-pity here? C'mon, Bean; be honest. Do you really think that you aren't needed anymore? You want to know what I really think? I think that you will be responsible for one of the most important jobs, and the success of our mission will depend directly on your completing it satisfactorily."

"You paint a pretty picture, Bill, but what am I to do? And if one more person tells me to be patient ..."

"Bean, why don't you go for a walk or whatever you creatures do for relaxation? I'm sure that you'll be apprised of your situation soon enough.

"If you think that *you* have doubts, how would you like to read my scribblings? I'm going to have to learn to write more selectively in the future; otherwise, I'll end up with reams and reams of rhetorical babble."

"I'd like that, if you really don't mind. Maybe I can introduce you to my ghost. It's possible he can help you out. He does have a propensity for writing about religion. Actually, I think he suffers a fixation on the subject."

"Well, if you want, here are the first pages. I'm curious as to your opinion."

From the Diary of the Reverend William Fellows

I don't know where to start.

I've never felt the need to keep a diary. My life has been one of quiet repose, with the exception of a brief expedition into the realm of fermented spirits—and that was not the kind of reminiscence one would like to either publish nor be reminded of. It was a past filled with insecurity and indecision aided by an aimless banging of my head against a wall of solid doubt.

The introduction of Maeve into the miasma of my soul provided the antidote necessary for my salvation. The gift of her presence opened up a new world for me and reawakened my faith in serving my fellow man. Patch was the cement that finalized my acceptance of the role I must play in my attempt to offer salvation for those in need.

Was this revelation worthy of the written word? I don't know. Perhaps it is if one considers it to be the catharsis of an erstwhile floundering soul which, in reality, intended the revelation to be enveloped in an aura of self-satisfaction?

When Jaindeaux first approached me to be the scrivener of this epic saga, I was a hit with a powerful feeling of doubt. My experience with the written word has been limited to the composition of weekly sermons; I have no experience in the conveyance of pages of historical proportions.

"Bill," she said, "The force that has been put together in this conflict will consist of millions of souls graciously enlisted in a faith-directed army of intense belief in the righteousness of man. This will be a powerful adjunct to the abilities inherent within my cadre of faeries."

I argued with Jaindeaux, stating that I, too, am a devout believer and should be included in her ranks.

Her reply elicited a feeling of compassion from Jaindeaux more intense than I have ever before received from any single person. It was as if all doubt had been erased from my mind and replaced with the confidence of purpose.

"Your position as an eyewitness to an impending clash I can only describe as being of apocalyptic proportions will be the only true accounting. It will be the definitive report to be read by future generations of man and will be utilized as a treatise in the battle of good versus evil.

"If perchance we should fall victim to the power of Lili-It and her soulless hordes, it will provide some introspection into the history of a species that was marked for greatness but fell prey to the enticement of the fabled apple on the tree of knowledge."

I was unable to respond to her explanation. If that was to be my contribution, then so shall it be.

"One more thing, Bill," she continued. "Your presence will be the only physical presence in attendance. This will not be a mano a mano bout filling the air with cries of victory or the wails of the vanquished, but instead a battle of wills versus the forces of won't. I don't intend to be flippant, for it will be a competition for the future dominance of the earth. Man needs a journal to function as a guide toward attaining his potential by overcoming adversity or demonstrating to whoever stumbles upon your words that there once existed a species endowed with wondrous gifts but who fell victim to the temptation of self-gratification.

"There is one thing that bothers me, and that is that history has provided him with the excuses he has utilized in bowing to negative enticements and, at the last moment, reversing those lures and achieving a temporary respite from his almost pathological need for aggression. The lessons learned are quickly forgotten, and history will be repeated once more. It will be repeated only if your species survives; otherwise, your endeavor will be yet another dust devil churning endlessly in a cyclone of despair. Mankind is endowed with the unfailing attribute of failure. He has the temerity to believe that he is infallible, and yet he never recognizes his failures; so the circle of repetition is endless. This battle we will partake of is just another result of his inability to grow and prosper from his achievements. It's as if success is too immense a gift to enjoy; therefore he should be punished for even thinking about attaining that level of satisfaction.

"We now have the power to gain a substantial foothold on evolution by defeating the spirit of darkness. If by this terrible battle, man can learn that there is no comfort in evil and self-righteousness, the cost will be worth it. Either way, we have no choice but to go forward to our destiny."

"Are you saying that my archiving of this conflict could be nothing more than *Bill's Fairy Tales*, which, in time, will be read to the children of whatever species retains possession of it as a bedtime story? Or perhaps it will be made into some three-dimensional cinematic production? I don't relish being made into a plastic action figure with movable arms and legs as kids present their own version of the day of reckoning."

I have so much more to ask Jaindeaux, but it will have to wait. My diary introduction has taken more effort than I had anticipated. If this is an example of what is to come, I can forecast a missal of monumental proportions.

I let the words of Bill's diary sink into my thoughts before answering him. I wanted to formulate my response and be able to temper, if necessary, any critique that might be forthcoming.

"I think that you've done a first-rate job by accomplishing two things. The first thing—and a very exemplary one at that—was a purging of your innermost feelings. The second was your skill in denoting detail, as in your interpretation of discussions with Jaindeaux. Your diary promises to be an acute account of the conflict—one which, by its sheer sensitivity, will be the definitive version for as long as people desire the truth."

"You're sure? It isn't too long-winded?"

"It's fine. I would venture a guess that my ghost would also approve of it.

"Tell me, Bill: how is Patch responding to the almost superhuman demands being placed upon her? Her alternating between innocence and maturity appears, at least to me, to have no lasting effect on her. Each personality, or whatever you would call it, is assumed without any complication and without any stress—and, interestingly enough, without any reference whatsoever to the other. In my experience, I have seen adults transform mentally and physically into children, but I have never observed the opposite. Patch demonstrates a metamorphosis almost as complete as that of the caterpillar evolving into the butterfly. She literally becomes an adult.

"You know, I wouldn't be the least bit surprised if your daughter isn't destined to be much more than a temporary manifestation of a warrior ordained to be humanity's salvation."

"You're scaring me, Bean. She's my daughter, and I want to experience every second of her childhood and revel in her growth to adulthood. The thought of her being taken away from us is very depressing."

"But if she has been chosen for an existence that rises far above man's feeble relationship with the cosmos, you will have no choice but to let her go. She will always be a daughter to you and Maeve, but she will become mother to the world.

"Even I am awed at that concept ... and Bill, it's only a concept. Who knows? Maybe she will revert to her childhood once these hostilities are over."

"Mother to the world of man? There isn't an aspirin large enough to ease that headache! If she is man's mom, who will be chosen to be her mate and father her children? In fact, what attributes will her children possess? What matter of creature will I be the grandfather of?"

"Hmm ... if you really think about it, that chronic headache could prevent that scenario from happening."

"There, you see? A little humor, and you feel better already. I apparently needed a little levity myself; I have to admit that I feel better also.

"Thanks for the help, and as a reward, I'll leave you to your pen."

With those parting words, I retreated to where my ilk went to relax.

"Arrkkk! Words ... words ... words: they are the bane of the deaf and dumb. And close the door behind you! Arrkkk!"

CHAPTER 109

"Bean."

"Jaindeaux."

"I knew that if I left you alone, you would arrive at what you seek by yourself."

"Arrive at what? What have I discovered?"

"Your assignment concerning Patch's future. You might not believe it, but the thoughts you shared with Bill come very close to being the truth. If we prevail, she will become a stature of perennial luminosity, regaling over whatever darkness survives with the light of her radiance; and you will be at her side for as long as she is needed to offer guidance and insight into whatever conflicts might arise. You and I will combine our resources: you with the final contact and strategy, and me with the spiritual aspect of her soul.

"In other words, you will have the overwhelming responsibility of participating in the future of humanity!"

In my stunned state, all I could say in reply to her announcement was, *"Moi?"*

Eventually, I managed, *"How does one prepare for that? I don't have the experience or the knowledge to undertake a task of such an overwhelming duty."*

"You underrate yourself, Bean. You have spent your entire existence—countless millennia, in fact—doing on a smaller scale that which I ask you to do now; of course, this time it will be of a much grander scope. You will be a success—of that I have no doubt.

"Keep doing what you have been doing for the time being and when the time comes for your participation, you will respond accordingly.

"I cannot enlighten you as to your future beyond that of the immediate, but it will be far and away the most ... forgive me, but for the first time, I am a loss for the correct adjective to define that moment. Have patience."

"Patience again? I would need an endless supply of the most powerful tranquilizer on the market to have all the patience asked of me in the past few days.

"Patience, indeed!"

CHAPTER 110

I supposed it was time for Leader to make his appearance, and I was not disappointed.

"Bean, you old flash in the sky, how is it with you? Still the moper? If I were able, I would take you in my arms and give you a pat on the back in an affectionate imp hug.

"I tell you, I've been busy coordinating all of our brethren into one cohesive element, and it is all falling into place rather smoothly. Old Lili-It doesn't stand a chance against us!

"Our people have forsaken their hibernation and have given themselves to us almost 100 percent. I can honestly say that at the time of reckoning, we may have billions of worshippers willing to give up their souls for the gift of peace. I'd give anything to be there when they confront the hellion and her escort! But I'll be here guarding Patch and her mortal image while her essence, as commander of our forces, faces Lili-It."

"I won't deny an underlying fear that gnaws at my ions: the fear of failure. It seems that our entire defense and offense is based upon conjecture, and nothing has been proven, at least to the extent required. The crux of the matter is that Lili-It has had time to perfect, or come close to perfecting, her tactics. With no noticeable impediment to her relentless march, she has persevered. We, on the other hand, are proceeding without any tried or true modus operandi, course of action, formula, plan, maneuver, or whatnot!

"Nervous? Yeah ... I'm a trifle nervous."

"Nervous is good, but failure is not in my vocabulary. We just have to work a little harder, that's all.

"You seem to forget that I have witnessed countless battles throughout the ages, and one fact that stands out is that the force that tries the hardest and the one with the most motivation usually goes home the winner ... and I'm already planning our victory party.

"So don't even think about failure, and don't ever mention it again to me.

"Now, git! Do something useful with yourself. *Tempus fugit* and all that stuff!"

I had never received a dressing-down like that before. I had visions of a puppy slinking away with his tail between his legs, his muzzle plying the carpet: "Bad dog!"

CHAPTER 111

I began to follow Patch around with a more solemn view toward accumulating as much of an insight into her psyche as possible. I was bewildered; she was just a little girl and behaved accordingly. I couldn't identify any resemblance to the icon that Jaindeaux had predicted she would become, with the exception of a few knowing glances in my direction from time to time.

I hadn't noticed any return to the mature presence she had introduced previously to the group.

To hell (ooops, wrong oath!) with Leader: I'm still nervous!

As the days went by, a noticeable air of excitement surrounded our family.

I hadn't been told when the day of reckoning would arrive, but with the absence of Leader and Jaindeaux, it must be very close.

Again, I detected no visible sense of anticipation from Patch. From Bill and Maeve, yes, but not from the prodigal daughter. As for me, the image of a holiday sparkler closely resembles my demeanor.

What I needed was the brain-numbing gibberish of one of Matt Christmas's guests. I wondered whether the minister was open to viewing the program.

There he was, at his desk, pencil in hand; staring at the wall, deep in thought.

Come on, Virgil. Say something.

As if to annoy me no end, the bird remained silent. I could swear he was smiling at me!

Okay; if that's what you want to do ... I can play also.

In an instant, I took possession of his birdbrain and let loose with a profundity such as would be expected from him. I was prepared to duck a shoe thrown at me in a demonstration of Bill's irritation.

"Arrkkk! All work and no play makes for a dull day, and a dull day is a day too dull to—"

Uh oh, here comes the shoe!

I guess I vomited out too many words.

"Virgil, what in blazes are you screeching about now? Or is it you, Bean?"

"It's Bean. I needed some company, and you were the only body around. Sorry.

"I was thinking: maybe a little Matt Christmas is in the offing. A little tension relief is called for. What say you?"

"You know," Bill said, stretching, "that might be just what the doctor ordered."

"Did I hear my name mentioned? Dr. Crank is here and at your service."

The wrong doctor, obviously.

"Where on earth did you get those suspenders? They look as though they could provide the support for a major suspension bridge."

"On earth? Who said anything about earth?"

"Very funny. Now lose the Crank getup, and tell us what's happening."

"Bean, that sense of humor again: missing!

"Things will escalate tomorrow or the day afterward—no later.

"Reverend, keep that pencil sharpened; *le grande adventure* **is about to commence."**

"Pens, not pencils, you nincompoop! How would I be able to sharpen pencils in the midst of war? Let's see: I might be able to get at least a segment of Christmas's broadcast."

After the television had gone about its usual warm-up rituals, the image of an Asian man appeared. He spoke with just the hint of an accent, peering out of tiny, frameless spectacles under a smoothly shaven, polished head. *This must be the promised Professor Saito Bokchoy—he of the bubbles.*

The program had already started, and we found ourselves somewhere in the middle of his talk. Matt Christmas was either completely absorbed in the professor's address, or—and I suspect it to be the true cause of his silence—his mind had been thoroughly blasted by the rhetoric.

"... So if the universe exists only as far as man is capable of physically acknowledging it, what exists beyond? Our personal universe exists as far as we are able to acknowledge it either visually or mechanically. If we move a mere millimeter in any direction, it changes, and a new universe is produced in the direction of that movement; an exact segment of the reverse universe is erased on the trailing end. The elliptical nature of earth's orbit creates constantly changing parameters in the dimensionality of its universe, allowing for an eternal altering of its borders.

"We do, however, have knowledge of other universes through the eyes and ears of others, but we do not include them within our personal sphere, instead only acknowledging their existence.

"Who says that the parallel universes have to be mirror images of ours? Could they be far more advanced or much more primitive and undeveloped? If they are far more advanced than ours, and if there are portals between the two, would that explain the phenomena called flying saucers? Or if such parallel universes are primitive in design, would that be the causation of our rare sightings of crypto-zoological creatures that have somehow evaded capture by traveling back and forth inter-dimensionally in random actions."

I could see Bill starting to rub his temples.

"If we indeed live in a bubble universe, as some physicists speculate, the universe within must rotate on an axis within the confines of an amoebic containment, or we would remain static, and gravity would cease to exist. Therefore, if we are able to travel within that bubble and in the same direction as the axis, but at the same speed, do we indeed remain motionless? If we are able to travel faster then that rotation, albeit in the same direction, do we advance to the future? If we were to travel fast enough, would we end up where we started but countless years in the future (à la Einstein), or perhaps enter into a void created by the ultimate demise of the bubble itself (as the membrane of its elastic exterior slowly disintegrates, as it is want to do), for nothing is permanent? If we travel too fast, we face the possibility of centrifugal force flinging us

out to the very edge of containment and facing a potential rupture in the membrane. This breakout would fling us out into the void until we either became a satellite of the bubble or another body seeking a place to corrupt.

"If we consider that the ultimate future is an absorption into another bubble universe or just sheer destruction, that voyage would prove that nothing is truly in our future. If, however, we travel, in the opposite direction do we return to the past? And, again, if we travel fast enough in reverse, could we conceivably run out of time and enter once again into the nothingness of pre-creation?"

If he rubs any harder, I'm afraid, he'll start a small brush fire!

"None of these scenarios would be a constant due to the very consistency and physical structure of the bubble, which is elastic in nature, much like a water balloon: forever changing its shape and creating a myriad of internal pressure changes. These changes would greatly affect the speed and direction of the various voyages, so nothing would be predictable and nothing would, or could, be repetitious inasmuch as we take our personal containment bubble with us. Every voyage would be an adventure into the unknown, creating fear of and respect for the results. The fear and the lack of knowledge of the unknown have been, and remain, the basis for religion, and religion has proven time and time again to be the trigger for violence. If violence contributes to the dissolution of countless personal bubbles, where does the energy from those bubbles amass?

"I wonder if our bubble universe, comprising countless smaller bubbles of human, flora, and fauna universes, could be described simply as a huge glass of seltzer that is expanding due to the vacuum of space and its inability to contain the pressures produced by its effervescence."

"Seltzer? We live in a glass of seltzer? I've got to turn it off; my head is about to split. Sorry, Bean—this one's really off the wall!"

"... and you have the temerity to affix me to the same wall?" Dr. Crank asked. "For shame upon you, my religioso and you, too, Bean. However, I will show some generosity and save a few inches on the partition for you, lest you garner space in the future!"

"Arrkkk! Boing, bing, and gadzooks! Where is the rain amid all that thunder? Arrkkk!"

"Go, everybody, go!" pleaded the minister. "And Virgil, zip your beak; I've got work to do!"

"Come, my compadre, we are not wanted in this man's bubble. Judging by his ire, I fear the bursting of said bubble would spray invectives hither and yon and rain pollution upon my delicate ears."

CHAPTER 112

Word spread very quickly among our cadre that our wait had come to an end, and the anticipation changed to exhilaration.

Maeve and Patch scooted around the house, packing things away, as if they would be gone for an eternity.

"Don't forget to take your sweater with you, sweetheart," Maeve said to her daughter. "You never know when you'll need it."

With a hug and a smile, Patch took the offering. To my amazement, she had demonstrated no overt reaction to the upcoming solemnities. She had continually behaved simply as a child enjoying a child's life.

Bill packed the pads and pens he had been accumulating for the past few days.

Food was laid out for Virgil, and a radio station was found with generic elevator music to keep him company.

"Bean," Bill asked, "should I put the TV on, so Virgil can watch Matt while we're gone? At least he'll have a human voice to talk to instead of that mesmerizing music."

"The TV will be fine, but be prepared to hear lectures of preposterous content when you return."

"When and if we return, his disjointed prattle will be more than welcome," Bill replied.

I wonder how Anna Walks With Grace was preparing for the great commune. Perhaps she was in the throes of an ancient ritual?

What an amazing woman; she managed to live in two worlds and was devout—and much respected—in both. She showed no ill effect from the awesome responsibilities heaped upon her graying head.

There exists among the societies of man a few chosen individuals who, by the sheer power of their unselfish and spiritual aura, offer a path to the salvation of those fortunate enough to bask in their company. Anna stands proud in that special group.

Tomorrow will see a world gathering together in the temples of their choosing to offer, unhesitatingly, their souls and corporeal existence in an effort to provide deliverance to a race which heretofore has shown nothing but disdain for its mortality.

This could very well by the final chapter in the tempestuous reign of one of nature's unfinished experiments.

Will the overseers of mankind be in attendance, and if so, will they opt to interfere in the conflict? Will man's God(s) be naught but a bystander as the future of his charges' battle for their place in the firmament? Is there … no, there must be a power that is responsible for this errant life form, as well as the countless other life forms that permeate this speck in the "ether capacious" (scintillate, scintillate, etc., etc.)."

Who, what, where, and when: the four horsemen of the Seekers remained mounted on a merry-go-round of evasive answers.

"Vamos en un galope Rocinante,[48] *for yonder lies a damsel in distress!"*

Tomorrow.

---

48   Spanish: "We go at a gallop, Rocinante." Rocinante is the name of Don Quixote's stalwart steed—not as the snorting charger Quixote sees her, but as the old, tired swayback that she truly is.

CHAPTER 113

The narrative from here on relies on the observation and understanding of Reverend Bill and what turned out to be a compilation of true and insightful reporting.

There will be, I'm sure, additions to the accounting by yours truly, as well as by Leader and, perhaps, Jaindeaux. But the reportage from an isolated noncombatant will prove to be the ultimate record.

From the Diary of the Reverend William Fellows

Hunger did not precede our breakfast; instead it was necessity that overrode the excitement within and compelled us to provide what little nourishment we could manage to consume.

We held hands as we walked the few yards to the mission house and toward our rendezvous with fate. No words were spoken; it was as if were alone in mind but joined in body. We might have walked through a wall of thorns and not felt a thing.

Automobiles of every make and vintage were parked haphazardly around the chapel and more continued to arrive, creating a Jackson Pollock masterpiece of metallic pigment on a canvas of hardtack and stunted grass.

Inside, the benches were filled with worshippers of every age and gender. They sat upright, and in deference to the sheer number of parishioners, silence ruled. Here, as with Maeve, Patch, and me, they were alone with their own thoughts.

I was curious about their thoughts. Was it fear of the unknown, was it elation, or was it determination that spurred them on toward their sacrifice? Whatever their motivation, they were here and resolute, every last one.

Almost to the man, heads turned toward us as and eyes followed us as we made our way to the front of the room and acquired our seats.

Once we were in place, attention was centered on the dais and the anticipation of what many believed would be a wondrous sight.

... and they were not to wait long; for a mist formed at the base of the altar and rose slowly skyward as the image of Giver of the Word appeared once more to the astonishment of the audience.

Cries of "Father!" reverberated throughout the assemblage.

"Aiee! He has returned as was foretold by our elders!"

The outpouring of affection was the cue for Anna to stand up and turn to the crowd. With tears in her eyes, she raised her arms in a gesture for silence. It took a few moments for the group to respond to her wishes, and silence once again reigned throughout the hall.

I attempted to imagine people; groups, whole congregations, cities, and whole countries all gazing upon a preordained site at their individual places of devotion, all awaiting the appearance of—and this is extremely difficult for me to voice—my daughter ... my Patch.

I was awakened from this daydream of mine by the figure of Giver of the Word gesturing to my little girl to take her place beside him. No—not beside him, exactly, but in front of him and facing the parishioners.

You read about supernatural occurrences, and you are presented with them via special effects in motion pictures, but what happened next was reality. All preconceived notions of one's belief system and of the mind's interpretation of visual stimuli vanished instantly. There was no rational explanation for what was happening, because no prior event existed to accurately aid in defining the moment.

I'll try to describe it to the best of my ability and employ whatever meager control of the English language I might possess, but my words cannot accurately convey the wonder of what was presented to us.

Giver of the Word raised his arms, as if offering a benediction for the congregants. As he held that position, a strong, white light enveloped Patch, and she grew in stature. Her uniform of jeans and a flowered blouse was replaced by a diaphanous gown of the purest white I have ever seen.

It occurred to me that this same vision was being received throughout the world at the same instant we perceived it.

A feather falling on a pile of cotton batting would have created a thunderous clap in defiling the silence that blanketed the chapel.

It was as if the crowd was acting as one entity in holding its breath at this mesmerizing scene before us.

The words she spoke next were delivered with quiet passion and were seemingly directed to each individual separately.

I understand that it is my responsibility to record everything I am witness to. A scene I can describe from a visual standpoint, but words are difficult. They come fast and furious, and I am not a practitioner of shorthand. In addition, we have the tendency to ponder certain words, ideas, and concepts, causing us to temporarily lose our concentration on the continuing dialogue.

So here, as my memory allows, are the words spoken by the figure I called daughter.

"My name is Patch.

"Throughout eternity, the land has been sullied by war, by famine, by plague, but it has always managed to survive. And despite those and many more impediments to its existence, it has fostered a rebirth of life.

"We can no longer rely upon this regeneration of purpose, for the land is slowly becoming totally devoid of life-giving nourishment. Our adversary is called Lili-It, and she is the fulfillment, the embodiment, and the accumulation of all that was evil for millions and millions of years ... and she is all-powerful!"

"What is she? She is not a physical being, although she started out as one. She is a force, a spiritual creature of diabolic design. She is the antithesis of light. Where she passes, darkness and death preside. She has no followers, just victims; and it is those victims who empower her to the extreme.

"Who am I? I exist on a metaphysical plane between the corporeal and the spiritual, and I am able to travel between both worlds. The degree of the strength of my spiritual embodiment depends upon the amassing of sympathetic souls in my sphere of influence.

"Today, with your help and confidence in the sincerity of our mission, the strength that emanates from my core will form the basis for our defeat of that unholy wraith.

"I ask you to cleanse your minds of any intrusive thoughts. Close your eyes, and direct your focus solely on the vision you have just witnessed. I ask only for your trust and your sincere belief in the righteousness of our cause. The concentration of your outpouring of love within my spiritual essence will imbue me with the assurance that we will succeed."

A mantle of warmth slowly and imperceptibly permeated the chapel, and it was as if all of our personal fears and uncertainties were erased and were replaced with a most welcomed imbuing of calmness.

I'm going to interrupt the previous entry from the minister's diary for a few minutes. Unfortunately he's only privy to what is accessible to him visually. He doesn't possess the ability to delve into the consciousness of us spirits, so I will apprise you of the preparations being put into place, the inclusion of which should clear up the questions that will undoubtedly present themselves as the Reverend Bill's narrative continues.

First of all, it appears that Patch will continue projecting her ethereal likeness into the minds of the congregants while at the same time communicating, via visual imagery, the progress of the conflict.

Jaindeaux will be at her side at the mission to provide support as an adjunct to both her spiritual influence over the people as well as her confrontation with Lili-It.

Maeve will remain with her daughter, even though Patch continues to exist in her angelic form. I can only describe Maeve as having abandoned all reality and intent on protecting the imperial segment of her own soul that was Patch.

And now we come to the question of how the minister will travel to the site of the holocaust.

There is no doubt that he will bear witness to the event, but will he be just a likeness complete with physical abilities, or will he indeed be present in his human guise?

That is your question, is it not?

To explain how he will be transported to the site, I have to ask you to open your mind to a concept that you might find intellectually implausible: the theory of mind over matter ... notably, telekinesis.

Okay, here's where I lose some of you. I'm not talking about bending spoons. I'm suggesting that solid objects can be moved from one location to another by employing the sheer power of the mind.

The very fact that you are still here attests to your acceptance of my presence, as well as that of Leader and Jaindeaux. We are nothing but energy in its pure elemental form. We are the children of what you call the big bang. To put it more simply, energy begets energy, and we are the begotten.

It was our force that moved stone and caused rivers to flow; it was our power that felt that this rock should be festooned with a diversity of life.

The beginning of the end of our guardianship of this world was the introduction of the species called humanity.

At first, he had both physical form as well as spiritual powers. He was a god: Zeus, Apollo, Athena, Minerva, Ra, all mortals with the ability of thought transference to both animate as well as inanimate subjects. They were the true masterpieces of creation.

However, as man's population on earth flourished, he became less interested in the gods and more interested in himself. As a result, his powers diminished to the point where they finally disappeared and were buried deep within his sub-consciousness.

Okay, before you try to move that sofa by staring at it, you might get better results with a dolly. When I said buried, I meant *buried*! Think of a grain of sand interred six feet beneath the Gobi desert; now that's what I meant by buried.

We faeries, on the other hand, retained those very powers, but we utilized them selectively and only in rare circumstances.

This is one of those rare and selective instances. Hence the minister (this is for you science-fiction fans) was transported to the edge of the encounter by Leader and enveloped in a protective force field.

CHAPTER 114

Patch and I teleported to the scene with no difficulty, and with us came the combined souls of millions upon millions of determined soldiers of light. We were positioned now to begin the battle for the ultimate control of humanity's' future legacy.

From the Diary of the Reverend William Fellows

The first thing that hits you is the smell.

Long before we approached THE PLACE, long before we saw the enemy, long before we heard the cacophony of battle, it was ... the smell!

How do I describe a smell as abhorrent as this one? It is a smell, a taste, a corruption of both nasal and throat membranes. It is a burning ... a congealing of mucosa too thick to spit out, too thick to swallow.

It is an ever-enlarging coagulate damming the spillways of your gullet.

It is pressure on the chest as if a thousand pounds of molten lava is slowly smoldering its way through to your lungs.

... and yet we went on, as if driven by some superhuman force intent on bringing this conflagration of evils to its final conclusion.

After successfully, but painfully, overcoming the noxious fumes, we developed a false sense of confidence—that is, until we spied, in the far distance, clouds of a motley gray boiling in a sky as dark as any hole in a stygian grotto. At the base of that living body of filth was a line of bright red slowly being assimilated into the cloud, becoming crimson sparkles mimicking the flickering of the stars in a distant nebula.

What happened to our bravado; our sense of invulnerability? It passed in an instant. Hesitation superseded any assurance that we had managed to generate. Insecurity gnawed its way into our hearts as we stumbled forward, mired in a pit of primordial ooze, destined to become specimens for future bone hunters.

How could we ever have thought that we would be able to conquer an adversary as commanding as the one we were going to face momentarily?

With our defeat would come the defeat of all mankind, and we knew that we must, but could never, prevail.

We have assigned our mortal souls to whatever destiny has in store for us.

I couldn't see Patch, nor could I see the armies, the battalions, the platoons, or the squads of her followers. I did feel ... how can I describe it? ... an energy in the air, similar to the pulsing of the ozone before a severe electrical storm, but much more noticeable.

There was no shouting, no roar of men going into battle. Instead the air was infused with the roar of a cyclone gone mad; but there was no wind, only the belief that I was encircled by a vast contingent of warriors. It was strange, but I didn't experience any fear, just the knowledge that I was somehow insulated from harm in a transparent, impenetrable bubble.

We knew that if Lili-It managed to reach the city of Jerusalem, the seats of the world's most populous religions would be destroyed forever, and with them the veritable hearts of devout followers.

If one removes the heart, the body dies, and with the death of faith comes the demise of any perceptible competition in Lili-It's march to oblivion.

A logical question would be, "What does she expect to garner as her victory reward? If all that is left is an orb of ash, where are the souls she would need to survive? Is she just a common—well, not so common actually—terrorist bent on entering Valhalla?"

I just do not understand her reasoning.

The strategy we were to implement was one of lure and containment. Patch and I would progress straight ahead and rouse the attention of Lili-

It while the vast majority of our militia, under the guidance of countless faeries, would encircle her in an effort to either slow her up or to stop her march completely. Electromagnetic energy and an outpouring of pure good would combine to create an impenetrable shield. The untainted, unselfish property of good is undeniably a power to be reckoned with.

It seemed like a viable plan, because if we stopped her forward progress, there would be no further souls for her to corrupt; therefore her power would gradually ebb.

As I said, it was a good plan initially, but as with all good intentions, snafus would eventually find a foothold here and there.

Our strength relied on the sheer number of allies that we felt confident would comprise our contingent. More would be beneficial, of course, but we could not dare to lose any noticeable quantity. We could not afford a hole in our shield, as we were spread thin enough.

But that was our first snafu: a well-planned and well-timed incursion into several large temples of worship by groups of fanatical suicide bombers shouting hysterical quotes from some obscure anarchic tenet successfully exterminated thousands of our worshippers and, in one split second, erased thousands of souls.

It doesn't matter who the bombers were or who directed them on their path of destruction; what mattered was that they were so frighteningly triumphant in their calling.

We immediately felt the loss through our spiritual connection to Jaindeaux, but what we didn't figure on was that the purveyors of death were so evil that, although their bodies had been incinerated, their souls were welcomed by Lili-It and consequently reinforced her already unspeakable power.

Despite the setback, we continued forward still, confident in our quest.

From the Diary of the Reverend William Fellows

Forward progress was slow but unrelenting. I guessed that we would reach Lili-It somewhat south of Jerusalem's center of religious devotion.

The insipid odor of death got stronger with each mile we consumed, and the roiling cloud cover seemed to expand its reach in all directions, getting more violent each second.

As frightening as it was, our march never faltered, despite the loss of those brave congregants. Yes, I also heard of that massacre through Leader's influence. I wanted to feel pain at the loss, but I was too involved in the proceedings at hand. I'll have time to mourn later on, and I'm confident in the knowledge that there will be many more souls to weep for.

At first I didn't trust my hearing, but as the miles crawled by, I started to hear an elegy of mournful despair radiating from that gray, repulsive obscurity. The air was filled with the cry of millions of souls in an atonal chorus of rage, of pain, of fear, of defeat, and in the background, much like the drone of a piper's dirge, of lives sacrificed.

And over that din, one could hear, with total clarity, the sound of insane laughter. It was enough for me, although protected by the bubble of invulnerability, to develop a dreadful chill in my body as the hairs on my neck sizzled.

… and still we marched.

CHAPTER 115

As Patch and I forged ahead, I received a communication from Jaindeaux. What with the loss of those martyred devotees and the intimidating view of Lili-It's domain, many of our erstwhile stalwart believers were starting to falter in their dedication. To counteract that potential disaster, Patch started a hymn so beautiful and yet so primitive that it overwhelmed the fear and uncertainty. The sound came not from the voice of a little girl but from the mesmerizing bowing of a violoncello, and it had the power to relegate any iota of despair and doubt to a cavern deep within the psyche.

Jaindeaux also notified me that Patch's charisma had grown in intensity and, when combined with her position of leadership, was elevating her as an object of worship. I am quite uneasy about that report, remembering a discussion we had a while ago about her elevation to godlike status. I'll keep my opinion to myself until I see what the future holds. Too many gods already dominate the minds and souls of man.

My attention was captivated not by the filth that composed the vile cloud, which seemed to have a life of its own, but by the cacophony of despair that emanated from it. That laughter, that insane laughter, I recognized as Whoever's glee from the chorus of anguish of which he was the composer and master conductor.

I felt hesitancy within Patch, a loss of confidence, as our wall of restraint started to give way. The stress of upholding sway over her followers and the terrible responsibility of putting a hold on Lili-It's incessant creep was starting to gnaw away at her self-assurance.

My pods of fellow imps and faeries managed to draw upon some superhuman (if that is the right adjective) effort and increased the strength of the barrier constructed in Lili-It's path. It succeeded, at least temporarily, in halting her insipid creep.

I didn't know how long that wall would hold, but this maneuver gave Patch a brief respite from her effort to combat her nemesis.

What we needed was an immediate resurgence of faith and the inclusion of additional forces to complement those that had persisted in our cause and to replace those whom we lost to eternity. I thought that we had enlisted all the devoted souls that were committed to us, so I was at a total loss as to where we can find any others.

From the Diary of the Reverend William Fellows

There was a brief moment when I felt we were moving backward. The desert provides few landmarks for me to fix upon, but the feeling was nevertheless there.

A spasm of fear shook my body as I envisioned the ultimate defeat of good over evil.

The scriptures forecast the final battle for man's salvation, called Armageddon. It is said that it refers to an area called Tel Megiddo,[49] which is located in the desert of northern Israel. Heaven protect us, we were but a few miles from that exact spot.

Coincidence? Or is it truly the biblical prophecy from Revelations come to life?

Damn it: who is this Lili-It, and why are we at this precise location? And my Patch ... why has she been appointed as the foil to Lili-It's ambitions?

The Mayans, Nostradamus, and many other prophets have predicted that the end of the world, as we have existed in for millennia, will reach its zenith at this precise time in history.

I cannot and will not accept those ominous divinings. For man to be relegated to mere songs chanted around the campfires of nomadic

---

49   Records describe Tel (or Mount) Megiddo as existing from 7000 BCE to 586 BCE at the crossroads of Egypt and Assyria. It was host to the struggles of Assyrians, Canaanites, Egyptians, Israelites, Persians, Philistines, and Romans. It is a historical area steeped in violent conflict. However, the actual battle of Armageddon is to occur at Jerusalem. See "Megiddo," http://www.bibarch.com/ArchaeologicalSites/Megiddo.htm.

tribes would mean the demise of God himself, and that is a notion which does not register within my heart!

Good will prevail! God will prevail! I cannot doubt it!

From the Diary of the Reverend William Fellows

I apologize for my emotional outburst. I forget that this is not a commentary on our times or a treatise on religion; this is a dispassionate accounting of a moment in history. My inexperience as a writer is evident, as is my true profession of that of a writer of sermons. I will attempt to be as dispassionate as possible and warrant this awesome responsibility.

Leader has managed to convey an image of Jerusalem as it appears in real time.

The noxious cloud was reaching the outskirts of the city, and with it came a storm of such intensity that no amount of canopies could afford shelter with any success.

From the Wailing Wall and the Dome of the Rock to the Chamber of the Martyrs, the Tomb of David, the churches of John the Baptist, and the Church of the Redeemer: Armenian, Christian, Jewish, and Moslem worshippers all filled the temples, churches, and mosques of their choice; the streets and alleys flooded with worshippers totally oblivious to their personal sect-borne hostilities. They were as one, and no recriminations as to cause of this potent calamity were voiced.

Despite the overbearing threat to their existence, these people, although from different worlds and conversing with different tongues and garbed in different dress, prayed in their own manner to the same God. The Tower of Babel, constructed over centuries by fear and suspicion, disintegrated before my eyes. The language of prayer and the desire for salvation from evil is the same in all languages.

But is this miracle of commonality enough to obliterate the menace that threatens to decimate the symbols of their belief structures? Perhaps even if their effort fails, for one brief moment, however futile, man will have emerged the victor by becoming as one.

Patch and I could see the unrelenting growth of Lili-It's sphere of influence. We soared far above the cursed desert and were able to see the death and destruction that was her trademark. It appeared as if the southern boundaries of Egypt, as well as Saudi Arabia and most of Jordan had already fallen victim. From what we could fathom, it looked as if she intended to encircle Israel from Mitzpe Ramon in the Negev to north of the Golan Heights, with the witch of the hellmouth herself charting a direct course toward the Eternal City.

Lili-It knew that with the total destruction of Jerusalem, our defenses would collapse, and we would present no further impediment of any worth to her domination and destruction of the world ... and it looked as if, at least at that moment, she might prevail.

From the Diary of the Reverend William Fellows

The destruction of Jerusalem has been a study in history repeating itself.

The area called Palestine was the beneficiary of conquests by Joshua in 1273 BCE and later by Babylonians, Egyptians, Syrians, Israelis, Romans, Christian Crusaders, Mongolians, and Turks. It has been sacked and destroyed time and again and yet rebuilt and renewed. The desecration was accomplished by mortals who appreciated the site for both its strategic and emotional benefits.

Lili-It, on the other hand, is not mortal, and the city's only significance to her is the advantage it offers as a potential weapon against us.

Perhaps in reply to my thoughts, Leader conveyed my bubble world to Jerusalem, where I would be able to witness the possibility of yet another devastation heaped upon the debris of centuries of previous tragedies.

The first thing I saw was a mass of pilgrims and common people intent on their prayers. It was, if I may say so, a rather encouraging sight. In contrast to this saintly scene, crowds of frightened citizens were making their way west by any means available, perhaps in the hope of reaching the Mediterranean Sea. I'm sure that they felt that the water would protect them from the hellfire that seemed sure to consume them.

Panic is a fearsome enemy with an indiscriminate life of its own; nothing can impede its progress, and no one is safe from its rapacious hunger. Kiosks were knocked over, and merchandise was dispersed without paying any mind as to their value, while the hawkers were trampled underfoot if they proved too slow in avoiding the stampede. Fear became so prevalent and the runners were so intent on escape that there was no evidence of looting. Hurrah for small things!

Women, children, and the elderly became victims of the onslaught and were trampled underfoot.

The holy paid no attention to the disturbance and continued their mantras of pious ministrations.

I am a man of God who has given himself to the preservation of life and the glory of the soul. It is impossible for me to be in the midst of all this carnage and yet offer no solace to the frightened and bereaved. Does the battlefield photographer deposit his feelings and concern for his fellow man in a locked vault as he goes about the business of recording the horrors that befalls the subjects in the bloody arena?

I wonder if that vault is on a time switch, allowing it to open periodically at a prearranged time, permitting the reporter to regain his humanity.

The cold, inanimate eye of the lens and its electronic chip of a brain stores memories and sights that retain no emotion from the carnage in its immediate zone of influence. It is the rationale for the reporter's dispassionate continuance of his mission. It is also unfortunate that what that electronic box records will provide confirmation and a brutal reminder of what we are capable of inflicting on our brothers and sisters. That chip can be destroyed, and all memories erased from its cold, dispassionate circuitry, but the images it shared with us cannot. There are times when I feel it would be desirable to have the gift of a removable chip within the confines of my mind.

The irony of the situation is that if Lili-It does succeed, pious or not; young or old, all will be fodder for her death machine. It was reminiscent of the siege of Masada,[50] where the doomed opted not to surrender but chose suicide instead to avoid the curse of slavery.

---

50   Masada, an ancient mountaintop fortress in Israel, was an outpost of zealot Jews in their rebellion against the Romans, and in the year AD 73, in a final act of rebellion, almost all of the defending Jews committed suicide rather than deliver themselves to Roman slavery.

After the majority of the runners dispersed, a small cadre of people remained, alone and in small groups, all facing south toward the inevitable presence of the cloud. I couldn't for the life me understand why they remained behind and why they had chosen not to join their fellow man in a last futile effort to survive.

A look of defiance was molded on their faces. They weren't going to surrender to the devil's handmaiden. And although they were of varied genders and varied nationalities, their defiance melted into one unit and was projected toward Lili-It.

My amazement was noticed by Leader and messaged to Patch and Bean. I found at later that this observation was in turn forwarded to Jaindeaux.

See for reference the Columbia Encyclopedia: Masada.

CHAPTER 116

Upon receiving our communication, Jaindeaux replied that the congregation had been receiving word of similar actions around the world. As if in response to our appeal for additional aid, even though we had accepted the fact that we had probably enlisted all who would be amenable to our plight, a new constituency presented itself.

"Bean," Jaindeaux said, "the only explanation I can offer is that when the message first went forth to the devout among man, it was also heard by the righteous among the nonbelievers. They in turn have concentrated their defiance and offered their strength of morality in conjunction with our original force."

"But where have they gathered? I feel no awareness of any large assemblage of souls anywhere, either through direct observation or through the conveyance of our fellow faeries."

"Not large groups, Bean, but individuals and small clusters scattered throughout the world. Somehow—and believe me, I don't know the reason—they have responded much as the crowd in Jerusalem.

"Their individual mind-sets parallel each other to the extent where, as in the Holy Land, they were able to bond as one and create a force to be reckoned with."

So what Jaindeaux implied was that (and it is a theory that I have pondered before) one doesn't have to belong to an organized belief system and give themselves up to the tenets of that structure to be considered a good person.

The rules and regulations governing morality and ethics are unnecessary if the individuals themselves are of a right and decent state of being.

This news reinforced Patch's esteem, and she became even more divine in her iconic demeanor.

From the Diary of the Reverend William Fellows

The silent fervor of the worshippers is somehow overpowering the din caused by the cyclonic winds of devastation. Is the power of silence more indefatigable than the blaring trumpets of an enemy's charge? Is it possible that we are slowly overcoming the might of Lili-It's advancement?

That maniacal laughter has, in my estimation, been replaced by an inhuman bellow of irrepressible rage.

… and still the people didn't waver, determination having replaced fear. Despite the unbearable din and the litter of man's existence swirling around and pelting them without sympathy, they did not waver!

What an honor, what a blessing to be included in that genre of God's grace!

The wind died down perceptibly as Patch and Bean forged ahead, confident leaders supported by an army of devoted followers who, in turn, were encouraged by the inclusion of souls from a diversity of beliefs; be they theistic in nature or self-proclaimed.

Millions upon millions of individuals had cast aside the thorny barriers of apathy and crumbled the walls of spiritual indifference to merge, finally, into an indestructible army of one. Are we truly so dissimilar that we ignore the similarities? We are all human beings and branches of the same tree gifted with a trunk sturdy enough to support us all. The salvation of our species has been revealed to us, can we but heed the message. That smell of death, of the decomposed bodies of Lili-It's sacrificial flock, had started to dissipate to be replaced by the sweet aroma of air newly born, as if from a post-storm inundation. A gentle breeze and the return of sunlight to the storm-ravaged city brought with it a renewed hope for an era of peace and understanding.

I followed the regeneration of life while encased in my bubble. As Lili-It was forced to retreat, the glory that was Patch caused the earth to renew its promise of life, and the land turned green once again.

CHAPTER 117

Patch and I continued pressing Lili-It through the parched and desecrated land she had defiled. The more progress we made, the weaker she became, and the weaker she became the more irate Whoever became. Angry he might be, but powerless he found himself. He might have had the option at one time to flee the state of affairs he was occupied in forming, but due to the intensity of his involvement with Lili-It, he now found himself irrevocably connected with her destiny. And as we pushed farther and farther back, toward her place of origin, her demise would be his—and, if we had our way, it would be severe.

I noticed that as our success increased, so did Patch's aura. I found it difficult to admit, but she was definitely achieving a godlike image and I, as with Whoever, was becoming more and more connected with her spirit. I dared not envision what this union would evolve into; the very thought of it was breathtaking in its potential effect on humanity.

We were caught up in a veil of sadness at the lives Lili-It had taken, and we felt powerless to replace them. But we felt that since the land was renewed and devoid of any negativity, it would be repopulated soon and with a renewal of positive energy. Where those lost souls had been sent, I did not know, but perhaps, or at least I fervently hoped, they would live on in the memories of those who survived.

CHAPTER 118

From the Diary of the Reverend William Fellows

It was as if I was honored by my maker in that I was privileged to bear witness to the rebirth of life from the ashes of the devil's spawn. The landscape indeed appeared as the original Genesis had been envisioned in my mind: a land not yet deformed by the avarice and the selfishness of man, where living in peace is the holy tenet.

Leader has successfully kept me in the dark as to my daughter's welfare. I can't help but fear that she will no longer be the little girl who ran after butterflies; the child who loved all things and adopted an abandoned bird; the kid who fell asleep in my nap while clutching a threadbare rag doll.

Who is she now? Will she still acknowledge Maeve and me as her parents? Although I basked in the success of our mission, I wept with the realization of our possible loss. I supposed I should feel pride and rejoice in the understanding that she would benefit mankind in one manner or another.

Looking around at the area we had stopped in, it dawned upon me that, according to the visions impressed on us prior to this action, we had reached the origin of the evil one's birth. Of all the reclaimed land that we had floated through, this was one spot that refused life. It was doomed to serve as a memorial to evil and to the base gift that it offered.

Surrounded by a wall of electromagnetic energy provided by countless imps and faeries, Lili-It and Whoever awaited their punishment, the former reduced from an arrogant wraith to a pitiful example of defeat.

Despite her loss, she remained defiant and stood erect, facing her conquerors and judges. No storm clouds enveloped her and no moans of anguish came from her victims; nothing could be perceived but the quiet and serenity of a land innocent and reborn.

What punishment would be inflicted on her and Whoever? Death by any means would prove to be insufficient and would not bring back the lives forfeited due to her transgressions. In reality, I didn't believe that Patch would agree to forfeit Lili-It's life. No matter how heinous the crime, the taking of another's life consciously and in retribution would be tantamount to murder; and that was against her ethos.

After much deliberation, it was decided that Lili-It and Whoever would remain on that barren plot of land forever, and it would be bathed in light and surrounded by representatives of all the species of animal and plant life that Lili-It had attempted to annihilate.

As a final touch, hymns of angelic reverie would fill the air above them without cease. Angelic reverie ... I wasn't sure what that would mean. Did Patch have the power to rise above the material world and summon heaven's troubadours? Was she suggesting that there is indeed a unique dimension of reality populated by beatific spirits?

"Tell me, Patch ... this 'angelic' thing you propose ... does it involve an actual entity or just a figure of speech? I have to admit that relying on the experience of my millions of years of existence on this planet, I have never encountered the appearance of surreal or supernatural beings emerging from the place you call heaven. What I have seen is the power of suggestion to induce such ethereal images in the minds of susceptible individuals. As a point of reference, I emphasize what you have managed to accomplish in creating the aura that was—and still is, may I add—the prime inducement in the formation of our devout followers."

"The true power of the mind and its limitless potential was a gift bestowed upon man at the beginning of time. You and your society of imps and faeries are the original legitimate life forms to inhabit earth. You said it before: pure energy creates by pure energy. Your decision to turn the barrenness of a rock into an object of visual and sensory delight was the prime reason for animal and plant life to emerge; and with that ambitious inspiration came man.

What I have done is within the realm of all humankind. The ability to rise above commonality and reach for the heavens is within them, it's just a step away from the re-attainment of their original supremacy over physical matter. Man has attempted to regain that ability, although not understanding the reason he has done so, by stimulating his unconscious by the infusion of both natural and artificial substances in a vain attempt to recall those memories from the past. However, as with all memories, they have the tendency to wheedle their way out periodically. Experimentation with hypnotic suggestion and mind-altering substances employed in an effort to induce psychotropic experiences proved to be an uncontrolled voyage into a comic book world of make-believe. Unless those memories can be attained through self-awakening, they will always be a false representation of once was.

"Bean, the God they search for is within themselves. They alone can control their destiny and have the power to do so."

"And you ...will you assume the pose of an object of pious devotion hoping to satisfy their demand for spiritual leadership?"

"No, Bean—not me alone. *We!*"

"We? What do I have to do with your ambition?"

"I don't think that your definition of ambition is to my liking. If my ultimate desire is to have man rise above his pettiness and reject the corruption of the many faces of religion he has blindly followed all these years; then yes, it is ambition! If I desire to offer man an object of devotion without the demands and control of false prophets, then yes, it is ambition!

"You see, if I want to coerce man into acknowledging what has been accomplished in the name of religion and the disparity of beliefs endemic to a credo of partisan doctrines, and have him join with his fellow man in the worship of one divinity ... again, it is ambition!"

"Once more: what do I have to do with this ... ambition?"

And what I feared came slowly to the mind of this once-simple sprite who has been altered by circumstance—or, perhaps, by preordination—to emerge into (and there is no use denying it any longer) a veritable God.

Patch continued her homily in an almost patronizing tone that had been seeped in patience. "Bean, you are the most unselfish and sensitive soul that I have ever come across. You give of yourself and demand nothing in return, and you use your gifts not for your own amusement but for the benefit of others.

"We have become very close these past days, and I rely greatly upon your guidance. It is those unselfish qualities that I call upon and plead with you to acquiesce to in helping me to achieve my so-called ambition. If you can accept that this ambition is just a means to an end—an end based upon a universal doctrine of belief in oneself—then you cannot refuse me.

In the past you have been satisfied with attending to the needs of one; now I offer you the opportunity to cater to the aid of millions, maybe even billions. Can you not see the good you could offer to those desiring direction in their lives? How can you refuse? I need you to complete my transformation!"

How can I refuse, she asks. Just a short time ago, I was a carefree imp enjoying the simplicity of a life that offered no complications I couldn't handle.

Then I found myself involved in a monumental cause of action against a harbinger of doom and her insatiable drive for the annihilation of all life on earth. Hey, I could have refused then ... but I didn't, as you well know.

Now I am faced with a choice that will alter my way of life forever. I am to become a deity worshipped by the society of man. What do I know about godliness?

I'll learn.

Patch needs me; how can I refuse?

If it's a God she wants, then a God I'll be.

Oye!

Meanwhile the monument to the futility of war shall be a daily reminder to any purveyor of darkness that no matter how powerful an angel of death becomes, and no matter how much damage it manages to accrue, it will be no match for the strength of the virtue and dignity of common man.

CHAPTER 119

From the Diary of the Reverend William Fellows

The battle is over, and we have triumphed in the end. Success is always marred by the sacrifice of those victims who gave of themselves willingly or as reluctant and powerless subjects of horror and brutality.

There shall be many tears shed for many a day in memoriam for those heroes.

Perhaps we have learned a valuable lesson about the senselessness of war. In the end, nobody really wins, since the number of losers far outnumber the winners. Death is a natural component of existence and should be a reward for a life well played. To be robbed of one's being by an external trigger of violence is anathema to all that we hold sacred.

It has been preached in sermons throughout the land that the obscenity of war and the devastation of disease are all part of God's great plan.

I am a member of his flock, and a most devoted one at that, but even I have had doubts about that theory. It is, and will always be, one of the premier premises of the tenets of religion that challenges the sincerity of my beliefs.

I see the punishment bestowed upon Lili-It and agree that it is Promethean[51] in concept. She will be doomed for all eternity

---

51   Prometheus was a Titan, a god of Greek mythology, who was punished by Zeus for stealing fire from him and giving it to mortals. He was doomed

to suffer the same retribution day after day after day. She must never be allowed to escape or to influence any protégé who might resume or improve upon her tactics. We must be vigilant, else we are doomed to repeat our mistakes.

It is only a matter of time before I am returned to my mission in New Mexico and to the bosom of my family. I don't know what to expect insofar as Patch is concerned. I'd like to say that I am prepared for the worst, but that is a relative concept. I can say, however, that I miss Maeve and my daughter as I would miss my own right hand—and that is the hand that penned this epistle.

My final entries will be concerned with our arrival and the conclusion of Patch's connection with the congregants. What will become of Jaindeaux, Leader, and Bean? It would be a pleasant diversion to spar with them intellectually from time to time, but I know that this will not be. I'm just a brief stop on an endless voyage to them, but I hope I will prove to be a memorable one.

We returned to the chapel and the gratitude of the people. Looking around, I noticed a few empty spaces on the benches, but all in all, the room remained full.

Maeve was still in front, gazing up at the angelic image of her daughter while Giver of the Word held his position behind her in a gesture of support.

The Reverend Bill arrived in a slight stupor, supported by the good Dr. Crank who also had in his possession a goodly amount of notebooks. Bill's notes and observations, I surmised.

"Ho, my honorable gentry. The battle has been fought with gusto, and evil has been vanquished. A rousing 'huzzah' is called for: HUZZAH!"

"Enough, Crank; it's time to mourn, not to cheer. We've lost many brave souls today who gave their lives unselfishly and in the name of their God. Let us mourn but also be joyous in the knowledge that their spirits shall be together in a hallowed place far from the pettiness of human existence."

---

to be tied to a rock where an eagle ate his liver every day only to have it grow back to be eaten again. Prometheus is credited with playing a pivotal role in the early history of mankind. See http://en.wikipedia.org/wiki/Prometheus

"Well said," Jaindeaux added while still in her guise of Giver of the Word. With that final pronouncement, Giver of the Word rose up slowly, with his arms outstretched, and faded into the white light bathing the altar. Many tears fell in the mission sanctuary, for he had been a great man.

It was Patch who spoke next. Her words were directed to all of her warriors throughout the world. Bathed in purity and haloed in grandeur, she easily imparted them to the throngs who had learned to regard her with awe.

"I look upon you with a feeling of admiration and with sincere appreciation for the sacrifices you have made.

"You look upon me as some sort of deity, as some sort of god. I am humble to receive such tribute, for I am but a symbol, a mirror image, of your own inviolability. If you choose to elevate me to the heights of sanctity, I will accept that honor if—and only if—it will bring us all together in the formation of a new world.

"You, my beloved, are the true gods. Due to your noble devotion to a cause that was most fearsome in its entirety, we have persevered. I bow my head most reverentially to you.

"Because you stood together and relegating your differences to that fading cloud of noxious content, you have already begun to unite your diverse beliefs into one innovative concept: a necessary first step in launching a lasting peace as the world's religions merge into one united faith while the holy places that were important to the faiths of the few become holy places to all and are revered as one.

"A new human race shall spring from your efforts, whereupon morality, ethics, a concern for the rights of all, and the joy that is nature are the predominant concerns among those whose aspirations cry out for peace.

"I shall be here for as long as you need me as a symbol of what your future holds in store for you. Once your minds are purged from the shackles that had you imprisoned for all those ages past, you will exult in your rediscovered freedom of thought.

"Go home to your loved ones now, and bask in their gratitude. You deserve all the accolades that will be heaped upon you. I ask you to spread the word of a new era in the ages of man. Become messengers of peace all.

"But before you leave your places of worship and scatter throughout the world, I should like to make known to you that the name Patch, as you refer to me by, was given to me by my parents as a loving derivation of my birth name. I would consider it an act of kindness if you refer to me by it from this moment on.

"My name is Pax."[52]

With the completion of her discourse, the congregants quietly rose and exited through the side door.

Anna Walks With Grace stayed behind to give support, if need be, to the Reverend Bill and Maeve. No one knew what the outcome with Patch would be.

The air was still as they waited for Patch to address them.

"Patch," I questioned, *"you must end the suspense. What do you intend to do?"*

"Bean," she replied, "we can never return to the way it was before this action commenced.

"I can never be that little girl again.

"We have been chosen by powers much greater than ours to see what destiny has shaped for us. If it means we will become gods, then that is what we shall be. It is our fate to be the teacher to a united world. We will show humanity that the true existence of what they have called God lies within, and we will educate them on how to access it and let them prosper from it. If man can achieve that level of consciousness, he can move mountains; he can travel the stars and rejoice in the discovery of new species of life encapsulated in what Professor Bokchoy refers to as our bubble of a universe. He can share his love for the unfortunate; he can cure disease; he can feed the hungry; he can form the building blocks for a new world!"

"Slow down, Patch—you're beginning to scare me! Your passion is a bit too zealous for me to accept comfortably; it borders on fanaticism."

"I'm sorry, Bean, but I am zealous when it comes to the good we can perform together."

"Okay, enough now with the cosmic syllogisms. What do you plan to do about Bill and Maeve and their daughter? I'm not sure whether they will be able to withstand the loss of Patch."

---

52   The Latin word Pax is defined in a number of ways:
1.   (When capitalized) the Roman goddess of peace: see Collins English Dictionary and Thesaurus
2.   From Middle English, from Medieval Latin, from Latin, peace: see Merriam-Webster Online Dictionary.

"Don't think that I haven't agonized over that question myself.

"What I intend to do hasn't been tried before. It will push our powers to a level I had never thought possible."

"You're scaring me again, Patch."

"No, no, listen. I—*we*—will project a virtual image of the young Patch just as she was earlier. As with Giver of the Word, she will be seen and heard by everyone. She will be treated as if she were a normal, lively, and bright young girl. She will have a corporeal presence so as to encourage displays of affection.

"I will take it upon myself to guide her growth into womanhood.

"For all intent and purposes, she will be a living, breathing entity. Only you and I will know the truth."

"Jaindeaux created the image of Giver of the Word as a visual projection and not meant to survive for any extensive period of time. What you suggest is tantamount to creating life itself! Aren't you carrying this godhead identity of yours a bit too far?"

"First of all, Bean, it's not *my* identity; it's our identity. And it's not playing God at all! We have the ability to accomplish wondrous feats by the sheer power of the mind; why not carry it a little further and produce an avatar, a clone, a facsimile, a … you get the idea."

"Intellectually and emotionally, I think we're treading on thin ice, and I'm afraid it will give way and we will drown in a sea of smugness. Smugness has a weight that can drag us down for good."

"It's true, but smugness can also give us the impudence—or impetus, if you wish—to attempt this envelope pushing.

"What say you? My parents … err, Patch's parents deserve the effort."

"Heck, let's go with it. What do we have to lose? It'll take a great deal of our combined energy to accomplish it, and if we fail, well, the world will go on just as it has for millions of years without us. We will be forgotten soon enough, for we are not irreplaceable. A new force will always arrive on the scene to confront the re-emergence of evil. That venomous worm will always manage to wriggle through our defenses. My only hope is that our replacements will have learned something from our efforts."

"Ever the optimist, eh, Bean? Enough of this banal chatter!"

And with the flippancy of a sideshow barker, she announced (telepathically, of course, as was our entire previous conversation), "… and here comes Patch!"

Well, not immediately, it seemed. She took it upon herself to first address Bill and Maeve.

"The time has come for us to end this life-altering experience. The gracious surrender of your daughter proved to be an intricate part of our stratagem. We could not have succeeded without her.

"Patch will be returned to you now as she was before. She will have no knowledge of the past few days, and she will no longer be looked upon as a spiritual healer. She will be just a little innocent girl once more. Love her and cherish what she is and take pride in what she will become."

I have no words for the Herculean effort it took to produce the child. For one brief moment, I thought we had extinguished our usefulness in fomenting our idealistic goal in affecting humanity's evolution. But it wasn't to be.

We took this emotional moment to fade into the light and leave the Fellows family to regain their attachments.

Jaindeaux was also preparing to depart.

"You've never answered our question as to who you really are. Who sent you, and where did you come from?"

"I have been called by many names by many people for many years. All I will tell you is that someone has to look after the lunacy of the human race and its unpredictable future. It was my responsibility from the original bang and will always remain so. You and your assemblage of imps and faeries did yourselves proud by following my directions at the source.

"Individually you did well, Bean. I will leave man and his prospects for survival to your good judgment. It's time now for the return of the Titans."

What could I say to that confession? *Hmmm* ... did she mean what I thought she did?

Titan ... visitor ... the concept stretched the imagination.

Anna Walks With Grace returned to the reservation filled with a greater confidence in the ambition of man to achieve peace and understanding in a conflict-free environment. She, too, would slowly forget the events of the past few days and continue her visits with the minister and his family. She would seek, but never regain, her visions of Giver of the Word.

And what of Leader, you ask?

Well, he has learned a lot about human nature, so I believe he'll avoid whatever clashes of diverse ideologies that may still survive and, instead of just observing it, take up where I left off.

The future promises that war will be nothing but an anachronism. Maybe a few isolated pockets of stubborn anarchists will take shots at one another, or isolated tribes of aboriginals will whack one another with sticks and stones, but a major confrontation with weapons of mass destruction? Optimistically, I don't think so.

There will be those people who will need help in adjusting to the new world order available at their beck and call. Politicians and lawyers will rank at the top of the to-do list. Perhaps the Golden Rule will replace the federal and judicial rules of conduct

Sadly, I have to say that we might have seen the last of Dr. Crank. With the departure of Leader, so goes Crank and his litany of absurdities. That leaves Virgil and the esteemed Matt Christmas to carry on the quackery that Bill will always employ for the morning respite from his mission chores.

As for Patch and I ... well, you know the overwhelming responsibility we have inherited. Enough said!

There is, however, one last favor that I ask of you: please, wish us luck. Your future depends upon it.

CHAPTER 120

From the Diary of the Reverend William Fellows

This might very well be the final entry in my journal. I have delayed writing for a few days in order to put my thoughts in order. I daren't wait any longer, because those very thoughts are beginning to fade.

Did all of this actually happen? Somehow I'm not sure.

Family life is as it always has been. Maeve and Patch remain my anchors, and an aura of joy resides in this house.

It seems as if I have just awakened from a dream, and yet, in reality, it appears as if peace has finally been achieved throughout the world, and we now stand on the threshold of a new awakening.

My last conversation with Bean offered not a definitive solution to universal woe, but hope.

"So, Bean, is it all over? Has man suddenly awakened to a new world bathed in the warmth of peace and tranquility, of morality and ethics? Can we now come together, hold hands, and sing 'Kumbaya'?"

"Do you mean right now? Today? This minute? The answer is no!

"Societal change doesn't happen with the speed of a big bang.

"Today, no, but tomorrow … well, only if you truly desire it. You were given a taste—a sample from a large buffet of incongruous and perhaps incompatible dishes, and now it's your turn to combine them and fashion a universal feast.

"Good-bye, Bill. A door has opened, and it takes but one step and then another to walk through.

"I hope you have learned something from our foray into battle: not all goals are windmills."

He was gone, and somehow I knew we would never cross paths again.

Was it all a dream? I guess tomorrow will provide that answer

He asked me if I had learned anything from our joust with evil.

I learned that Armageddon is just a word and not a promise.

I learned that we can adjust to change and thrive in it.

I learned to put my trust in the sincerity of others.

If the memories of the final battle will fade, who will ever read this tome? In fact, who will want to?

Was there truly a Bean or a Dr. Crank or a Jaindeaux? Did Patch really form the basis of a new deity, a new world order?

Were they just an invention of the mind for a people disgusted with the status quo and desirous of change?

One result of the "dream" is that my attachment to the old God will have to be rethought. An enlightening has taken place, but I still believe we must have a supreme being worthy of our devotion. It doesn't matter if that entity is male or female or even an abstract thought. We were the result of a wondrous creation, and it is the responsibility of the family of man to give praise to whom praise is due.

My mind and body is exhausted from the strain of whatever did occur during the past week. My only respite right now is to switch on that old TV of mine and catch Matt Christmas; it's time for a brain freeze.

"… Aha!" Matt said. "How about this concept for the cause of global warming?

"For centuries, man has mined for minerals and pumped and removed billions upon billions of tons of oil and ore from the bowels of the earth. What if—and this is pure conjecture, of course—that the removal and redistribution of physical weight caused a change in the dynamic balance of the planet, which in turn caused a minute shift in either the orbit of the planet or a change in its tilt? Could this slight modification be the cause of the alteration of our heretofore

normal weather patterns, affecting the lives and the future of its inhabitants?"

Click!

"Not 'aha,' but bah! Some things never change …"

"Arrkkk! Shut the door behind you on the way out! Arrkkk!"

SOME FINAL THOUGHTS

I choose to write in the realm of fantasy, whereupon the subject matter is totally controlled by the author. In this way, I can create a semblance of hope, happiness, and peace among my characters, in my world … and maybe, vicariously, among my readers. I can manipulate my story to fulfill whatever situation demands to be scribed.

I sincerely believe that the concept of Bean is embedded in the soul of each and every one of us. We sincerely want to exist in a world where trust in and compassion for our neighbors is a natural projection of our being. The fear of receiving misanthropic labels has caused many of us to cover those qualities with a blanket of fear woven with the threads of suspicion, paranoia, and the unrelenting drive for the accumulation of material gain.

For me to achieve this aura of Bean-inspired bliss, I have had to venture into darkness while incurring the demise of many innocent souls. This was an unhappy foray for me but an important one, **"for nothing of value is as precious as one that is earned by sacrifice."**[53]

While their physical forms were shattered, their souls reached out as one, and, uniting with our combined determination to survive, met and defeated the evil will of the malevolent maiden and her spirit cohort. Where darkness had ruled, light now shines upon an earth reborn, and the hope for man's future has been rekindled.

In my story, that is—fiction and fantasy, not reality.

---

53   Stephen Stuart, *Rantings* (2009).

438

The concept of world peace, of a world where there is no want and everyone is equal, and where the desire for knowledge and the need for religious support are one and the same, is the reflection of the naive and not the stuff of reality. It is the rhetoric of the few and the inaccessibility of the many.

With Bean and Patch, I have attempted to put those wishes in the forefront of man's evolutionary progress. With the decline of aggression, he is presented with the necessary keys to open the door of salvation. Naive? Of course it is, but you can't deny that it is a fine and noble thought

Man is not a creature of complacency.

He is a territorial beast whose territory could be measured in either land or in material possessions. He is too restless to be complacent. His wants far exceed his needs, and this leads to frustration—and, inevitably, conflict.

In contrast to Book One, "The Wonder of All That Is: The Story of Bean", I have attempted to play down any passionate discourse on contemporary life. To quote William Shakespeare, who said it better than I can ever hope to,

Tomorrow and tomorrow and tomorrow, creeps in the petty pace from day to day to the last syllable of recorded time, And all our yesterdays have lighted fools the way to dusty death. Out, out, brief candle! Life's but a walking shadow, a poor player and then is heard no more: it is a tale told by an idiot, full of sound and fury, signifying nothing.[54]

As for the concept of mind over matter, there has been a great deal of research into that phenomenon with surprisingly positive results. If the reader is interested in further research, I would recommend accessing articles in the field of noetic science, as well as available literature on the subject of paranormal healing (a list of some helpful and informative Web sites will be noted in an addendum at the end of this narrative).

---

54   William Shakespeare, *Macbeth*, Act 5, Scene 5.

The subject of science versus religion has been among the forefront of the great controversies throughout recorded time. In the past, you could have been burned at the stake for heresy by just thinking about it; today you are only ostracized at the stake of an indomitable theology.

Is there room for both hypotheses? I'll let you decide.

Woe is the soul living in the darkness of ignorance for he shall consume the nourishment of a stone.[55]

Research into the workings of the human mind is in its infancy. Science has only just begun to realize its vast and untapped potential. Is the bending of a spoon, supposedly by thought transference, just a charlatan's trick, or have a few select people mastered some minor control of its immense prospective? Can the total control of the power of thought transform man into God?

It's a concept straight out of science fiction … or is it?

Inasmuch as I am fond of reciting quotations, here is one by Albert Einstein:

The religion of the future will be a cosmic religion. It should transcend a personal God and avoid dogmas and theology. Covering both the natural and the spiritual, it should be based on a religious sense arising from the experience of all things, natural and spiritual, as a meaningful unity. Buddhism answers this description.[56]

---

55 Stephen Stuart, *Rantings* (2010)
56 Albert Einstein. See "Buddhism in the Eyes of Intellectuals," http://www. buddhanet.net/budintel/buddhism/cosmic.htm

Finally, I could have written an entire volume just on the quotations and observations of Miguel de Cervantes. He was one of the greatest of thinkers and, unbeknownst to many, the author of many oft-repeated bons mots. I beseech you, the reader, to delve into the writings of that most insightful of men. I guarantee that you will not be disappointed. What better way to end my narrative than to quote, once again, Senor Cervantes?

"Too much sanity may be madness.
And maddest of all,
to see life as it is and not as it should be."[57]

---

57   Miguel de Cervantes: http://www.quotes.net/authors/
      Miguel+de+Cervantes

POSTSCRIPT

For those of you who will miss the guests on the minister's favorite TV show, I'll include a program (actually just a brief synopsis) that he missed while encapsulated in his bubble at war's edge.

From Matt Christmas's favorite visitor, Professor Saito Bokchoy, comes this gem, which, I must explain, is not a gem of wisdom from yours truly, but actual thoughts from the esteemed academician.

If you are intellectually in sync with him, please enlighten me in as basic a rhetoric as you can. I have no idea what he is talking about!

> *... here is another concept: what if we travel perpendicular to the direction of the rotation of our bubble? We are now faced with two variables. One would be the rotation itself, and the other would be a departure from the scenario that is the now. But taking into consideration an adjustment for the rotation, thus remaining in a true perpendicular status, do we view the present from various adjuncts until we return to our starting point? This could conceivably offer alternatives, plausibly offer parallel universes, and perhaps tender solutions to present situations owing, of course, to our ability to alter the speed of the perpendicularity, or reverse it and return to the now with a different approach to present-day conundrums. A benefit to this approach would be an angular departure from the perpendicular, which would result in unlimited coefficients of present/future prospects (the same aspects of view would occur if we angled in reverse: this would afford us the ability to study the image of the present by appraising the seeds of the past and would also allow us to*

modify the direction of the future). This would present even greater possibilities as to the alteration of the present and its influence on the future and could produce scenarios that would, in fact, provide significant impetus to our changing of the present.

I wonder if *he* is a result of a wormhole excursion?

Nevertheless, I hope you enjoyed our visits with the intelligentsia, and you have my wishes that they somehow enlarged your knowledge base and provided you with some food for thought.

"Don't laugh at the absurd, For the ridiculous is divine."[58]

---

58   Stephen Stuart, *Rantings* (2010).

ADDENDUM

As promised, here are a few references dealing with the power of thought:

1. **"Empirical Explorations of Prayer, Distant Healing, and Remote Mental Influence"**: William G. Brand, Institute of Transpersonal Psychology; as copyrighted in an article appearing in the Journal of Religion and Psychical Research, Vol. 17, No. 2, April, 1994: pages 62-73.

2. **"Einstein's "Cosmic Religion":**
   see; http://openparachute.wordpress.com/2008/03/07/einsteins-cosmic-religion/ (1/21/2010)

3. **"Paranormal Medicine: Mind Over Matter in the Genesis and Cure of Disease"**: Howard Eisenberg, M.D.: Director of the EGO program at York University, Toronto, Canada. Reprints available from: Rosedale Medical Centre, 600 Sherbourne Street, Suite 609, Toronto, Ont. M4X 1L5. (Can. Fam. Physician 23: 1524 December 1977).
   see: http://www.ncbi.nlm.gov/pmc/articles/PMC2379031(1/21/2010)

4. **"The Power of Thought":**
   see; http://www.rosicrucian.com/zineen/pamen049.htm (1/20/2010).

5. **"What is Noetic Science?"** Cassandra Vieten
   see: http://www.huffingtonposr.com/cassandra-vieten/what-is-noetic-science_b_28779.html (1/20/2010).